THE CITY IN AMERICAN LITERATURE
AND CULTURE

The city's "Americanness" has been disputed throughout US history. Pronounced dead in the late twentieth century, cities have enjoyed a renaissance in the twenty-first. Engaging the history of urban promise and struggle as represented in literature, film, and visual arts, and drawing on work in the social sciences, *The City in American Literature and Culture* examines the large and local forces that shape urban space and city life and the street-level activity that remakes culture and identities as it contests injustice and separation. The first two sections examine a range of city spaces and lives; the final section brings the city into conversation with Marxist geography, critical race studies, trauma theory, slow/systemic violence, security theory, posthumanism, and critical regionalism, with a coda on city literature and democracy.

KEVIN R. MCNAMARA, Professor of Literature at the University of Houston–Clear Lake, is editor of *The Cambridge Companion to the City in Literature* (2014) and *The Cambridge Companion to the Literature of Los Angeles* (2010) and author of *Urban Verbs: Arts and Discourses of American Cities* (1996).

CAMBRIDGE THEMES IN AMERICAN LITERATURE AND CULTURE

Twenty-first-century America puzzles many citizens and observers. A frequently cited phrase to describe current partisan divisions is Lincoln's "A house divided against itself cannot stand," a warning of the perils to the Union from divisions generated by slavery. America seems divided in almost every way, on almost every attitude. Civic dialogue on issues often seems extremely difficult. America is an experiment always in process, a remarkable union of 300 million diverse people covering all races and faiths. As a forum in which ideologies and interpretations abound, Literary Studies has a role to play in explanation and analysis. The series **Cambridge Themes in American Literature and Culture** addresses the key cultural themes that have brought America to its current moment. It offers a summation of critical knowledge on key cultural themes as well as an intervention in the present moment. This series provides a distinctive, authoritative treatment of the key literary and cultural strains in American life while also pointing in new critical directions.

Titles in the Series

War and American Literature Edited by Jennifer Haytock, SUNY–Brockport

Gender in American Literature and Culture Edited by Jean Lutes, Villanova University, and Jennifer Travis, St. John's University

Apocalypse and American Literature and Culture Edited by John Hay, University of Nevada

The City in American Literature Edited by Kevin R. McNamara, University of Houston–Clear Lake

THE CITY IN AMERICAN
LITERATURE AND CULTURE

EDITED BY

KEVIN R. MCNAMARA

University of Houston–Clear Lake

CAMBRIDGE
UNIVERSITY PRESS

CAMBRIDGE
UNIVERSITY PRESS

University Printing House, Cambridge CB2 8BS, United Kingdom

One Liberty Plaza, 20th Floor, New York, NY 10006, USA

477 Williamstown Road, Port Melbourne, VIC 3207, Australia

314–321, 3rd Floor, Plot 3, Splendor Forum, Jasola District Centre,
New Delhi – 110025, India

79 Anson Road, #06–04/06, Singapore 079906

Cambridge University Press is part of the University of Cambridge.

It furthers the University's mission by disseminating knowledge in the pursuit of
education, learning, and research at the highest international levels of excellence.

www.cambridge.org
Information on this title: www.cambridge.org/9781108841962
DOI: 10.1017/9781108895262

First published 2021

A catalogue record for this publication is available from the British Library.

Library of Congress Cataloging-in-Publication Data
NAMES: McNamara, Kevin R., 1958– editor.
TITLE: The city in American literature and culture / edited by Kevin R. McNamara.
DESCRIPTION: New York : Cambridge University Press, 2021. | Series: Cambridge themes in
American literature and culture | Includes index.
IDENTIFIERS: LCCN 2021007097 (print) | LCCN 2021007098 (ebook) | ISBN 9781108841962
(hardback) | ISBN 9781108815321 (paperback) | ISBN 9781108895262 (ebook)
SUBJECTS: LCSH: American literature – History and criticism. | Cities and towns in literature. |
City and town life in literature. | Cities and towns – Social aspects – United States. | Cities and
towns – Political aspects – United States. | BISAC: LITERARY CRITICISM / American /
General | LITERARY CRITICISM / American / General
CLASSIFICATION: LCC PS169.C57 C586 2021 (print) | LCC PS169.C57 (ebook) | DDC 810.9/
3587309732–dc23
LC record available at https://lccn.loc.gov/2021007097
LC ebook record available at https://lccn.loc.gov/2021007098

ISBN 978-1-108-84196-2 Hardback

Contents

Illustrations

Contributors

SOPHIA BAMERT is a PhD candidate in English at UC Davis whose research addresses literary geography, critical race studies, and cities in American literature. She has been a visiting exchange lecturer at the Obama Institute for Transnational American Studies at Johannes Gutenberg Universität, Mainz. Her work has been published in *The Nathaniel Hawthorne Review* and the collection *American Literature in Transition, 2000–2010* (Cambridge, 2018).

WILLIAM BOELHOWER, cofounder and former coeditor of the journal *Atlantic Studies*, is currently Visiting Professor in the Department of Linguistic and Comparative Culture Studies, University of Ca' Foscari, Venice (Italy). He has translated and written on the cultural writings of Antonio Gramsci and Lucien Goldmann. His books include *Through a Glass Darkly, Ethnic Semiosis in American Literature* (1992) and *Atlantic Studies: Prospects and Challenges* (2019). He has written essays in the areas of multiculturalism, migration studies, citizenship and human rights, cartography, the cultural history of the sea, and cultural geography.

ANA MARÍA MANZANAS CALVO is Professor of American Literature and Culture at the Universidad de Salamanca, Spain. Her publications include *Hospitality in American Literature and Culture* (2017), *Occupying Space in American Literature and Culture* (2014), and *Cities, Borders, and Spaces in Intercultural American Literature and Film* (2011), all of them coauthored with J. Benito. She has edited collections of essays, such as *Literature and Ethnicity in the Cultural Borderlands* (2002) and *Border Transits* (2007).

JOSEPH ENTIN teaches English and American studies at Brooklyn College, City University of New York. He is the author of *Sensational Modernism: Experimental Fiction and Photography in Thirties America* (2007) and coeditor, with Sara Blair and Franny

Nudelman, of *Remaking Reality: U.S. Documentary Culture after 1945* (2018) and, with Robert Rosen and Leonard Vogt, of *Controversies in the Classroom: A Radical Teacher Reader* (2008). His current research examines literary and cinematic narratives of precarious labor.

JOHN FAGG is Senior Lecturer in American Literature and Culture at the University of Birmingham. He is the author of *On the Cusp: Stephen Crane, George Bellows and Modernism* (2009) and several articles, chapters, and catalog essays on late nineteenth- and early twentieth-century American art and literature, including "Chamber Pots and Gibson Girls: Clutter and Matter in John Sloan's Graphic Art" (*American Art* 29.3), which received the 2014 Terra Foundation International Essay Prize and the 2016 Arthur Miller Centre Best Essay Prize. He is working on a monograph *Re-envisioning the Everyday: American Genre Scenes, 1905–1945*.

FRED L. GARDAPHÉ is Distinguished Professor of English and Italian/American Studies at Queens College/CUNY and the John D. Calandra Italian American Institute. He is a Fulbright Fellow (University of Salerno, Italy, 2011) and past president of the Italian American Studies Association (formerly AIHA), MELUS, and the Working Class Studies Association. His books include *Italian Signs, American Streets: The Evolution of Italian American Narrative* (1996), *From Wiseguys to Wise Men: Masculinities and the Italian American Gangster* (2006), *The Art of Reading Italian Americana* (2011), and *Read 'Em and Reap* (2017). He is cofounding/coeditor of *VIA: Voices in Italian Americana*, editor of the Italian American Culture Series of SUNY Press, and frequent contributor to the *Fra Noi*, *L'italoamericano*, and *i-Italy* magazine and television.

SEAN GRATTAN is author of *Hope Isn't Stupid: Utopian Affects in Contemporary American Literature* (2017). His next monograph investigates representations of scale in contemporary literature from the very large of apocalypticism and ecological crisis to the smallness of wearable wellness technology.

THOMAS HEISE is the author of three books, the monograph *Urban Underworlds: A Geography of Twentieth-Century American Literature and Culture* (2011), the experimental novel *Moth; Or How I Came to Be with You Again* (2013), and the collection *Horror Vacui: Poems* (2006). His essays have appeared in *African American Review, Modern Fiction Studies, Twentieth-Century Literature, Journal of Urban Cultural Studies, American Literary History*, and elsewhere. He is a professor in the Department of English at Pennsylvania State University (Abington).

DAVID HENKIN has lived in cities his entire life, more than half of it in San Francisco. Since 1997, he has taught the social and cultural history of the United States at the University of California, Berkeley and is the author of *City Reading* (1998), *The Postal Age* (2006), and (with Rebecca McLennan) *Becoming America* (2014), as well as numerous articles and a forthcoming book on the history of weekly life.

HSUAN L. HSU is Professor of English at the University of California, Davis. His publications include *Geography and the Production of Space in Nineteenth-Century American Literature* (Cambridge, 2010), *Sitting in Darkness: Mark Twain's Asia and Comparative Racialization* (2015), and *The Smell of Risk: Olfactory Aesthetics and Atmospheric Disparities* (2020), along with numerous articles and edited projects on topics in literature, cultural geography, race studies, and the environmental humanities.

ARIN KEEBLE is Lecturer in Contemporary Literature and Culture at Edinburgh Napier University in Scotland. He has published two monographs, *The 9/11 Novel: Trauma, Politics and Identity* (2014) and *Narratives of Hurricane Katrina in Context: Literature, Film and Television* (2019), and has published scholarly essays in *Modern Language Review*, *Critique*, *Canadian Review of American Studies*, *Comparative American Studies*, *European Journal of American Culture*, *Reconstruction*, and *Punk and Post-Punk*. Dr. Keeble is currently working on a new book on contemporary literary narratives of terrorism.

KATHY KNAPP is Associate Professor of English at the University of Connecticut. She is the author of *American Unexceptionalism: The Everyman and the Suburban Novel after 9/11* (2014). Her work has appeared in *American Literary History*, *Los Angeles Review of Books*, *Modern Fiction Studies*, and *Twentieth Century Literature*. She is co-book reviewer editor of *Twentieth Century Literature*.

KEVIN R. MCNAMARA is Professor of Literature at the University of Houston–Clear Lake. He is the editor of *The Cambridge Companion to the Literature of the City* (Cambridge, 2014) and *The Cambridge Companion to the Literature of Los Angeles* (Cambridge, 2010) and the author of *Urban Verbs: Arts and Discourses of American Cities* (1996) and other essays on literature, cities, and culture.

ERIK MORTENSON is a literary scholar, writer, and translator. He is the author of three books: *Capturing the Beat Moment: Cultural Politics and the Poetics of Presence* (2011), which was selected as a *Choice* outstanding academic title; *Ambiguous Borderlands: Shadow Imagery in Cold War American Culture* (2016); and, most recently, *Translating the Counterculture: The Reception of the Beats in Turkey* (2018).

JAMES PEACOCK is Senior Lecturer in English and American Literatures at Keele University in the United Kingdom. He specializes in contemporary fiction and has particular interests in literary depictions of urban neighborhoods, gentrification, and notions of community. He is the author of *Brooklyn Fictions: The Contemporary Urban Community in a Global Age* (2015).

ANDREW PILSCH is Associate Professor of English at Texas A&M University, where he teaches and researches rhetoric and the digital humanities. Pilsch's first book, *Transhumanism: Evolutionary Futurism and the Human Technologies of Utopia* (2017) won the Science Fiction and Technoculture Studies Book Prize for that year. His research has been published in *Amodern, Philosophy & Rhetoric* and *Science Fiction Studies*. His current project is a media archeology of the software bug.

DOUGLAS REICHERT POWELL is Professor in the Department of English and Creative Writing at Columbia College Chicago, where he teaches writing, literature, and cultural studies. He is the author of *Critical Regionalism: Connecting Politics and Culture in the American Landscape* (2007) and, most recently, *Endless Caverns: An Underground Journey to the Show Caves of Appalachia* (2018).

CARLO ROTELLA, Professor of English at Boston College, is the author of *The World Is Always Coming to an End: Pulling Together and Apart in a Chicago Neighborhood* (2019), *Playing in Time: Essays, Profiles, and Other True Stories* (2012), *Cut Time: An Education at the Fights* (2003), *Good with Their Hands: Boxers, Bluesmen, and Other Characters from the Rust Belt* (2002), and *October Cities: The Redevelopment of Urban Literature* (1995). He contributes regularly to the *New York Times Magazine*; his work has appeared in *The New Yorker, Harper's*, and *The Best American Essays*; and he has received a Guggenheim fellowship and the Whiting Writers Award.

JOHN CARLOS ROWE is USC Associates' Professor of the Humanities and Professor of English and American Studies and Ethnicity at the University of Southern California, where he has served as Chair of the Department of American Studies and Ethnicity (2008–11) and Chair of Comparative Literature (2016–17). He was Professor of

English and Comparative Literature at the University of California, Irvine, from 1975 to 2004, where he was a founding member of the Critical Theory Institute. He is the author of *Henry Adams and Henry James: The Emergence of a Modern Consciousness* (1976), *Through the Custom-House: Nineteenth-Century American Fiction and Modern Theory* (1982), *The Theoretical Dimensions of Henry James* (1984), *At Emerson's Tomb: The Politics of Classic American Literature* (1997), *The Other Henry James* (1998), *Literary Culture and U.S. Imperialism: From the Revolution to World War II* (2000), *The New American Studies* (2002), *Afterlives of Modernism: Liberalism, Transnationalism, and Political Critique* (2011), and *The Cultural Politics of the New American Studies* (2012). He is editor of *The Vietnam War and American Culture* (1991), *New Essays on* The Education of Henry Adams (1996), *"Culture" and the Problem of the Disciplines* (1998), *Post-Nationalist American Studies* (2000), *Selections from the Writings of Ralph Waldo Emerson and Margaret Fuller* (2003), *A Concise Companion to American Studies* (2010), and *Henry James Today* (2014), and coeditor of *Re-Framing the Transnational Turn in American Studies* (2011), *A Historical Guide to Henry James* (2012), Lindon Barrett's *Racial Blackness and the Discontinuity of Western Modernity* (2014), and Günter H. Lenz's *A Critical History of the New American Studies: 1970–1990* (2016). His current scholarly projects are *Our Henry James, The Ends of Transnationalism*, and *Sailing Lessons: Thinking across the Pacific*.

RUTH SALVAGGIO, Professor Emerita of English and Comparative Literature at the University of North Carolina, Chapel Hill, is the author *Hearing Sappho in New Orleans: The Call of Poetry from Congo Square to the Ninth Ward* (2012), along with other books and essays on the literatures of the early Atlantic world, feminist theory, and poetry. Her essays on New Orleans gravitate around varied kinds of recuperative poetics in the city.

JESÚS BENITO SÁNCHEZ is Professor of American Literature and Culture at Universidad de Valladolid. His main field of research is multiethnic American literatures. He is General Editor of the Brill series Critical Approaches to Ethnic American Literature. With Ana María Manzanas, he has coauthored four books: *Hospitality in American Literature and Culture* (2017), *Occupying Space in American Literature and Culture* (2014), *Cities, Borders, and Spaces* (2011), and *Intercultural Mediations* (2003). He served as President of the Spanish Association for American Studies from 2011 to 2015.

BRIAN TOCHTERMAN is the author of *The Dying City: Postwar New York and the Ideology of Fear* (2017). He is Associate Professor of Sustainable Community Development in the Department of Social Responsibility at Northland College in Ashland, Wisconsin, where he teaches courses in the history and theory of urban planning and sustainable community development as well as the intersection of popular culture and social and political change. His research interests lie primarily in post–World War II urban and cultural history.

JOHANNES VOELZ is Heisenberg Professor of American Studies, Democracy, and Aesthetics at Goethe-Universität Frankfurt, Germany. The author of *The Poetics of Insecurity: American Fiction and the Uses of Threat* (Cambridge, 2018) and *Transcendental Resistance: The New Americanists and Emerson's Challenge* (2010), he has also edited several volumes of essays and special issues, among them "Security and Liberalism," a themed issue of the journal *Telos* (2015).

Acknowledgments

It is always a pleasure to work with Ray Ryan, Edgar Mendez, and the rest of the staff at Cambridge University Press, including, this time, Victoria Parrin, who guided the project from manuscript to print, and it was particularly exciting to work on what was at the time a series in the making. Preliminary discussions with Ray and feedback from the anonymous readers at each level of the review process helped sharpen the project's focus. Nothing, of course, did more for that goal than the superlative work of the chapters' authors; I am especially grateful for their goodwill, dedication, and willingness to entertain my occasional suggestions. Finally, I am very grateful to Sam Arnold-Boyd (Cascade Indexing) for the wonderful index that she supplied and to my colleagues on the Faculty Research Support Fund Committee at the University of Houston–Clear Lake for defraying its cost.

We thank Joan Annsfire for permission to use portions of "Strike Day in Oakland" (2011); Gina Ferrara for permission to use portions of "Where a Great Heron Wades," published in *Amber Porch Light* (CW Books, 2013); Brenda Marie Osbey for permission to use portions of "Mother Catherine," published in *From All Saints: New and Selected Poems* (LSU Press, 1997), Katherine Soniat for permission to use portions of "Toppled Columns, Blue Sky and Sea" published in *Alluvial* (Bucknell University Press, 2001), the University of Illinois Press for permission to use lines from Norman R. Shapiro's translation of Camille Thierry, "You," published in his book, *Creole Echoes: The Francophone Poetry of Nineteenth-Century Louisiana* (2004), and Elizabeth Guzman, on behalf of Sybil Kein, for permission to use portions of "Erzuli," published in *Gumbo People* (Margaret Media, 1999). Lines from "Gae, Gae Soulangae" from *Creole: The History and Legacy of Louisiana's Free People of Color*, edited by Sybil Kein, 2000, are used by permission granted by LSU Press. "New Orleans," copyright 1983 by Joy Harjo, from *She Had Some Horses* by Joy Harjo, is used by permission of W. W. Norton and Company, Inc. Danez Smith, "Dinosaurs in the Hood" from *Don't Call Us Dead*, copyright 2017 by Danez Smith, is reprinted with the permission of The Permissions Company, LLC on behalf of Graywolf Press, Minneapolis, Minnesota, graywolfpress.org. Felix Stefanile, "The Bocce Court on Lewis Avenue," from *Songs of the Sparrow: The Poetry of Felix Stefanile* (Bordighera Press, 2015), is reprinted by permission of the estate of Felix Stefanile, Thomas P. Adler, executor. "The Great Figure," by William Carlos Williams, from *The Collected Poems: Volume I, 1909–1939*, copyright 1938 by New Directions Publishing Corp., is reprinted by permission of New Directions Publishing Corp.

For the epigraphs in Chapter 5, the passage from Norma E. Cantú, "Living on the Border: A Wound That Will Not Heal," in *US-Mexico Borderlands*, the 1993 Folklife Festival book, is used by permission of the Smithsonian Institution. The passage from the English translation of Henri Lefebvre's "Philosophy of the City and Planning Ideology" is used by permission of the translator, Elizabeth Lebas. The excerpt from *Tropic of Orange* (Coffee House Press, 1997) is used by permission of Coffee House Press. Copyright © 1997 by Karen Tei Yamashita. To Stathis Gourgouris, I extend my thanks for permission to use his words from "Democracy Is a Tragic Regime," *PMLA* 129.4 (2014) as epigraph to the Coda.

For permission to use Louis Lozowick's *59th Street Bridge, New York* (1922), many thanks are in order: to the Lozowick estate's executor, the Mary Ryan Gallery; to the Kunin Collection and especially its registrar, Jenny Sponberg, who kindly arranged to have the canvas photographed on short notice; Robert Cozzolino and Dan Dennehy at the Minneapolis Institute of Art for supplying the photograph; and to Jennifer Marshall, Associate Professor of Art History at the University of Minnesota, who answered an out-of-the-blue email and put the editor in touch with the people he needed to reach.

The Five Points (ca. 1827), by an unknown artist, is reproduced courtesy of the Metropolitan Museum of Art; Robert Edmund Jones, program cover for *The Pageant of the Paterson Strike* (1913), is courtesy of the American Labor Museum, and Joseph Stella's *Battle of Lights, Coney Island, Mardi Gras* (1913–14), is courtesy of Yale University Art Gallery. John Marin, *Street Crossing, New York* (1928), copyright 2008 Estate of John Marin/Artists Rights Society (ARS), New York, is reproduced by permission of The Phillip Collection, Washington, DC. John Sloan, *Election Night* (1907), is reproduced by permission of The Memorial Art Gallery of the University of Rochester. Craig Ruttle's photograph, *Student Gun Protests*, is reproduced by license from Shutterstock.

Introduction

Kevin R. McNamara

A symbolic city upon a hill has echoed through US national mythology and political discourse since John Winthrop first invoked it in "A Model of Christian Charity" (1630) to warn that the world's eyes would be on the Puritan settlers and their failure would "open the mouths of enemies to speak evil of the ways of God."[1] While later invocations retain this claim of moral exemplarity, they typically revise Winthrop's caution into certainty of a destiny foretold and, more than occasionally, into a celebration of American diversity. Thus, at the end of his presidency, Ronald Reagan substituted individual opportunity for religious obligation and recast that city as a center of commerce "teeming with people of all kinds living in harmony and peace. [. . .] And if there had to be city walls, the walls had doors and the doors were open to anyone with the will and the heart to get here." Reagan's polis of immigrants resonates with Walt Whitman's description of the United States as a "a nation of nations" and the cultural pluralism of Horace Kallen's "Democracy vs. The Melting Pot" (1915), if not Randolph Bourne's more forthrightly multicultural "Trans-national America" (1916).[2]

The city of nations has always been contested by another strand of national mythology that regards the urban as alien to a national character defined by the experience of settler colonialism and embodied in the self-reliant yeoman farmer. "Americans are the western pilgrims," J. Hector St. John de Crèvecoeur intoned in a canonical passage from his *Letters of an American Farmer* (1782). Once they were Europeans, and in seaboard cities they may so remain. On the western lands, however, they exchange their "ancient prejudices and manners" for the local standards and are "melted into a new race of men," soil-nurtured and taintless. Theirs are the norms and ideals to which new settlers conform.[3] At one level, then, when Americans talk about the city, they are talking about the kind of society that they want to live in, the sort of people they wish to live among.

By the 1970s, the city's place in the national imaginary seemed settled. Events and cultural representations of "the *Taxi Driver* period," to borrow Marshall Berman's phrase that invokes the casual violence and psychopathy of Martin Scorsese's 1976 classic in the depraved-city genre, seemed to signal the city's death throes.[4] In seeming confirmation of Lewis Mumford's decades-long Jeremiad forecasting the city's progress from polis to metropolis to megalopolis to congested necropolis choking on "the burden of its own magnified expenses," the *New York Daily News* headline blared "FORD TO CITY: DROP DEAD" on October 30, 1975, when the president declined to help New York avert bankruptcy.[5] No matter that the urban crisis was fueled by government policies (e.g., the Federal Home Loan Bank Act of 1932, Housing Act of 1934, and Servicemen's Readjustment Act of 1944 [the GI Bill]) that established the economic infrastructure for suburbanization, or that corporations were moving industrial jobs to lower-tax, nonunion US regions or offshore, all of which produced a *decongestion* borne out by population data.[6] No matter, either, that urban areas for decades have subsidized rural areas at the federal and state levels, or that even after cities won home rule, rural-weighted state legislatures continue to constrain municipal governance.[7] The era's lurid headlines and popular depictions of urban crime captured the public imagination with its images of urban doom. If *Taxi Driver* represented the urban present, *Blade Runner* (Ridley Scott, 1982) quickly became a metaphor for the city's future.[8]

As the 1990s began, a posturban US geography was conjectured in response to these visions of decline. Necklaces of new development on the urban periphery would blend office parks and mid-rise office buildings with moderate density housing and amenities to suit residents' lifestyle expectations. These edge cities (Joel Garreau, *Edge City: Life on the New Frontier* [1991]), would be origin and destination for daily commutes and nights on the town, as drivers skirted dilapidated metropolitan centers.[9] In the meantime, at least, the mall had become "The New Downtown," Witold Rybczinski insisted, because it preserved the "public order" that cities had sacrificed to "police indifference and overzealous protectors of individual rights." The history of mall development in the United States does not support the causality that Rybczinski proposes, yet his list of deplorables – "boorish adolescents, noisy drunks and aggressive panhandlers" – well captures the sort of grievances that motivated white flight even as it avoids overt reference to race.[10]

Rybczinski's story also implicitly acknowledges a change in the definition of citizenship and belonging that arose with neoliberal governance.

Firstly, malls are not public spaces but spaces of exclusion for people who do not, or cannot, look and act the part of the shopper. Secondly, they definitely are not political spaces where the people to gather to discuss the issues of the day. Steven Downs learned that lesson when he was escorted from the Crossgates Mall in the Albany, New York, suburbs for wearing a t-shirt that read "Give Peace A Chance" during the run-up to the Second Iraq War – despite that he purchased the shirt from one of Crossgates' shops.[11] The pleasure that Rybczinski's good citizens experienced in malls before the days of active-shooter events and the mallpocalypse – which has spawned a subgenre of ruins photography – was insulation from the anxiety of being discomfited by the sorts of difference or substantive disagreement that animate the public sphere.

By *Blade Runner*'s year of 2019, however, the city's comeback was widely touted. The twenty most productive metropolitan areas were generating 53 percent of the nation's gross domestic product.[12] Development booms in San Francisco, Seattle, and New York could make the real estate-led financial crisis of 2008 seem another lifetime, another world. New York City mayor Bill de Blasio felt sufficiently flush in that year to reject Amazon's proposal to establish a second headquarters in Queens. Rust-Belt Pittsburgh, an archetypal industrial city and subsequently a prime example of postindustrial decline as it shed double-digit percentages of its population each decade from the 1950s through the 1980s, today boasts a diversified economy driven by its medical, academic, and financial sectors. The former Steel City's rejuvenation as "a global innovation city" committed to climate leadership seems to validate Richard Florida's argument in *The Rise of the Creative Class* (2002) that cities' viability rests on their ability to attract people who create "new ideas, new technology, and new creative content," along with the financial, legal, and business professionals who underwrite, protect, and disseminate those products, as well as cities' success at providing the mix of cultural and recreational amenities necessary to retain that class.[13]

The limits of this sunny account are apparent in the fate of such Rust Belt cities as Detroit, Youngstown, and Gary, and the condition of New Orleans a decade and a half after Hurricane Katrina, which, despite the city's importance as a port, is the most prominent example of how federal and state governments routinely shortchange cities. These cities' fates remind us, as Florida somewhat concedes in *The New Urban Crisis: How Our Cities Are Increasing Inequality, Deepening Segregation, and Failing the Middle Class-and What We Can Do About It* (2017), that urban revival is concentrated in what he calls superstar cities, whose leading enterprises function within multinational networks of production, finance, and trade rather than as nodes in regional or even national production and distribution networks. These global cities outcompete regional cities, which continue to experience disinvestment by states, the federal government, and the private sector.

The ill effects of the urban revival are not limited to still-declining second- and third-tier cities, however. If the city's future is no longer *Blade Runner*, then neither is it the diverse yet close-knit-neighborhood ideal embodied by Jane Jacobs's West Village, anchored by the White Horse Tavern, then "a smoky place with a mixed clientele of artists, dock workers, meatpackers, gays, and nurses from a nearby hospital," Richard Sennett recalls, not a pilgrimage site for literary tourists. If the streets were "run-down, with a visible population of rats," and thus clearly marked by decline in the eyes of lenders and urban planners, such neighborhoods were nevertheless vibrant and viable, Jacobs trenchantly argued.[14] Superstar cities' real-estate booms destroy these neighborhoods as they inexorably price out of local markets their working classes, their artists, writers, musicians, and assorted bohemians that who were the archetypal urban creative class, Increasingly, they price out their middle-class families as well.

The older urban landscapes that Sennett has described as a "a thick impasto of experience[s]" of difference – the populace, certainly, but also built environments layered with history and stained with evidence of use – give way to nostalgic simulacra of urbanity that appeal to tourists and new, upscale residents.[15] A James Rouse-inspired festival marketplace that inverts the relation of the heritage site and its gift shop to conjure soft-focus tableaux of local history as marketable ambiance for themed shopping and entertainment experiences, a retro stadium that incorporates elements of the disused industrial landscape into its design, and a privately managed downtown park, preferably with a view patterned on New York's High Line, or, if not, then certainly programmed to attract a targeted demographic (who may rent the park for private events) instead of to gather the citizenry in its diversity, all define a way of urban life and a topography of induced urban memory that becomes normative.[16]

As these projects spur further nearby development, they displace yet more residents and businesses, and they exacerbate existing racial and class divisions. The quality-of-life issues that Rybczinski cited in his paean to the mall return, except that instead of urbanites fleeing homeless panhandlers, they now demand that the homeless and panhandlers be removed. Meanwhile, developers remake neighborhoods to accommodate the amenities of "suburban life in the city."[17] Not only in New York and San Francisco, but also in nonboom cities such as Houston, new high-end apartments and condominiums feature rooftop parks with dog runs and outdoor movie nights – even if they are sited across the street from public parks; onsite gyms, restaurants, and lounges further reduce the need to interact with the city. The city is thus redefined by the creative-class strategy that, like neoliberalism generally, conceives cities in market terms, not as experiments in people of different backgrounds living together and governing themselves.

In the country at large, the cultural divide between multiethnic, more liberal cities and whiter, more conservative exurban farm and factory towns was exacerbated by hysterical backlash against election of Barack Obama and disparate rates of economic recovery from the Great Recession. Reaction included the Tea Party and Constitutional Sheriff movements and the mainstreaming of once-fringy white- and religious-nationalist movements that crystallized around the campaign and presidency of Donald Trump, who tirelessly stoked racial and regional resentment and animosity. Despite being the most urban-identified of presidents and someone who embodies all the moral flaws ascribed to urbanites by centuries of country-party ideologues, Trump claimed electoral victory by running against cities as enclaves of feckless elites, as zones of "American carnage" inhabited by immigrants and minorities, and as responsible for the loss of individual autonomy and a climate of moral drift. All in all, his rhetoric reprises (far more vulgarly) the dominant themes of what T. J. Jackson Lears calls "the crisis of cultural authority" at the previous turn of the century.[18] In the election and mishandled-pandemic year 2020, and with the powers of the presidency at his disposal, Trump augmented his rhetoric with rolling paramilitary deployments to American cities targeting, first, protesters against police violence and then black and brown urban populations.[19]

The simultaneous ascendance and vilification of the American city fairly demands a fresh look at what the city means and has meant in US literature and culture. The twenty essays written for this volume bring the resources of literary and cultural history and criticism to bear on the representation cites and city life and what these texts tell us about the city's promise and its unresolved problems. The organization of the first two sections takes its cue from architect Robert Venturi and planner Denise Scott Brown's definition of the city as "a set of intertwined activities that form a pattern on the land."[20] Section one considers particular kinds of urban space, while section two focuses on the experience of the city from diverse subject

positions and efforts to find or to impose patterns of significance on the
city. The division is hardly absolute; we may find patterns by studying built
landscapes and the flows they induce (the work of urban planning), while,
conversely, we can see ephemeral patterns of human activity over time
change the meaning, function, and appearance of built space, as when new
waves of residents refunction existing infrastructure to support their ways
of life. Neighborhoods and bohemias may both be conceptual spaces
formed by social behaviors and senses of common identity, yet they are
also mappable (although bohemia is mobile) and marketable by real estate
agents, planners, and politicians, while neighborhoods become slums
through policy choices that accelerate disinvestment and out-migration,
or gentrified by an influx of speculative capital and wealthier residents.
Nevertheless, the division allows more sustained considerations of the
spatial relations and patterns of experience characteristic of cities.

In the opening two chapters, David Henkin examines the role of the
printed word in conceptualizing the social structure and field of experience
of the emerging public sphere as the US city transitioned from premodern
to modern – from knowable community to world of strangers – in the
nation's first half century or so; then, John Fagg examines the arts of the
urban public sphere as they develop over the ensuing two centuries,
focusing on the street as site where denizens enact the everyday politics
of belonging together and the spectacular politics of mass protest. The
following quartet of chapters discusses the elemental space of city life, the
neighborhood. Carlo Rotella begins the unit by proposing a literature of
neighborhood, a space compounded of bounded location and affective
associations that give it meaning; people make neighborhoods, he argues,
yet neighborhoods also shape the lives they support. The neighborhoods
that most interest him are products of histories and memories of migration,
industrialization, and subsequent deindustrialization. Thomas Heise next
critiques the discursive process by which certain neighborhoods become
ghettos and *slums*, the shifting connotations and uses of those terms, and
ways they have shaped and continue to inflect public attitudes toward
those spaces and their inhabitants. Ana María Manzanas Calvo and Jesús
Benito Sánchez turn our focus toward the space between neighborhoods.
Deploying the Derridean analytic of *hostipitality*, they read intracity borders as contact zones in which relations between those who belong and
those who are marginal, precarious, or excluded are negotiated in narratives
that either reinscribe or undermine the border's effectivity. James Peacock
then takes up a specific the conflicts generated by the spatial and discursive
practices of gentrification. Reading novels of gentrification, he shows how,

at their best, such narratives meld attention to perspective, affect, and (inter)personal conflict with attention to larger social and economic transformations going on in cities and render textured and nuanced accounts of a process often seen, as he says, through a lens of "Manicheanism and moral reductionism."

Of the section's final three chapters, two move beyond the city in different directions. Kathy Knapp considers suburbia – the lifestyle descriptor associated with extra-urban domicile, not the element of political geography whose instances range from spectacularly wealthy to "inner-city" poor, from overwhelmingly white to single-minority ethnoburbs – by way of the aesthetic and pedagogical work performed in *The New Yorker*'s pages by female fiction writers who imagined a version of postwar liberalism's aspirational suburbs less isolated and alienating than the contemporaneous version imagined by John Cheever, John Updike, and other male writers in that magazine. Knapp then extends her revisionary analysis with a turn to writers more recent and ethnically diverse whose work remodels those suburbs for equally diverse inhabitants and a recent online spat about who "owns" the literary suburbs. John Carlos Rowe crosses national borders in order to conceive the transnational city with attention to how US neo-imperialism both destructively "Americanizes" cities elsewhere and some of the consequences of those overseas adventures on the cities of the homeland. In this way, he foregrounds what is overlooked when the transnational city is understood through its imbrication in the global circulation of capital and information or a focus on the diasporans and refugees that populate the world city without acknowledging the US role in uprooting peoples.

Ruth Salvaggio closes the first section with an examination of the transnational culture of rim cities that suggestively complements William Boelhower's chapter on the emergent biopolitics of the industrial city that opens the section on urban lives; both chapters attend to the patterns that collective life makes at the scale of the city. Focusing on New Orleans, Salvaggio elaborates an ecopoetics of place whose dominant element is water, the key to the city's geography and development, and a controlling metaphor for a culture constituted as the confluence of indigenous, African, and European peoples, music, poetry, and song. Boelhower examines Modernist and immigrant aesthetic representations of the emergent technological order of the twentieth-century metropolis, finding in them aesthetic expressions of the new anthropology that Marx had forecast and Gramsci confirmed: that crowds, technology, and media would give rise to a field of forces as much or more than an arrangement of spaces, thus, in its own way, to liquid cities defined for inhabitants by the experience of vertigo.

Those immigrants figure in the following two chapters. Joseph Entin's examination of US labor literature focuses on immigrant workers' importance to the labor movement and their hope to redraw the social geography of capitalist cities as one of three moments in the laboring city's literary history, along with the Great Depression and the waning of labor solidarity since the Reagan-era onset of the postindustrial economy. Using Italian American fiction and poetry as his focus, Fred Gardaphé follows the ambivalent path toward suburban whiteness traveled by descendants of white immigrants of the late nineteenth and early twentieth centuries as they migrated from ethnic enclaves, and how that experience is formally represented in the transition from realist to modernist narrative structures, and he engages with authors and critics who argue for forward-looking ethnic memory concerned less with reasserting lost ethnic ways than recovering traditions of critical engagement with American society and culture common to the earlier narratives. In a chapter conditioned by the shifting class and racial geographies discussed by Entin and Gardaphé, Brian Tochterman engages the evolution of realism over more than half a century of crime fiction and film, attending to these stories' role in framing popular understanding of urban problems and their solutions (including models of white masculinity from Philip Marlowe to Mike Hammer and Dirty Harry), the political exploitation of these narratives, African American cinematic responses to the world those narratives project, and the rise of the critically engaged crime series typified by David Simon and Ed Burns's string of Baltimore-set dramas.

Moving from what Tochererman calls the death-wish city to apocalyptic urbanism, Sean Grattan deploys Kim Stanley Robinson's Hurricane Sandy–influenced novel *New York 2140* (2017) as a window onto the discourse of apocalypse. The question this chapter pursues is what comes after the end, what modes of postapocalyptic and post-anthropocentric living might then arise because, Grattan notes, even as the apocalyptic genre portrays the destruction of one world through irreversible choices made that predate the narrative present, it clears a space to imagine new social forms better suited to the ends of life. The section closes with Erik Mortenson's critical engagement with twentieth-century bohemias, particularly the Beat movement's opposition to then-dominant cultural and social norms, the ways that revolt was recaptured as style, and the question of what remains today of interest in bohemia as a resistive and creative space and a utopian gesture.

The final section's five chapters place contemporary theory and literary texts (broadly construed) in dialogue to explore how theories inform our understanding of representations of urban space, life, and processes, as well as how literary texts may challenge and revise theories. Sophia Bamert and Hsuan L. Hsu supplement literary studies' spatial turn, which draws on the work of Marxist geographers with work in critical race theory to produce a more robust account of literature that engages the spatial imaginaries and practices responsible for the distribution of space and population in American cities. In a cognate study of two post–Hurricane Katrina texts, Arin Keeble argues the need to supplement trauma theory, which rewards readers with its attention to the manifold vectors of urban trauma – violence, uprooting, catastrophe, precarity – at which literature has always excelled, with the analytic of systemic and slow violence that lays bare the less-visible factors that often precipitate, and at other times intensify, traumatic effects on cities and urban populations, which both Dave Eggers's *Zeitoun* (2009) and David Simon and Eric Overmyer's *Treme* (2009–13) undertake to foreground.

Johannes Voelz places Michel Foucault's security dispositif in dialogue with a literary image of security mechanisms derived from city literature to examine the management of circulation in cities; rather than simply confirm the presence of a security dispositif, Voelz explicates the limitations of security theory as applied to literary fiction, which, he argues, evinces a structural need for moments of insecurity and free circulation. Approaching the question from a different angle, Andrew Pilsch crosses between science fiction, primarily Ann Leckie's *Imperial Radch* trilogy, and speculative theoretical interventions into urban systems, notably Benjamin Bratton's *The Stack* (2016), to limn the possibilities of an intelligent city no longer conceived, as it long has been for philosophers, planners, social scientists, and literary critics, as a spatial expression of Western humanism. Douglas Reichert Powell closes the section with an "outsider" view that argues for the importance of dialogue between urban studies and critical regionalism. While aesthetic regionalisms of the first half of the twentieth century regarded the city as the threating Other of, the nation's regional cultures, Powell deploys critical regionalism's practice of relation to diversify Appalachia and to relate it to the Rust Belt, inner cities, and the principally urban media ecology whose representations significantly determine how these regions are perceived via Appalachian artists' and writers' critical engagements with J. D. Vance's monolithic construction of Appalachian culture in *Hillbilly Elegy*, a polemical memoir published in 2016 and quickly embraced by pundits as explaining the year's

presidential election. The volume closes, with a coda that asks what
American literary history may teach us about the practice of democracy
as an undertaking of collective self-governance and and an ethical orientation toward others.

Despite best editorial efforts, three planned chapters did not materialize.
A chapter on the narratives of urban form and city life that have guided
urban planning and the cities they created – such as the City Beautiful's
emphasis on unifying the whole and creating public space, the City
Efficent's emphasis on speed and commerce, the Garden City's and New
Urbanism's nostalgic communitarianism, Jane Jacobs's city of neighborhoods – would have highlighted the context implicit in the literary and
cinematic texts discussed here. The other two chapters concern subjects
nevertheless discussed elsewhere in this volume. African American writers,
directors, and African American urban experience are, indeed, well represented throughout the volume, but the literary, visual, and musical history
of the African American city, its Afrofuturist projections, and the struggle
for rights and recognition, in the forefront as I write in the month after the
police murders of George Floyd and Breonna Taylor, deserves the sustained attention of a chapter.[21]

Likewise, issues potentially germane to the topic of ecological criticism
are notably developed in Sean Grattan's extended treatment of Kim
Stanley Robinson's climate crisis novel, Arin Keeble's discussion of two
Hurricane Katrina narratives, Sophia Bamert and Hsuan Hsu's engagements with environmental racism, and Ruth Salvaggio's ecopoetic
approach to New Orleans as a rim city, the last of which takes us notably
beyond the frame of the city as degraded space common to much American
ecocriticism, perhaps a legacy of the agrarian exceptionalism that has run
through the disciplinary imaginaries of American studies and American
literary studies and a strand of urbanist thought stretching from the garden
city to New Urbanism.[22]

If the political and cultural divide between urban and rural provides
something of an occasion for this volume, some caveats must be enumerated. First, if conservatives are now foremost in denigrating cities, there
have been – and still remain – significant strains of left anti-urbanism.
Second, as Reichert Powell rightly cautions, no region is nearly as homogeneous as this dichotomy would have it, and third, rural American
regions, notably Appalachia, have been dogged by accounts of pathological
monoculture similar to the diagnoses proffered for inner-city poverty.

With respect to the first caution, the historiography of American literary
history and the disciplinary history of American studies reveal a tradition of

progressive antiurban sentiment that helps us to answer the question headlining Will Wilkinson's 2018 critique of the apportionment of US political representation, "Why Do We Value Country Folk More than City People?" In the same broad terms that the headline uses, a political scientist might note that we always have; the three-fifths clause and the composition of the Senate and Electoral College wrote rural bias into the Constitution, while state-level redistricting still, to borrow Wilkinson's phrase, "effectively gives extra votes to dirt."[23] The literary and cultural answer runs through histories of canonization and myths of American character that were not always politically conservative. In fact, a central strain in American studies for decades valorized the rural as a voice of democratic dissent raised by a "minority of political radicals, writers, artists, clergymen, and independent intellectuals" against narratives of "progress disseminated by spokesmen for the dominant economic and political elites," whose fortunes derived from industrialization and the proletarianization of labor.[24]

Two foundational texts of this history roughly bracket Lears's years of crisis in cultural authority. Raised in still-frontier Wisconsin, Frederick Jackson Turner wrote "The Significance of the Frontier in American History" (1893) as a eulogy for an ethos shaped by that "line of most rapid and effective Americanization," whose denizens' "impulses [were] stronger, their wills less restrained" than were easterners' – or even Crèvecoeur's sentimental farmer – and whose confidence in their equality with all others and jealousy of their rights were unrivaled.[25] In this soil lay the roots of American democracy, Turner insisted, not in transplanted institutions. He salved his anxiety about its survival in the absence of a frontier and in the presence of immigrants who were never born again in the American loam by insisting that the frontier character had by 1890 been so "wrought into the very warp and woof of American thought" that it necessarily would survive industrialization. As evidence, Turner improbably offered Andrew Carnegie, Mark Hanna, John D. Rockefeller, and other Gilded Age titans who hailed from the West or moved there, despite the manifest threats their careers and politics posed to ideals of individual self-reliance and social equality that he celebrated.[26]

A generation later, Kansas-bred Vernon Louis Parrington shifted focus from the hypermasculine frontiersman back to the frontier yeoman when he cast American history as a contest between physiocrats and financial and manufacturing interests – lengthened shadows of Thomas Jefferson, cast not as a slaveholder but a leader of yeomen in battle with Virginia's planter aristocracy, and Parrington's bête noire, Alexander Hamilton, as the force

of centralization behind the First Bank of the United States, the Society for
Establishing Useful Manufactures, and violent suppression of the Whiskey
Rebellion – in his magisterial *Main Currents in American Thought: An
Interpretation of American Literature from the Beginnings to 1920*
(1927–30).[27] Parrington hoped to write a history of the people's overcom-
ing of the interests. To his credit, he sought to relocate the resistive,
egalitarian strand of the American character in the post–Civil War era
among urban laborers rather than Gilded Age magnates, yet this effort of
Main Currents's third volume fits poorly with its first 900 pages, over
which hovers the image of Jefferson, contemptuous as he "looked into the
future [where] he saw great cities rising to breed their Roman mobs, duped
and exploited by demagogues, the convenient tools of autocracy[,] and
count[ed] the cost in social-well-being."[28] In short, the interdependence of
urban life and the centralization required for effective unionization equally
cut against grain of the national character Parrington sought to preserve.

   The mythic West retained its hold on US literary history during the
Cold War, less as frontier than as pastoral. Robert Spiller organized *The
Cycle of American Literature* (1955) as a story of two rolling frontiers, the
European settler-colonists' "conquest of the continent" and the machine's
conquest of "the garden of the world in the West," a phrase rejuvenated five
years earlier by Henry Nash Smith's study of the western lands as the basis
of American identity, *Virgin Land*. Throughout these decades, Mumford
maintained his stream of monographs and articles advancing his critique of
American urbanism and technology in the name of the garden city, which
wed the organic metaphors of urban growth used by his mentor, Patrick
Geddes, with a Jeffersonian understanding of democratic society whose
monoculture is evident in *The City* (Ralph Steiner and Willard Van Dyke,
1939), a promotional film screened at the New York World's Fair, to which
Mumford contributed an "overheated commentary."[29] To this body of
work Leo Marx added his elegiac study of the war between technology and
the American pastoral ideal, *The Machine in the Garden* (1964).

   Amidst an upsurge of historically grounded attention to city literature in
the 1990s, Richard Lehan's *The City in Literature: An Intellectual and
Cultural History* (1998) injected Spenglerian pessimism (which he wrongly
attributed to Mumford) into the frontier myth and the narrative of urban
decline.[30] Reading F. Scott Fitzgerald's *The Great Gatsby* (1925), Lehan
accepts Nick Carraway's implicit assessment that the city forecloses the
"sense of wonder [. . .] hope, [. . . and] desire" that Nick ascribes to Gatsby
and that, Lehan suggests, Turner had thought "inseparable from America"
itself. Rather than creating a new race and destiny in the "Hamiltonian"

city, Lehan continues, the city makes of race "an incomprehensible chaos."[31] (So, also, for language, Mumford had cautioned; the "babble of tongues" unleashed by "the great influx of non-English-speaking immigrants" furthers the undermining of regional cultures initiated by the machine.[32]) Recycling the agrarian myth that "the promise of America was betrayed [. . .] during the Civil War, when Jefferson's vision gave way to that of Hamilton," Lehan ignores how Fitzgerald's narrative undermines myth: the war made the Carraways when a great uncle sent a substitute into battle and ran a thriving wholesale hardware business that would have helped to provision the state's troops; besides, those Dutch sailors were traders.[33]

Lehan's selection of authors never hints at it, much as the selection of "classic" American literature never registered the urban voice,[34] but New York's "incomprehensible urban chaos" was a mosaic of ethnic communities themselves apprehensive about the city's encroachments on *their* communal ways even as nativists, assimilationists, pluralists, and what we would now call multiculturalists debated immigrants' and ethnic Americans' proper fate in leading weeklies and monthlies. To view these changes as incipient chaos is to ignore the agency of fragmentation in the making of selves and the remaking of culture. "The means to self-development," Sennett argues, lies in responsiveness to "ever more complex, fragmented experience," and the city, where "all the secret ambitions and all the suppressed desires find somewhere expression," as the pioneering urban sociologist Robert E. Park observed, is the ideal location for that undertaking. So Edgar Allan Poe's convalescing narrator of "The Man of the Crowd" (1845) discovers as he "hurl[s] himself headlong into the midst of the throng, in pursuit of an unknown, half-glimpsed, countenance that has, on an instant, bewitched him" by exceeding his catalog of known urban types. So Sherwood Anderson's George Willard affirms when he leaves the grotesques of *Winesburg, Ohio* (1919), hoping "paint the dreams of his manhood." And so, Ralph Ellison wrote of "a world so fluid and shifting that often within the mind the real and the unreal merge, and the marvelous beckons from behind the same sordid reality that denies its existence."[35] For eastern pilgrims such as George, hopeful members of the Great Migration, or men and women who leave the old neighborhood in search of knowledge, love, or other adventure, the promise of the city is the possibility of self-authorship.

Much of the freedom for self-invention derives from what Lewis Wirth, Park's student, called urban society's "heightened mobility." City life is discontinuous; the people one works with, plays with, worships with, and lives among, most often are different. Solidarities around labor and class are more often multiethnic, whereas ethnic identity is familial, communal, and frequently religious, but it almost inevitably crosses class boundaries. Among these groups and across myriad other affiliations motivated by avocational interests or instrumental objectives, city dwellers' relative status will fluctuate. Wirth seems not to have imagined that urbanites would be capable of mapping the web of relations in which they are enmeshed because the myriad groups "are tangential to each other or intersect in highly variable fashion."[36] The lightness of attachment and the prevalence of monofunctional relationships contributes to the atomization and anonymity of social life beyond the intimate community but thereby also loosens the norms and constraints that such communities enforce.

The complexity of this lived experience places urbanites in an aesthetic relationship with their cities; they create their selves through the process of representing their urban worlds and the patterns of their engagements within them. Whitman was attuned to the erotic possibilities latent in crowded thoroughfares, and he used it to ground his persona's democratic ethos. His celebration of the "flash of eyes offering me love, / Offering response to my own," and the

> Numberless crowded streets, high growths of iron, slender, strong, light, splendidly uprising toward clear skies,
>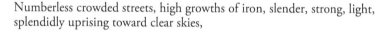
> The down-town streets, the jobbers' houses of business, the houses of business of the ship-merchants and money-brokers, the river-streets,
> Immigrants arriving, fifteen or twenty thousand in a week,
> The carts hauling goods, the manly race of drivers of horses, the brown-faced sailors,
> ·
> The mechanics of the city, the masters, well-formed, beautiful-faced, looking you straight in the eyes,
> [. . .] Broadway, the women, the shops and shows,

reveal both what Jason Frank describes as an "eroticized impersonality" that highlights "a queer proximity between cruising and citizenship," and what Iris Marion Young called the erotics of the city in "the wide sense" of all its sensuous phenomena that spark "the pleasure and excitement of being drawn out of one's secure routine to encounter the novel, strange, and surprising."[37] Frank O'Hara's poetry of distracted ambling continues that erotic engagement with the aleatory city; it stages the mutually constitutive play of mind and scene that organize perception into figures of thought and affect, an aesthetic democratic in the breadth of elements it arrays on a single plane. Its painterly analogy might be Robert Rauschenberg's *¼ Mile or Two Furlong Piece* (1981–98), a visual and aural environment in which the beholder becomes a stroller who makes chance connections among recycled material from the streets and images that are both a collective record of the times and a retrospective of Rauschenberg's oeuvre. In this way, *¼ Mile or Two Furlong Piece* mimics everyday tactics of place-making in the city, both the ways that city dwellers sift visual data into useful order and the way that the physical city takes shape from incidental juxtapositions of structures that accrete over time and are repurposed to accommodate (sub)cultural preferences or needs.

Whitman, O'Hara, and Rauschenberg thus explore some of the utopian possibilities of discovery and invention latent in the modernist city without borders and the generative potential within in the contingency of the everyday. Yet as my brief descriptions of the chapters to come suggest, the volume will more often attend to the representations of US cities as they are and have been, and how those utopian possibilities have been frustrated by the ends to which the physical, social, and cultural spaces of American cities have been shaped and how they, in turn, shape the consciousness and experience of city dwellers;[38] how writers and artist depict the conflicts and exclusions through which urban space is policed, and the modes of transgression, negotiation, and collaboration that remake space in ways that bring the city's myriad constituencies closer to realizing the city's promise as a site for individual self-creation and collective self-determination.

Notes

1. John Winthrop, "A Model of Christian Charity," in Alan Heimert and Andrew Delbanco, eds., *The Puritans in America: A Narrative Anthology* (Cambridge: Harvard University Press, 1985), p. 91.
2. Ronald Reagan, Farewell Address to the Nation, January 11, 1989, *The American Presidency Project*, www.presidency.ucsb.edu/documents/farewell-address-the-nation; Walt Whitman, Preface to *Leaves of Grass* (1855), in Justin Kaplan, ed., *Poetry and Prose* (New York: Library of America, 1996), p. 5.
3. J. Hector St. John de Crèvecoeur, Letter III, *Letters from an American Farmer* (Mineola, NY: Dover, 2005), p. 26.
4. Tony Monchinski, "Big Apple Redux: An Interview with Marshall Berman," *Cultural Logic* 8 (2001), http://ojs.library.ubc.ca/index.php/clogic/article/view/191963/188908, p. 9.

5. Lewis Mumford, *The Culture of Cities* (1938; New York: Harcourt, 1970), p. 279. *New York Daily News*, October 20, 1975, 1.

6. "In 1959," William Julius Wilson noted, "less than one-third of the poverty population in the United States lived in metropolitan central cities. By 1991, the central cities included close to half the nation's poor" (Wilson, *When Work Disappears: The World of the New Urban Poor* [1996; New York: Vintage, 1997], p. 12). In the new century, rates of suburban poverty have accelerated, with the largest concentration in older suburbs and the fewest people living in poverty in the newest suburbs (Scott W. Allard, *Places in Need: The Changing Geography of Poverty* [New York: Russell Sage Foundation, 2017], p. 58).

7. On the early twentieth-century struggle for home rule, see, e.g., Frederic C. Howe, *The City, the Hope of Democracy* (New York: Scribner's, 1905), pp. 158–76, 300–313. On recent attempts (often under the aegis of the Koch Brothers-funded American Legislative Exchange Council) to undermine local governance, see, e.g., Emily Badger, "Blue Cities Want to Make Their Own Rules. Red States Won't Let Them," *New York Times*, July 6, 2017, www.nytimes.com/2017/07/06/upshot/blue-cities-want-to-make-their-own-rules-red-states-wont-let-them.html. Most recently, Republican governors in Texas, Georgia, and other states, and courts in Wisconsin, overruled municipalities' plans for responding to the COVID-19 pandemic.

8. On *Blade Runner*'s city, see McNamara, "Los Angeles, 2019: Two Tales of a City," in John N. Duvall, ed., *Productive Postmodernism: Consuming Histories and Cultural Studies* (Albany: SUNY Press, 2002), pp. 123–36.

9. Garreau more recently dismissed reports of urban resurgence as "six cities [. . .] where the children of the people who read *The New York Times* live," while "the vast majority of Millennials" live "in the suburbs, like sensible human beings," a choice that expresses the "almost unlimited value [that Americans place] on individualism and freedom" (quoted in Jake Blumgart, "Return to Edge City," *CityLab*, April 10, 2018, www.citylab.com/design/2018/04/return-to-edge-city/552362/).

10. Witold Rybczynski, *City Life: Urban Expectations in a New World* (New York: Scribner, 1995), p. 210. Between 1945 and 1960, the urban population grew by 0.1 percent, while the suburban population grew 45 percent; with that shift and the rise of car ownership, public transportation use declined by nearly two-thirds between 1945 and 1965, and downtown shopping areas suffered from lack of convenient parking. Malls were already well established by the early 1960s; 1,600 shopping centers had been built by 1956, and another 2,500 were under construction. By 1963, 80 percent of Americans owned a car. (See Jon C. Teaford, *The Twentieth-Century American City: Problem, Promise, and Reality* [Baltimore: Johns Hopkins University Press, 1986], pp. 98–110.)

11. Winnie Hu, "Mall Case Creates Antiwar Celebrity," *New York Times*, March 7, 2003, B:4. In *Lloyd Corp v. Tanner* (1972), the Supreme Court ruled that mall owners have the right to curtail political speech; however, *PruneYard Shopping Center v. Robins* (1980) permits states to protect political

speech in malls. On the legal history of the mall's shift from "public" to private space, see Lizabeth Cohen, "From Town Center to Shopping Center: The Reconfiguration of Community Marketplaces in Postwar America," *American Historical Review* 101.4 (1996), 1068–72.

12. US Bureau of Economic Analysis, "Gross Domestic Product by Metropolitan Area, 2017," *Bureau of Economic Analysis*, www.bea.gov/news/2018/gross-domestic-product-metropolitan-area-2017.

13. Richard Florida, *The Rise of the Creative Class: And How It's Transforming Work, Leisure, Community, and Everyday Life* (New York: Basic, 2002), p. 8. On Pittsburgh, see Scott Andes, et al., *Capturing the Next Economy: Pittsburgh's Rise as a Global Innovation City* (Washington, DC: Brookings Institution, 2017).

14. Richard Sennett, *Building and Dwelling: Ethics for the City* (New York: Farrar, Straus, and Giroux, 2018), pp. 81, 79. One of Jacobs's major contentions throughout *The Death and Life of Great American Cities* (1961) is that what on the surface appear to be run-down areas are often stable neighborhoods that are undone by both disinvestment and redevelopment strategies that destroy the spaces and rhythms of collective life.

15. Sennett, *The Conscience of the Eye: The Design and Social Life of Cities* (New York: Knopf, 1990), p. 127.

16. See, e.g., M. Christine Boyer, "Cities for Sale: Merchandising History at South Street Seaport," in Michael Sorkin, ed., *Variations on a Theme Park: The New American City and the End of Public Space* (New York: Hill and Wang, 1992), pp. 190–91; and Bart Eeckhout, "The 'Disneyfiction' of Times Square: Back to the Future?," *Critical Perspectives on Urban Development* 6 (2001), 379–428. CityWalk, a walkable representation of a baby-boomer Los Angeles that never existed, built on the Universal Studios lot on the other side of the Hollywood Hills, is the apotheosis of this trend; see McNamara, "CityWalk: Los(t) Angeles in the Shape of a Mall," in Dirk De Meyer et al., eds., *The Urban Condition: Space, Community, and Self in the Contemporary Metropolis* (Rotterdam: 010 Press, 1999), pp. 186–201.

17. Roman Speron, quoted in Candace Jackson, "The Suburbs Are Coming to a City near You," *New York Times*, May 18, 2019, www.nytimes.com/2019/05/18/opinion/sunday/the-suburbs-cities.html.

18. Donald Trump, Inaugural Address, January 20, 2017, *The American Presidency Project*, www.presidency.ucsb.edu/documents/inaugural-address-14; T. J. Jackson Lears, *No Place of Grace: Antimodernism and the Transformation of American Culture, 1880–1920* (New York: Pantheon, 1981), p. 3.

19. See, among others, Ronald Brownstein, "Trump Is Determined to Split the Country in Two," *The Atlantic*, July 22, 2020, www.theatlantic.com/politics/archive/2020/07/trumps-portland-offensive-fits-long-pattern/614476/; Quinta Jurecic and Benjamin Wittes, "Nothing Can Justify the Attack on Portland," *The Atlantic*, July 21, 2020, www.theatlantic.com/ideas/archive/2020/07/nothing-can-justify-attack-portland/614413/; and David Smith, "Trump Announces

'Surge' of Federal Officers into Democratic-Run Cities," *The Guardian*, July 22, 2020, www.theguardian.com/us-news/2020/jul/22/donald-trump-federal-officers-police-surge-chicago.

20. Robert Venturi, Denise Scott Brown, and Steven Izenour, *Learning from Las Vegas: The Forgotten Symbolism of Architectural Form*, rev. ed. (Cambridge, MA: MIT Press, 1977), p. 76.

21. Black authors' absence from "Urban Borders, Open Wounds" reflects an editorial decision premised on the contents of the absent chapter.

22. But see, e.g., Michael Bennett and David W. Teague, eds., *The Nature of Cities: Ecocriticism and Urban Environments* (1999); J. Scott Bryson, "Surf, Sagebrush, and Cement Rivers: Reimagining Nature in Los Angeles," in McNamara, ed., *The Cambridge Companion to the Literature of Los Angeles* (New York: Cambridge University Press, 2010), pp. 167–76; Catrin Gersdorf, "Nature in the Grid: American Literature, Urbanism, and Ecocriticism," in Stefan L. Brandt, Winfried Fluck, and Frank Mehring, eds., *Transcultural Spaces: Challenges of Urbanity, Ecology, and the Environment* (Tübingen: Narr, 2010), pp. 21–40, and "Urban Ecologies: An Introduction," *Ecozon@* 7.2 (2016), http://ecozona.eu/article/view/1151/1224; and, at a broader scope, McNamara and Timothy Gray, "Some Versions of Urban Pastoral," in McNamara, ed., *The Cambridge Companion to the City in Literature* (New York: Cambridge University Press, 2014), pp. 245–60.

23. Will Wilkinson, "Why Do We Value Country Folk More than City People?," *New York Times*, June 27, 2018, www.nytimes.com/2018/06/27/opinion/republicans-democrats-trump-urban-rural.html. This is not to say that the rural is uniformly conservative, Christian, and white, but electoral effects derive from majorities, and districts often are drawn at the state level to benefit the party in power.

24. Leo Marx, *The Machine in the Garden: Technology and the Pastoral Ideal in America* (New York: Oxford University Press, 1990), p. 393.

25. Frederick Jackson Turner, *The Frontier in American History* (New York: Henry Holt, 1921), p. 34; Turner, "The Significance of the Section in American History," *Wisconsin Magazine of History* 8.3 (1925), 262, quoting John Archibald Campbell of Alabama, who did "not wish to increase the number [of states] until the New States [sic] already admitted to the Union become civilized"; Turner omits to note that behind Campbell's anxiety is the potential antislavery sentiment of newly admitted Western states (Campbell, letter to John C. Calhoun, November 30, 1847, in J. Franklin Jameson, ed., *Correspondence of John C. Calhoun* [Washington, DC: Government Printing Office, 1899], p. 1141).

26. Turner, *Frontier in American History*, p. 264.

27. Dana D. Nelson reads the rebellion as an instance of commons democracy and mentions Hamilton's role in its suppression in *Commons Democracy: Reading the Politics of Participation in the Early United States* (New York: Fordham University Press, 2016), pp. 53–67.
Hamilton is miscast as Machiavellian schemer, but he fares no better as multicultural democrat. To Jefferson's proposal to grant citizenship to

"every one manifesting a bona fide purpose of embarking his life and fortunes permanently with us," Hamilton responded by tracing Rome's fall to "her precipitate communication of citizenship to all of Italy" and noting that in France "[a] foreigner" had "erected a despotism on the ruins of a Republic." He concluded, in now Trumpian terms, "*It is certain*, that had the late election been decided entirely by native citizens [. . .], the man [i.e., Jefferson] who ostentatiously vaunts that the *doors of public honor and confidence have been burst open to him*, would not now have been at the head of the American nation" (Jefferson, First Annual Message to Congress, December 8, 1801, in Julian P. Boyd, et al., eds., *Papers of Thomas Jefferson*, 44 vols. to date [Princeton, NJ: Princeton University Press, 1943–], 36:64; Lucius Crassus [Hamilton], "The Examination Number VII" [January 7, 1802], in Harold C. Syrett, ed., *The Papers of Alexander Hamilton*, 27 vols. [New York: Columbia University Press, 1961–87], 25:494, 494, 494, 493; Hamilton's italics).

28. Vernon Louis Parrington, *Main Currents in American Thought: An Interpretation of American Literature from the Beginnings to 1920*, 3 vols. (New York: Harcourt, 1930), 3:46, 3:174, 3:173, 1:346.

29. Howard Gillette, Jr., "Film as Artifact: *The City* (1939)," *American Studies* 18.2 (1977), 76.

30. Lehan writes that "Oswald Spengler and Lewis Mumford saw a short-circuiting process once the city becomes disconnected from the nourishing vitality of the land" (Richard Lehan, *The City in Literature: An Intellectual and Cultural History* [Berkeley: University of California Press, 1998], p. 6), but he neglected Mumford's own countermyth of the garden city and humanized technology. Mumford's biographer notes that while "Mumford agreed with Spengler that Faustian [technological] culture had entered the 'winter' of its development," he nevertheless "saw a brilliant post-Faustian world, a great revival of the regional and the organic outlook" in its aftermath (Donald L. Miller, *Lewis Mumford: A Life* [New York: Grove Press, 1989], p. 302).

31. Lehan, *City in Literature*, pp. 207, 207, 215, quoting Spengler, *The Decline of the West* [1918–23], 2 vols., trans. Charles Francis Atkinson (New York: Knopf, 1926), p. 131.

32. Mumford, *Culture of Cities*, p. 360.

33. Lehan, *City in Literature*, p. 208. Lehan appears unaware of Parrington's criticism of the American farmer who "had never been a land-loving peasant, rooted to the soil and thriving only in daily contact with familiar acres" but is instead "half middle-class, accounting unearned increment the most profitable crop, and buying and selling land as if it were calico" (Parrington, *Main Currents in American Thought*, 3:26).

34. Leo Marx later attributed the absence of urban voices from "classic American literature" to the fact that US cities, unlike their European counterparts, "embody relatively few features of any social order other than that of industrial capitalism" (Marx, "The Puzzle of Antiurbanism in Classic American Literature," in Lloyd Rodwin and Robert M. Hollister, eds., *Cities of the*

Mind: Images and Themes of the City in the Social Sciences [New York: Springer, 1984], pp. 166, 180).

35. Sennett, *Conscience of the Eye*, p. 127; Robert E. Park, "The City as Social Laboratory" (1929), in Everett Cherrington Hughes, et al., eds., *Human Communities: The City and Human Ecology*, vol. 2 of *The Collected Papers of Robert Ezra Park* (Glencoe, IL: Free Press, 1952), p. 87; Charles Baudelaire, "The Painter of Modern Life" (1863), in Jonathan Mayne, ed. and trans., *"The Painter of Modern Life," and Other Essays* (London: Phaidon, 1964), p. 7; Sherwood Anderson, *Winesburg, Ohio* (New York: Heubsch, 1919), p. 303; Ralph Ellison, "Harlem Is Nowhere," in *Collected Essays*, ed. John F. Callahan (New York: Modern Library, 1995), p. 322.

36. Lewis Wirth, "Urbanism as a Way of Life," *American Journal of Sociology* 44.1 (1938), 16.

37. Walt Whitman, "City of Orgies" (1860), *Poetry and Prose*, p. 279; Whitman, "Manahatta" (1860), ibid., pp. 585–86; Jason Frank, "Promiscuous Citizenship," in John E. Seery, ed., *A Political Companion to Walt Whitman* (Lexington: University of Kentucky Press, 2011), p. 175; Iris Marion Young, *Justice and the Politics of Difference* (Princeton, NJ: Princeton University Press, 1990), p. 239.

38. Caren Irr suggests that modernism's open city has in more recent fiction been replaced by a city medieval in its spatial and social relations (Irr, "Neomedievalism in Three Contemporary City Novels: Tobar, Adichie, Lee," *Canadian Review of Comparative Literature* 42 [2015], 441).

City Spaces

CHAPTER I

Antebellum Urban Publics

David Henkin

In 1775, the former colonial governor of Pennsylvania, then sixty-five, congratulated himself on knowing by name "every person white & black, men, women, and children, in the city." Since Philadelphia had a population around 15,000 during James Hamilton's tenure as governor, we might read his assertion with caution, but the fact that a prominent Philadelphian could even entertain such a boast suggests a particular experience and ideal of urban community. Less than seventy years after Hamilton made this claim, the reformer and cultural critic Lydia Maria Child would complain of only seeing two faces she recognized in "eight weary months [. . .] in the crowded streets" of New York. In many ways the shift from a premodern to a modern city is best captured by those two experiences.[1] In the United States, the transition took place with dramatic speed.

At the dawn of American independence, US cities were few, compact, and lightly populated. They were socially distinctive, to be sure: ethnically heterogeneous compared to towns and villages, riven by more overt forms of class conflict, and politically combustible in ways that shaped the course of revolution. But Philadelphia, New York, Boston, Baltimore, Newport, and Charleston – the only places in the new republic with populations of more than 10,000 – retained the basic characteristics of colonial port towns. Philadelphia, the largest city in British America at the time of the Revolution, covered less than one square mile, extending no further than seven blocks from the shore of the Delaware River and easily traversed on foot. In population (about 10,000–40,000), as in size, early American cities more nearly resembled our college campuses than our urban communities. As such, they were regulated by personal contact and facial recognition. Hamilton's self-aggrandizing and nostalgic recollection was essentially that of being his campus's big man.

By contrast, Child's New York in the 1840s, which by then had long eclipsed Philadelphia as the nation's leading city, represented a different kind of urban space. Home to more than 300,000 residents (the figure would exceed half a million by the end of that decade), the urban settlement stretched up the lower half of the island, well beyond the limits of what one could comfortably cover on foot in a couple of hours. New York was extreme, but not unique. By 1860, nine different US cities had crossed the population threshold of 100,000. The walking city of the early national era had given way to the antebellum world of strangers, epitomized by the anonymous crowd of unrecognizable, even illegible faces.

Although only a small percentage of Americans lived in big cities during the middle of the nineteenth century, those communities epitomized and symbolized new forms of impersonal social connectedness that reverberated in the nation's political, economic, and cultural life more generally. More specifically, the experience of urban crowding and anonymity had profound implications for the meaning of publicness, especially among participants in American print culture. Because authors, editors, and publishers in the nine largest cities in the United States accounted for the overwhelming majority of its literary output, the preoccupations and sensibilities of those who inhabited the urban world of strangers dominated American literature, journalism, and other forms of print entertainment. And in part for this reason, books, periodicals, and newspapers from the period thematized a new understanding of the public sphere. Whereas eighteenth-century urban authors were more likely to embrace Enlightenment models of publication and public exchange as occupying (or creating) an abstract, neutral space (albeit nationally or regionally distinctive) where *pseudonymous* authors could efface their private identities, many of the most popular, influential, or enduring antebellum American authors took the *anonymous*, promiscuous, cacophonous, and transitory city itself as the model for what it meant to engage or circulate in public.

The bustling spaces of the mid-nineteenth-century US city, both unprecedentedly dense and unprecedentedly sprawling in the North American context, had not been part of the national blueprint. Although disproportionately urbanites themselves, the founders and framers had mostly celebrated the fact that the new nation was, by contemporary European standards, overwhelmingly rural. In 1800, only six places in the young nation had populations of more than 10,000, and less than 4 percent of the nation lived in them. At a time when London held 865,000, Paris 548,000, Lisbon 350,000, and Vienna 232,000, there were no remotely comparable big cities in the United States – and to the first generation of American leaders, this was a source of pride and optimism. The integrity and stability of the republic depended, they insisted, on a dispersed citizenry of white, male landowners. And the absence of large cities would spare the United States from political intrigue, excessive democracy, mob rule, class conflict, and Old World corruption.

Nonetheless, the new nation became urban – not immediately, but still unmistakably. The proportion of Americans living in communities with populations more than 2,500 had remained roughly constant (about 5–6 percent) throughout the last quarter of the eighteenth century and into the very beginning of the nineteenth. But in the 1820s, the figure was rising sharply (8.8 percent by 1830), initiating the United States' century-long demographic shift from a minority-urban to a majority-urban society. The principal source of this transformation in the antebellum period was the attraction of economic opportunities in America's proliferating and growing towns and cities on rural migrants in the Northeast and both rural and urban immigrants from northwestern Europe. Because migrants chose disproportionately (but by no means exclusively) to relocate to cities in the North and West, the United States became more urban, even as its rural population grew.

Alongside this process of urbanization, another pattern emerged as well. The individual cities where Americans lived got much bigger (a development that typically accompanies urbanization, but does not have to), reaching population levels unseen in the history of the continent, outstripping Cahokia, Mexico City, and all the cities in British America. At the outbreak of the Civil War, New York (which then included only Manhattan) counted more than 800,000 residents. At more than 565,000, Philadelphia's population was more than ten times what it had been fifty years earlier. Brooklyn, Baltimore, Boston, New Orleans, Cincinnati, St. Louis, and Chicago all boasted six-digit populations. And San Francisco, which had been a tiny commercial village at the time of the mid-century gold rush, counted more people a decade later than had lived in any US city in 1800. These were the nation's ten major metropolitan centers at the end of the antebellum era, and together they incubated and represented new forms of urban life in the experience of the masses of men, women, and children who inhabited or visited them.

What made these cities qualitatively different from their early national predecessors was not simply that they were bigger and more crowded. Because the nation's big cities were dominated by newcomers and were extending urban settlement into areas that had been farmland within recent memory, they were, in multiple senses and from multiple perspectives, profoundly unfamiliar. In practical terms, traversing an unstable cityscape and encountering unrecognizable faces from unknown backgrounds became a standard and expected feature of everyday urban life. Symbolically, the anonymous urban crowd also underscored the larger problem of what was unknown, unknowable, or knowable only in the most general terms in big cities.

Beyond their staggering size, at least three subtler infrastructural developments, beginning in the years 1825–35, marked the emergence of the modern world of strangers in big antebellum cities. Unlike the major technological breakthroughs typically associated with nineteenth-century modernization, none of these developments depended directly on steam or electricity, nor did they entail breathtaking acceleration or the annihilation of distance. Yet they were central to distinguishing the antebellum metropolis from the seaport walking city of earlier periods, to differentiating urban experience from the experience of the nonurban majority, and to identifying what was broadly resonant and unsettling about modern life more generally. All three provided themes for Americans' literary encounters with the urban public.

The first of these urban innovations was fixed-route public transit, which allowed strangers to navigate the city without having to know (or communicate with) other people. Although historians often emphasize transportation innovations that accelerated the pace of streetcar service and expanded the commuting radius of walking cities, in many respects, it was the fixity of a route rather than speed (which increased slowly and varied widely) or locomotive power that defined a transit system as meaningfully public in this era. When horse-drawn omnibuses began regular service along New York's Broadway in 1829, the streets opened up to fare-paying strangers in a recognizably modern way. Within a few years, urban transit companies were operating omnibuses in Boston, Philadelphia, Baltimore, New Orleans, Washington, DC, and Brooklyn. Omnibuses were soon joined by street railway cars, also powered by horses but larger, faster, and much more definitively fixed in their routes, which became the dominant form of urban transportation by the middle of the century.

Urban transit systems certainly expanded the distances people could conveniently travel between home and work. But they did other things as well, enabling anonymous circulation in public space while thrusting strangers together in microcosms of the larger promiscuous crowd. An 1860 description of London's omnibuses reprinted for *New York Times* readers familiar with the phenomenon captured some of the socially subversive features of early public transit:

> There is something irresistibly comic in an omnibus full of utter strangers. Face to face they sit, and their muscles are perfectly rigid; they nod forward,

like an old dame dozing, at every jolt of the omnibus, and threaten each other with their noses; they stare vacantly at the brims of each other's hats or bonnets; their hands are crossed upon the handles of their sticks or umbrellas; and they speak never a word. [. . .] You there see man in his primitive state, not of nudity, of course, but of incivility.[2]

But if the silent anonymity of bus riders struck some observers as uncivil, it also represented a new code of public life, a set of agreements that urban space did not require personal introductions or legible identities.

The second major innovation in antebellum urban culture was commercial nightlife, something that remains a defining characteristic of modern cities. In earlier periods, city streets were largely empty after dark, but by mid-century, restaurants, bowling alleys, oyster bars, saloons, cheap theaters, dance halls, and various kinds of commercial sex venues had become standard features of the urban nightscape. Gaslight, which appeared first on the streets of Baltimore in 1816, spread to other cities in the 1820s, serving the needs of a growing market for late-night entertainment. By later standards, gas lamps provided only partial illumination and created none of the spectacle that would be associated with electrified cityscapes at the end of the century. But gaslight opened new worlds of nocturnal activity, available to strangers with money. And its limited illumination made gaslight a compelling figure in the writings of mid-century observers and reformers seeking to describe what went on in cities after dark in lurid and sensational terms. One popular journalist, chronicling *New York by Gaslight*, decried "the fearful mysteries of darkness in the metropolis – the festivities of prostitution, [. . .] the haunts of theft and murder, the scenes of drunkenness and beastly debauch."[3]

A third crucial piece of new cultural infrastructure in antebellum urban life hit closer to home for those who wrote about cities and crowds in the United States. Although newspapers had appeared in American cities throughout the eighteenth century and had expanded considerably during the early national era with the support of subsidized postage and the encouragement of national political parties, the modern relationship between the press and the urban populace had yet to emerge before the 1830s. Newspapers were produced in cities (the 1828 publication of the *Cherokee Phoenix* in Cherokee country/rural Georgia was a rare exception to this pattern), but they did not address the mass of residents in their places of publication, nor did they concern themselves with urban life. Readers might be local or distant, but in either case, they tended to be prosperous elites, businessmen interested in commodity prices or ship arrivals, or (depending on the newspaper) party faithful seeking national or foreign news from a congenial ideological perspective. In 1833, however, a journeyman printer named Benjamin Day presented New Yorkers with a new product, promising on his masthead "to lay before the public, at a price within the means of every one, ALL THE NEWS OF THE DAY, and at the same time afford an advantageous medium for advertising."[4] Within months, his daily *Sun* was the most popular paper in the city, offering a smaller, cheaper product to a mass readership and employing an army of newsboys to hawk individual copies in public space. The penny paper business model quickly spread to other big cities, with similarly spectacular results. The *Boston Daily Times* took only a few weeks to earn the highest circulation in that city, while the *Baltimore Sun* amassed a circulation three times its nearest competitor's before it was nine months old.

Cheap urban dailies initiated new, less-affluent readers into modern habits of news consumption. Some early penny papers also had ties to working-class politics, but after the Panic of 1837, many went out of business. The survivors attracted readers from different classes and usually disclaimed any formal identification with particular political parties, appealing instead to a wide local readership by offering popular fiction, descriptions of city life, sensational crime stories, and classified advertising that helped ordinary people find work, entertainment, services, and consumer products. Significantly, the city itself was both the setting and the primary subject in much of that content, cementing a geographical identification between the producers and imagined readership of the news that would persist in American print journalism. And because the cheap dailies addressed their readers not primarily as fellow merchants, businessmen, and lawyers but as big-city dwellers, their frequent invocations of "the public" (as in Day's masthead) referred implicitly to a vast, anonymous urban populace.

Alongside those three new urban institutions – fixed-route transit, commercial nightlife, and cheap daily newspapers – two older ones expanded dramatically during the second quarter of the nineteenth century. One was the wage system, which had been practiced to some extent in American cities since their inception but had been marginal compared to other forms of compensating, organizing, and disciplining urban labor (including slavery, apprenticeship, and providing room and board) before this period. The other, partly related to the wage system, was the boardinghouse, where unrelated strangers shared lodgings and meals for short periods. These two arrangements became dominant in large northern and western cities during the antebellum years (and even in New Orleans, Baltimore, and St. Louis, where chattel slavery flourished, wage-paying and boarding proliferated rapidly) and marked the arrival of the modern city. Like omnibuses, gas lamps, and cheap dailies, both wage payments and boardinghouses provided useful themes and powerful material and symbolic resources for representing city life in print.

Writing about the phenomenon of the big city spread across the American literary landscape. Many of the most popular antebellum authors – Fanny Fern, George Lippard, Ned Buntline, Maria Cummins, George Thompson, and others – set their poems, stories, and novels in urban space, frequently emphasizing the new practices and institutions that facilitated the circulation of strangers. The canonical authors of the American Renaissance were similarly engaged with urban themes and content. Some examples are well studied, such as the representations of the crowd in Walt Whitman's *Leaves of Grass* (1855), Herman Melville's *Pierre* (1852), and Edgar Allan Poe's trilogy of Dupin stories. Poe's extensive quotations from the New York penny press coverage of a violent death in "The Mystery of Marie Rogêt" (1842) underscore the close relationship between literary and journalistic representations of the city and their shared interest in the social relations particular to the urban world of strangers. A slightly earlier Poe story, "The Man of the Crowd" (1840), set in London, focused even more directly on the forms of spectatorship and the crises of legibility associated with such social relations. So did Melville's "Bartleby, the Scrivener: A Story of Wall Street" (1853), which shared Poe's particular interest in the mysterious resistance of the urban stranger to sympathetic identification.

But the distinctive imaginative responses of singular authors to the conditions of public life in the large cities in which they wrote and published may be less instructive than the broad conventions with which they wrestled and the popular forms of urban representation by which they were surrounded. In addition to the daily newspaper itself, three disparate but related genres helped to frame the mid-century American literary encounter with what was unwieldy, unfamiliar, or simply difficult to grasp about urban growth. The least literary-seeming were the official city guides and directories (the first of which appeared in 1794 in Philadelphia) that listed local businesses and offered practical information, often under the imprimatur of the municipal government. By 1840, city directories had become familiar texts and standard urban amenities, typically seeking to represent a city's major public buildings and institutions as evidence of civic order and anchors of prospective economic growth. Many of these guidebooks featured pictures, enlisting the skills of leading lithographers and photographers to offer readers a sense of the frenetic metropolis as a manageable, legible entity.

By contrast, other, more popular mid-century guides to the metropolis tended to dramatize, rather than contain, the chaos of urban life, promising to expose the hidden dangers and pleasures of the city to a readership that could remain at a safe distance. Prominent among these were works of melodramatic fiction: the city-mysteries novels modeled on Eugene Sue's *Les Mystères de Paris* (1842). From the mid-1840s on, many of the most successful works of nineteenth-century American fiction fit comfortably within this category. Ned Buntline's *Mysteries and Miseries of New York* (1848), like its counterparts appearing first in serial installments in the popular press, was reprinted in a book format that quickly sold close to 100,000 copies. A slew of titles followed in its wake, turning every American city into the object of literary unmasking. Some of these novels, such as Henry Boernstein's *The Mysteries of St. Louis* (1851), Emil Klauprecht's *Cincinnati; or, The Mysteries of the West* (1854–55), and Ludwig von Reizenstein's *The Mysteries of New Orleans* (1854–55), were published originally in German by immigrant authors. Other works that did not explicitly invoke Sue in their titles nonetheless belong to this genre, including the quasi-pornographic *Venus in Boston* (1849) by George Thompson and George Lippard's *Quaker City; or, The Monks of Monk-Hall* (1844–55), which was the bestselling novel written by an American before *Uncle Tom's Cabin*.

Alongside these novelistic unmaskings of crime, vice, and corruption in the big city proliferated a host of texts offering ostensibly nonfictional sketches or exposés. In rhetoric and imagery, these urban guides shared much with the melodramatic fiction. In place of an omniscient narrator, authors like George Foster, James McCabe, and Junius Henri Browne invoked the privileged access of the urban connoisseur. Less commonly, as in Maria Monk's fraudulent anti-Catholic provocation *Awful Disclosures of the Hôtel Dieu Nunnery* (1836), an author might also claim the authority of firsthand traumatic experience. But the classic sensationalist journalist was male, intrepid, and aloof, in some cases modeled on British or (less often) Continental traditions of detached literary spectatorship. Armed with these sensibilities and the authority of having insider access to unfamiliar places, the narrator guided readers on tours of nightlife, demimondes, and slums.

Despite the obvious differences between such journalistic surveys of places and people in the contemporary city and the lurid fictional tales of crime and tragedy that composed the city-mysteries genre, the links between the two types of literature are sufficiently tight that scholarly discussions of urban sensationalism often confuse the two. Significantly, the titles often offer little help in sorting out the genres. Texts like *Sunshine and Shadow in New York* (1868), *Lights and Shadows in San Francisco* (1876), and *Boston Inside Out!* (1880), to name but a few representatives, were not novels at all but rather guidebooks. McCabe's *Lights and Shadows of New York Life* (1872), for example, even partook of elements of official city directories, interspersing sensational descriptions of vice with architectural illustrations, biographies of leading journalists and tycoons, and explanations of the workings of city government.

The emphasis on light and darkness in all these urban guides indicates their shared preoccupation and marketing strategy. While alluding to the pleasures and perils of the artificially illuminated nocturnal cityscape, the sun and shade metaphors also framed the interplay between the concealed and the revealed city. Urban connoisseurs and novelists offered to decode and demystify the city by lifting the veil of darkness under which it lay shrouded. At the same time, the contrast between light and darkness served a political purpose as well, insofar as it evoked a contrast between two halves of the city. Much as muckraking journalists of a later era would use light and darkness to tell sensational stories of how the other half of a city lives, antebellum critics were fond of juxtaposing the extremes of opulence and degradation that coexist in cramped urban confines. Matthew Hale Smith's sensational guide to *Sunshine and Shadow in New York* aligned rhetorically with Lippard's fictional *New York: Its Upper Ten and Lower Million* (1854).

Certainly, readers consumed city directories, urban exposés, and melodramatic novels for different reasons and with different expectations. But all three genres addressed, exploited, and encouraged the same perception that cities were vast entities in need of decoding. Why exactly cities needed such decoding was not always clear. Perhaps because cities remained anomalous social arrangements in an overwhelmingly rural nation, they could be treated as distant and unfamiliar destinations to a mass readership residing elsewhere. Alternatively, because cities were so sprawling and overpopulated, they seemed distant and unfamiliar to local readers as well, most of whom were themselves newcomers. Certainly, many sketches and novels implied that cities were marked by deceptive or opaque surfaces and that guides were needed to penetrate those surfaces. Both city-mysteries novels and sensational urban journalism tend to move from streets and exteriors into the enclosed spaces of houses, brothels, and saloons. If daily newspapers tended to focus on streets, docks, and plazas and to equate the urban public with the urban outdoors (a tendency characteristic of Whitman and Poe as well), authors like George Foster and George Lippard destabilized that equation. The broadly visible inter-actions of anonymous strangers in urban space were to them mere camou-flage for power relations that lay hidden from view.

Yet despite their interest in power relations, in conflicts over wealth and politics, and in the racial, religious, and sexual animosities that have animated generations of writers about the urban public, the camouflage itself was – and remains – paradoxically foundational. The public life of jostling, agglomerated, exposed, dimly illuminated, constantly counted, and inconsistently legible bodies – sometimes outdoors, sometimes under-ground, sometimes buried under the weight of labor or commerce or legal surveillance, sometimes transgressively spectacular – continues to structure the settings for our city stories.

Notes

1. James Hamilton, quoted in "Diary of James Allen, Esq., of Philadelphia," *Pennsylvania Magazine of History and Biography*, IX (July 1885), p. 185; Lydia Maria Child, *Letters from New-York* (London: Richard Bentley, 1843), p. 92.
2. "Omnibuses," *Chambers's Journal*, April 14, 1860, 228; "Omnibuses," *New York Times*, May 26, 1860, 8.
3. George G. Foster, *New York by Gaslight and Other Urban Sketches*, ed. Stuart M. Blumin (Berkeley: University of California Press, 1990), p. 69.
4. *New York Sun*, September 3, 1833, 1.

CHAPTER 2

Intersections
Streets and Other Democratic Spaces

John Fagg

Five Points. That name, which in the four-square grid-plan city of New York insists on an excess of intersection, conjured, in David Henkin's words, "perhaps the dominant pejorative symbol of urban intensification and social heterogeneity in antebellum America."[1] Five Points was associated with cramped tenements that housed recent Irish and African American arrivals to the city, and with crime and vice; it was there that Davy Crockett witnessed "Black and white, white and black, all hug-em-snug together," and there too that he "saw more drunk folks, men and women, that day, than I ever saw before."[2] Crockett's emphasis on what he was able to see is significant. In his account of streets as sites of "public reading" Henkin observes that Edward Clay's 1837 lithograph, *The Times*, depicts Five Points as "a collage of writing – a bazaar of spurious print claims covering a multitude of surfaces" and Tyler Anbinder similarly notes that in George Catlin's painting *Five Points* (ca. 1827), as in prints and paintings made after it (Illustration 2.1), "grocery" signs indicate liquor for sale while "prostitutes brazenly solicit customers."[3] The neighborhood's vibrant, notorious street culture made visible its demographics and encouraged observers to come to conclusions about its character. During his brief spell as editor of the *Aurora* in 1842, Walt Whitman alluded to the Five Points, "the neighborhood of the Tombs," in a report, "Incidents of last Night," that moved from a confrontation there "between some squads of Irish, and a number of Americans, whom they insulted grossly" to the announcement of the day's election result outside Tammany Hall, "where we found the crowd great, and the passages and walks in front filled with an immense mass of people."[4] In the space of a few blocks and a few paragraphs Whitman observes tensions within the city's heterogeneous population and a broad public's involvement in the (supposedly) democratic process out in the open in the street.

2.1 Unknown artist (after George Catlin), *The Five Points* (ca. 1827). Oil on wood panel. Bequest of Mrs. Screven Lorillard (Alice Whitney), from the collection of Mrs. J. Insley Blair, 2016. Courtesy of the Metropolitan Museum of Art.

Whitman's experiences as a reporter were among those he drew on as he turned to poetry in which he embraced "the rush of the streets," told of lovers "Jostling me through streets," and "[found] letters from God dropped in the street."[5] Whitman sang city streets, ferries, bridges and other meeting points as sites of encounter, exchange, and reciprocity: "If you meet some stranger in the street and love him or her, do I not often meet strangers in the street and love them?"[6] That embrace of the street was not, though, without its complications. As Anbinder explains, "The racial and political pressures that had been building up in New York during the first two years of the [Civil War] exploded in the spring of 1863,"[7] with the Draft Riots in which Five Points mobs attacked African American residents and their properties and violence erupted on a still greater scale in neighborhoods farther north. "So the mob has risen at last in New York," Whitman wrote his mother from Washington, DC. "The passions of the people were only sleeping, & have burst forth with terrible fury, & they have destroyed life and property." This was, a later letter declared, "the devil's own work."[8] The radical freedom for erotic, communal and democratic expression that the poet found in city streets also facilitated violent and destructive acts. At the same time the street's invitation to look and to draw conclusions gave license to prejudiced and pejorative ways of seeing. Citing the rapid growth and diversification of Manhattan's population, Karen Karbiener suggests that "here, perhaps more than anywhere else on earth during Whitman's day, residents were driven to possess a global awareness, challenged to recognize and tolerate difference, and tested to the limits of their humanity."[9] In an 1868 letter, Whitman described a visit to Five Points as "instructive but disgusting – I saw one of the handsomest white girls there I ever saw, only about 18 – blacks & white are all intermingled."[10]

Whitmanian chants and catalogs provide a "native" mode for singing diverse, bustling, complex cities that later writers combined with the practices of the flâneur and the literary impressionist assimilated from Europe. This chapter considers twentieth- and twenty-first-century Americans working in these ways, often quite explicitly after Whitman, who found verbal and visual languages for the intersection on city streets of individuals and crowds, of what might be objectively reported and what can only be felt and limned, and of lived everyday experience and political expression. In political discourse and in city planners' schemes "the street" can become an abstraction: the locus of commonplace opinion or a site of grassroots protest; a space for public interaction or privatized commercial transaction. What Main Street thinks. Ask the man on the street. Take to the streets. Urban regeneration. Multidimensional street-level culture. Poetry, prose, painting, and photography flesh out and complicate the lived experience of American urban spaces to reveal the messy complexities of street life. Street art and writing reveal a politics that can be felt and intuited by strolling the sidewalk or dipping into a barroom, though these sites can also project false fronts and false promises of community. The street becomes the space in which to find community or register detachment from it. It becomes, too, the space of visible, physical action in which individuals and groups come together, spontaneously or in organized protest, or come apart as order breaks down and confrontation and rioting take hold. However policed and regulated, the street holds the promise of unofficial, untrammeled democratic feeling and expression, of the best and the worst that this phrase might mean.

Among the impressions of streets seen for the first time in decades in *The American Scene* (1907), Henry James found "our vast crude democracy of trade" expressed in "the new, the simple, the cheap, the common, the commercial, the immediate, and, all too often, the ugly."[11] Against this stood Trinity Church, once "the pride of the town and the feature of Broadway," whose architecture fitted "a patient pedestrian sense and permitting thereby a relation of intimacy" recalled the knowable, human-scaled city Whitman addressed in his 1888 poem "Broadway":

> Thou portal – thou arena – thou of the myriad long-drawn lines and groups!
> (Could but thy flagstones, curbs, facades tell their inimitable tales;
> Thy windows, rich and huge hotels – thy side-walks wide;)
> Thou of the endless sliding, mincing, shuffling feet![12]

In 1905, Trinity Church stood at the intersection "just where Broadway receives from Wall Street the fiercest application of the maddening lash." Venturing down Wall Street, James, the "restless analyst," struggled to derive meaning from his sensory perceptions of the built environment and its people: "'the state of the streets' and the assault of the turbid air seemed all one with the look, the tramp, the whole quality and allure, the consummate monotonous commonness, of the pushing male crowd, moving in its dense mass with the confusion carried to chaos for any intelligence, any perception; a welter of objects and sounds in which relief, detachment, dignity, meaning, perished utterly and lost all rights." The things that drew Whitman to crowds, including the surrender of individual identity to the mass, repelled James. Elsewhere, and most significantly in Central Park, James saw benign and even utopian possibilities, but the mix of crowd and commerce on Wall Street prompted patrician disdain for America's democratic citizenry. The passage ends by likening the scene to "the heaped industrial battlefield" and with the crowd's "will to move – to move, move, move, as an end in itself, an appetite at any price."[13] In such accounts the street serves as an index of democracy's negative potential, the unchecked momentum of a faceless, unknowable mob.

Writing in the year James published *The American Scene*, the painter John Sloan used the same language of density and chaos to describe Manhattan crowds in his November 5, 1907, diary entry:

> After dinner I went out again and saw the noisy trumpet blowers, confetti throwers and the "ticklers" in use – a small feather duster on a stick which is pushed in the face of each girl by the men, and in the face of men by the girls. A good humored crowd, so dense in places that it was impossible to control one's movement.[14]

In a painting made from memory some days later, *Election Night* (1907; Illustration 2.2), Sloan visualizes both the detail and the general sensation of his prose. As in Whitman's newspaper report of the scene outside Tammany Hall, election results have brought people out onto the streets

2.2 John Sloan, *Election Night* (1907). Oil on canvas 26 ⅜ x 32 ¼ in. (67 x 81.9 cm).
Memorial Art Gallery of the University of Rochester, Marion Stratton Gould Fund.

and brought forth a carnivalesque remaking of the city now illuminated by
electric light. While not overtly marked as partisan, the crowd's febrile mix of
excitement and menace is charged by participation in the democratic process. In the first decade of the twentieth century, Sloan and other Ashcan
School painters treated with measured enthusiasm the sensations of being
jostled, assailed, and overwhelmed by urban crowds from which James had
recoiled. Their street-level visual aesthetic often cast painter and viewer as
vicarious participants in playful crowds of city dwellers "behaving as if they
know they will be observed by strangers and at times positively enjoying it."[15]
    The Sixth Avenue El and, to the left, the Herald Building locate the
scene of *Election Night* near to Sloan's own Chelsea neighborhood, a dozen
blocks from his apartment. As art historian Alexis Boylan has argued, the
Ashcan School tended to elide signs of difference in picturing a "generic
whiteness" and creating "a vision of New York that is almost exclusively
populated by white men."[16] While he was, in *Election Night* and elsewhere,

more attentive to women's bodies and presence than his peers, Sloan's positive take on the election night street crowd is in part a product of his perceived proximity to the people he paints. As a June 7, 1910, diary entry suggests, Sloan was equally engaged but less at home in other neighborhoods: "I took a walk thro' the East Side – most interesting afternoon – I went thro' the section between Brooklyn and W'[illia]msburg [*sic*] bridges. Life is thick! colorful. I saw more than my brain could comprehend, a maze of living incidents – children by thousands in the streets and parks. [...] The Jews seem to predominate in this section."[17] James had been similarly bemused by the "intensity of the material picture in the dense Yiddish quarter" and in response intensified his language of mass and texture: "it was the sense, after all, of a great swarming, a swarming that had begun to thicken, infinitely, as soon as we had crossed to the East side and long before we had got to Rutgers Street. There is no swarming like that of Israel when once Israel has got a start, and the scene here bristled, at every step, with the signs and sounds, immitigable, unmistakable, of a Jewry that had burst all bounds."[18] While "swarming" risks lapse into anti-Semitic tropes, James saw an individuality and distinctive personhood on the streets of the Lower East Side resistant to the reification witnessed on Wall Street. Both he and Sloan, in walking Lower East Side streets and looking at them closely, came to a more nuanced understanding, without wholly shedding their touristic distance from the scene.

"Hester Street," the first chapter of Anzia Yezierska's *Bread Givers* (1925), ends with ten-year-old Sara Smolinsky positioning herself on a bustling Lower East Side corner. Sara's cry of "Herring! Herring!" is "louder than all the hollering noises of bargaining and selling." Her performance prompts a passing woman to mock, "Also a person [...] also fighting already for the bite in the mouth," but this clearly is a moment of coming to selfhood for Yezierska's protagonist. Perceived from the position of a participant, the street scene that seemed daunting to young Sara and other to outsiders like James and Sloan is remade: "The pushcart peddlers yelling their goods, the noisy playing of children in the gutter, the women pushing and shoving each other with their market baskets – all that was only hollering noise before melted over me like a new beautiful song."[19] This figuring of street sound as song is akin to the metaphor of the "intricate sidewalk ballet" with which Jane Jacobs would later characterize the "complex order" that lay beneath the "seeming disorder of the old city."[20] From this coming to possession of self and street on the Lower East Side, *Bread Givers* follows Sara to the point where she is at home and herself anywhere in New York. On her return to the city from college, Sara "walked, for the first time in

[her] life, on Fifth Avenue, devouring with [her] eyes the wonderful shop windows."²¹ Tyrone Simpson argues that Sara's college schooling in the ways of whiteness "opens up the exclusive metropolitan spaces to this erstwhile nonwhite ethnic. No longer confined to the carceral, ghettoized region of the cityscape, Sara is poised to exercise her rights as a modern white subject and consumer citizen."²² *Bread Givers* thus offers an ambivalent account of assimilation into the homogenous "democracy of trade" that James hoped the Jewish American community might prove resistant to. It also suggests that ways of seeing and of being seen on the street were shaped by the relation of observer and observed to American cities' patchwork of racial and ethnic enclaves.

Nowhere was this more keenly felt than on the streets of Harlem, Bronzeville, and other northern urban neighborhoods that became home to African American men and women during the Great Migration that began in the late 1910s. "A stranger who rides up magnificent Seventh Avenue on a bus or in an automobile must be struck with surprise at the transformation which takes place after he crosses One Hundred and Twenty-fifth Street" wrote James Weldon Johnson in 1925. "Beginning there, the population suddenly darkens and he rides through twenty-five solid blocks where the passers-by, the shoppers, those sitting in restaurants, coming out of theatres, standing in doorways and looking out of windows are practically all Negroes; and then he emerges where the population as suddenly becomes white again."²³ The demographic shift of the preceding decade is made apparent to even the casual urban observer moving through Harlem. The street, as it had been for James and others, is the vantage point from which the urban population can be apprehended and its meaning deduced.

Recalling his own arrival in Harlem in 1921, Langston Hughes wrote that "At every subway station I kept watching for the sign: 135TH STREET. When I saw it, I held my breath. I went up the steps and into the bright September sunlight. Harlem! I looked around. Negroes everywhere! [. . .] I took a deep breath and felt happy again."²⁴ That rhapsodic moment of first encounter with Harlem streets resonates through African American literature of the period. Rudolph Fisher's "City of Refuge" (1925) begins with King Solomon Gillis stepping up from the same subway station where, "slowly, spreadingly, he grinned at what he saw: Negroes at every turn; up and down Lenox Avenue, up and down 135th Street; [. . .] here and there a white face drifting along, but Negroes predominantly, overwhelmingly everywhere. There was assuredly no doubt of his whereabouts. This was Negro Harlem."²⁵ Reacquainting himself with the neighborhood in

Home to Harlem (1928), Claude McKay's Jake goes "for a promenade on
Seventh Avenue between One Hundred and Thirty-fifth and One
Hundred and Fortieth Streets. He thrilled to Harlem."[26] Fisher's Gillis
has been led to believe that "In Harlem [. . .] you had privileges, protected
by law" and is likewise thrilled to see an African American policeman
directing traffic.[27] But his assumption of community and security based on
these initial perceptions proves false as his trust is betrayed and he is made
the fall-guy in a criminal operation. The twist in Fisher's tale anticipates
the shift from euphoria to disillusionment that Farah Jasmine Griffin
identifies as a recurring feature of African American migration narratives
that move through confrontation with the urban landscape to "a consideration of the sophistication of modern urban power."[28]

   If all these descriptions record or recall the heady potential of Harlem in
the 1920s, subsequent accounts and experiences echo the betrayal that
Fisher foresaw. Hughes's 1940 memoir *The Big Sea* moves from initial
euphoria to the sense of a moment and opportunity lost; by his 1951 poem
"Harlem," the atmosphere on the streets is that of rotten meat, running
sores or an explosive force. In his 1948 dispatch from "The Harlem
Ghetto," James Baldwin moves from reportorial objectivity, wherein "the
buildings are old and in desperate need of repair, the streets are crowded
and dirty, there are too many human beings per square block," to an
extended simile for the way those streets feel: "All of Harlem is pervaded
by a sense of congestion, rather like the insistent, maddening, claustrophobic pounding in the skull that comes from trying to breathe in a very small
room with all the windows shut."[29] In his recollection of the moments
prior to the 1943 Harlem Riots, Baldwin corroborates Hughes's sense of
a neighborhood "infected by waiting." The "congestion" would not be
apparent to "the white man walking through Harlem" but the "poison"
was palpable to those who inhabited and truly knew the streets. "The
avenues, side streets, bars, billiard halls, hospitals, police stations, and even
the playgrounds of Harlem – not to mention the houses of correction, the
jails, and the morgue – testified to the potency of the poison," Baldwin
declares, his catalog of neighborhood sites grounding his claims in specific
experience.[30] In these shifting positive and negative appraisals of Harlem,
writers move from what they feel at street level to what it tells them about
the social and political conditions of African American life.

   Taking Langston Hughes's first, deep, life-giving, breath as an exemplary instance, Sidney Bremer argues that, "In Harlem Renaissance
literature, African America's capital city is organic, not mechanical. It is
fleshy – and embodied in lively colors, tastes, and sounds." She places this

urban vision in contrast with "the mainstream American image of the city as a machine boxed off from nature."[31] While many early twentieth-century writers followed James's "heaped industrial battlefield" metaphor and deployed military and mechanistic imagery, other streams beside Harlem Renaissance writing embraced the living street. The influential journalist and critic James Huneker, an early advocate of Sloan's painting, developed an embodied urban imagery in the 1915 collection *New Cosmopolis*, casting Central Park as "The Lungs," the subway as "The Matrix," and bars and restaurants as "The Maw of the Monster." His sketches revisit in several instances the scenes of James's "New York Revisited," but with a journalistic sensibility more restless and less analytical, more of the city and willing to go with the flow of its streets. At Coney Island, his impressions of the crowd come from its midst, "where the mob is thickest, where your ear-drums are shattered by steam-organs, and the yelling of barkers"; at Steeplechase Park, he abandons detached observation as on the rollercoasters "you cast aside your hampering reason and become a plain lunatic."[32]

Surveying the urban scene from the vantage point of 1938, the Federal Writers' Project's *New York Panorama* explained that, "Forecast by such lively wine salesmen of the arts as James Huneker, a more thorough school of cultural commentators whose origins were mainly literary set out in the early 1920's to re-examine the pattern of New York as a prefiguration of the new America."[33] The 1913 Armory Show brought European postimpressionism to New York en masse and to the bemused, outraged attention of mainstream audiences for the first time, establishing a dialogue between the fragmented visual language of cubism and the scale and tumult of New York. The French artist Francis Picabia hailed New York as "the cubist, the futurist city" and sought to express his sense of "your stupendous skyscrapers, your mammoth buildings and marvellous subways," as well as the streets with "their surging, their unrest, their commercialism, and their atmospheric charm."[34] In turn, American artists associated with Alfred Stieglitz's 291 gallery including John Marin and Max Weber depicted the mix of crowds and buildings in idioms that eschewed Sloan's realism for forms of abstraction. In Marin's 1928 watercolor, *Street Crossing, New York*, translucent figures occupy a fractured streetscape of semi-legible signs, jarring overhanging buildings and fragments of city life (Illustration 2.3). This reciprocal exchange with the European avant-garde – "a jump spark crackled between New York and Paris" in the period according to *New York Panorama* – fostered a confident, cosmopolitan American urbanism, whose tenor was caught in Paul Rosenfeld's *Port of*

2.3 John Marin, *Street Crossing, New York* (1928). Watercolor, black chalk, and
graphite on off-white watercolor paper, 26 ¼ x 21 ¾ in; 66.675 x 55.245 cm. Acquired
1931; © 2008 Estate of John Marin/Artists Rights Society (ARS), New York. The
Phillip Collection, Washington, D. C.

New York (1924), a series of fourteen essays on Stieglitz, Marin, and other
members of their circle.

Port of New York is, as Celeste Connor demonstrates, a statement of the
Stieglitz circle's Whitmanian "democratic ethos" and "antirational,
mythopoetic mode" which emphasized intuition and sensory
perception.[35] For Rosenfeld, New York had once been a place as alien
and unknowable even to long-term residents as it had appeared to the
returning James. "It was," he writes, "as useless trying to feel yourself
through the crowding towers of the lower town, and feel a whole, as it
was trying to feel yourself through the forbidding people in the streets."[36]
But gradually and in unspecified moments a new feeling for the city

emerges, which Rosenfeld's third person attributes to the figures celebrated in his essays, to his wider generation of artists and intellectuals, or perhaps to all 1920s New Yorkers. As the earlier alienation had been most palpable amidst "crowding towers" and forbidding crowds, so this new condition was made apparent at street level: "the fundamental oneness we have with the place and the people in it, that is sensible to us to-day in the very jostling, abstracted streets of the city. We know it here, our relationship with this place in which we live."[37] In such articulations, as the Federal Writers' Project later observed, Rosenfeld, in league with Randolph Bourne, Van Wyck Brooks, Lewis Mumford and others, "forged a concept of the city, a unity for the city, out of the collective character and history of its inhabitants."[38] This was an intellectual and highly theorized project that was nonetheless grounded in the lived and sensory experience of the street.

Rosenfeld looked beyond New York and New Yorkers to Carl Sandburg and Sherwood Anderson as writers who exemplify this feeling for urban energy but whose affiliations were with the Midwest. Rosenfeld found exuberant mythopoetic expression in Sandburg's ode to Chicago. Singing the "Stormy, husky, brawling, // City of the Big Shoulders" the poet lets "the sheer noise, the banging of the jazz, the 'rhythmic oompa of the brasses,' colored and emphatic and cruel phrases, raging and gorgeous slang of the American streets, saturate him, thrill grim, rough, sardonic joy up in him."[39] The speaker in Sandburg's "A Teamster's Farewell" invokes the policemen's whistles, horses hooves and the "slamming roar of the street" that he will "hunger for" when incarcerated.[40] Sound and slang are not overwhelming as they had been for earlier writers of the urban scene: the cacophony is merely the shared experience of daily life that binds a community together; the city's capacity for cruel words and brawling violence part and parcel of its swagger and scale. "Passer-By" similarly celebrates anonymous voices that "rose and blent" in "the city's afternoon roar." In this poem's attention to shoe soles on sidewalks and in "Clark Street Bridge," which begins, "Dust of the feet," the physicality of walking becomes part of the city experience too.[41] "Clark Street Bridge," "Halsted Street Car" and, with its opening reference to Maxwell Street, "Fish Crier" all locate Sandburg's *Chicago Poems* at specific points within the city's downtown grid. The ear-to-the-ground, feet-to-the-street sensibility of these early poems informed and was informed by Sandburg's practice as one of the few journalists attuned to the violent mood of the city, which he detailed in the newspaper reports collected as *The Chicago Race Riots, July 1919* (1919).

This grounded, rhapsodic, physical urbanism led Rosenfeld to hail Sandburg as a Whitman figure for twentieth-century Chicago, and

Anderson, likewise, sought to play that role. His "Song of the Soul of Chicago" in *Mid-American Chants* (1918) begins, "On the bridges, on the bridges – swooping and rising, whirling and circling – back to the bridges, always the bridges." The soul of the city is located in its thoroughfares and intersections; something unnamed and nebulous runs free here in the nonlinear motions familiar from other descriptions of city crowds. That unfettered movement is associated at the end of the poem with a nascent political order: "We want to give this democracy thing they talk so big about a whirl."[42] The first stanza of the first poem in *Mid-American Chants* runs,

> I am pregnant with song. My body aches but do not betray me. I will sing and hide them away. I will tear them into bits and throw them in the street. The streets of my city are full of dark holes. I will hide my songs in the holes of the streets.[43]

This explicitly urban variant on Whitman's entreaty at the close of "Song of Myself" – "If you want me again look for me under your bootsoles" – locates poetry in, of, and from the street as central to Anderson's effort "to begin to write out of the people and not for the people."[44] Sandburg and Anderson crafted an avowedly populist poetics in the 1910s and 1920s that in the 1930s came to resonate with the populism and propaganda of the New Deal and the Popular Front.

Sandburg's long 1936 poem, *The People, Yes*, moves from a cataloging and ventriloquizing of the everyday lives and thoughts of the people, which, as in Whitman, suggests a kind of communal consciousness, to a more direct, programmatic insistence on organized political protest. Brian Reed argues that in this populist vision, "the 'people' will only free themselves once they cease thinking of themselves as individuals, set aside their arbitrary personal preferences, and take reification to an extreme by uniting as a mass. The people, empowered as a collective, will then 'march.'"[45] The early years of the Depression saw mass marches and pickets, from the 1932 Bonus March in Washington, DC, to the 1934 San Francisco General Strike, turn from orderly protest to violent confrontation. In a fevered dispatch from San Francisco, Tillie Olsen (then Lerner) interpolates eye-witness reports of "Bloody Thursday": "the policemen, finding their gas bombs and gas shells ineffective poured lead from their revolvers into the jammed streets [. . .] from intersection to intersection the battle moved, stubbornly the rioters refused to fall back." In the aftermath of this violent confrontation Olsen "walked down Market that night. The savage wind lashed at my hair. All life seemed blown out of the street; the few people hurrying by looked hunted, tense, expectant of anything." As in the aftermath of the New York Draft Riots and 1919 Chicago Race Riots, here the San Francisco waterfront has been made over and, as is apparent to a sensibility attuned to the way streets feel, defamiliarized by violence. "Somehow I am down on Stuart and Mission, somehow I am staring at flowers scattered in a border over a space of sidewalk, at stains that look like rust, at an unsteady chalking – 'Police Murder.'" The next day, at the funeral procession for murdered workers, a "pregnant woman standing on a corner" resolves, "We'll not forget that. We'll pay it back . . . someday," while "on every square of sidewalk a man was saying, 'We'll have it. We'll have a General Strike.'"[46] Over subsequent decades American city streets played host to an era of mass organized protest and both nonviolent and violent confrontation with authority that ran from the New Deal through spontaneous uprisings to the Civil Rights and antiwar movements.

In "Notes of a Native Son" (1955), James Baldwin observed that during the 1943 Harlem Riots, "The mob did not cross the ghetto lines. It would have been easy, for example, to have gone over Morningside Park on the West Side or to have crossed the Grand Central railroad tracks at 125th Street on the east side, to wreak havoc in white neighborhoods."[47] Two decades of tireless organization and mobilization later, Baldwin was an at once moved and skeptical participant in the 1963 March on Washington. In *No Name in the Street* (1972) he recalled that in the glow of Martin Luther King Jr.'s speech and the massed commitment of the marchers, "That day, for a moment, it almost seemed that we stood on a height, and could see our inheritance; perhaps we could make the kingdom real, perhaps the beloved community would not forever remain that dream one dreamed in agony." Believing in retrospect that this "polite" protest was a mistake, Baldwin explained that "the original plan had been to lie down on airport runways, to block the streets and offices, to immobilize the city completely."[48] Another dissenting voice from the street, Malcolm X, informed by the Nation of Islam's determination to avoid direct confrontation with authority and a hustler's disdain for King's faith that the check would be cashed, shared Baldwin's doubt that the spectacle of a brief, peaceful, racially integrated occupation of the capitol would bring positive change.

A similar skepticism toward mass demonstrations emerges in *The Book of Daniel* (1971). E. L. Doctorow, "the epic poet of the disappearance of the American radical past," introduces Old Left street politics with a traumatic walk through midtown Manhattan as the lawyer Ascher drags a young Daniel and his still younger sister Susan up subway steps and along 42nd

Street.[49] As in the later "ALONE IN THE COLD WAR with Franny and Zooey" section of the novel, the street is a harsh, defamiliarized environment for the siblings: "Where they stood, in the mouth of the precipitous entrance to the subway, two winds converged, the hot underground draft rising to caress their faces and the cold blast of the street cutting their backs. Dust, paper, soot, swirled along the ground." They traverse 42nd Street to where a vast crowd has gathered and are hoisted onto a stage erected at the intersection of 40th Street and Broadway: "Flushed and breathless, dizzied by the motion like the roar of the sea, they stared out at the crowd, a vast hideous being of millions of eyes that seemed to undulate in the canyon of the street, splashing life and sound and outrage in great waves up on the platform."[50] The crowd chants "FREE THEM!" in protest against the incarceration and eventual execution of Daniel and Susan's parents, the Isaacsons – fictionalized versions of Julius and Ethel Rosenberg. Viewed from the perspective of a disoriented child, this politically mobilized street appears monstrous. Doctorow's novel then characteristically flips from the early 1950s to an account of the 1919 Red Scare – full of the kind of street brutality reported by Sandburg and Olsen – in the PhD thesis Daniel is writing in the late 1960s.

The Book of Daniel's entry into New Left street politics comes, similarly, with a train ride and a walk, quite consciously located within the flâneur tradition by the subheading, "A Tour of the City." Daniel takes the subway from the Upper West Side to Union Square then walks east to meet Artie Sternlicht. The journey takes him along Fourteenth Street, "the most dismal street in the world," with "all the stores of cheap shoes and cheap clothes going past Union Square like an assembly line of cheap hopes." The Jamesian sense of the crudely commercial passes as Daniel turns south at the intersection with Avenue B. Tompkins Square Park "is crowded. This is not 14th Street, this is the community." Dog walkers, handball players, old Ukrainian women, and "burned-out head[s]"; kids play, radios blast; a "blonde-haired girl [sits] on the pipe fence. Her ass, in jeans, hangs over the pipe fence. Four black guys surround her. One talks to her earnestly. She stares straight ahead."[51] This is the democratic crowd that, away from the commerce of Wall Street, James was able to envision in Central Park; this is the mix of races and classes that antebellum observers remarked on in the Five Points; and, in Doctorow's/Daniel's prurient attention to the white woman and black men, this is the same troubling response.

Holding forth in his apartment Sternlicht disparages "dudes who march down the street and think they're changing something" and advocates alternative forms of political action until an exchange with friends in the street below brings everyone out onto the fire escape.

> Avenue B is humming. Cars come through the narrow street, people are out in the hot night. Two blocks away is the park at Tompkins Square and from it emanates a pulse of energy composed of music and shouting and the heat of many people. The world came to America down Avenue B. The bar across the street is crowded and Daniel can see through its window the old polished wood and tarnished mirrors, and the light of the TV screen. He suddenly sees the Lower East Side with Sternlicht's vision: it is a hatchery, a fish and wildlife preserve.[52]

Sternlicht imagines a New Left politics emerging out of this ferment. He identifies himself as a Digger; speaks in response to earnest questions posed by a "girl reporter" for *Cosmopolitan*; and references a forthcoming attempt to levitate the Pentagon, which would in fact take place in October 1967. All this makes the scene proximate to Joan Didion's famous essay, "Slouching towards Bethlehem," which appeared in the September 23, 1967, *Saturday Evening Post* and which details her trips to another intersection, Haight-Ashbury, a West Coast counterpart to this Lower East Side.

Didion's first *Post* essay of 1967, "Farewell to the Enchanted City," pays close, prose-poetic attention to the feel of New York City streets, as when, eating fruit at 62nd and Lexington, "I could taste the peach and feel the soft air blowing from a subway grating on my legs and could smell lilac and garbage and expensive perfume and I knew that it would cost something sooner or later."[53] While "Slouching towards Bethlehem" is less concerned with sensory perceptions of the Haight, Didion's New Journalism insists on her presence, there, on the street, getting "the word" from the crowds of dropouts and dreamers. This approach was not, as Louis Menand observes, particularly successful because "The hippies she tried to have conversations with said 'Groovy' a lot and recycled flower-power clichés. The cops refused to talk to her. So did the Diggers." Just as Sternlicht twists and evades the reporter's questions so Didion's interlocutors obfuscate and spin pronouncements at once rote and hyperbolic. She later told an interviewer, "That piece is a blank for me still."[54] Haight-Ashbury does not contain the evidence of or insight into "social hemorrhaging" that Didion is looking for; its politics remain vague, nebulous, and secondary to the main aim of getting high.[55] The street as site of either community or political ferment is, here, as in Doctorow's novel, or indeed Rudolph Fisher's "City of Refuge," a false front.

The month before their attempt to levitate the Pentagon, Abbie Hoffman and others had entered the New York Stock Exchange and showered the brokers with cash. One participant, Stew Albert, described this as "a new way to demonstrate, a theatrical turn of politics that invaded sacrosanct places and turned them into a stage set full of props for our use."[56] The blurring of, and dialogue between, political activism and street theater or performance art is a central concern of Don DeLillo's later novels, including *Cosmopolis* (2003) in which various forms of art and activism are encountered in the course of a limousine ride through Manhattan's hypercongested streets. Enacting the theatrical turn, masked men and women hurl rats, chant "a specter is haunting the world," and storm the Nasdaq building. "They were protesters, anarchists, whoever they were, a form of street theater, or adepts of sheer rampage."[57] Their slogans and actions resonate with the 1999 anti-WTO mass actions in Seattle and the theatrical interventions of the anti-corporate-globalization movement described by Naomi Klein in *No Logo* (1999). Surveying the scene through the sunroof of his heavily armored (but heavily defaced) limousine and then via the numerous screens and feeds within, DeLillo's protagonist, the billionaire currency trader Eric Packer, finds these actions an ingenious and exhilarating spectacle. When one of the protesters self-immolates, Packer's "Head of Theory," Vija Kinski, calls it "an appropriation."[58] Here and elsewhere *Cosmopolis* compresses themes and images familiar from DeLillo's previous novels into a single day and two-hundred pages, so that theoretical and political positions are more starkly and directly stated.

This compression applies both to the presentation of the street as a site of political action and as one of human encounter and interaction. "There were days when he wanted to eat all the time, talk to people's faces, live in meat space. He stopped looking at computer screens and turned to the street." That street is 47th Street between Fifth and Sixth Avenues, and Eric finds the Diamond District's "intensely three-dimensional" com-merce antiquated: "In the grain of the street he sensed the Lower East Side of the 1920s." *Cosmopolis* is shot through with Eric's sense of the physical world as so obsolete that even words like "phone" and "computer" sound "backward and dumb." In the novel's free indirect discourse, this attitude seeps into description of the surrounding city: "There were tourists pressing through the theater district in all the words that make a multitude. They moved in swirls and drifts, shuffling in and out of megastores and circling vendors' carts."[59] Where, in the openings of *Mao II* (1991) and *Underworld* (1997), DeLillo had given paragraphs and pages to "the words that make a multitude," here the spectacle of streets and crowds can be parsed, abbreviated.

Cosmopolis, or at least its protagonist, expresses disdain but also nostalgia for those who shuffle and circle in the meat space of the street. The novel's plot and crosstown journey are driven by Eric's need for a haircut in a barbershop with "Associations. Calendar on the wall. Mirrors everywhere" that is situated on "a grim street" in Hell's Kitchen where his father grew up "in loud and close company, in railroad flats," and where he "was compelled to come and let the street breathe on him."[60] This is, for reviewer Tom Shippey, an "iconic setting, the old-time barbershop out of Norman Rockwell, where you got your shoes shined and caught up with the neighbourhood gossip."[61] The barbershop scene is followed by another seemingly overdetermined moment of urban communion, in which Eric encounters and then strips and joins "three hundred naked people sprawled in the street."[62] The vague explanation is that this is a film shoot but, lacking context, as the extras have not been told what they are doing and the production is about to shut down, it feels more like an art happening.

Specifically, as several commentators have noted, it evokes the work of Spencer Tunick who, by the early 2000s, was becoming known for photographing volunteers naked and en masse in iconic urban locations. Early works in this vein, like *New York* (1997) made at 5:00 AM in Times Square and *Barriers II* (1998), which poses approximately one hundred prone bodies on the Williamsburg Bridge, convey both abjection and transgression. Tunick was arrested and had his camera confiscated and made photographs that juxtapose vulnerable naked flesh and cold unyielding concrete. Lying naked Eric "felt the textural variation of slubs of chewing gum compressed by decades of traffic. He smelled the ground fumes, the oil leaks and rubbery skids, summers of hot tar." To be in the street so freely is as challenging and uncomfortable as it is emancipatory. It takes these heightened, artificial conditions for Eric to reconnect with the physical world and his fellow New Yorkers, so that he desires "to set himself in the middle of the intersection, among the old with their raised veins and body blotches and next to the dwarf with a bump on his head."[63]

As participants in Tunick's shoots attest, the experience builds "a great sense of community"; as the artist himself told CNN in 2018, "People want a sense of freedom when it comes to their bodies and public space – that governments . . . and corporations don't own your body."[64] By this point in his career Tunick's work tends to scale and spectacle, to thousands rather than hundreds of bodies, and to collaboration with city arts festivals and major sports events. For Vija Kinski in *Cosmopolis* the rat-hurling protesters "don't exist outside the market."[65] In Dana Spiotta's *Eat the*

Document (2006) the flash mobs and hacked advertisements of late-1990s teenage antiglobalization protesters are at once enacting a playful activism and playing at being activists. Tunick now offers a complex aesthetic in which bodies and cities come together in some version of the urban sublime but also low-stakes provocation in which the site and tactics of political protest are turned to the ends of personal expression. Undressing is a step in Eric's rapid divestment and downsizing and leads him to finally make love to his wife, Elise Shifrin, who also happens to be among the crowd. Tunick's website now asks potential participants to identify their skin color on a light-dark palette, but white flesh dominates his earlier, riskier photographs. Mass public nudity, in *Cosmopolis* a form of release for wealthy white Manhattanites, requires confidence in the way one's body will be perceived and addressed.

By detailing the aggression and suspicion that seep into everyday encounters between African American customers and white baristas or between black and white subway passengers Claudia Rankine shows how the perception of black bodies alters the stakes of the public sphere from the smallest transaction up. Toward the end of *Citizen: An American Lyric* (2014) something like Jane Jacobs's "eyes on the street" vision of urban community provides rare succor, as "Closed to traffic, the previously unexpressive street fills with small bodies" and a father stands watch over his child among the mass. "You were about to enter your building, but do not want to leave the scope of his vigilance."[66] But that site of expressive community is for African Americans, as Rankine testifies in a subsequent essay, at once a site of surveillance, vigilance, and unending (self) policing: "no driving your car, no walking at night, no walking in the day, no turning onto this street, no entering this building, no standing your ground, no standing here, no standing there, no talking back, no playing with toy guns, no living while black." On Canfield Drive in Ferguson, Missouri, "After [Michael] Brown was shot six times, twice in the head, his body was left facedown in the street by the police officers." Rankine echoes earlier African American skepticism regarding street protest, which may be "ultimately to our own detriment, because protest gives the police justification to militarize, as they did at Ferguson."[67] Rankine's "The Condition of Black Life Is One of Mourning" was reprinted in Jesmyn Ward's collection of James Baldwin-inspired essays, *The Fire This Time*, alongside Daniel José Older's "This Far: Notes on Love and Revolution." Older uses Baldwin's "This Far and No Further" (1983) to frame his account of the "whole year of protest" that followed Ferguson: "a culminating mass of days and nights, bodies laying down in intersections, symphony halls, strip malls, superhighways across the country, stopping traffic and business-as-usual, declaring by their very presence: 'No further,' and again, 'No further.'"[68] To lie down in the image of Michael Brown at a Black Lives Matter die-in is to assert the absolute stakes of the street as the site of resistance.

Two distinct, interconnected strands in Rebecca Solnit's writing and practice – walking the city as a radical flâneuse and participating in a range of recent movements, including the 1999 anti-WTO mass action, Occupy, #MeToo and the anti-Trump "resistance" – attest to why the street is worth the risk. In *Wanderlust* (2000), Solnit describes returning from rural New Mexico to San Francisco to see the street afresh: "Every building, every storefront, seemed to open onto a different world, compressing all the variety of human life into a jumble of possibilities made all the richer by the conjunctions."[69] In *The Battle of the Story of the Battle of Seattle* she and her brother David Solnit tell the story of "a huge, unanticipated, powerful – and rowdy – demonstration and blockade" that was "met by escalating violence from police, who used tear gas, rubber bullets, truncheons and direct assaults" on November 30, 1999, in order to counter the prevailing official histories that insist on that day as one of activist violence.[70] Introducing a history of Occupy Wall Street, Solnit builds on her on-the-spot dispatches posted from Occupy sites that identified the street encampments as symbols of an awakening political consciousness. She counsels against judging grassroots movements by their immediate outcomes or a means-end logic: to be together in the street might be enough; to be part of Occupy was "to be warmed by that beautiful conflagration that spread across the world, to be part of that huge body that wasn't exactly civil society but was something akin and sometimes even larger."[71] This sense of civil society is articulated against later-twentieth and early twenty-first-century threats to the street as democratic space that range from the privatization of what once was public and the implementation of defensive architectures and surveillance technologies to the heavily militarized shutdowns of the anti-WTO and Occupy protests.

Zuccotti Park housed a 4,000-volume library that was ransacked by the NYPD, and Occupy spawned a poetry movement recorded in print and open online anthologies. Occupy Oakland activist, poet and former librarian Joan Annsfire calls forth the moment

> A human tide of people swept into the port.
> We moved as one, wound up and over the bridge and came down,
> came out, came across, danced and chanted;

like straw spun into gold, anger and pain transformed into victory
that moment, that day, that army of the 99 percent.

In contrast to the cool detachment of DeLillo's observers or Tillie Olsen's
impassioned survey of the aftermath of protest turned to violent conflict,
these lines record the euphoric surge of being amidst the march, of being
a visible and vulnerable part of a politics larger than oneself. The vast
outpouring of language from Occupy draws on a long tradition of finding
selfhood in the crowd and thus intuiting the potential of the street.
Introducing a selection of Occupy poems including Annsfire's "Strike
Day in Oakland" (2013), scholar Pamela Annas suggests that "The ghosts
of Emily Dickinson and Walt Whitman, each an expert on occupation,
hover over the camps."[72]

Spiotta's *Eat the Document* ends with a tentative opening into the
possibilities of online activism, alive in the mid-2000s to the ways in
which such a move might be assimilated into or already indistinguishable
from the market. In a 2018 response to a question about the role of social
media in recent political movements, Solnit suggests that *Wanderlust* is
about "what it means to be out in the open whether you're communing
with the non-human world [. . .] or with your fellow human beings in the
city, and so much of what the internet has done is encourage us to stay
home and only connect through these kind of corporate-mediated
things."[73] This commitment to the street over social media may itself be
a form of privilege, to be set against the emphasis that so many contributors
to *The Fire This Time* place on the counterpublic value of Black Twitter.
On March 24, 2018, Our Lives mobilized more than 1 million people in
over 450 marches through American streets to protest against gun violence.
Many marchers carried placards – "Books not Bullets," "Congress should
grow a set of" followed by an image of some balls – that recall both David
Henkin's sense of antebellum city streets as sites of "public words" and
"public reading" as well as Occupy's fusion of protest and poetry.[74] The
placards' intricate messages – "The 1st Amendment doesn't protect all
speech. So why should the 2nd Amendment protect all guns?" – and
small lettering suggest that they were intended less to be seen in the
moment on the street than to be photographed and circulated online.
But who held them and where – on Pennsylvania Avenue in DC, in
downtown Houston, Texas, or at West 65th Street and Central Park
West (Illustration 2.4) – matters too. Those signs operate at the intersection of the lived, layered, interpersonal experience of the street and a
potentially vast, fragmented, impersonal online audience. Any anonymous

2.4 Craig Ruttle/AP, *Student Gun Protests* (2018). Craig Ruttle/AP/Shutterstock.

"keyboard warrior" can post a comment but there is a deeper commitment in physically making the sign and carrying it to the protest and standing by it in public out in the open in the street.

Notes

1. David M. Henkin, *City Reading: Written Words and Public Spaces in Antebellum New York* (New York: Columbia University Press, 1998), p. 162.
2. Davy Crockett, *An Account of Col. Crockett's Tour to the North and Down East* (Philadelphia: E. L. Carey and A. Hart, 1835), pp. 48, 49.
3. Henkin, *City Reading*, pp. 1–3, 162; Tyler Anbinder, *Five Points: The 19th-Century New York City Neighborhood That Invented Tap Dance, Stole Elections, and Became the World's Most Notorious Slum* (New York: Free Press, 2001), p. 25.
4. [Walt Whitman], "Events of Last Night," *New York Aurora,* April 13, 1842, 2.
5. Walt Whitman, "Song of Myself," *Leaves of Grass,* 1855 ed., in Justin Kaplan, ed., *Walt Whitman: Complete Poetry and Collected Prose* (New York: Library of America, 1982), pp. 27, 80, 85.
6. Walt Whitman, "Leaves of Grass," in *Complete Poetry,* p. 90.
7. Anbinder, *Five Points,* p. 314.
8. Walt Whitman to Louisa Van Velsor Whitman, July 15, 1863, and August 18, 1863, in Edwin Haviland Miller, ed., *The Collected Writings of Walt Whitman:*

The Correspondence, 6 vols. (New York: New York University Press, 1961–77), pp. 1:117, 1.136.

9. Karen Karbiener, "Brooklyn and Manhattan," in Joanna Levin and Edward Whitley, eds., *Walt Whitman in Context* (Cambridge: Cambridge University Press, 2018), p. 19.

10. Walt Whitman to Henry Hurt, October 2, 1868, in *Correspondence*, 2:53.

11. Henry James, *The American Scene* (London: Chapman and Hall, 1907), p. 67.

12. Walt Whitman, "Broadway," in *Complete Poetry*, p. 624.

13. James, *American Scene*, pp. 78, 83, 84.

14. John Sloan, Diaries, 1906–13, *Delaware Art Museum*, www.delart.org/word press/wp-content/uploads/2017/07/1906-to-1913.pdf, p. 254.

15. Rebecca Zurier and Robert W. Snyder, "Picturing the City," in Rebecca Zurier, Robert W. Snyder, and Virginia M. Mecklenberg, eds., *Metropolitan Lives: The Ashcan Artists and Their New York* (Washington, DC: National Museum of American Art; New York: Norton, 1995), p. 137.

16. Alexis L. Boylan, *Ashcan Art, Whiteness, and the Unspectacular Man* (New York: Bloomsbury, 2017), p. 11.

17. Sloan, *Diaries*, p. 712.

18. James, *American Scene*, pp. 130–31.

19. Anzia Yezierska, *Bread Givers* (New York: Persea Books, 1975), p. 22.

20. Jane Jacobs, *The Death and Life of Great American Cities* (1961; Harmondsworth, UK: Penguin, 1994), p. 60.

21. Yezierska, *Bread Givers*, p. 238.

22. Tyrone R. Simpson II, "'The Love of Colour in Me': Anzia Yezierska's 'Bread Givers' and the Space of White Racial Manufacture," *MELUS*, 34.3 (2009), 109.

23. James Weldon Johnson, "The Making of Harlem," *The Survey*, March 1, 1925, 635.

24. Langston Hughes, *The Big Sea* (New York: Knopf, 1940), p. 81.

25. Rudolph Fisher, *The City of Refuge: The Collected Stories of Rudolph Fisher*, ed. John McCluskey (Columbia: University of Missouri Press, 2008), p. 35.

26. Claude McKay, *Home to Harlem* (Boston: Northeastern University Press, 1987), p. 10.

27. Rudolph Fisher, *City of Refuge*, p. 36.

28. Farah Jasmine Griffin, *"Who Set You Flowin'?" The African-American Migration Narrative* (New York: Oxford University Press, 1995), p. 10.

29. James Baldwin, "The Harlem Ghetto," in Toni Morrison, ed., *Collected Essays* (New York: Library of America, 1998), p. 42.

30. Baldwin, "Notes of a Native Son," in *Collected Essays*, pp. 73, 78.

31. Sidney H. Bremer, "Home in Harlem, New York: Lessons from the Harlem Renaissance Writers," *PMLA*, 105.1 (1990), 49, 50.

32. James Huneker, *New Cosmopolis: A Book of Images* (New York: Charles Scribner's Sons, 1915), pp. 157, 154.

33. Federal Writers' Project, *New York Panorama: A Comprehensive View of the Metropolis* (New York: Random House, 1938), p. 18.

34. Quoted in Arthur Jerome Eddy, *Cubists and Post-Impressionism* (Chicago: A. C. McClurg, 1914), p. 96.

35. Celeste Connor, *Democratic Visions: Art and Theory of the Stieglitz Circle, 1924–1934* (Berkeley: University of California Press, 2001), pp. 42–43.

36. Paul Rosenfeld, *Port of New York: Essays on Fourteen American Moderns* (New York: Harcourt, Brace, 1924), p. 287.

37. Ibid., p. 292.

38. Federal Writers' Project, *New York Panorama*, p. 18.

39. Rosenfeld, *Port of New York*, p. 72.

40. Carl Sandburg, *Chicago Poems* (New York: Henry Holt, 1916), p. 17.

41. Ibid., pp. 13, 12.

42. Sherwood Anderson, *Mid-American Chants* (New York: John Lane, 1918), pp. 62, 63.

43. Federal Writers' Project, *New York Panorama*, p. 11.

44. Walt Whitman, "Song of Myself," p. 88; Sherwood Anderson, *Notebook* (1926), quoted in Connor, *Democratic Visions*, p. 42.

45. Brian M. Reed, "Carl Sandburg's *The People, Yes*, Thirties Modernism, and the Problem of Bad Political Poetry," *Texas Studies in Literature and Language*, 46.2 (Summer 2004), 185.

46. Tillie Olsen [Lerner], "The Strike," *Partisan Review*, 1.4 (Sept.–Oct. 1934), 6, 7, 8, 9.

47. Baldwin, "Notes of a Native Son," p. 81.

48. Baldwin, *No Name in the Street*, in *Collected Essays*, pp. 439, 440.

49. Fredric Jameson, *Postmodernism; or, The Cultural Logic of Late Capitalism* (London: Verso, 1991), p. 24.

50. E. L. Doctorow, *The Book of Daniel* (1971; London: Picador, 1982), pp. 18, 22.

51. Ibid., pp. 136, 136–37, 137.

52. Ibid., pp. 143–44.

53. Republished as "Goodbye to All That," in Joan Didion, *Slouching towards Bethlehem* (1968; New York: Farrar, Straus, and Giroux, 2008), p. 228.

54. Louis Menand, "Out of Bethlehem: The Radicalization of Joan Didion," *The New Yorker*, August 24, 2015, www.newyorker.com/magazine/2015/08/24/o ut-of-bethlehem.

55. Didion, "Slouching towards Bethlehem," in *Slouching*, p. 85.

56. Larry "Ratso" Sloman, Michael Simmons and Jay Babcock, "OUT, DEMONS, OUT!: The 1967 Exorcism of the Pentagon and the Birth of Yippie!," *Arthur* 13 (November 2004), http://arthurmag.com/tag/stew-albert/.

57. Don DeLillo, *Cosmopolis* (London: Picador, 2003), p. 88.

58. Ibid., p. 100.

59. Ibid., pp. 63–64, 64, 82–83.

60. Ibid., pp. 15, 159.

61. Tom Shippey, "Cooling Connections," *The Times Literary Supplement*, May 2, 2003, 23.

62. DeLillo, *Cosmopolis*, p. 172.

63. Ibid., pp. 174, 176.

64. Martha Hayes, "'I Kept My Eyes Firmly above the Chin': Peter Stanford Poses Nude for Artist Spencer Tunick, 17 July 2005," *Guardian*, August 26, 2016, www .theguardian.com/artanddesign/2016/aug/26/spencer-tunick-naked-art-newcas tle-photograph; "Hundreds Strip Off in Melbourne for Controversial Mass Nude Photos," *CNN Style*, July 9, 2018, http://edition.cnn.com/style/article/spencer-tunick-nude-art-installation-australia/index.html.

65. DeLillo, *Cosmopolis*, p. 90.

66. Claudia Rankine, *Citizen: An American Lyric* (London: Penguin, 2015), p. 149.

67. Claudia Rankine, "The Condition of Black Life Is One of Mourning," in Jesmyn Ward ed., *The Fire This Time: A New Generation Speaks about Race* (London: Bloomsbury, 2019), pp. 146, 149, 147.

68. Daniel José Older, "This Far: Notes on Love and Revolution," ibid., p. 200.

69. Rebecca Solnit, *Wanderlust: A History of Walking* (London: Verso, 2001), p. 171.

70. Rebecca Solnit, "The Myth of Seattle Violence: My Battle with the *New York Times*," in Rebecca Solnit and David Solnit, eds., *The Battle of the Story of the Battle of Seattle* (Chico, CA: AK Press, 2010), p. 58.

71. Rebecca Solnit, "Obstacles and Miracles," in Nathan Schneider, *Thank You, Anarchy: Notes from the Occupy Apocalypse* (Berkeley: University of California Press, 2013), p. 12.

72. Joan Annsfire, "Strike Day in Oakland," *Radical Teacher* 96 (Spring 2013), p. 23; Pamela Annas, "Preface," "Poems from the Occupy Movement," ibid., p. 22.

73. *Shakespeare and Company presents Rebecca Solnit*, June 28, 2018, www .youtube.com/watch?v=r23r7hhjThU.

74. Henkin, *City Reading*, pp. 1–3.

CHAPTER 3

The Literature of Neighborhood

Carlo Rotella

Like a neighborhood in relation to a city, the literature of neighborhood is a subset of the larger category of urban literature. When you call a work of literature "urban" you take on an obligation to show how the writing responds to the possibilities and challenges presented by the traits that make a city a city. Social scientists have been refining their list of those traits for more than a century; it includes density, anonymity, central place function, high property values, cosmopolitanism, hybridity, the concentration of trade and capital, the production of culture and knowledge, serving as a seat of government, and more. Neighborhoods appear on the list, too, because they are an urban universal, showing up throughout history wherever human beings have settled in substantial numbers. All these general traits that make any city a city present writers with opportunities to tell stories, experiment with form, make meaning, and otherwise exercise the literary imagination. (I say "writers" and "writing" for the sake of concision, but my broad construction of literature goes beyond novels, short stories, poems, and nonfiction to include movies, music, and more.) The same is true of particular aspects of history, landscape, population, or other features that may be distinctively specific to a particular city – unique attributes that make, say, Milwaukee different from Baltimore or El Paso.

We can adapt this definition of urban literature to cover smaller units that compose a city, zeroing in on how literature exploits qualities that make a neighborhood a neighborhood. So, what are those qualities?

To begin with, *neighborhood* is a several-faced, sometimes contradictory term. It literally refers to a spatial relationship (if X is nigh – near – to Y, then X is in the neighborhood of Y), but in common usage *neighborhood* means both a place and a feeling among its residents, both a physical landscape and the flows of people and resources and ideas moving through it. A neighborhood is also both durable and transient. The infrastructure of streets and buildings may be there for the long haul, but any particular order – any particular way of life and the set of material arrangements supporting it – housed in this container is always taking form, in the process of disappearing, or both at once. And the term *neighborhood* can shrink or stretch in scale to fit a small cluster of buildings or an expansive quarter of the city composed of many named subunits that qualify as neighborhoods in their own right.

We tend to think of ourselves as living in neighborhoods, but the reverse holds just as true: neighborhoods live in us. They aren't just neutral stages on which we act out our lives and feel the effect of large-scale forces. Rather, as the eminent sociologist Robert Sampson puts it, neighborhoods are "important determinants of the quantity and quality of human behavior in their own right," affecting residents in ways that can be teased apart from overlapping influences like income and race.[1] The places in which we live shape us in long-lasting ways, called neighborhood effects, which show up across the life course in everything from child mortality to school performance to economic attainment to life expectancy. Neighborhood effects also show up in less easily quantified aspects of perception and mentality that we usually think of as personal character, like altruism, sensitivity to disorder, and attitude toward the rule of law.

With all that in mind, we can come at the literature of neighborhood from any or all of several different angles. We can track how neighborhood effects and other such processes show up in plots, themes, and character systems. We can examine how literature responds to changes in the city, the dynamic of succeeding and persisting orders that adds up to the history of neighborhoods. We can consider the ways in which we use neighborhood to think about topics like community or justice or difference. We can parse truth and beauty in the neighborhood literature for their own sake, for art's sake. No matter which approaches we take, we inevitably engage what neighborhood *means*. In considering examples of writing and filmmaking that bear the marks of the characteristic traits of neighborhoods and exploit their meaning-making possibilities, the selection that follows does not attempt to range across the most important works, periods, or cities. A sample, not a survey, of literature's engagement with some defining aspects of neighborhood, it proceeds by showing how we can read a variety of books and movies together with each other and with the history and sociology of the city.

Looking back at the mid-twentieth century, we can assemble a cohort of novels and other books that together paint a composite portrait of the neighborhoods of the American city as it reached the end of an era. The cohort includes, among others, Richard Wright's *Native Son* (1940) and *Lawd Today* (1963); Betty Smith's *A Tree Grows in Brooklyn* (1943);

Gwendolyn Brooks's poetry collection *A Street in Bronzeville* (1945); Ann Petry's *The Street* (1946); Nelson Algren's *The Man with the Golden Arm* (1949); Alfred Kazin's memoir *A Walker in the City* (1951); Ralph Ellison's *Invisible Man* (1952); Harriet Arnow's *The Dollmaker* (1952); *For Love of Imabelle* (1957), *Cotton Comes to Harlem* (1965), and other crime stories by Chester Himes; Paule Marshall's *Brown Girl, Brownstones* (1959); and Warren Miller's *The Cool World* (1959). Each of these books devotes a significant share of its energies to imagining a neighborhood and using it as a stage for action and reflection. These are the kind of books that contemporary reviewers credited with saying important things about city life, the American scene, "the way we live now."

One central element of the urban moment was a growing sense that the industrial city that had taken center stage in American culture as it boomed in the late nineteenth and early twentieth centuries had reached full maturity, with decline approaching or already under way. Organized around turning raw materials into finished goods in factories, physically dominated by railroad tracks and port facilities and tight-packed districts of workers' housing arranged around manufacturing plants and a monumental downtown, this city bore the marks in its form and function of the great processes that drove urban growth after the Civil War. Urbanization, industrialization, and immigration (which we can extend to include internal migration) had conjured the marvel of Chicago out of prairie and swamp, turned New York City into what many regarded as the world's foremost economic and cultural center, and made global manufacturing capitals out of places like Dayton and Birmingham. Realists, modernists, proletarian writers, and others had set themselves to the task of mapping and chronicling the industrial city, including two of its most distinctive neighborhood orders: the urban villages that housed immigrants in transition from the Old Country to America; and the Black Metropolis, exemplified by Bronzeville in Chicago and Harlem in New York, that grew from the encounter between the aspirational energies of black migrants from the rural South and the constraints imposed by a segregated society. These orders had reached their full flowering by mid-century and had begun to show signs of aging out.

In *A Walker in the City*, Kazin returns to Brownsville in Brooklyn, where he was raised in an intensely parochial urban village of Jewish immigrants from eastern Europe. Visiting the kind of place that upwardly mobile white ethnics at mid-century were already beginning to think of as the Old Neighborhood, Kazin's memoir looks back with both nostalgia and bitterness to his childhood in the 1910s and 1920s, the great theme being his

movement from this closed world of "five city blocks" to what he once
regarded as "beyond": to greater Brooklyn, Manhattan, the republic of
America and the republic of letters.[2] It's a story of assimilation that also
tries to hang onto particularistic roots, to preserve within that
Americanness an identity extending back through the Old
Neighborhood to the Old Country.

Such tensions, centering on the scale of neighborhood, give Kazin's
memoir much of its inner life. On the one hand, moving outward from the
home into the neighborhood is a step in the direction of the wider world,
including Brownsville's connection to diasporic Judaism. On the other
hand, the neighborhood's in-turned quality stands in contrast to another
set of cosmopolitan possibilities available on the metropolitan scale –
possibilities represented by schools, museums, newspapers, the subway
system, and above all the Brooklyn Bridge. In a pivotal passage, Kazin
remembers rising up on the bridge as an adolescent, the crowds dropping
away below and the vista of lower Manhattan and downtown Brooklyn
opening up before him, the scale of his perception and experience expanding until he achieves a transformative epiphany: "Where in this beyond are
they taking me?" Compare that to the return to the neighborhood in the
next sentence: "Every day the battle with the back wall of the drugstore
began anew."[3] He's referring to handball, but he's also contrasting the
expansiveness of the metropolitan with the claustrophobia of the local
figured by that wall. The urban village may attract the nostalgic walker in
the city for a return visit to the roots that give him a distinct identity, but by
mid-century it has already slipped away in his wake. He's in motion – he's
a Manhattanite now, a New York intellectual, an American through and
through – and the neighborhood's orders are also in motion, as evidenced
by new housing projects and black residents.

Petry's *The Street*, a classic neighborhood novel, maps mid-century
Harlem in ways that reveal the constraints on the prospects of its protagonist, the young single mother Lutie Johnson. Her modest aspirations to
a decent living and a better life for her son, Bub, focus at first on her search
for an apartment. In a larger sense, she's trying to find a viable place for
herself within the neighborhood's interlinked economic, cultural, and
political structures. In the novel's opening scene, she's apartment-
hunting on 116th Street between Seventh and Eighth Avenues, out on
the street in a position of maximum exposure to the forces at play in the
neighborhood: the cold November wind, the lustful attention of men, and
the influence of Junto, the white kingpin who exercises power through
a behind-the-scenes network extending well beyond Harlem. Throughout

the novel, Lutie's attempts to secure shelter and independence only expose her to greater danger and control by others. When she and other Harlemites try to move up in the world, they discover that the game is rigged against them; when they leave the neighborhood, they find their trajectory bending back inexorably toward it. Harlem as Black Metropolis may well be a vibrant cultural capital, a promised land for migrants from the South like Lutie's family, but it is also a trap, a dead end.

One principal way the novel develops this theme is through the "drama of representation," a literary work's more or less veiled reflection on the processes that produced it. *The Street* is full of images of creativity that raise questions about authorship: a musician trying to figure out whether he has composed a new melody or reproduced one he has heard somewhere; Lutie trying to find her voice by singing along with the jukebox, solo, and in front of a band; the rage-filled super of Lutie's building, Jones, tracing the outlines of several mailbox keys and then merging the copies into a synthesis that "wasn't really a copy" but "seemed to embody all the curves and twists of the others."[4] Characters struggle with the problem of who gets to create a representation of their life, to what extent such a creation might be original or derived from another author's work, and who benefits from it. Lutie, trying to shape her own narrative, discovers that while the blues tradition and other aspects of black culture may produce stories that her neighbors in Harlem find vivid and meaningful, those stories lack authority in the wider world. Her singing, for instance, moves audiences at the corner saloon who share her experience but doesn't succeed in securing the money she needs to get out of Harlem. Compare that to the written representation of Lutie's life provided by an Italian American immigrant family via a letter of recommendation that (temporarily) gets her out of Harlem and into a job as a domestic in suburban Connecticut.

Lutie's comparisons of herself to Benjamin Franklin, whose autobiography provides a template for American narratives of self-making, underscore how her attempts at self-authorship keep running up against the limits of race and gender given form in the boundaries of Harlem and the forces bearing down on her on 116th Street. "You better get your dinner started, Ben Franklin," she says to herself, dismissing her daydreams of triumphant self-authorship as she walks home from her subway stop. On the way she passes children chanting "Down in Mississippi and a bo-bo push!" as they jump rope on the sidewalk, and then she encounters Bub, working as a shoeshine boy.[5] The street scene, with its references to Franklin and Mississippi and menial work that portends frustrated upward mobility, exemplifies how *The Street* uses its depiction of the neighborhood to show that the mature Black Metropolis has failed to deliver on the promise it once seemed to extend to migrants from the South.

In the decades after the Second World War, as the urban village and the Black Metropolis continued to show signs of breaking up and giving way to succeeding orders, neighborhood literature responded to the challenge of representing cities in transition. This often took the form of stories of decline, but we can also see neighborhood literature tracing the contours of the urban present and future as it took shape. From Claude Brown's account of his adventures in heroin-plagued Harlem and Beat-era Greenwich Village in *Manchild in the Promised Land* (1965) to the *Godfather* movies' (Francis Ford Coppola, 1972, 1974, 1990) account of the Corleone family's trajectory from Lower East Side immigrant idyll to assimilation, fragmentation, and regret in suburban Long Island and beyond, those stories bear the marks of deep shifts in urban life.

A second great folk migration to a second mid-century promised land, of white city dwellers to the booming suburban periphery, interlocked with the migration of African Americans from the rural South to the inner city. At the same time, US cities underwent a great shift in form and function as the industrial city began to age out in earnest, with manufacturing jobs departing northern inner cities to relocate in the suburbs, southern states, and other countries. The postindustrial metropolis, primarily organized not around turning raw materials into finished products but around handling information and providing services, rose around and through the receding industrial city. The emerging order's distinctive forms – highways and airports rather than rail lines and port facilities, steel-and-glass office towers rather than redbrick factories, high-rise housing rather than tenements or bungalows – layered over earlier cityscapes. Government policies pushed the process via urban renewal initiatives like slum clearance and the construction of monumental housing projects, and by fostering suburban growth with highway construction and loan practices encouraging home ownership. The transformation also brought new layers of neighborhood order: the second ghetto, the signature form of which was those towering housing projects; the postwar barrio, fed by fresh migrations from Puerto Rico, the Dominican Republic, Mexico, and other parts of Latin America; professional and neobohemian districts filled with college-educated knowledge workers; the white-ethnic enclave, a fortified remnant of the urban village no longer embedded in a patchwork of similarly Old World-derived neighborhoods; and suburbs growing with such speed that by the 1980s they had collectively reset the norms of American life.

The literature of neighborhood bears the marks of these changes and exploits creative possibilities opened up by them. Shifting from New York (the setting of both *A Walker in the City* and *The Street*) to Chicago, we can trace the consequences of the postindustrial city's emergence in, for instance, Mike Royko's *Boss* (1971), in which the dean of US metro columnists offers a nonfiction portrait of the greatest machine mayor of his time, Richard J. Daley, who presided over the unmaking of the neighborhood order that had shaped him and his city. We can see the change as well in the difference between Gwendolyn Brooks's early poetry, celebrated for its exquisitely wrought observations of life in the kitchenette buildings and on the street corners of Bronzeville, and her later work, which pursues an aesthetic of the second ghetto in portraits of Blackstone Ranger gang members whose "country is a Nation on no map," "sisters who kept their naturals," and a Rangerette who "sighs for Cities of blue and jewel/Beyond her Ranger rim of Cottage Grove."[6] In David Mamet's play *The Old Neighborhood*, middle-aged Jewish characters whose families moved away from the South Side of Chicago during the great white flight of the 1960s look back at the urban village they left behind in their socioeconomic wake and lament its passing. "Oh, Bobby, it's all gone," says one. "It's all gone there. You knew that."[7] In *The Hottest Water in Chicago* (1992), the essayist Gayle Pemberton takes a walk through Mamet's old neighborhood, South Shore, and surveys the shuttered storefronts, heaps of garbage, and idlers on its desolate main drag, 71st Street – visible consequences of the capital flight that attended the departure of Mamet's characters and their neighbors.

Stuart Dybek is the writer whose work most richly captures the layering of Chicago's – and perhaps any American city's – neighborhood orders. Born in 1942, Dybek grew up in Pilsen/Little Village, a formerly industrial area southwest of the Loop where residents with roots in Bohemia, Poland, and other eastern European places gave way in the 1950s and 1960s to those with roots in Mexico and Central America. Dybek's short stories and poetry, a body of work spanning half a century, return again and again to the seemingly bottomless well of inspiration provided by coming of age in a neighborhood in transition. The ghosts of an older city appear to Dybek's characters as "apparitions in broad daylight": peddlers with horses and wagons; a "mute knife sharpener pushing his screeching whetstone up alleys"; El trestles, bridges, and tenements encased in decades of pigeon droppings; a Brigadoon-like restaurant that serves life-saving sauerkraut soup; grandparents and other Old World figures whose incantatory foreign speech, music, and folkways seem at once alien and intensely familiar.[8] These ghosts appear in the wrinkles and gaps of an emerging neighborhood order. Factories and icehouses close down, jukeboxes ring with Mexican polkas and waltzes that sound eerily similar to the Polish and Czech tunes they have replaced, blues-derived music and other aspects of black culture pervade the scene as African American neighbors move into adjoining areas, and young people coming of age have to reckon with a new set of facts of life that include the realization that schooling – not the manual work done by parents and grandparents – provides the best shot at achieving upward mobility.

The drama of representation follows a similar logic in Dybek's work. "Blight," one of his finest stories, tracks a crew of postadolescent friends, nascent storytellers who experiment with poetry, fiction, songwriting, and musicianship as they navigate a difficult historical moment, "those years between Korea and Vietnam," and a layered landscape in the throes of transformation.[9] The city has slapped the label of Official Blight Area on the neighborhood and begun tearing down its aging factories, railroad tracks, truck docks, industrial dumps, scrapyards, and workers' housing to make room for expressways and other urban renewal projects. Hallucinatory glimpses of Mayor Daley give visionary form to the decisive influence of downtown interests on the neighborhood. Feeling at once grounded and adrift, the characters try to make sense of their situation by turning it into narrative, into literature, into beauty. "Blight" can be read as an account of how its narrator, Dave, wandering this transitional neighborhood scene with his friends, assembles the wherewithal to narrate the story by filling his toolkit with a syncretic variety of literary equipment made available to him in encounters with Old World, Mexican, and black cultures; youth culture's beatniks and hippies; and a college literature course taught by a professor whose Chicago accent changes the opening of Shelley's "To a Skylark" from "Hail to thee, blithe Spirit!" into "Hail ta dee, blight Spirit!" The story Dave tells is not just of the urban village's decline but also of opportunities for meaningful, even ecstatic, experience available in the overlaps of persisting and succeeding neighborhood orders. It is also a story of striking literary gold: the drama of representation locates creative opportunity, as well, in the neighborhood's mishmash of cultural possibilities.

In the story's final scene, Dave has moved away from the neighborhood, presumably to some professional or (small-b) bohemian area father north, but he comes back for a visit. He's in a bar, the Carta Blanca, when the jukebox stops playing and he hears "the bells from three different churches tolling the hour." Because the bells don't "agree on the precise moment," their ringing overlaps – a figure that resonates with the overlap of neighborhood orders that shaped the sensibility shared by Dave and his friends. The bells trigger an epiphany in which he first remembers the terror of disoriented dreams "in which I was back in my neighborhood, but lost, everything at once familiar and strange," and finally finds the terror transmuted into wonder: "and then in the dream I would come to a corner that would feel so timeless and peaceful, like the Carta Blanca with the bells fading and the sunlight streaking through, that for a moment it would feel as if I had wandered into an Official Blithe Area."[10]

As the postindustrial city matured in the final decades of the twentieth century and the opening years of the twenty-first, the shape of its social and cultural landscape became easier to discern. Its characteristic neighborhood orders displayed a range of familiarity and novelty to which the typological terms commonly available as descriptive labels – ghetto, barrio, yuppie, hipster, gentrified, and so on – did not always do justice. Neighborhood literature took on the task of mapping this emergent city with greater nuance: in, for instance, the contrast of downtown Manhattan's professional-bohemian loft districts to the post-1965 immigrant enclaves of Queens in Chang-rae Lee's *Native Speaker* (1995), the rendering of the borderland between North Oakland and Berkeley as an interracial contact zone in Michael Chabon's *Telegraph Avenue* (2012), or the mosaic of racial and artistic formations in Boerum Hill and other parts of Brooklyn in Jonathan Lethem's *The Fortress of Solitude* (2003).

One city that experienced a postindustrial renaissance in neighborhood stories was Boston, which had been a cultural capital and manufacturing center in the nineteenth century before entering a long decline that spanned much of the twentieth. Boston remained a provincial backwater until the 1980s, when a so-called New Boston began to emerge, a city centered on its flourishing education, high-tech, biotech, and finance sectors. As this developing layer matured, Boston's reputation in the nation and the world changed again, thanks not only to its economic revival but also to increasingly widespread recognition that educational institutions, with which Boston had long been uniquely well endowed, were ever more essential engines of growth in the postindustrial city. Another significant factor contributing to Boston's revived cultural identity and growing prominence was an improbable movie boom, encouraged by a state tax credit incentive, that put fanciful renditions of Boston neighborhood stories, manners, and mores into global circulation.

Though the Boston of Harvard, MIT, and other educated elite precincts does show up repeatedly (as in the beginning of *The Social Network* [David Fincher, 2010]), and though information-handling knowledge workers do appear (as in *Fever Pitch* [Peter Farrelly and Bobby Farrelly, 2005], in which a teacher and a tech wiz meet cute), a handful of neighborhoods associated with deeply rooted remnants of the industrial-era Irish American urban village have been heavily overrepresented in Boston movies. Southie (South Boston), Charlestown, parts of Dorchester, and aging districts of workers' housing in outlying former manufacturing hubs like Lowell form the heartland of the composite geography mapped by movies that make a substantial effort to establish a Boston feel. The list includes *The Friends of Eddie Coyle* (Peter Yates, 1973), *The Brinks Job* (William Friedkin, 1978), *The Verdict* (Sidney Lumet, 1982), *Good Will Hunting* (Gus Van Sant, 1997), *Monument Ave.* (Jonathan Demme, 1998), *Next Stop Wonderland* (Brad Anderson, 1998), *The Boondock Saints* (Troy Duffy, 1999), *Mystic River* (Clint Eastwood, 2003), *Fever Pitch*, *The Departed* (Martin Scorsese, 2006), *Gone Baby Gone* (Ben Affleck, 2007), *Black Irish* (Brad Gann, 2007), *What Doesn't Kill You* (Brian Goodman, 2008), *Shutter Island* (Scorsese, 2010), *Edge of Darkness* (Martin Campbell, 2010), *The Town* (Affleck, 2010), *The Company Men* (John Wells, 2010), *The Fighter* (David O. Russell, 2010), *Ted* (Seth MacFarlane, 2012), *The Heat* (Paul Feig, 2013), *Black Mass* (Scott Cooper, 2015), *Spotlight* (Tom McCarthy, 2015), *Patriots Day* (Peter Berg, 2016), *Manchester by the Sea* (Kenneth Lonergan, 2016) – plus various sequels, television shows like *Wahlburgers* and *SMILF*, and yet more films and shows currently in production (like Showtime's *City on a Hill*) that will have been released by the time this chapter sees publication.

As Dennis Lehane (several of whose novels have been adapted into Boston movies) and others have pointed out, the movies' idealization of Boston's avatars of the Old Neighborhood has taken place as the areas of the city that once exemplified the industrial neighborhood order have lost much of the white-ethnic and blue-collar tribal culture rooted in manual labor and a set of institutions that included the parish church, saloon, union hall, immigrant social club, and neighborhood-level organizational strata of the white-ethnic political machine.[11] Contemporary Boston is a majority-minority city, and educated professionals from elsewhere have descended in force on former white-ethnic enclaves.

In the Boston movies, though, the Old Neighborhood retains its potency, a theme that has grown familiar to the point that it has been routinely parodied by comedians on late-night TV. From an aerial establishing shot of a neighborhood we drop down into a landscape of close-set triple-deckers that house insular, no-r-pronouncing Sullivans and McSomebodies whose connections to the neighborhood equip them with weapons-grade accents, class resentment, and urban skills. In *The Town*, Doug MacRay (Affleck) eludes an FBI lockdown of Charlestown by taking to the rooftops, commandeering a city bus, and otherwise deploying regular-guy local knowledge to prohibitive advantage. In both *Gone Baby Gone* and *The Departed*, the mere association of the runty protagonist with the Old Neighborhood (Dorchester in the former, Southie in the latter) causes other characters to quail in his presence even when they have the advantage in force.

These movies deploy the equipment of genre fantasy to consider – among many other subjects – what has been gained and lost in the changes that shaped the postindustrial city. They are, in part, *about* the possibilities opened up by this transformation. Sometimes that aboutness can be found right on the surface of the movie: there's a scene in *The Company Men* in which a man walking through a silent, rusting, broken-windowed shipyard rhapsodizes about a lost masculinity founded in manual labor. Sometimes it is buried a little deeper, as in a scene in *The Fighter* in which Charlene (Amy Adams) confronts Micky (Mark Wahlberg) at his apartment. The neighborhood vista, established in a long shot of wood-frame walkups in the foreground with brooding redbrick buildings that once housed textile mills in the background, establishes the context for Micky's prowess as a boxer and also for the characters' vulnerability. Lowell has made them tough, but it has also made them fear that they might be losers. Sometimes the meditation on change comes in drastically compressed form, as when Krista (Blake Lively) explains to Doug in a neighborhood bar in *The Town* that encroaching new immigrants ("Somalians") and knowledge workers ("yuppies") need to be reminded that there are still "serious white people in Charlestown." And *Good Will Hunting* remains the mother of all Boston movies because it resolves the tensions between old and new Bostons by imagining a character from Southie who has impeccable blue-collar neighborhood credentials and is also smarter than the eggheads at MIT and Harvard. As he says to an improbably snooty grad student, "You dropped a hundred and fifty grand on a fuckin' education you could have got for a dallah fifty in late chahges at the public library."

There are some recent signs of curdling in the Boston movies' attitude toward the neighborhoods and working-class white masculinity they have conventionally idealized. For instance, *Black Mass*, a nasty little gangster movie, and *Spotlight*, an Oscar-winning prestige production on the model of *All the President's Men* (Alan Pakula, 1976), share a thematic emphasis on systemic rottenness at the core of the Old Neighborhood. And comedies like *The Heat* and Seth Meyers's much-viewed trailer for an imaginary movie called *Boston Accent* make fun of the in-turned parochialism that has been transmuted into a heroic virtue by the Boston movie boom. The rise of Donald Trump may well have taken some of the bloom off the notion of a potently unreconstructed white working-class identity – though the viral "Be a Masshole, not an asshole" political ad, in which a buzz-cut regular guy straight from Boston-movie central casting ("'Manhattan clam chowdah'? The fuck is that?") defends transgender rights in a bar, would suggest that such an identity can also be invoked in support of conventional blue-state purposes. Despite or perhaps in part *because* of the varying and potentially conflicting ideo-logical resonances of white working-class identity, Boston remains one of Hollywood's go-to locations when it wants to think about locality. A handful of neighborhoods in Boston have, in that sense, come to stand for the very idea of "the local." Their vigorous global circulation via Hollywood's distribution networks have helped restore Boston's status as a cultural capital.[12]

Like cities, the stories we tell about them accrue in layers. Though the shock of the new attracts literary attention, persistence is often a stronger force than succession in shaping our storytelling routines, especially when it comes to neighborhood. That's because it is typically easier to recognize signs of the established order's enduring qualities or its incipi-ent fall than to assemble a coherent vision of the emergent future from piecemeal glimpses of its arrival. Looking back through the neighbor-hood literature stretching back to the middle of the twentieth century, we can see emergent orders in abundance, but we can also discern a powerful investment in the notion that familiar older orders still exert a shaping force on city life. This is in keeping with what social science tells us about the "stickiness" of neighborhood effects: a neighborhood's reputation tends to last even through repeated trans-formations of its social order, and even an exhausted order that has receded into the underlying structure of a neighborhood can still exert an influence on what comes next: subsequent landscapes, stories, ways of knowing the world or being in it. To move through a neighborhood, in the material world or on the page or on the screen or in the mind's eye of memory or fantasy, is simultaneously to inhabit multiple superseded versions of that place, each exerting its own ghostly neighborhood effects.

Notes

1. Robert J. Sampson, *Great American City: Chicago and the Enduring Neighborhood Effect* (Chicago: University of Chicago Press, 2012), p. 22. See also Rotella, *The World Is Always Coming an End: Pulling Together and Apart in a Chicago Neighborhood* (Chicago: University of Chicago Press, 2019), pp. 1–23.
2. Alfred Kazin, *A Walker in the City* (New York: Harcourt, 1979), p. 17.
3. Kazin, *A Walker in the City*, p. 108.
4. Ann Petry, *The Street* (Boston: Beacon, 1985), p. 292.
5. Petry, *The Street*, p. 64.
6. Gwendolyn Brooks, *Blacks* (Chicago: David Company, 1987), pp. 447, 459, 449.
7. David Mamet, *The Old Neighborhood* (New York: Random House, 1999), p. 29.
8. The knife sharpener appears in Stuart Dybek, *The Coast of Chicago* (New York: Knopf, 1990), p. 85; the restaurant appears in Dybek, *Childhood and Other Neighborhoods* (New York: Viking, 1980), pp. 122–38.
9. Dybek, *The Coast of Chicago*, p. 42.
10. Dybek, *The Coast of Chicago*, p. 71. In greater depth, see Rotella, *October Cities: The Redevelopment of Urban Literature* (Berkeley: University of California Press, 1997), pp. 108–15.
11. Dennis Lehane, "Introduction: Tribalism and Knuckleheads," in Dennis Lehane, ed., *Boston Noir* (New York: Akashic, 2009), pp. 12–13.
12. See Rotella, "The Boston Movie Boom of the 21st Century," in Johan Andersson and Lawrence Webb, eds., *The City in American Cinema: Post-Industrialism, Urban Culture and Gentrification* (London: Bloomsbury, 2019), pp. 153–74.

CHAPTER 4

Writing the Ghetto, Inventing the Slum

Thomas Heise

The US literature of the "ghetto" and "slum" from the late nineteenth century to the present has been an aesthetic and ethnographic project arising and evolving in response to profound changes in the life of the American city. It is a literature that has changed, as well, with shifts in the modes of writing that novelists, memoirists, muckraking journalists, and sociologists have made as they grappled with the social meanings and lived experience of the ghetto and slum for residents, city dwellers at large, suburbanites, and Americans more generally. As this chapter will show, the ghetto and the slum are simultaneously real and imagined places. They are, on the one hand, material domains built from the practices of bank redlining, segregation, and municipal neglect. Yet, on the other hand, they are discursively invented realms, places of mythic struggle or nightmarish social decline, as well as mere everyday life, places scripted into being and instantiated by the rhetorics of the genres producing them as analytical and experiential sites for researchers and readers.

The literature of the American ghetto and slum is vast and nearly as unmappable as the terrain it seeks to discover, understand, police, and in some cases imaginatively preserve. What an overview of the literature makes clear is that while any individual text may tell a story of the ghetto and the slum, there is no single, overarching narrative of these zones. Instead, one finds competing stories testifying to the diverse perspectives of insiders and outsiders and the divergent, yet sometimes overlapping, aims of social scientists and novelists who, when confronted with these often-bewildering urban spaces, set about trying to understand them formally and ideologically. The social-science discourse of the ghetto and slum evolves over the century (although it remains depressingly unchanged in many ways) and, on the whole, evinces little definitional consensus or methodological unity. So, too, is the literary writing of these urban zones of great variance, ranging across themes and styles. If a composite story emerges, it is one of fissures and contradictions. It is the story of the slum and ghetto as a miasma of immoral contagion, but also a terrain of cultural and linguistic vibrancy, energy, and vitality; as the ground-zero of social disorganization, but also a place of new social reorganization along lines of ethnic and racial difference; as a domain of inassimilable hetero-geneity, but also a space of ethnic acculturation; as a zone characterized by poverty and pathology, but also as a home to cultures characterized by pride and activism; and finally, if not exhaustively, as a fortress of social isolation, but also a site where embryonic transformations of American life are first detectable. These contradictory understandings within and between texts in the discourse reveals the unsettled and historically chan-ging nature of the ghetto and slum, as well as the fact that the social-science and imaginative literature that takes them as its subjects is itself a contested terrain riven by competing scripts of empathy, revulsion, fear, and philanthropy.

The divergent strains in this composite story underscore the capacity of these urban environments to condense, heighten, and dramatize social, cultural, and economic fears, and perhaps less frequently, hopes and dreams. Rather than providing a sweeping survey, this chapter offers targeted readings of selected works that articulate the changing definitions, representations, motifs, and meanings of the ghetto and slum from the period of late nineteenth-century industrialization that gave birth to America's diverse ethnic enclaves through the period of mid- to late twentieth-century deindustrialization that saw the emergence and consoli-dation of the nation's racially homogenous ghettos. It will consider first the representation of these locales in the influential work of Chicago School sociologists in the 1920s and 1930s, then turn to depictions of ethnic urban wards by Jacob Riis, Abraham Cahan, and Theodore Dreiser, and con-clude with a consideration of the depictions of the racial ghetto in postwar sociological discourse and in work by Nelson Algren, Ralph Ellison, and Claude Brown. What becomes evident from a consideration of this col-lective body of writing is that the commonalities and differences of the ghetto and slum arise from shared, if shifting, historical processes (changes in production, immigration flows, federal governance) that shape and reshape cities and citizens. By bringing a historical and spatial analysis to the discourse we obtain a fuller understanding of its complex, if sensation-alistic, representations of urban crisis, ethnicity, race, and poverty. Much of this literature turns out to be a literature of the double binds ethnic and racialized subjects face over competing loyalties to family and community, on the one hand, and to self-independence and self-advancement, on the other, narratives that are also stories of spaces, of leaving the neighborhood or sticking it out to put down roots. They are narratives of how communities survive and thrive, how culture is emplotted and uprooted, and how the transformation of urban orders through decline, suburbanization, and renewal gives rise to backward-glancing nostalgia and new structures of feeling that imagine a different future for the slum and the ghetto. In short, these writers are part of a contentious conversation about the American city and the activities of making and unmaking places. Some of them write from the outside looking in and others from the inside looking to get out. Regardless of the perspective, they engage with the formal challenge of signifying urban spaces that are difficult to apprehend because of their internal social complexity, and because of their ever-evolving transformation by external forces, from local practices of slum clearance, ghettoization, and urban redevelopment, to global patterns of capital and labor migration impacting city life.

Any study of the literature of the slum and ghetto must contend with the fact that the terms are freighted today with offensive overtones. This was true, too, for reform activists in the late nineteenth century. The Chicago School sociologist Andrew Lind, for example, remarked that nineteenth-century social workers rejected the terms for "possessing invidious connotations which disqualified them for scientific or practical use." Jane Addams in *Twenty Years at Hull House* (1910) "religiously avoids the two words," observed Lind.[1] However, sociologists throughout the twentieth century rarely paused to contemplate disqualifying connotations and instead freely used the terms. Compounding matters is the definitional flexibility of the words. In Progressive Era discourse, *slum* and *ghetto* were often deployed interchangeably. Louis Wirth, for instance, contended that *ghetto* could signify any number of ethnic or racial enclaves: "Chinese, Negro, Sicilian, or Jewish." Yet these were areas that Riis and others labeled not as ghettos but as slums. If the terms were used inconsistently in the first half of the century, by the second half there was starker clarity, although pathologizing connotations remained. Mid-twentieth-century demographic changes, which led to "extensive concentrations of blacks in northern cities," profoundly altered the urban landscape and the language for labeling it.[2] The ghetto lost its ethnic associations, and from the 1950s onward was applied almost exclusively to so-called inner-city neighborhoods housing a black underclass.

While for some late nineteenth- and early twentieth-century urban intellectuals the slum and the ghetto were relatively indistinct from one another, for others there were critical differences, most alarmingly in their levels of social cohesion. A central trope of sociological writing in the 1920s and 1930s is the slum's utter disorganization. In the view of outsider experts, it was the antithesis of a community, where social bonds were ephemeral and fractured. In *The City* (1925), Robert Park described the slum as a zone of instability, littered with dilapidated rooming houses, brothels, and cheap hotels, where "vagrant and suppressed impulses, passions, and ideals emancipate themselves from the dominant moral order." Harvey Zorbaugh expanded on these descriptions of the slum's nonnormativity. "The slum harbors," he wrote, "many sorts of people: the criminal, the radical, the bohemian, the migratory worker, the immigrant, the unsuccessful, the queer and unadjusted," "prostitutes," "outlaws," "hobos," and "men and women of unstable or problematical character."[3] Such catalogs are a feature of the era's writing in which wrapping one's mind around slum life's pell-mell nature necessitates naming all of its human types. The geographer Jean Brunhes likewise remarked that the slum's "masses" were "veritable nomads who pass from room to room and from house to house," leaving behind "a certain social anarchy [that] follows inevitably from the ever-rising tide and the ever-repeated flood of these unattached beings" with "no moral home." For these experts, slum life was at best itinerant and was at worst run amok. Early twentieth-century discourse was rife with pathologizing images of the slum as bleak, amoral, and as a place riddled with "high rates of birth, infant mortality, illegitimacy, and death." For Park and Zorbaugh, the slum wasn't so much the creation of capitalist structures of social and spatial inequality as it was of the "well-defined types of submerged humanity" who lived there.[4] Such claims would not dissipate over the century, but would harden into the postwar culture-of-poverty thesis that laid blame for immiseration at the feet of those suffering from it the most.

In contrast, the early twentieth-century ethnic ghetto was praised for its stability, homogeneity, and rootedness, all the qualities the slum supposedly lacked. In the ghetto, Park contended, "the group" – a word that connotes cohesion, unlike the slum's *masses* – "is able to live its life according to its own standards, and maintain its own cultural traditions untouched and unspotted from the world." The ghetto's insularity, a byproduct of its cultural homogeneity, permitted it to play a role as a place of stability, as well as transition. Or as Lind argued, its "habitual and customary patterns of life [. . .] conserve and foster the only cultural standards which the immigrant can understand" during a "trying period of readjustment to a new culture and civilization." The ghetto was metaphorically likened to a "decompression chamber" facilitating "the survival and adjustment of immigrants" and eventually leading to assimilation, a process Cahan would dramatize in his novella *Yekl* (1896).[5] To the extent that industrial modernity was a maelstrom of confusion, the ghetto was figured as a staging ground for immigrants to ease the pains of acculturation, thus differing sharply from the slum's status as a space of anomie.

Underpinning the Chicago School sociologists' thinking was an ecological theory of urbanization processes whereby the slum's environment determined human behavior. It was an idea that naturalist writers Stephen Crane, Theodore Dreiser, and Frank Norris decades earlier had dramatized in stories about the corrosive influence of the city. This stress on environmental causes of nonnormative behaviors indicated a paradigm shift from earlier nineteenth-century reformers' understanding of the slum through the lens of Christian morality. "A filthy city always has been and always will be a wicked city," proclaimed the influential preacher and editor Thomas De Witt Talmage, who proselytized about "the great remedial influence" of "the Gospel of Christ." Park and Ernest Burgess instead wrote analytically of the slum's "divergent moral code," using a methodology of "description and explanation" without castigating the slum as sinful.[6] For them, the industrializing city was "a laboratory or a clinic" for examining "human nature and social processes," in particular "the pathology or disorganization typical of city life." In essence, the city was a complicated social-science problem whose social orders needed to be empirically mapped, zoned, and expertly managed.[7]

For Chicago School sociologists, a central technology for visually managing the city was the map charting the development of the urban field in concentric rings. The most famous of them were Burgess's radial maps that plot the city's zonal social geography from central business district to suburban periphery, amounting, in effect, to a map of waves of capital rippling across the landscape. Other sociologists, such as Clifford Shaw, used maps to anatomize individual neighborhoods by tracking delinquency, disease, and poverty block by block. A common element of literary depictions of the slum and ghetto, as well, is the narrative mapping of tenements, streets, and neighborhood by which writers plot the coordinates of class, ethnicity, and race. Riis maps "The Bend," "Chinatown," "Jewtown," and "the color line in New York."[8] Cahan charts Jewish life on Hester Street, while Dreiser tours the rough-and-tumble Bowery, and Crane in *Maggie: A Girl of the Streets* (1893) plots the world of Rum Alley and Devil's Row. For sociologists, pinpointing the slum's coordinates was a step toward understanding and imaginatively containing it. With its putatively high rates of social disorganization, the slum was designated as "a zone of deterioration" that shared a border with more established immigrant ghettos. Where one zone ended and another began was a worrying question given the "tendency of each inner zone to extend its area by invasion of the next outer zone," wrote Burgess.[9]

The 1920s and 1930s witnessed a flurry of studies by "sociologists [who] discovered" the slum and the ghetto, or at least imagined they did.[10] The truth was that writers, reformers, and social workers already had arrived on the scene in the mid-to-late nineteenth century. This "discovery" motif, with its affects of shock and bewilderment, is age-old and recurrent in US urban discourse, stretching at least from Riis's *How the Other Half Lives* (1890) to Michael Harrington's *The Other America* (1962) and beyond in exposés where the nation discovers again the invisible poor who have always been among us. The early nineteenth-century mercantile city had a condensed spatial form where middle, working-class, and poor populations lived cheek by jowl. But by century's end, when Riis was writing, this urban spatial order and social structure was morphing into a new form. Mass immigration and industrialization were creating a more unevenly developed city that was distended in new directions with the flight of the middle class and their wealth away from the urban core. It is in the context of this "decidedly modern" urban form that Riis's "other half" isolated in slums and ghettos was to be rediscovered.[11] The further hollowing out of the city later in the mid-twentieth century – through accelerated suburbanization, urban renewal, and the red-lining of African Americans in underresourced areas – similarly laid the groundwork for the discovery of the so-called black underclass in the 1950s and 1960s.

Riis opened his study of the harrowing conditions in New York by tearing aside the veil of ignorance shielding the middle class from knowledge of the city's grueling poverty, disease, and congestion: "Long ago it was said that 'one half of the world does not know how the other half lives.'" Equipped with a camera and new flashcube technology, he set about exposing "the hot-beds of the epidemics," "the nurseries of pauperism," and the "enormously swelling population held in [. . .] galling bondage" in the slums.[12] The startled faces staring out from his photographs document not only the appalling circumstances of nineteenth-century poverty but also the pathos of those whose lives have been literally thrust into the light by Riis, who made a habit of barging into apartments without warning. Contextualizing these photographs is Riis's lurid, sentimentalizing prose, which tells a "story [that] is dark enough [. . .] to send a chill to any heart." It is an effort to render the lower wards legible, but it often makes them more inscrutable. "That was a woman filling her pail by the hydrant you just bumped against," Riis explains, enjoining the reader, "Come over here. Step carefully over this baby – it is a baby, spite of its rags and dirt."[13] Not merely descriptive information, Riis's prose here seeks to impose the discomforts of life in the slum on the reader.

Riis's exposé is shot through with voyeurism, racism, and xenophobia, leading some twentieth- and twenty-first-century readers to dismiss the text outright. At times, slum life appears unredeemable. "A vast human pig-sty" is how he describes the Italian area of the Mulberry Bend. He portrays the Chinese as completely incapable of assimilating. Riis comments on the "unmistakable physiognomy" of Jews, and derides them for their industriousness while lambasting other ethnics for laziness. With such descriptions in mind, it is easy to forget that Riis was actually a liberal reformer railing against "exorbitant rents" and the "greed and reckless selfishness" of landowners in an effort to raise the consciousness of an "enlightened public" to rein in the human costs of capitalism. He set his sights on the squalid tenements, whose poor sanitation, lightless rooms, and overcrowded conditions were dehumanizing. In Riis's eyes, the poor were "shiftless, destructive, and stupid," but that is "what the tenements have made them." "All life eventually accommodates itself to its environment," he remarked, expressing an emergent theory of ecological determinism whereby spatial conditions molded character.[14]

The poor were victims of circumstance for Riis. As a reformer rather than a radical, he sought solutions within "the 'system' that was the evil offspring of public neglect and private greed." The answer to the city's social problems, he thought, was better housing, model tenements that were "*sufficiently separate, decent, and desirable.*"[15] To this end, Riis successfully advocated for new laws that would improve existing tenements and compel developers to build new ones with better ventilation and sanitation. But such solutions failed to root out the underlying causes of poverty. The slum remained, both as a material place in the city and an imagined place in the minds of those who wrote about the city.

It's hard to read *How the Other Half Lives* without coming away with the impression that what offended Riis the most about the immigrant slum was its apparent disorder. Images of squalor were almost de rigueur in slum literature. Writer and labor activist Abraham Cahan deployed them in *Yekl.* The streets of Cahan's Lower East Side overflow with "sickening piles" of garbage; the fire escapes of the overcrowded tenements are "festooned with mattresses," and the whole atmosphere is "laden with nausea." However, it is important to note that Cahan historically contextualizes such scenes by informing readers that the Jews of "the Ghetto" are "refugees" from the brutal pogroms in Russia and anti-Semitism in Europe, and that they are dignified "people torn from a hard-gained foothold in life and deep-rooted attachments by the caprice of intolerance or the wiles of demagoguery."[16] They live and make do in the overcrowded ghetto, Cahan suggests, because there remain few other places this community is welcomed, or even, tolerated.

If for Riis the squalor of the slum was not just a material reality but also a symbolic reflection of the people who lived there, Cahan saw a neighborhood whose residents were neither pathological nor exotic. They were ordinary people – "artisans, merchants, teachers, rabbis, artists, and beggars" – struggling to construct a new community in a foreign land. *Yekl* tells this story through a domestic plot, that most familiar framework of realistic fiction. When the novella begins the increasingly acculturated Jake, who is enjoying his bachelor life in New York, is reluctant to pay for the passage over for his wife Gitl and their son Yosselé, yet eventually agrees. Yet upon their arrival at the Immigration Bureau, he is immediately struck by her "uncouth and un-American appearance." The story closes with their divorce, Jake's impending marriage to a more Americanized woman, and Gitl's plan to use her settlement to open a grocery business, a sign of her own budding American entrepreneurialism. Nowhere is there the lurid sensationalism of so much writing on the Yiddish quarter. Cahan's Lower East Side is a self-sufficient "compact city within a city." Only on rare occasions do his characters cross the threshold of "the Ghetto of the American metropolis." The marital and economic tensions of Jake and Gitl unfold in an elaborately networked community knitted together by neighborly alliances. Insular, yes, but chaotic, no. For Cahan, the ghetto is a place of social and political organization where workers, such as Jake and his shopmates fight off exploitation by "threatening a strike," where residents borrow capital from each other to build a new American future, and where neighbors, such as Gitl, Mrs. Kavarsky, and Fanny, share gossip and information to help with adapting to life in the United States.[17]

Cahan provided an insider account of the Yiddish quarter, but in subsequent years writers from the outside, such as Dreiser, would continue to return to the area to lend another perspective. *The Color of a Great City* (1923) comprises Dreiser's impressionistic snapshots, "very brief pictures" of New York between 1900 and 1915, a period he calls his "early adventurings" in the Bowery and surrounding areas. Whereas Cahan's novella depicted a new America in the making, "a human hodgepodge with its component parts changed but not yet fused into one homogenous whole," Dreiser's work, published nearly thirty years later, looks back on turn-of-the-century

New York only to mourn that so much of what Cahan described as coming into being was "fast vanishing." "The haphazard must, and in the main does, give way to the well-organized," Dreiser reasons, lamenting the advances of the Progressive Era that transformed the heterogeneous immigrant district into just another neighborhood. His frank preference is for "the east side and the Bowery" of the past, "unrelieved as they were by civic betterment and social service ventures of all kinds" in contrast to "the beschooled and beserviced east side of to-day."[18] For Dreiser, New York City in the 1920s is too modern, clean, orderly, and efficient.

As local-color writing, Dreiser's work aestheticizes the city, a point made plain by his book's title. To put a sharper point on it, it aestheticizes poverty and ethnic differences that once made the slums and ghettos of New York vibrant in Dreiser's mind. Late nineteenth-century New York, with its "astounding areas of poverty and beggary," and with its "Jews," "Italians," "Germans, Hungarians, French, Polish, Swedish, Armenians all with sections of their own" offered Dreiser "greater social and financial contrasts that it does now." The "rich, dark, colorful threads to the rug or tapestry which is New York" had become, in his mind, washed out. Rather than pathologizing the poor, *The Color of a Great City* romanticizes their social and material inequality, reimagining their lives and struggles for a writer desperate for personal revitalization. "Bums," Dreiser remarks, "have always had a peculiar interest for me." "They take life with too jaunty an air to permit one to be distressed about them," he claims. In another sketch on poverty, he lays bare the source of his fascination: "I have even been beset by a nervous depression which has all but destroyed my power to write."[19] The supposed physical vitality of the poor – the way they "take life" – inspires the middle-class subject, as it had Dreiser's contemporary Hutchins Hapgood, who admired how the Jewish ghetto "helps you to see the limitations of respectability. [. . .] It wears away the unnecessary, calls aloud for essential humanity." Through his writing, Dreiser textually preserves what was disappearing materially in a modernizing New York. As he did so, the poor, whose slums were "vanishing," served as symbolic labor that reconstructed a strenuous, middle-class masculinity some Progressive Era writers believed was on the wane.[20]

Dreiser never claimed his sketches of the "polyglot city" were studies in urban sociology, but others noticed similarities between them and the work produced by the Chicago School that combined "the verve of journalism with the restraint of science" and that borrowed the local-color detail found in the work of literary writers. Reviewing Zorbaugh's *The Gold Coast and the Slum* (1929), Rupert Vance called it "worthy of

a title once used by Theodore Dreiser, 'The Color of a [Great] City.'"
Vance's analogy underscores the observation by literary scholar Carlo
Rotella that "urban intellectuals" of many stripes "set out in various
ways, and often at cross purposes, to explore the literary possibilities and
social consequences" of a changing urban order.²¹ The emergence in the
late nineteenth and early twentieth centuries of the immigrant slum
spurred an aesthetic and ethnographic project to understand the industrial
city. But this project recalibrated into an even more urgent mode in the
postwar period when demographic shifts and structural transformations –
such as large-scale deindustrialization, a second Great Migration from the
South, and a concomitant white exodus to the suburbs – gave rise to the
black ghetto. These changes, along with locally discriminatory policies,
such as slum clearance, urban renewal, and highway construction through
black neighborhoods, produced unprecedented concentrations of racial
poverty and "a new spatial order" bearing "little resemblance to the
American city in the past."²² Not surprisingly, what emerged with the
black ghetto was an outpouring of sociological and policy discourse, such
as Kenneth Clark's *Dark Ghetto* (1965), Daniel Patrick Moynihan's *The
Negro Family* (1965), and Oscar Lewis's *A Study of Slum Culture* (1968), that
centered on urban crisis and decline.

Whereas the discourse on the slum anatomized the ethnic poor into
myriad urban types, the new discourse on the postwar ghetto largely
focused on a single specter, a so-called underclass of African Americans
mired in an intractable "culture of poverty," a thesis that dominated
academic and policy writing. The causes of poverty, Oscar Lewis implied,
were not primarily structural, but cultural and psychological. "Slum culture," by which he meant the culture of the black ghetto, was a nightmare
of "resignation and fatalism," where residents "lack[ed] impulse control"
and evinced a "high tolerance for psychological pathology."²³ The punish-
ing conditions of the ghetto warped one's mind, he contended, leading to
a downward spiral of despair that manifested in the fetid streets and
violence of the inner city. In effect, Lewis circularly argued that delinquency and cultural pathology were the outcome and the cause of the
insalubrious living conditions of black urban Americans. In a critique of
Lewis's victim-blaming thesis, Michael Katz notes how it "conjured up
a mysterious wilderness in the heart of America's cities" and how it robbed
its population of agency apart from bare survival in "a terrain of violence
and despair."²⁴ Much of the postwar sociological discourse implied that
escaping the black ghetto – unlike the earlier ethnic ghetto – through
acculturation into the mainstream of American life was nearly impossible.

As the "increasingly vehement national conversation about cities in the 1950s and 1960s called into question every form of urban order – not only the political, social, or architectural but also the representational," explains Rotella, the metaphor of a perverse underclass was one representational strategy for both clarifying and mystifying the complex processes of ghettoization.[25]

As the industrial urban order began to be dismantled, Nelson Algren's novel *The Man with the Golden Arm* (1949) furnished a transitional text dramatizing its decline and prefiguring its replacement. Steeped in the terrain of Chicago realism, the novel never pulls back for a wide-angle view of "urban renewal, deindustrialization, or suburbanization," but, instead, maintains a narrow "representational range" from the perspective of grifters detached from the industrial labor force in the blighted Polish neighborhood of working-class tenements on the Near Northwest Side (the neighborhood that Zorbaugh closely examined two decades earlier) as it is about to turn into a racial ghetto. Algren's close-up view is the product of "research, observation, and precise description of urban types, languages, terrains, and processes," much like the work of the Chicago sociologists with whom he shared the city.[26] Feelings of anxiety, claustrophobia, and malaise permeate the text, portending some ominous, if still inchoate change, which the character Sophie imagines as "a sense of imminent doom." Algren's Chicago is one of shadows and smoke. "It's goin' up! Loop 'n all!," Sophie predicts, and breathlessly pleads, "Why don't we move out of the neighborhood," adding "the spades are moving in." Algren's characters pine for "the old days" when their "crummy neighborhood" was "less crowded" and the city at large was less "crippled" and less "insane." "All had gone stale for these disinherited," he writes of the city's poor. Sophie's husband Frankie begins the novel with an addiction to morphine, accidentally kills his dealer, and then flees to "the narrow Negro streets," where he commits suicide.[27]

Drug addiction, crime, and racial succession drive Algren's novel. Even still, the ghetto remains on the text's periphery, more of a fear and a future threat than a present-day reality. Yet for postwar African American writers, the struggles and humiliations of the racial ghetto were all too real. For Ralph Ellison in "Harlem is Nowhere" (1948) conditions in America's most famous black neighborhood were so dire – "casual violence," "crumbling buildings," "garbage and decay" – as to leave him searching for language commensurate to a reality "indistinguishable from the distorted images that appear in dreams." His contention that Harlem was "nowhere" suggested it lacked any identifiable qualities of a community. It was "the very bowels of the city" and a place of "labyrinthine existence," representations unfortunately reinforcing sociological inscriptions of the ghetto as inescapably foul, even as Ellison argued the roots of its impoverishment lay in the city's racist exclusions that "exploited [Harlem] politically and economically."[28] It was a perspective he would greatly amend with his more nuanced portrait of Harlem in *Invisible Man* (1952) with its intricate pastiche of realism, mythological substructures, and black folkloric rituals. Images of black abjection and political passivity are few in *Invisible Man*. The novel, rather, portrays the neighborhood as the site of heroic black struggle for individual self-creation, a place rich in culture, and as a terrain divided by political ideologies tearing it asunder as it seeks collective empowerment.

One of the searing images in the final pages of *Invisible Man* is the torching of "a huge tenement building," a disease-ridden "deathtrap" in Harlem, by African American rioters who burn to the ground the immiserating architecture that Riis a half-century earlier thought could be reformed. "You wouldn't fix it up. Now see how you like it," one of the protesters exclaims after flicking a match into a room soaked with kerosene. Ellison's hero ultimately rejects such violent collective protests and pledges to play a more "socially responsible role."[29] He does so primarily through writing his own story of survival and maturation, one that inscribes into being an intelligent and determined black masculinity that contrasts starkly with sociological the depictions of black eccentricity and pathology that circulated freely in the postwar period. In his writings and public statements throughout the 1960s, Ellison would wholly reject the discourse of black pathology and push back against the labeling of Harlem as a ghetto. For Ellison, Harlem and America's other historically black districts were places deeply saturated with art, myth, and memory, and they were just as complexly networked and socially cohesive as ethnic enclaves of earlier eras.

Ellison's aim was to shift the national conversation in which Harlem was the epicenter of America's urban crisis. But not all African American writers agreed that that story had been fully told. The most shocking ghetto narrative – at least for many white readers – was Claude Brown's bestselling *Manchild in the Promised Land* (1965). In order to capture the harrowing realities of postwar Harlem, Brown shed the artifices of fiction and turned to the form of first-person memoir with an unvarnished, at times vulgar, prose conveying the gritty authenticity of street life. The "promised land" of the title bitterly evoked the dream of racial liberation for the hundreds of thousands of African Americans who had migrated from the Jim Crow South.[30] While Brown's coming-of-age story is his own, it is also a generational tale belonging to those migrants' children, who were growing up not in a promised land but a dilapidated neighborhood walled in by segregation. Juvenile delinquency, gun violence, heroin addiction, broken families, Brown's memoir had it all, leading to accusations that he catered to white voyeurism, but also to praise for authenticating a black reality too often ignored.[31] "Harlem was getting fucked over by everybody," Brown exclaimed. *Manchild*'s dramatic opening sentence – "Run!" – is a fearful imperative to flee the ghetto, which Brown eventually does but not before cycling in and out of reform schools and liberal social-service institutions that consistently fail him. "I gave my gun away when I moved out of Harlem. I felt free," he confesses. Yet Brown's escape for his own survival comes with feelings of disconnection that are a persistent strain in the literature of the slum and ghetto: "I was losing whatever hold I'd had on my old stamping ground, my home town, my family, and my friends." For all its grit, *Manchild* is washed in sepia-tinted hues of nostalgia for the old neighborhood. "The Harlem that I had dreamed of and wanted to get back to seemed gone," he writes.[32] As the 1960s wore on, black pride and black separatist power movements would resignify the ghetto yet again, stressing a distinctive Afrocentric dignity and beauty in a fierce rebuttal to depictions of black life as tragic. This development was another example of how writers across the twentieth century aesthetically responded to the city divided and redivided by class, race, and ethnicity.

Into the twenty-first century urbanization, immigration, economic inequality, and de facto segregation continue to transform our material and social landscapes, and in doing so, they continue to engender a literary and political discourse that, broadly speaking, is about *place* and the process of place-making. In light of the preceding historical and discursive overview, we might understand the rhetoric of the 2016 US presidential campaign and the first years of the Trump administration, not as something sui generis, but as the latest recrudescence of the most insidious manifestations of a discourse that has longed wedded race and ethnicity to urban geography. The forces that led to the election of Donald Trump were manifoldly complex. But their core was a rural revolt fueled by the latest eruption of an incendiary racist and xenophobic rhetoric that conflates racial and ethnic minorities with crime, drug use, disease, pathology, invasion, and, of course, the city itself. Yet if the contrasting image of an archipelago of welcoming and multicultural cities across the United States in the twenty-first century brings comfort, it is belied by the fact that the leading source of today's anti-urban populism is himself a born-and-bred

New Yorker. His rapid rise to power is a sign that deep divisions endure not only between the country and the city, but within the urban terrain as well.

In the twenty-first century, US literature is growing more diverse, as is the nation, despite efforts to materially and rhetorically wall off its territory and its traditions. Undoubtedly, the spatial imagination of the century's new writers will continue to explore the systematic workings of race, ethnicity, and urban space as did their forerunners whose writings of the slum and ghetto dramatized the affective dimensions – stories of settlement, struggle, celebration, and dislocation – of these ever-evolving geographies that constrain and liberate the imagination.

Notes

1. Andrew W. Lind, "The Ghetto and the Slum," *Social Forces* 9 (1930), 206.
2. Louis Wirth, "The Ghetto," *The American Journal of Sociology* 33 (1927), 71; Jacob Riis, *How the Other Half Lives* (New York: Norton, 2010), p. 9; David Ward, *Poverty, Ethnicity, and the American City,1840–1925: Changing Conceptions of the Slum and Ghetto* (Cambridge: Cambridge University Press, 1989), p. 5.
3. Robert E. Park, "The City: Suggestions for the Investigation of Human Behavior in the Urban Environment," in Park, Ernest W. Burgess, and Roderick D. McKenzie, eds., *The City* (Chicago: University of Chicago Press, 1967), p. 43; Harvey Zorbaugh, *The Gold Coast and the Slum* (Chicago: University of Chicago Press, 1983), pp. 11, 32.
4. Jean Brunhes, *Human Geography* (Chicago: Rand McNally, 1920), p. 543; Zorbaugh, *Gold Coast*, pp. 9, 129.
5. Park quoted in Lind, "Ghetto and the Slum," 206; Lind, "Ghetto and the Slum," 208–9; Ward, *Poverty*, p. 170.
6. Thomas De Witt Talmage, "From *The Night Sides of City Life*," in Thomas A. Gullason, ed., *Maggie: A Girl of the Streets* (New York: Norton, 1979), pp. 71, 73; Park, "The City," p. 45; Park and Burgess, *Introduction to the Science of Sociology* (Chicago: University of Chicago Press, 1969), p. 29.
7. Park, "The City," p. 46; Louis Wirth, "A Bibliography of the Urban Community," in Park, Burgess, and McKenzie, *The City*, p. 199; Ward, *Poverty*, p. 92.
8. Riis, *How the Other Half*, pp. 35, 55, 63, 85.
9. Park, "The City," pp. 54, 50.
10. Lind, "Ghetto," 206.
11. William Sharpe and Leonard Wallock, "From 'Great Town' to 'Nonplace Urban Realm': Reading the Modern City," in Sharpe and Wallock, eds., *Visions of the Modern City: Essays in History, Art, and Literature* (Baltimore: Johns Hopkins University Press, 1987), p. 3.
12. Riis, *How the Other Half*, pp. 5, 6, 5, 6.

13. Ibid., pp. 6, 29, 30.
14. Ibid., pp. 35, 63, 17, 152, 154, 93.
15. Ibid., pp. 6, 5.
16. Abraham Cahan, *Yekl and the Imported Bridegroom* (New York: Dover, 1970), pp. 13, 14.
17. Ibid., pp. 34, 24, 13, 45.
18. Theodore Dreiser, *The Color of a Great City* (1923; Syracuse, NY: Syracuse University Press, 1996), p. ix; Cahan, *Yekl*, p. 14; Dreiser, *Color*, pp. ix, 132, ix.
19. Dreiser, *Color*, pp. 7, ix, 6, 35, 37, 78.
20. Hutchins Hapgood, *The Spirit of the Ghetto* (Cambridge, MA: Harvard-Belknap Press, 1967), pp. xx; Dreiser, *Color*, p. ix.
21. Dreiser, *Color*, p. xiii; Rupert Vance, "Reviewed Work: The Gold Coast and the Slum," *Social Forces*, 8.2 (1929), 321; Carlo Rotella, *October Cities: The Redevelopment of Urban Literature* (Berkeley: University of California Press, 1999), p. 4.
22. Thomas Sugrue, "The Structures of Urban Poverty: The Reorganization of Space and Work in Three Periods of American History," in Michael Katz, ed., *The "Underclass" Debate: Views from History* (Princeton, NJ: Princeton University Press, 1994), p. 116.
23. Oscar Lewis, *A Study of Slum Culture: Backgrounds for La Vida* (New York: Random House, 1968), pp. 10, 11.
24. Michael Katz, "The Urban 'Underclass' as a Metaphor of Social Transformation," in M. Katz, ed., *The "Underclass" Debate* (Princeton, NJ: Princeton University Press, 1994), p. 4.
25. Rotella, *October Cities*, p. 7.
26. Ibid., pp. 67, 50.
27. Nelson Algren, *The Man with the Golden Arm* (New York: Seven Stories Press, 1996), pp. 235, 235, 29, 116, 259, 96, 21, 294.
28. Ralph Ellison, "Harlem Is Nowhere," in *Shadow and Act* (New York: Quality Paperback Book Club, 1994), p. 295.
29. Ellison, *Invisible Man* (New York: Vintage, 1982), pp. 533, 534, 568.
30. Claude Brown, *Manchild in the Promised Land* (New York: Touchstone, 2012), p. ix.
31. Rotella, *October Cities*, p. 305; Nathan McCall, introduction, *Manchild*, p. vii.
32. Brown, *Manchild*, pp. 179, 1, 182, 205, 109.

CHAPTER 5

Urban Borders, Open Wounds

Ana María Manzanas Calvo and Jesús Benito Sánchez

> The pain and joy of the borderlands – perhaps no greater or lesser than the emotions stirred by living anywhere contradictions abound, cultures clash and meld, and life is lived on an edge – come from a wound that will not heal and yet is forever healing. These lands have always been here; the river of people has flowed for centuries. It is only the designation "border" that is relatively new, and along with the term comes the life one lives in this "in-between world" that makes us the "other," the marginalized.
>
> Norma E. Cantú, "Living on the Border: A Wound
> That Will Not Heal" (1993)

> Planning as ideology formulates all the problems of society into questions of space and transposes all that comes from history and consciousness into spatial terms. It is an ideology which immediately divides up. Since society does not function in a satisfactory manner, could there not be a pathology of space?
>
> Henri Lefebvre, "Philosophy of the City
> and Planning Ideology" (1968)

There is a pain and a joy associated with living on an edge, writes Norma Cantú. Both emotions stem from what she terms "a wound that will not heal and yet is forever healing." Cantú refashions Gloria Anzaldúa's vision of the Mexican American borderlands as an open wound, and concatenates the tracing of the border and the creation of the category of the Other. There is no border fence or barbed wire in the city, but city planning implements an ideology that divides and separates, resulting in what Henri Lefebvre identifies as "a pathology of space."[1] As Janette Turner Hospital eloquently comments, "there are divisions and boundary lines that fissure any state more deeply than the moat it digs around the nationhood. [. . .] Yet on every side there are also doors to a wider place, a covert geography under sleep where all the waters meet."[2] This chapter explores these dividing mechanisms and fissures that dig deeply around and through the country, as it relocates the image of the border as un-healing wound to the urban landscape. The analysis uproots the border from the perimeter of the country, from the traditional dyad in which it is embedded (this country/that country; inside/outside; north/south) and releases it in the urban landscape. The premise of this reconsideration of urban borders is that just as the category of space has been mobilized in the work of geographers such as Doreen Massey, it is possible to transfer this process of destabilization to the concept of the border and the shifting categories of crossers and gatekeepers. Space, Massey claims, is always "under construction," always "in the process of being made. It is never finished; never closed."[3] Similarly, it is possible to claim that borders are always in the process of being reconfigured, never finished, never closed, always in the midst of being drawn but also blurred.

Significantly, *order* is part of the word *border*. A border separates and, in so doing, carries out a visual rearrangement of space. The inescapable result of order building, writes Zygmunt Bauman, is that it casts some parts of the extant population as "out of place," "unfit," or "undesirable."[4] The links between order making, spatial control and racial subordination have been eloquently clarified by George Lipsitz:

> From the theft of Native American and Mexican lands in the nineteenth century to the confiscation of Black and Latino property for urban renewal projects in the twentieth century, from the Trail of Tears to the Japanese Internment, from the creation of ghettos, barrios, reservations, and "Chinatowns" to the disproportionate placement of toxic hazards in minority neighborhoods, the racial projects of U.S. society have always been spatial projects as well.

A basic tenet that splits space in two undergirds the correlation between racial and spatial terms: "The white spatial imaginary idealizes 'pure' and homogeneous spaces, controlled environments, and predictable patterns of design and behavior." In order for these "pure and homogeneous spaces" to exist, "'impure' populations have to be removed and marginalized," allocated to what we can call infected spaces.[5] This spatial distribution is clear in Jacob Riis's *How the Other Half Lives*, which gave visibility to the tenements and slums in New York City. In the introduction, Riis refers explicitly to the line that segregated different populations in the city: "The boundary line of the Other Half lies through the tenements."[6] This pitting of pure/impure, homogeneous/heterogeneous spaces and populations illustrates the hierarchical dimension of space distribution and its accompanying ideological regime.

The limits and dimensions of these infected or impure spaces configure the contours of urban borders. They may not be apparent at first, but their presence is quietly productive. If we do not see them, Patricia Price claims, it may be because we are not looking in the right places, or because we are failing to recognize them when we encounter them. Borders and demarcations have turned inconspicuous, flexible, and fluid, and may go undetected. For Price the location of boundaries requires thinking about lines of separation as more fluid sorts of places, since they do not stay put in visible geographical manifestations according to traditional geometrics. Drawing from Price, we claim that urban borders function in a *transverse* fashion, conflating visual, architectural, economic, and racial segregation.[7] They may get activated in the face of the "wrong" kind of crosser, whenever s/he is entering the domestic or pure spaces on which the dominant culture models itself. In fact, the unwelcomed crossers bear the coordinates of a "shifting boundary."[8] The border, simply put, is where the migrant or the ethnic body is. This destabilization of the geopolitical line allows us to revise traditional spatial categories such as inside versus outside and here versus there, and to assess how those dichotomies relate to pure versus infected spaces.[9] Although situated within the country, infected or diseased spaces are outsides within the inside. As Jacques Derrida and Hélène Cixous have put it, "One can be inside without being inside, there is an inside in the inside, an outside in the inside and this goes on infinitely."[10] More recently, Sandro Mezzadra and Brett Neilson have explored the ambiguities between inclusion and exclusion, a gray area that is not sufficiently explained in the dyad in/out. Although the characters in the literary works we set out to analyze are within the perimeter of the country, they illustrate what Mezzadra and Neilson call a "differential inclusion" that reveals different "degrees of internality and externality, which substitute and blur the clear-cut distinction between inside and outside that was produced by the traditional border of the nation-state."[11] The characters will never enjoy the hospitality that the United States administers to desirable guests. Such a problematic hospitality cannot be untangled from its parasitical other, hostility, and resembles Derrida's aporetic concept of hostipitality.[12] There are, this chapter illustrates, multiple ways of hostipitalizing the Other in the urban landscape. Spatial segregation and the accompanying practices originating outside the immigrant communities, what Raúl Homero Villa terms "barrioization" (from *barrio*, Hispanic Arabic **bárri* "exterior," and classical Arabic *barrī* "wild"), however, contrast with "barriology," the way that migrants perceive themselves, their spaces in the city and the community-sustaining practices they engage in from within the community.[13] Such practices cross ethnic boundaries and allow for multiethnic identities. They also offer multiple instances of multicultural collaboration and polyphonic discourses, as the works of Karen T. Yamashita and Li-Young Lee, among many others, demonstrate.[14]

In what follows, we disaggregate different strands of urban border narratives to assess how they are reconceptualized and resemanticized by those living on those urban edges or wounds. We look at borders not only in their "ordering" dimension but also as sites that allow for reordering strategies of self-definition and articulation. As a result, the outsides in the insides may become new insides within the inside. This double perspective allows us to acknowledge the productivity of boundaries as well as their violation and subversion.[15] In the midst of these two processes, the urban borders we examine, as Cantú remarks, will not heal but are always in the process of healing.

Concentric Borders: Hosts, Guests, and Discursive Lines

Helena Viramontes's "The Cariboo Café" (1995) stands as a paradigmatic example of a concentric border that keeps being reconfigured. Significantly, Viramontes does not include the crossing of the geopolitical boundary, as if the perimeter of the country were secondary to the inner borders the characters are bound to encounter once inside the country. We are told that the family in the story arrives "in the secrecy of night" as befits displaced people. As in other renditions of immigrant experiences such as Sandra Cisneros's *The House on Mango Street*, the dream of creating a home and a finer future proves hard to achieve; in the meantime, the family has to be content with occupying a geography of invisibility where the children play "in the back alleys, among the broken glass."[16] Yet these diseased spaces are their only protection against the police and the threat of deportation. Fear turns the border inward and brings the national contour within, creating externalities within the country. The perils of the outside become all too real when the protagonists, Sonya and Macky, lose the key to the apartment and become homeless. Significantly, there is no home in the story, just temporary occupations of nonhomes where the children and the nameless woman from Central America seek refuge, namely, the Cariboo Café and a hotel. Thus, the story moves from the hostility of the country to the hospitality industry.

As an example of a fungible and portable border, the Cariboo Café is carefully watched by a border keeper, the café owner. Although he claims that he will never put up signs restricting entry to his café, the welcome to his business is immediately compromised by the way he conceptualizes his customers as "scum" that has to eat. Upon seeing the woman, he automatically places himself on the side of the safe, the legal, and the fair ready to stop the potentially abusive guest. The fact that she speaks Spanish is enough to identify her as illegal, as belonging south of the border. Illegality is automatically associated with an "immigrant" language as opposed to English, the language of the land. Just as the white imaginary idealizes "pure" and homogeneous spaces, it seems possible to argue that it also idealizes "pure" and allegedly homogeneous languages, i.e., English, while removing and relocating "impure" populations, along with their languages to infected spaces. Thus, the cook voices the well-known isomorphism of a country that views itself as white, English-speaking, and Anglo-Saxon. However, his reaction to Spanish as an illegal language is problematic; the language itself brings echoes of intimacy with his ex-wife, and Spanish words pepper his own discourse. This act of code-switching implies a crossing over into the "guest" language that seems to suspend his linguistic and ideological gatekeeping activities. The opposition between host/guest-parasite, legal/illegal, inside/outside opens to the wide range of possibilities between alleged polar opposites. The arrival of the police, however, reinstates the boundary within the café, and the place of reunion turns into the space of separation.

The drawing of different boundaries to contain the immigrant Other and the discursive border between English and Spanish reverberate in Junot Díaz's *This Is How You Lose Her* (2012). There is nothing secretive about the arrival of the Dominican family in "Invierno," just a prosaic pick up at JFK Airport. Ramón, as *pater familias*, finally reunites with his family after years of separation and drives them to London Terrace. Like the children in Viramontes's "The Cariboo Café," Ramón's family will live in specific neighborhoods that expel immigrants while folding them in. As if to emphasize its status as infected space, London Terrace stands only two miles away from a landfill. The location provides more than spatial coordinates, for it places the migrants next to the refuse of society. Revealingly, the material, undesirable waste of society is lumped together with its social excrescence. To this outer perimeter, Díaz adds an inner circle within the apartment, as Ramón reveals himself as a disciplinarian who makes sure his authority is never questioned. Observing silence when the father is at home, and forbidden to leave the apartment, mother and sons gradually assume the role of the hostage. To this physical enclosure, Díaz adds a linguistic one. As the kids start learning English through programs such as *Sesame Street*, the mother tries out English words on the father at dinnertime. Her efforts, however, are immediately dismissed, for only he is to take care of English. Ramón presents himself as the linguistic administrator who allocates languages to the different speakers in the apartment. Bakhtin has argued that "language, for the individual consciousness, lies on the borderline between oneself and the other. The word in language is half someone else's. It becomes 'one's own' only when the speaker populates it with his own intention, his own accent, when he appropriates the word, adapting it to his own semantic and expressive intention."[17] When the mother utters her first English words, she makes them her own but is immediately informed by her addressee that those words are not for her to appropriate. She simply is not to learn. The scene recalls the discursive boundary between the café owner and the unnamed woman, between English and Spanish. What is significant about "Invierno" is that even if Ramón and his wife belong to the same cultural and ethnic group, he uses his knowledge of English to regulate his wife's access to the language. The average woman, he concludes, "can't learn English."[18] Díaz situates Ramón's bilingualism side by side with the enforced monolingualism of the mother, automatically transformed into the linguistic Other. Thus, Ramón adds the gender divide to the home. English is for men, Spanish for women. Similarly, from a guest language Spanish becomes a hostage language, sealed and immobilized by English, and restricted to the private realm of the apartment.

What happens when immigrants want to break out of those infected spaces and settle in middle-class neighborhoods? Díaz's "Otravida, Otravez" (2012) deals with that effort as Yasmin chronicles Ramón's attempts to buy a house in the quieter parts of Paterson, New Jersey. Significantly, Yasmin equates house-hunting with interviewing for a visa. Like a checkpoint at a geopolitical boundary, both visa interviews and the process of purchasing a home enact an encounter between self and Other, host and guest; both reverberate with images of openness and closure, inside and outside. In both scenarios, someone belonging to the out-there is seeking entrance to the in-here. Any attempt at crossing into a pure space (or less infected one), however, activates the gatekeeper's power over the one seeking entrance. Even if, as Yasmin claims, the houses they look at are in terrible condition, and are "homes for ghosts and for cockroaches and for us, los hispanos,"[19] the couple finds that no one is ready to sell to them. As migrants, Yasmin and Ramón carry their own border, and seem to take their outside within the inside. Eventually, however, they meet an elderly homeowner who served in the Dominican Republic's Civil War and is finally willing to sell to them. In bringing up the American invasion of the

Dominican Republic in April 1965, like American financing of the Nicaraguan Contras in Viramontes's "The Cariboo Café," the author points to the parallel process of the inside taken out. Both writers remind us that, as Saskia Sassen argues in *Guests and Aliens* (1999), even if the immigration-receiving countries behave as though they were not parties to the process of immigration, in fact they are actual partners. Yasmin and Ramón finally fulfill the dream of home ownership. They have been admitted into an inner circle and, as Ramón comments, they can begin to live. Díaz, however, does not close this story with a triumphant entrance into a less infected space. For Ramón, owning a house marks another line of division between his inside and the outside, between the new owners and the Others who still belong in the category of the displaced. Situated on the inside, Ramón reinstates the boundary against an outsider that is already a priori a *hostis*, the intruder that threatens with dispossession.

This image of the host or owner barricading against the Other reverberates in Viramontes's "Neighbors" (1995). The opening of the story situates the protagonist, Aura Rodríguez, at the center of a series of concentric circles: "Aura Rodríguez always stayed within her perimeters, both personal and otherwise, and expected the same of her neighbors."[20] The neighborhood does not carry the implications of a tightly knit community that supports the individual but is described as a graveyard where Aura has to protect herself against a new generation of youngsters, the Bixby boys, who throw empty beer-cans into her yard as they blast a tape from a red Impala. Significantly, the car does not take advantage of the mesh of freeways surrounding and partitioning the community. It remains stationary, a relic from the 1960s that has forgotten its primary purpose. Mobility, like the echoes of political struggle of the late 1960s, has subsided in the claustrophobic barrio. What remains is a sense of latent violence that Viramontes escalates in a three-step fashion as Aura activates different versions of the boundary. An unknown woman who happens to know Aura's name starts and closes the series. When she stops at Aura's gate and asks for her neighbor's whereabouts, Aura feels the need to scrutinize her. Gone is the "solidarity of the subaltern,"[21] the barrio-based network of support that used to welcome the newcomer to the barrio. It is what Ernesto Galarza would call *asistencia* in *Barrio Boy* (1971). Not charity or social welfare, he clarifies, but a helping hand given and received on trust.[22] Far from creating this nexus, Aura responds by assuming the role of the gatekeeper. Nervous under Aura's scrutiny, the woman rummages through her bags "like one looking for proof of birth at a border crossing."[23] Only when she manages to produce written proof of her destination, Fierro's house, is she granted permission to enter. Aura activates the border mechanism a second time when, tired of the Bixby boys, their laughter, and their loud music, she calls the police on them and does not allow Toasty, one of the youngsters, to seek refuge in her house.

Aura's carefully watched gate is a refracted image of a major if inconspicuous wall that encapsulates the barrio, the freeway. This horizontal separation comes into focus when Viramontes introduces Fierro on the on-ramp crossing. Lewis Mumford characterized Los Angeles as "an undifferentiated mass of houses, walled off into sectors by many-laned expressways, with ramps and viaducts that create special bottlenecks of their own."[24] The word choice – "walled off" – is significant, for it foregrounds the role of freeways and expressways as dividing mechanisms.[25] Contemporary postmetropolises like Los Angeles, Edward Soja writes, face a process of conceptual and material *unbounding* that has broken down old boundaries. Paradoxically this process has resulted in the creation of constellations of carceral cities where police substitutes for polis.[26] "Neighbors" makes clear the correlation between the police state and the physical regulation of space, the cluster of multiple lanes, on-ramp crossings, and overpasses. Viramontes dismantles the triumphant narrative of the freeway as the singular architectural and engineering monument of LA's contemporary public image to concentrate instead on its effects on the communities it displaces, fragments and isolates. Barriology in "Neighbors" is severely restricted, and apart from Fierro's unconditional hospitality to the unknown woman whose name he is unable to remember, there is no reimagining the barrio as a community-enabling place; no sustaining practices or ethos engaged in counterpointing the external barrioization of the neighborhood. The principle of the polis, which Galarza, Gallego, and Samora describe as points of intercourse, exchange and reciprocity, is nonexistent, and the crossings in the story seem to favor police control.[27] As opposed to the gospel of mobility the freeway proclaims, Viramontes settles on the description of a stagnant community, plagued by crime and distrust of the Other, that has internalized the workings of the urban border.

Barrios: Segregation and Congregation

What the map cuts up, the story cuts across.
Michel de Certeau, *The Practice of Everyday Life* (1980)

Buzzworm had a plan. Called it gentrification. [...] Sort where people living there become their own gentry. Self-gentrification by a self-made set of standards and respectability. Do-it-yourself

gentrification. Latinos had this word, *gente*. Something translated like
us. Like *folks*. That sort of gente-fication. Restore the neighborhood.
Clean up the streets. Take care of the people.

Karen T. Yamashita, Tropic of Orange

These examples of urban wounds, with the redrawing of boundaries
enforced by dominant *barrioizing* forces, stand side by side in contemporary literature with stories that, as Michel de Certeau mentions, manage to
cut across spatial and ideological demarcations. This remapping stems
from a revisionary process from below, what Buzzworm terms urban *gente-
fication*. As the works of Karen T. Yamashita and Ernesto Quiñonez
illustrate, what initially appears as the infected spaces of segregation
become the repossessed spaces of congregation and belonging. In *I Hotel*
(2012) Yamashita foregrounds the differential inclusion of Asian migrants,
suspended between the welcome of the Golden Gate Bridge (equivalent to
the Statue of Liberty on the East Coast) and the hostility of two detention
islands, Angel Island and Alcatraz. As the beneficiaries of hostipitality, the
migrants settled "in old and new ghettoed communities" such as
Manilatown and Chinatown.[28] Permeable and porous from the outside
and hermetic from the inside, these immigrant towns were seen from the
outside as what Dalia Kandiyoti terms "migrant sites," spatial units whose
content is frequently assumed to be fixed, and which resemble the concept
of the disciplined, planned, controlled or striated spaces of Foucault and
Deleuze and Guattari.[29] Within this bounded territory, Yamashita zooms
in on the International Hotel in San Francisco, a landmark in the history of
the city, a symbol of Asian American activism, and a bulwark against the
gentrification of the city. In its third incarnation, from 1907 to the forceful
eviction of its tenants in 1977, the Hotel housed elderly Filipino and
Chinese immigrant bachelors who had migrated to the United States to
work prior to World War II. Because of antimiscegenation laws, exclusion
acts prohibiting Asian immigration, and a life of constantly mobile migrant
labor, they were unable to find spouses, and settle in the United States.[30]
Just as the Mexican American community in Sacramento provides beds
and meals for the different waves of refugees in Galarza's *Barrio Boy*
through the *asistencia*, the historical International Hotel offered a similar
safety net for the Filipino and Chinese immigrants who, after toiling for
fifty years, retired to nothing. From the outside, however, life in a hotel was
envisioned as openly contrary to the pure and healthy spaces the nation-
state models itself on. Homes, from this perspective, are the personal spaces
in which the nation-state is produced and reproduced, whereas the hotel

simply brings exteriority within. In fact, according to the narrative voice, a famous scholar who studied hotel life warned that when there are no homes, there will be no nation. But the question is what did he mean by home and what did he mean by nation?[31] These open questions challenge the notion of one home and one nation, the concepts that Yamashita revisits in this monumental novel, until we enter the last hotel room/novella just before the last guests are forcefully evicted on August 4, 1977. By that time, the narrative voice claims, the hotel guests had already figured out that they were not part of the authoritative version of the national home: "We were already the displaced people in the city's plan to impose a particular meaning of *home* and a particular meaning of *nation*."[32]

Strictly speaking, a hotel is no home. A nonplace in Marc Augé's formulation, a hotel is a temporary abode, an example of commercial hospitality.[33] From this perspective, it stands as a dislocating localization where the outside is brought within, only to remain part of the outside. This is the traditional reading of the hotel Yamashita revises and scales up as she traces how the United States deals with its immigrants (sojourners, FOBs, refugees, exiles), and allocates them to ghettos, detention islands, and concentration camps. At the same time, the hotel becomes a trope that illustrates the kind of hospitality the country is ready to provide when immigrants are no longer useful. Mireille Rosello argues that a commercial logic pervades the relation between the immigrant Other and the host country. If the migrant's stay is regulated by a time frame or a contract, there is no reason, argues Rosello, to identify the nation-state as a house. The "so-called hospitality of nations," the critic clarifies, "may more closely resemble commercial hospitality." Given this clarification, it seems more accurate to imagine the state as a hotel, rather than as a private house. This reconceptualization changes the nature of the guest, who immediately becomes a "paying guest."[34] If the country is conceptualized as a hotel, the question is what becomes of the hotel?

In *I Hotel*, what was initially an instance of surgical separation from the healthy spaces of the nation is repossessed. It is reconstructed as the basis of a privileged standpoint from which to theorize the relationship between a country and its immigrants. The hotel undergoes a process of contami-Nation and becomes the opposite of its initial meaning, as the tenants fashion a multicultural "WE the people of the International Hotel" that provides a home and new articulations of belonging. Contrary to the scholar who claimed that when there is no home, there will be no nation, the I Hotel demonstrates that home and nation are elusive concepts. As a desti-Nation, the hotel became a microcosm traversed by people in movement seeking different forms of political membership "into existing polities."[35] Their staying at the perpetual threshold questioned the traditional categories of belonging through national citizenship and suggested new modalities of inclusion. An experimental mode of membership, a mini-nation that liquefied territoriality and sovereignty, the I Hotel offered the right to have rights. Significantly, when the hotel guests were evicted from the hotel-home to make room for a parking lot and office buildings in the aggressive process of "Manhattanization" of what used to be Japantown, Chinatown, and Manilatown, there was no plan to house them. For more than two decades after its demolition in 1979, the site of the I Hotel remained an empty hole on Kearney Street.[36] Since August 2005, the site harbors the Chinatown Community Development Center's International Hotel Senior Housing.

Resistance against the blindness of capitalism and its effects on ethnic communities is at the heart of Ernesto Quiñonez's novels. In *I Hotel*, Yamashita presents the tenants of the International Hotel joking about the alleged name of the latest owner of the hotel – Enchanted Seas Corporation, an investment company operated by a mafia godfather from Thailand – and wondering how such a remote company can know about them. The remarks point at the disconnect between the I Hotel as lived and experienced by tenants and activists, and place as conceptualized by a ghost owner who buys up all the hotels around the I Hotel. The actual new owner, Four Seas Investment Corporation, bought the International Hotel from the San Francisco-based Milton Meyer and Company. With strong ties to Chinese businessmen and lawyers in Chinatown, it never revealed what it wanted to do with the International Hotel. What was obvious throughout the litigation process was that the corporation was not concerned about the housing and welfare of the immigrant communities.[37]

Similarly, in *Bodega Dreams* (2000) and *Chango's Fire* (2004), Quiñonez presents the recurrent presence of what Manuel Castells calls the "space of flows" in East Harlem as opposed to "the space of places,"[38] the barrio as a center of stability and local resistance. As in *I Hotel,* the forces of capitalism and the market represent the threat of placelessness, removal, and uprooting for the Puerto Rican community. If global capitalist flows thrive on the porosity of borders and the constant relocation of capital and resources, the protagonists of Quiñonez's novels struggle to undo that process by securely locating themselves on the map, in very conspicuous sites with clear geographic coordinates. Puerto Rican narratives, Kandiyoti claims, are recurrently located in the barrio, an urban space which figures as a "central topos." Quiñonez, like Yamashita, repossesses the previously discarded or abject spaces of the city. What was initially felt to be accursed, the interiorized outsides of the city, is affirmed and reconstructed as the basis for a poetics of location, the *aquíness* of the writing.[39] The threat of capitalist displacement figures prominently in *Bodega Dreams*. Low-income Latinos living in Spanish Harlem are on the verge of eviction because of increasingly high rents, leaving room for the gentrification of the neighborhood. Willie Bodega, the character whose dreams the novel dramatizes, will use those capitalist forces of dispersal and dislocation to re-root and re-place the barrio and its Latino inhabitants. Bodega uses money from his drug trafficking operations to strike deals with city officials in charge of urban planning, in an effort to stop the gentrification of the barrio. Like Buzzworm's in Karen T. Yamashita's *Tropic of Orange*, his dream is to fashion a "do-it-yourself" gentrification, a process of "gente-fication" that renovates the barrio while saving it for a social class of Latino professionals born and raised there.[40]

This act of physical re-placement runs parallel to a literary and ideo-logical process of occupation, for *Bodega Dreams* is modeled on F. Scott Fitzgerald's *The Great Gatsby* (1925). If corporate capitalism and gentrifi-cation threaten to occupy East Harlem, the novel dramatizes a metafictional reverse move, as a Puerto Rican occupies the central space of Western culture, a space assumed to be inaccessible to the ethnic Other. The way toward emplacement, toward undoing the forces of capitalist deterritorialization, however, becomes both a promise and a threat. Bodega's reappropriation of the barrio as a cultural space of resistance against placelessness, inevitably falls prey to similar capitalist dynamics. As David Harvey cautions, "Movements of opposition to the disruptions of home, community, territory, and nation [. . .] run up against a seemingly immovable paradox." Such initiatives, clarifies Harvey, "open themselves to the dissolving power of money as well as to the shifting definitions of space and time arrived at through the dynamics of capital circulation. Capital, in short, continues to dominate, and it does so in part through superior command over space and time."[41] The paradox the novel illus-trates centers on the question of how to align economic empowerment with ethnic identity and spatial resistance.

A similar quandary is at the heart of Quiñonez's second novel, *Chango's Fire*, another instance of "space consciousness" in the face of urban renewal, from Robert Moses's leveling of the "Bronx slum" and the creation of what the protagonist calls "Latino reservations"[42] to its gentri-fication into Spa Ha. As in *Bodega Dreams*, the laws of the international market have brought down the tacit borders that used to enclose the barrio as pathological space, and have transformed its streets into the visual manifestation of the space of flows, with chain stores lining the streets. The issue is how the inhabitant of the barrio can appropriate and digest the push and pull of the market, and how Julio, the narrator, can articulate his own "space of places." Rather than mobility, Julio, like Chino in *Bodega Dreams*, repositions *place* at the center of his experience and identity. For him "place refers to the experience of, and from, a particular location with some sense of boundaries, grounds, and links to everyday practices."[43] Hence he is intent on creating a *cordon sanitaire* that preserves the neighborhood against a threatening guest and the globalizing forces that build on "placelessness as practice and ideology."[44] This is the precarious balance the novel illustrates, for if, on one hand, the barrio is in the process of "being appropriated and commodified by commercial culture," it is also "being rearticulated for the creation of oppositional 'resistance cultures'" on the other.[45] Significantly these two possibilities are represented in the protagonist's building. Maritza's Church, the church of the stranger, the *arrivant*, the "illegals," occupies the first floor; Julio and his parents live on the third floor. They account for the old wave of migration that settled in the barrio in the first decades of the twentieth century. Helen, the new white tenant, occupies the second, sandwiched between two different contingents that articulate versions of resistance cultures.

Quiñonez dramatizes the clash between old and new owners in a new version of a border encounter right at the entrance to their building. Helen needs to verify that the young man *does* live there and politely but firmly requests him to ring the bell. Like Aura in "Neighbors," she requires proof or identification before allowing entrance. Julio, for his part, ponders on his feelings about white people encroaching on *his* neighborhood. There were hardly any white people when he was growing up. Each contingent was allocated to a specific part of town and made automatically unwelcome in another. "You'd be arrested on the very spot where you had set foot on their lawns," Julio comments.[46] Spatial demarcations, according to Buzzworm, an African American character in Yamashita's *Tropic of Orange*, did not have to be officially drawn; everybody knew that if you stepped over the invisible front line, you could get implicated, arrested, jailed, or killed. If you stepped back, you would just be invisible. Similarly, Ernesto Galarza remarks: "only when we ventured uptown did we feel like aliens in a foreign land."[47] As opposed to these feelings of foreignness when crossing the boundaries of ethnic communities, the scene at the entrance presents a permutation of roles: whites have become the new guests, and Puerto Ricans have morphed into the unwilling hosts in what seems to be a forced visitation, another byproduct of the global city. Helen's standing at the threshold, filling the role of a gatekeeper, suggests that some groups are mobile and potentially always at home while others must be controlled or filtered in unexpected border encounters. For Julio, this questioning at the entrance to his building is an instance of the always limited welcome that awaited Puerto Ricans in the United States. Despite the open invitation engraved at the foot of the statue of Liberty, Puerto Ricans have never been welcomed into the great American Dream. Emma Lazarus's verses, in fact, seem undercut by another series of invisible lines that Julio repeats to himself: "But not on my block. / Not in my suburb. / Not in my building."[48] The reiteration of negatives automatically creates spaces of containment and exception, a differential or conditional inclusion that has been traditionally reserved for the migrant or newcomer.

Julio's efforts to repossess the formerly diseased spaces of East Harlem and to maintain a *cordon sanitaire* against the push and pull of the market is not without a darker side. Like Bodega, he illustrates how oppositional movements to the disruption of home, community and territory run up against a seemingly unavoidable paradox and open themselves to the dissolving power of money. Apart from his job at the construction site, Julio supplements his income with his job as an arsonist for a shady Irish landlord. He does so, he claims, for the same reason his boss does it – for the money – thus perpetuating the cycle of fire he decries. The fact that fire consumes his building at the end of the novel destabilizes his claim to a fixed sense of place. Like Chino in *Bodega Dreams*, Julio does not find his place in the barrio but has to make a place for himself through complex negotiations.

Conclusion: "What then may I do / but cleave to what cleaves me"

The workings of the urban border and its pathological division of peoples and places allow vistas into a complex and multilayered un-healing wound. As a conclusion to this chapter we focus on the image of the wound as envisioned by Li-Young Lee's "The Cleaving" (1990). Lee rearranges the multiplicity of border narratives in a poem situated in a butcher shop in Chinatown, New York. To the outer spatial segregation Lee adds visual images of fragmentation and cutting that situate the reader in the midst of the wound. The butcher shop, Chinatown, and the experience of migration are turned outside in to reveal graphic images of severed flesh. Watching the butcher chop meat makes the poetic voice reflect on the transcultural experience of migration. There is no welcoming of immigrants in the target country, just an exploration of the middle process, the in-between. Lee dissects the open wound and dwells on the duplicity implicit in the title: "Cleaving" can mean either clinging to and joining or tearing apart and separating; it metaphorically evokes bleeding and scarring, as well as the splitting and rejoining of the self's spaces. In Lee's poem the metaphoric un-healing wound becomes flesh, as the narrative voice concatenates the physical cutting of the interpersonal self, and the act of halving a duck. The particularly disturbing sight elicits images of a split self, of ghettoized communities, outsides in the inside, and of the "junk of the poor"[49] crossing the sea. As Lee obstinately retains the first-person singular in the poem, the "I" becomes both a graphic parallel of the vertical motion of the knife and the visual image of fragmentation. Toward the end of the poem the "I" itself splits into cleaver and cleft, into "I" and "eye," into "I" and a multilayered "We." The Chinese butcher becomes an African, a Jew, an Asian, and a Bedouin in an example of multicultural and multiethnic crossings. The split self fingers the open wound and the fracture therein, and acknowledges the image of cutting as inherent to the creation of the self and as the occasion for alternative reordering and repossession. Cutting, parting, cleaving, and separating – in both corporeal and social terms – allow for the transformation and the communion of opposites. The personal and the communal, place and displacement, wound and scar, the sanitized and the abject, past and present, are all brought to life in the poem and kept open, in process, as a reclaimed and repossessed wound that "will not heal and yet is forever healing."

This exercise of repurposing and reconfiguring the traditional normative ordering of opposites is key to the reassessment of the urban border. The border narratives that we analyze in this chapter cleave to what cleaves them, as the writers occupy a border in process and write from within the border. What does it mean to write from the perspective of the urban border? What was initially felt to be a curse – the ordering of spaces into pure and impure, healthy and infected – becomes repossessed to constitute a privileged standpoint and a self-fashioning from within. Galarza, Viramontes, Díaz, Yamashita, Quiñonez, and Lee, among many other writers, manage to repossess the wound and transform it into a place and site of enunciation. Walter Mignolo terms "border thinking" the moments in which "the imaginary of the modern world system cracks."[50] Arguably the modern world system cracks when the order implicit in border-making breaks down and when it is no longer possible to hold traditional dichotomies such as host/guest; inside/outside; one side/the other; here/there.

Notes

1. Henri Lefebvre, "Philosophy of the City and Planning Ideology," in *Writings on Cities*, trans. Eleonore Kofman and Elizabeth Lebas (Oxford: Blackwell, 1996), p. 99.
2. Janette Turner Hospital, *North of Nowhere, South of Loss* (St Lucia: University of Queensland Press, 2003), p. 57.
3. Doreen Massey, *For Space* (Los Angeles, CA: Sage, 2005), p. 9.
4. Zygmunt Bauman, *Wasted Lives: Modernity and Its Outcasts* (Cambridge: Polity, 2004), p. 5.
5. George Lipsitz, *How Racism Takes Place* (Philadelphia: Temple University Press, 2011), pp. 52, 29, 30. Lefebvre makes a similar distinction between healthy and diseased spaces in *Writings on Cities*, p. 99.
6. Jacob A. Riis, *How the Other Half Lives: Studies among the Tenements of New York* (1890; London: Penguin, 1997), p. 2.
7. Patricia Price, *Dry Place: Landscapes of Belonging and Exclusion* (Minneapolis: University of Minnesota Press, 2004), p. 118. The notion of transversality entails "thinking/beyond geometric, Euclidean spaces and towards borders as more fluid sorts of spaces, both real and imagined" (ibid., p. 119). This transversal perspective is akin to the term *borderscapes*, which, in Chiara Brambilla's words, goes beyond the "the flat and two-dimensional surface of the map," for they are "multidimensional and mobile constructions" (Holger Pötzsch, "iBorder, Borderscapes, Bordering: A Conversation – Chiara Brambilla and Holger Pötzsch," *Society and Space Online* (2015), http://societyandspace.org/2015/03/05/iborder-borderscapes-bordering-chiara-brambilla-and-holger-potzsch/).
8. Homi Bhabha, *The Location of Culture* (London: Routledge, 1994), p. 163.
9. Gaston Bachelard, *The Poetics of Space*, trans. Maria Jolas (Boston: Beacon Press, 1994), p. 212.
10. Jacques Derrida and Hélène Cixous, "From the Word to Life: A Dialogue between Jacques Derrida and Hélène Cixous," *New Literary History* 37.1 (2006), 5.
11. Sandro Mezzadra and Brett Neilson, "Between Inclusion and Exclusion: On the Topology of Global Space and Borders," *Theory, Culture and Society* 29.4/5 (2012), 62, 68.
12. Derrida, "Hostipitality," trans. Barry Stocker and Forbes Morlock, *Angelaki* 5.3 (2000), 3–18.
13. "Barrio," *Diccionario de la lengua Española*, Real Academia Espaola Online; Raúl Homero Villa, *Barrio-Logos: Space and Place in Urban Chicano Literature and Culture* (Austin: University of Texas Press, 2000), p. 6.
14. Critics have noted Afro–Asian solidarities as well as the connections between the International Hotel struggle and the occupation of Alcatraz; see, e.g., Nathan Ragain, "A Revolutionary Romance: Particularity and Universality in Karen Tei Yamashita's *I Hotel*," *MELUS* 38.1 (2013), 137–54.
15. Dalia Kandiyoti, *Migrant Sites: America, Place, and Diaspora Literatures* (Hanover: University Press of New England, 2009), p. 44.

16. Helena Maria Viramontes, "The Cariboo Café," in *The Moths and Other Stories* (Houston: Arte Público Press, 1995), p. 65.
17. Mikhail M. Bakhtin, *The Dialogic Imagination: Four Essays*, ed. Michael Holquist, trans. Carril Emerson and Michael Holquist (Austin: University of Texas Press, 1992), p. 293.
18. Junot Díaz, *This Is How You Lose Her* (London: Faber, 2012), p. 124.
19. Ibid., p. 63.
20. Viramontes, "Cariboo Café," p. 109.
21. Villa, *Barrio-Logos*, p. 36.
22. Ernesto Galarza, *Barrio Boy* (South Bend, IN: University of Notre Dame Press, 2005).
23. Viramontes, "Neighbors," in *The Moths*, p. 110.
24. Lewis Mumford, *The City in History* (New York: Harcourt, 1961), p. 510.
25. Judy Baca and the workspace SPARC, founded by Baca in 1996, stands as an example of barriology. Baca's mural art on the walls of Los Angeles barrio housing projects and on the Internet reinscribes Chicano history in the barrio and, in so doing, offers an example of spatial repossession. Chela Sandoval and Guisela Latorre call these artistic manifestations "digital artivism," the convergence between "activism" and digital "artistic" production (Chela Sandoval and Gustavo Latorre, "Chicana/o Artivism: Judy Baca's Digital Work with Youth of Color," in Anna Everett, ed., *Learning Race and Ethnicity: Youth and Digital Media* [Cambridge, MA: MIT Press, 2008], p. 81).
26. Edward Soja, *Postmetropolis: Critical Studies of Cities and Regions* (Oxford: Blackwell, 2000), p. 218; Soja, *Thirdspace: Journeys to Los Angeles and other Real-and-Imagined Places* (Oxford: Blackwell, 1996), p. 22.
27. Cited in Villa, *Barrio-Logos*, p. 12.
28. Karen Tei Yamashita, *I Hotel* (Minneapolis, MN: Coffee House Press, 2010), pp. 58, 602; Estella Habal, *San Francisco's International Hotel: Mobilizing Filipino American Community in the Anti-Eviction Movement* (Philadelphia: Temple University Press, 2008), p. 9.
29. Gilles Deleuze and Félix Guattari, *A Thousand Plateaus: Capitalism and Schizophrenia*, trans. Brian Massumi (Minneapolis: University of Minnesota Press, 1987), p. 40.
30. Yamashita, *I Hotel*, p. 609.
31. Ibid., p. 590.
32. Ibid., p. 590.
33. Marc Augé, *Non-Places: Introduction to an Anthropology of Supermodernity*, trans. John Howe (London: Verso, 1995), pp. 77–79.
34. Mireille Rosello, *Postcolonial Hospitality: The Immigrant as Guest* (Stanford: Stanford University Press, 2001), pp. 34, 35.
35. Seyla Benhabib, *The Rights of Others: Aliens, Residents and Citizens* (Cambridge: Cambridge University Press, 2004), p. 1.
36. Habal, *San Francisco's International Hotel*, pp. 3, 4.
37. Ibid., pp. 77–80.

38. Manuel Castells, *The Rise of the Network Society* (Oxford: Blackwell, 2000), pp. 408–9.
39. Kandiyoti, *Migrant Sites*, p. 157; see Kandiyoti's "Poetics of Aquí," ibid., pp. 164–66.
40. Yamashita, *Tropic of Orange* (Minneapolis, MN: Coffee House Press, 1997), p. 83.
41. David Harvey, *The Condition of Postmodernity: An Inquiry into the Origins of Cultural Change* (London: Blackwell, 1990), pp. 238–39.
42. Ernesto Quiñonez, *Chango's Fire* (New York: Harper, 2004), p. 6.
43. Arturo Escobar, "Culture Sits in Places: Reflections on Globalism and Subaltern Strategies of Localization," *Political Geography*, 20.2 (2001), 152.
44. Kandiyoti, *Migrant Sites*, p. 158.
45. Douglas Massey and Nancy A. Denton, *American Apartheid: Segregation and the Making of the Underclass* (Cambridge, MA: Harvard University Press, 1993), p. 82.
46. Quiñonez, *Chango's Fire*, pp. 15–16.
47. Yamashita, *Tropic of Orange*, p. 217; Galarza, *Barrio Boy*, p. 239.
48. Quiñonez, *Chango's Fire*, p. 16.
49. Li-Young Lee, "The Cleaving," in *The City in Which I Love You* (Rochester, NY: BOA Editions, 1990), p. 80.
50. Walter Mignolo, *Local Histories, Global Designs: Coloniality, Subaltern Knowledges, and Border Thinking* (Princeton, NJ: Princeton University Press, 2002), p. 23.

CHAPTER 6

Gentrification

James Peacock

Cabbagetown, Atlanta, in the last decade of the twentieth century. A forty-something African American man watches gentrification in action. He sees "ash-brick factories now being converted into trendy lofts to make way for the chi-chi Yuppies swarming in" and reflects on the racial and class configurations attendant on neighborhood change: "The poor white trash in Cabbagetown despised chi-chi Yuppies a tad less than they hated niggers. They had more in common with the blacks, but you could never convince them of that."[1] Sardonic observations like these, taken from Nathan McCall's black comedy *Them* (2007), abound in gentrification stories set in cities across the United States, and they demonstrate both the distinct power of literature to represent urban transformation, and the distinct challenges that transformation poses to writers. On the one hand, the novel's abiding interest in multiple subjectivities, perception and affect, its potential for combining lyricism with ethnography, can allow for a nuanced treatment of gentrification in all its messiness and avoid the Manicheanism and moral reductionism of some critical debates. It can portray the "individuation of perception" that Sarah Schulman maintains is the antidote to the homogenization – of consumption, class, ethnicity, sexuality – inherent to gentrification.[2] On the other hand, one must recognize that the subjectivities being represented are themselves partly shaped by larger political and socioeconomic forces, and that gentrification, as the authors of *Gentrifier* (2017) argue, carries "explanatory power" only when understood as a product of coincidental larger trends and not as "an all-encompassing belief system."[3] Part of the difficulty in talking about gentrification is its multivalency: it has come to denote not only changing demographics in urban space, but also, among many other phenomena, collective loss of memory, the death of bohemian thinking (*bohemian* itself, as Erik Mortenson shows in Chapter 15, being an "overdetermined" idea, but one that he allies to nonconformity and spontaneity), or neoliberalism more generally.[4] From its original coinage by British sociologist Ruth Glass in 1964, referring to the displacement of "working class occupiers" by the middle classes in areas of inner London, *gentrification* has acquired, like *country* and *city*, and like *suburbanization*, as Kathy Knapp demonstrates in Chapter 7, a host of ideological values.[5]

The challenge for gentrification novels, then, is to balance agency and structure in their portrayals, to demonstrate that if gentrification is driven in part by "cultural choice and consumer preference," then those preferences are inseparable from policy decisions and global market forces.[6] According to Peter Moskowitz, "We talk about gentrification at the interpersonal level because that's how we see it in our daily lives – rents mysteriously rise, an art gallery opens one day, then hipsters follow. But in every gentrifying city there are always events, usually hidden from public view, that precede these street-level changes."[7] Adept as they are at representing interpersonal encounters, the best gentrification novels (complex, dialogic systems in themselves) also reveal the concomitant workings of politics and capital beyond the street, the block, the neighborhood. They show that people actively make choices, for a huge variety of reasons, to live in particular communities, but also, as Miranda Joseph persuasively argues in *Against the Romance of Community* (2002), that capital and community are supplementary, not conflicting realms. Such novels balance critique – primarily of gentrifiers – with a desire to humanize rather than demonize.

In the passage from *Them* just quoted, the juxtaposition of active and passive verbs adumbrates the play of structure and agency. Factories "being converted" by unspecified actors – enabled, presumably, by civic planning decisions, private investment, the decline of manufacturing industry – invite the influx of the affluent middle class. The verb *swarming* shows the novel's internal focalization. It encapsulates the narrator's dismissive attitude to the invaders, and signals the ironies to come later, when a white couple moves in next door and forces him to confront his tendency to dehumanize the racial other. Most importantly, the passage betrays his assumption that *all* yuppies are white. Although he is prepared to consider links between class and race, his intersectionality is limited at this early stage of the narrative. Ostensibly born of his own experience and empirical observation of a changing Atlanta, it must also be understood as a cliché (as evidenced by the hackneyed term "trendy lofts"), and therefore as shaped, at least in part, by the preexisting, prevailing discourses surrounding gentrification and the divisions it inspires. This is not to say that in the broadest terms the narrator's observations are *wrong* (or that clichés have no basis in truth), only that subsequent events will add nuance by demonstrating the complex negotiations of structure, agency, and lived experience.

This chapter explores such negotiations in a range of gentrification stories from Paula Fox's excoriating dark comedy *Desperate Characters* (1970) to Michael Chabon's epic of Oakland soul fans, *Telegraph Avenue* (2013), with reference to genre and mode. Following Rick Altman, it conceives genre neither as a taxonomy of fixed structures nor, at the opposite extreme, as a concept so anarchic as to be practically nonexistent, but as a form of textuality emerging through negotiations between communities comprising individual genre consumers with specific preferences, and the industries producing texts for consumption. Thus, the (re)formulation of genre is "a never-ceasing process, closely tied to the capitalist need for product differentiation."[8] What gives readers pleasure – the generic content – is inseparable from the text's status as a material commodity. Choices are made according to individual pleasure but also according to what has been produced and offered for consumption. In turn, the industry continually audits its products according to choices made by communities of consumers. Through the symbiosis of these two processes, genres evolve.

The idiosyncratic ways that authors use genre can be regarded as evidence for their ethical orientations toward subcultural groupings and clashes of communities.[9] Because it develops, like gentrification, through interactions of structure and agency, and because it, too, is both material and ideological, genre is useful in studying gentrification novels, which are expressly concerned with contiguous, overlapping or conflicting communities and with the material, ideological and affective elements of urban change. Starting with a brief survey of genre and mode in a range of novels and continuing with closer readings of selected texts, this chapter demonstrates ways in which these texts make important contributions to understanding gentrification as it is experienced within communities. Moreover, as fictional characters map the built urban landscape in ways linked to their own subject positions (and to the genre characteristics of their stories), they reveal gentrified environments to be texts in themselves, laminated with multiple meanings.

The term *gentrification story* does not refer to a monolithic genre. Urban transformation has been explored through coming-of-age narratives, detective thrillers, comedies of manners, romances, social novels, and historical fictions. Nor does a singular modality pertain. Although satire has been an important recurring mode in novels from *Desperate Characters* and L. J. Davis's *A Meaningful Life* (1971) through to twenty-first-century texts such as *Them* and Lucinda Rosenfeld's *Class* (2017), it is but one of many modes employed in the dissection of gentrifier culture and its casualties. The gothic, detective fiction's saturnine ancestor, emerges in crime fiction interested in the inequality attendant on gentrification, a prime example being the work of Thomas Boyle. His *Only the Dead Know Brooklyn* (1986) ends with a central character, who has recently survived the attentions of a psychopathic murderer, lying in a Park Slope brownstone, disturbed "by the intermittent sounds of his next-door neighbor stripping paint from his cherrywood shutters, punctuated by water dripping from the toilet bowl into a bucket."[10] Here, the very work of renovation, the implied fetishization of architectural features considered "authentic" (a key, contested term in all discussions of gentrification, as we shall see) is rendered grotesque, uncanny.

If the history of gentrification fiction has a strong realist line, befitting stories concerned with the material aspects of urban change – brownstone renovation, school zones, retail choices – it is a realism often inflected by magical *ostranenie*, fabulism, hauntings and comically exaggerated picturesque. These modes offer revealing insights into affective experiences and perceptions of gentrification, the structures of feeling engendered by material alterations in the urban environment, as well as implying resistance to a conception of gentrification as capitalist realism. Thus they provide means of discussing complex negotiations between structure and agency or, as Raymond Williams argues, between external social formations already established and understood, and "the kind of feeling and thinking which is indeed social and material, but each in an embryonic phase before it can become fully articulate."[11] And so the *rusalka* (a mermaid from Slavic folk tales) who magically appears to help the protagonist of Amy Shearn's motherhood comedy *The Mermaid of Brooklyn* (2013) after her husband's disappearance, also hypostasizes her anxieties about class and racial conflicts in Park Slope, Brooklyn. Likewise, the magic ring that confers invisibility upon white kid Dylan Ebdus, protagonist of Jonathan Lethem's *The Fortress of Solitude* (2003), and the power of flight upon his black friend Mingus Rude, expresses Dylan's as-yet unarticulated guilt at the whitening of Gowanus as it becomes Boerum Hill. More broadly, in Matt Godbey's terms, it speaks to "the complex relationship between gentrification, race, and middle-class white identity" in Lethem's novel.[12] Similarly, the ghosts that populate Ivy Pochoda's *Visitation Street* (2013) represent the histories of communities in danger of being occluded as Red Hook gentrifies.

The contemporary gentrification picturesque comes in many forms, but these forms share with their nineteenth-century ancestors such as William Dean Howells's *A Hazard of New Fortunes* (1890) an aestheticizing impulse toward what Carrie Tirado Bramen calls "variety," which "bypasses the extremes of [cultural] heterogeneity and uniformity by finding a middle ground [that] creates a sense of relative stability without monotony."[13] Urban picturesque promulgates a vision of local-colorful, heterogeneous neighborhoods at an early, bohemian stage of gentrification, under threat from "supergentrification," the broad shift from independent establishments to global brands and extreme wealth.[14] When comforting variety is signaled by a character's surveying of shops and services, a mode emerges that one might call the "consumer picturesque," as exemplified by the protagonist of Kitty Burns Florey's *Solos* (2004), reflecting on Williamsburg: "They pass the sushi place, the Mexican restaurant, the video store, the Syrian deli, the Polish bakery [. . .] the new baby shop that has a pair of studded black leather booties in the window, and Marta's beauty salon, whose faded pink-and-green sign has probably not been retouched since 1966."[15] Emily Lime's wanderings are a form of taxonomic cognitive mapping, one in which shop signs become a metonym of ethnic diversity, providing the (white, middle-class) individual with a sense of local and global belonging through commodity consumption. In Amy Sohn's *My Old Man* (2004), the consumer picturesque is reconfigured as the sexual picturesque. The transformation of Brooklyn's Cobble Hill into a neighborhood of white yuppies is temporarily staved off by the diverse romantic choices of protagonist Rachel Block's rampaging housemate Liz Kominsky: "One other cause Liz worked very hard for was minority men. The whole two months I'd known her, every guy I'd seen coming or going from her apartment was Arab, Latin, or black."[16]

Both *Solos* and *My Old Man* employ picturesque as a critique of gentrification's homogenizing effects. In both cases, however, the characters' preoccupation with consumer preferences as benchmarks of variety and authenticity invites a concomitant critique of romantic views of community founded just as firmly on notions of commodity and capital, and in the end just as internally contradictory and exclusive as the supergentrification against which they fight. What Sharon Zukin dubs the "schizoid quality" of authenticity is key to understanding these contradictions. As Zukin argues, *authenticity* oscillates between seemingly competing visions: it derives from, "on the one hand, being primal, historically first or true to a traditional vision, and on the other hand, being unique, historically new, innovative and creative."[17]

Yet these visions can be reconciled through judicious elision. Emily Lime can describe the late-industrial Williamsburg that existed before the arrival of artists and eccentrics as "an urban wilderness of warehouses and factories," and the new luxury apartments as "untrue to the spirit of Brooklyn in general and Williamsburg in particular" because in her eyes her prelapsarian idyll is both traditional and innovative.[18] Unwilling to accept that she is a gentrifier present as part of larger historical and economic forces (as hinted at by the warehouses and factories she cursorily dismisses), Lime displays a nostalgia for the present, reinforced by the historical present of the narration, that attempts to mythologize her narrow view of neighborhood and arrest historical change. As reference to the "wilderness" implies, this is a frontier novel with a colonialist mindset, disguised as a local-color picturesque. Likewise, *My Old Man*, for all its rambunctiousness, ends conservatively. Having had an affair with Block's father, Kominsky enters therapy, admitting, "I violate boundaries because I'm afraid no one will like me if I don't relate to them sexually."[19] The sexual picturesque is a pathology to be cured; boundaries – between family and friends, whites and blacks, authentic "holdovers" from the 1970s and inauthentic hipster newcomers – must be reinforced.[20] Once again, a picturesque becomes a frontier novel, differences clearly defined.

For the sake of argument, this chapter has up to now employed a false dichotomy. In truth, picturesque gentrification novels are *always* to some extent frontier narratives, too; to be more specific, a novel's implied orientation toward gentrification can be understood by examining the play between these two modes, one of which inclines (often factitiously) toward variety, inclusivity, aestheticization, one toward material difference and exclusivity. The relationship between the picturesque and the frontier depends on the stage of gentrification being depicted, as well as narrative point of view and texts' complex mapping of genres. If one accepts that genres carry ideological use-value, are produced through difference and are inherently unstable, then one can accept their utility in exploring representations of urban landscapes also (re)produced through interactions between competing ideologies and material circumstances. According to Suleiman Osman, for example, Brownstone Brooklyn "was neither completely real nor invented" but was "a tectonic cityscape with the architectural and social imprints of multiple economic stages."[21] As the following examples show, gentrified neighborhoods in stories set in Brooklyn, Atlanta and Oakland share this layered character. What is especially important is the ways in which different socioeconomic groups seeking versions of authenticity in gentrifying neighborhoods make legible particular features of the landscape in order to distinguish themselves and their neighborhood vision. After all: "Authenticity differentiates a person, a product, or a group from its competitors; it confers an aura of moral superiority, a strategic advantage." It is, in Schulman's terms, a way of masking domination "from the dominant themselves."[22]

At the start of *Desperate Characters*, the cathexis of architecture, tasteful furnishings and objets d'art affords Otto and Sophie Bentwood an aura of superiority in their new Brooklyn neighborhood. Readers' attention is drawn to "the old cedar planks of the floor," the "Victorian secretary" and a "bookcase which held, among other volumes, the complete works of Goethe and two shelves of French poets," as well as "an earthenware casserole filled with sautéed chicken livers, peeled and sliced tomatoes on an oval willowware platter Sophie had found in a Brooklyn Heights antique shop." We also observe the Bentwoods' self-consciousness, the way Otto "regard[s]" the dining table, the "deliberation" with which Sophie unfolds a linen napkin.[23] A carefully constructed picture of middle-class accumulation, sophistication, and authenticity, this opening scene communicates a studied cosmopolitanism achieved through an interior picturesque suited to a couple who share a name with a furniture style.

References to the "slum street" behind their house and a fellow newcomer from Manhattan as "a brave pioneer" signal the Bentwoods' awareness that they are outsiders, that this is a frontier environment and that their beautiful interior functions partly as insulation against the material realities outside. Sophie is even perspicacious enough at this stage to realize that "it doesn't take courage. It takes cash."[24] As Elizabeth Gumport says: "As fixated as they are on the appearance of their houses, characters in early gentrification novels recognize that there are consequences to their labor. The newcomers are not immune to guilt."[25] This is why Sophie feeds the imperturbable cat that arrives as an emissary from the slum street and becomes so central to the narrative. When the cat bites Sophie on the hand, drawing blood and thus casting her as a gentrifying Lady Macbeth, it is tempting to view the bite as symbolic of the locals' revenge on the presumptive and self-isolating gentrifiers, a kind of opening salvo in a frontier skirmish. And yet this would be far too simplistic; it would fall into the trap Fox deliberately sets – that of subscribing to the Bentwoods' symbolic system, and Sophie's desire to sublimate her guilt and prejudices through the symbolically charged animal. Moreover, when the sudden arrival of a black man in their home later in the novel lays bare their prejudices, his exasperated description of his white middle-class neighbors as "inhospitable cats" inverts the symbolism and complicates the relationship between self and other. So the bite, the accompanying pain, and the blood are better understood as representing a sudden, violent invasion of the material into an exquisitely constructed interior (matched by the novel's perfect prose) full of fetishized commodities so artful as to be absolutely abstracted. The cat bite stands for the inevitable failure of the Bentwoods' symbolic system. If, as Sophie's friend Leon says, civilization occurs when "you take raw material and you transform it," then the bite is the moment when the abstract carapace of the gentrifiers' picturesque interior is transformed back into crude raw materials, the smooth surface of skin into ragged, damaged flesh.[26]

Throughout the novel, the couple's agency is directed toward an aesthetic utopian vision, but they are constantly being reminded of the material circumstances upon which that vision rests, the larger economic structures at play in the background, ones which they try to disavow. In a fancy kitchen shop, Sophie desires an omelet pan; the description of it highlights this tense play of abstraction and materiality: "it sat, substantial as its own metal, in a hazy domestic dream: a middle-aged couple sitting together over their *omelette aux fines herbes*, two glasses of white wine." When the shopkeeper informs Sophie that another pan is "made better," thus drawing attention to the labor involved, she panics and leaves instead with an egg-timer.[27] In *Desperate Characters* the frontier upon which the gentrifiers live is not simply the one separating slum street from gentrifying block, black from white, rich from poor; it is also that between concrete materiality and the abstraction required to turn commodities into an exclusive vision. Each rude interruption of the Bentwoods' life – the stone thrown through the window of a friend's house, the return of the cat, the green plastic airplane in the hands of a near-naked black man stumbling down their street, the ransacking of their Long Island farmhouse – reminds them how porous this frontier is, how supplementary the relationship between materiality and abstraction. At an early stage of gentrification, and still in a minority, they are unable to assimilate these intrusive elements successfully into a picturesque vision: the frontier narrative keeps invading. Moreover, Fox refuses to let the beauty of her own writing stand outside its own materiality: when Otto grabs an ink bottle and throws it violently against the wall at the close of the novel, the black ink running down the wall reminds us of the physical substance of the words we have read, and by association the labor of creation.

Desperate Characters sets the template for the gentrification story's yoking of the picturesque and the frontier to explore negotiations between materiality and ideology, structure and agency. Despite being told from the gentrifiers' perspective and allowing a measure of sympathy for the Bentwoods' plight, the novel's ironic distance and insistence on its own materiality achieve a critique of their ideological disavowals. Fox's frontier tale has many descendants, including Brooklyn motherhood comedies set at a later stage of gentrification, in which an established middle-class picturesque appears to come under threat from outsiders. In *The Mermaid of Brooklyn*, for example, a child breaks her arm in a Park Slope playground, causing the narrator to reflect on the presence of boys from the poorer, "other side of the park," as if "they themselves had imported free-floating violence over from the projects, like a flu virus." Hence the frontier is reimagined and reinscribed in the playground.[28] In the way its lead characters obsess over interior details, Brian Platzer's *Bed-Stuy Is Burning* (2017) explicitly shows the influence of Fox: "Aaron owned those windows. He and Amelia did together. They owned the stained-glass windows and the original woodwork surrounding them."[29] Where it differs from Fox, and where ultimately it fails as a bourgeois critique, is in its choice of genre. After an African American neighbor is shot dead on their stoop and a poor local teenager occupies the couple's upstairs office, it becomes a home-invasion thriller. Thus, whatever degree of satire is aimed at the gentrifiers, narrative resolution arrives with the expulsion of outsiders (the poor, the ethnically different) from the sacred space of the renovated home.

Although it, too, culminates in a violent encounter derived from crime thrillers, McCall's *Them* provides a more balanced frontier narrative. Set in Atlanta's Old Fourth Ward, birthplace of Martin Luther King Jr., its protagonist is an African American man called Barlowe Reed who lives in the ward and is concerned about the "wild rumors, about *them* coming through the neighborhood, snooping around for who knows what." His deliberate othering and diminishing of "them" is challenged in Part Two of the novel by his interactions with Sandy Gilmore, a white woman who moves next door with her husband, intent on "building bridges." Although her noble intentions are challenged by the "imaginary boundary to her yard" that becomes a physical boundary when her increasingly paranoid husband builds a wrought-iron fence, the gradual thawing of their relationship is a key element of *Them*'s nuanced treatment of the issue.[30] McCall avoids reducing the novel merely to a sentimental story of unlikely friends: he carefully places both the Gilmores' decision to move and Reed's resistance to their arrival in a wider structural and historical context. Ironically, the Civil Rights history of the Old Fourth Ward is both the source of pride for its black residents and a key attraction (along with house prices) to liberal white gentrifiers, a point the Gilmores' real estate agent is happy to emphasize. Moreover, Reed himself, we discover, is an incomer, who moved to Atlanta from the "small and small-minded town" of Milledgeville as a young adult, like many black Americans escaping poverty and prejudice in rural areas. McCall also introduces Marvetta Green, a property developer and African American gentrifier. Taken individually, these elements are interesting if not conclusive. Considered together, they complicate the narrative of neighborhood invasion by locating it in a longer historical narrative of migration, by demonstrating how real estate agents and banks exploit "authentic" black histories as marketing tools, by exploring in detail the (sincere) agency of gentrifiers and locals, and, thus, by blurring the implied frontier between blacks and whites, gentrifiers and locals, them and us.

When no easy distinction between insider and outsider is initially possible, as with Michael Chabon's *Telegraph Avenue*, frontier imagery is a less viable approach to urban mapping. Chabon's story takes place in 2004 as Oakland experiences incipient gentrification. Centered on Nat Jaffe and Archy Stallings's "neighborhood institution" and "church of vinyl," Brokeland Records ("Brokeland" is both the neighborhood's nickname and an indicator of the store's financial status), *Telegraph Avenue* is a sprawling social novel, a family saga, and an affectionate dissection of subcultural obsession, its two main characters vinyl addicts with an encyclopedic knowledge of soul and jazz-funk records and an immaculately audited shop window "vaccinated against all forms of bullshit."[31] Like Lethem's *The Fortress of Solitude*, in which the white protagonist sees black characters in stylized terms as "scribbling in flesh" or "cartoon squiggle[s],"[32] *Telegraph Avenue*'s picturesque elements tend to be human – mythologized, fantastic figures in a realistic landscape. They include Stallings's father Luther, a legendary Blaxploitation actor; keyboard player Cochise Jones with his "octave-and-a-half hand, its nails like chips of piano ivory"; and Gibson Goode, former quarterback and now successful boss of Dogpile Music, a man not averse to wearing "heavy tortoiseshell sunglasses with dark green lenses."[33] Goode poses an existential threat to Brokeland Records when he announces plans to open a Dogpile megastore on Telegraph.

The stage is set for a battle between independent shop and chain store, between bohemia and gentrification, between authentic and inauthentic. On one side is Stallings, "the last coconut hanging on the last palm tree on the last little atoll in the path of the great wave of late-modern capitalism," a man whose very surname connotes delaying the inevitable. On the other, there is Goode, eyes behind funky shades intent on "the cold business of empire." Stallings frequents the old neighborhood businesses such as Neldam's bakery, soon to close down, with its "old-fashioned sincerity, a humble brand of fabulousness"; Goode, by contrast, can afford "to open a *bangin* used vinyl store, five times as big as Brokeland and tenfold deep [. . .] bankrolled by his media empire, his licensed image, his alchemical touch with ghetto real estate."[34] Goode stands for reinvention, regeneration, and *danger*: he is also called "G-Bad."

Yet the situation is more complicated, the battle lines blurred. Goode's declared motivation for opening Dogpile is "to restore, at a stroke, the commercial heart of a black neighborhood cut out during the glory days of freeway construction in California," the place where he was born and visited regularly throughout his life. In one of the novel's most surreal, picturesque scenes, Goode invites Stallings for a ride in his Dogpile zeppelin, hoping to make him a job offer. Surrounded by fantastical people, including "a Harryhausen negro, mythic and huge [. . .] the dude from *The Golden Voyage of Sinbad*," he proves himself perfectly capable of indulging in the same nostalgia for old Oakland – House of Wax record store, the laundromat, purchasing classic Luke Cage comics – as Stallings. In the gondola suspended from an envelope described, significantly, as "formed from some black polymer glossy as a vinyl record," Goode shows himself to be authentic within the parameters established by Jaffe and Stallings: black, soul and funk-loving, wedded to original vinyl and, as Oakland businessman Garnet Singletary describes him, "a semi-local product."[35]

Telegraph Avenue, then, problematizes notions of authenticity based on Stallings's brand of "sheepish nostalgia" and on fixed cultural markers of race.[36] Goode and the music he purveys encapsulate the complexity of blackness as a signifier: black music is both innovative and traditional, he tells Stallings, and working in Dogpile represents a chance to reeducate black youth in the wonders of the form rather than sell records "for some white dentist or tax attorney to take home and hang on his wall." His withering assessment of Brokeland's current clientele is corroborated by the protest meeting convened there by Jaffe: a "motley gathering of freaky Caucasians united [. . .] only by a reflexive willingness if not a compulsion to oppose pretty much anything new" in "a city that was largely black and poor and hungry for the kind of pride-instilling economic gesture" Goode's store represents. Though Jaffe has a horror of "black-acting white men," his attempt to bribe Singletary into supporting the protest with a plate of fried chicken is especially uncomfortable.[37] Reflecting, perhaps, the author's self-consciousness about his own love of African

American culture, the novel subverts a narrative of gentrification (especially common in Brooklyn novels) of wholesale usurpation of nonwhite populations from urban neighborhoods, opting instead to highlight an equally insidious process of cultural appropriation by bohemian white liberals – a gentrification of the soul, if you will – bound up in myth and nostalgia for a perceived authentic blackness. Such an impulse extends even to the midwifery business run by Gwen and Aviva, Jaffe's and Stallings's partners, laconically described as "Black midwife and a million white mommies."[38]

If the African American cultural signifiers are a version of picturesque, Chabon contrasts them with a panoramic picturesque which expands the novel's horizon beyond obsessed-over spaces such as the record store, revealed for the first time from Goode's zeppelin. As the ship soars, Stallings, feeling "unhooked," looks down: "Oakland fell away beneath them. The Bay Area shook out its rumpled coverlet, gray and green and crazy salt pans, rent and slashed and stitched by feats of engineering." Later, he spies "the giant oil tanks of Richmond, ranked along the slopes like second-hand turntables."[39] His simile is an attempt to anchor the panoramic view in his obsessions, but he is nonetheless forced to consider, literally and metaphorically, the bigger picture – the shifting layers of industry, engineering and natural features composing the landscape over time. This spatial expansiveness suggests a temporal scope developed in the novel's impressionistic middle section, "A Bird of Wide Experience," in which a parrot once belonging to Cochise Jones embarks on an Oakland odyssey, connecting the lives of diverse characters in diverse neighborhoods. More than a literary flight of fancy, it, too, opens a more expansive social viewpoint that transcends a restricted set of cultural obsessions. It maps the picturesque back onto the social novel.

The examples of *Them* and *Telegraph Avenue* provide a revealing contrast to texts such as *Solos* and *My Old Man* and allow us to form some conclusions about late twentieth- and early twenty-first-century gentrification novels. In their determination to situate their characters in a neighborhood landscape subject to continuous imprinting and layering, McCall's and Chabon's texts not only show the involutions of structure and agency, they also challenge a linear trajectory of gentrification. Moreover, though they include characters suffering from nostalgia, the implied ethics of such novels moves away from the nostalgia Gumport argues is endemic in contemporary gentrified fictions.[40] The combination of genres, modes, and levels of reality – notably the picturesque and the frontier – is part of the strategy of avoiding a narrow, nostalgic worldview predominantly based on a gentrifier's perspective. In this respect, *Telegraph Avenue* in particular shares much with Lethem's *The Fortress of Solitude* (2003), which combines a realist bildungsroman with superheroic powers and subcultural imagery derived from graffiti and hip-hop. Most significantly of all, the spatial expansiveness of Chabon's novel corresponds to the spatial and temporal scope of Lethem's, its tracking of a longer neighborhood history from pre-gentrification to a stage of firmly established bourgeoisification, and its occasional superhero's-eye-view of the Brooklyn streets. Both authors also dramatize self-consciousness about their problematic racial politics, the risk of appropriating "authentic" urban signifiers of blackness inherent in their writing.

The need to historicize, not to be trapped in nostalgia (for the past or present) leads to a counterintuitive final thought: that some of the most incisive gentrification stories of recent years choose not to tackle gentrification directly but instead its prehistory. Examples include Ernesto Quiñonez's *Bodega Dreams* (2000), which portrays a Spanish Harlem native's attempts to regenerate his neighborhood from within in order to resist the predations of white developers and settlers. It contains many of the contradictions of the ghetto narrative Thomas Heise identifies in Chapter 4: poverty and criminality, local pride, and activism. It also, as Sean Moiles demonstrates, accurately depicts the neoliberal policies of free-market privatization that allow gentrification to flourish.[41] (For a more detailed analysis of Quiñonez's work, see Ana María Manzanas Calvo and Jesús Benito Sánchez's treatment in Chapter 5.) Jacqueline Woodson's coming-of-age story, *Another Brooklyn* (2016) inherits from Paule Marshall's *Brown Girl, Brownstones* (1959) a focus on postwar African American or West Indian communities in New York. By returning to gentrification's prehistory – migration from the south, white flight from the inner cities – it renders it a ghost haunting the textual margins, and reveals the varied lived experience of populations eventually marginalized and moved out. Like all coming-of-age stories, its subject is memory. The most insightful contemporary gentrification narratives, in different ways, insist on long memory, and a longer, more complex view of history. In so doing, they deny what Moskowitz calls gentrification's "ability to erase collective memory," any assumption that it is, in Schulman's terms, "normal, neutral, and value free," and any sense of its inevitability or completeness.[42] They offer, if only imaginatively, the possibility of alternatives.

Notes

1. Nathan McCall, *Them* (New York: Atria, 2007), p. 12.
2. Sarah Schulman, *The Gentrification of the Mind: Witness to a Lost Imagination* (Berkeley: University of California Press, 2012), p. 17.
3. John Joe Schlichtman, Jason Patch, and Marc Lamont Hill, *Gentrifier* (Toronto: University of Toronto Press, 2017), pp. 12, 11.
4. For gentrification as loss of memory and empathy, see Schulman, *Gentrification of the Mind*; for gentrification as the death of bohemianism, also see Schulman and Chapter 15 of this volume.
5. Ruth Glass, *London: Aspects of Change* (London: MacGibbon, 1964), p. xvii.
6. Neil Smith, *The New Urban Frontier: Gentrification and the Revanchist City* (New York: Routledge, 1996), p. 55.
7. Peter Moskowitz, *How to Kill a City: Gentrification, Inequality, and the Fight for the Neighborhood* (New York: Nation Books, 2017), p. 9.
8. Rick Altman, *Film/Genre* (London: BFI, 1999), p. 64.
9. See James Peacock, *Jonathan Lethem* (Manchester: Manchester University Press, 2012), pp. 5–10.
10. Thomas Boyle, *Only the Dead Know Brooklyn* (London: Hodder and Stoughton, 1986), p. 282.
11. Raymond Williams, *Marxism and Literature* (Oxford: Oxford University Press, 1977), p. 131.
12. Matt Godbey, "Gentrification, Authenticity and White Middle-Class Identity in Jonathan Lethem's *The Fortress of Solitude*," *Arizona Quarterly* 64.1 (2008), 132.
13. Carrie Tirado Bramen, *The Uses of Variety: Modern Americanism and the Quest for National Distinctiveness* (Cambridge, MA: Harvard University Press, 2000), p. 23.
14. On supergentrification, see Sharon Zukin, *Naked City: The Death and Life of Authentic Urban Places* (New York: Oxford University Press, 2010), p. 9.
15. Kitty Burns Florey, *Solos* (New York: Berkley Books, 2004), p. 2.
16. Amy Sohn, *My Old Man* (New York: Simon and Schuster, 2004), p. 25.
17. Zukin, *Naked City*, p. xii.
18. Florey, *Solos*, pp. 51, 23.
19. Sohn, *My Old Man*, p. 297.
20. Ibid., p. 13.
21. Suleiman Osman, *The Invention of Brownstone Brooklyn: Gentrification and the Search for Authenticity in Postwar New York* (New York: Oxford University Press, 2011), p. 22.
22. Zukin, *Naked City*, p. xii; Schulman *Gentrification of the Mind*, p. 27.
23. Paula Fox, *Desperate Characters* (London: Flamingo, 2003), p. 3.
24. Ibid., pp. 4, 5.
25. Elizabeth Gumport, "Gentrified Fiction," *N+1* (November 2, 2009), http://nplusonemag.com/online-only/book-review/gentrified-fiction/.
26. Fox, *Desperate Characters*, pp. 98, 84.

27. Ibid., p. 74.
28. Amy Shearn, *The Mermaid of Brooklyn* (New York: Touchstone, 2013), p. 40.
29. Brian Platzer, *Bed-Stuy Is Burning* (New York: Atria Books, 2017), p. 36.
30. McCall, *Them*, pp. 38, 69, 154.
31. Michael Chabon, *Telegraph Avenue* (London: Fourth Estate, 2012), pp. 271, 284, 4.
32. Jonathan Lethem, *The Fortress of Solitude* (London: Faber and Faber, 2003), pp. 118, 124.
33. Chabon, *Telegraph Avenue*, pp. 47, 297.
34. Ibid., pp. 246, 297, 147, 308.
35. Ibid., pp. 14, 296, 295, 43.
36. Ibid., p. 392.
37. Ibid., pp. 310–11, 266, 255.
38. Ibid., p. 489.
39. Ibid., pp. 300, 309.
40. Gumport's argument is too sweeping; she includes novels such as *The Fortress of Solitude* that are precisely about the dangers of white liberal nostalgia for imagined authenticity.
41. Sean Moiles, "The Politics of Gentrification in Ernesto Quiñonez's Novels," *Critique: Studies in Contemporary Fiction*, 52.1 (2011), 116.
42. Moskowitz, *How to Kill a City*, p. 176; Schulman, *Gentrification of the Mind*, p. 51.

CHAPTER 7

House Rules
The New Yorker *and the Making of the White Suburban Liberal Woman*

Kathy Knapp

Given the large-scale catastrophes that have transformed the landscape in the United States and around the globe during the first two decades of the twenty-first century – interminable war, worldwide economic meltdown, the ongoing refugee crisis, the rise of nationalism, devastating natural disasters, and climate change, for starters – it may be risible to say that in the United States, at any rate, the twenty-first century might also be called the suburban century. But it is true that around 2000 suburbanites became the majority of the nation's population, and their numbers have been rising ever since; 52 percent of Americans identify their neighborhood as suburban, as opposed to either urban (27 percent) or rural (21 percent). Less clear is what constitutes a suburb because there is no official federal definition.[1] The persistent image of massive postwar developments like Levittown notwithstanding, the suburbs are hardly monolithic. We have come up with various labels to differentiate between kinds of suburbs – first-ring, industrial, and Sun-Belt suburbs; ethnoburbs and gated communities, to name a few. And it is not just the landscapes that vary. Suburban populations have become increasingly diverse, with immigrants bypassing the city altogether to live outside its limits. Furthermore, suburban populations are aging along with their infrastructure, and more people in poverty live in suburbs than in cities.[2]

Against this backdrop, there is a certain kind of suburbia that persists in our imagination, as if a mirage: far from the mass-produced houses of Levittown and the like, this is a leafy green place, dotted with sparkling pools and picket fences, the air hanging fragrant but heavy with the ephemeral anxieties of its lily-white inhabitants, overcome as they are with a pervasive sense of displacement, debilitated manhood, marital woes, and perceived personal and professional slights.[3] To riff on the title of Ben Yagoda's history of the magazine, this is the world *The New Yorker* made because, arguably, we owe this strangely enduring collective vision to the hundreds of stories by John Cheever and John Updike that it published, which chronicle again and again the suburban malaise we have come to recognize as the special province of white male privilege. Critics have done a pretty thorough job of eviscerating Updike, Cheever, and their followers for casting the white affluent homeowners they depict as the victims of "sentimental dispossession," as Catherine Jurca has described it.[4] Somewhat more sympathetically, Timothy Aubry has noted that Cheever's fiction in particular functioned much like the self-help books that were just becoming popular in the 1950s in the way that they taught readers "how to be properly miserable" – how to nurture, in other words, a "salutary self-irony" that would set them apart from the gray-flannelled masses.[5]

Given the dramatic demographic changes in the suburbs since the postwar era, what can the affluent, educated, but willfully disengaged white male suburbanite possibly have left to teach us? It's fair to say that especially under the leadership of William Shawn, who took over as the magazine's editor in 1952 and reigned decisively but discreetly until 1987, the magazine initially sought to mold its readership in its own image, which a 1946 marketing pamphlet describes as "intelligent, well-educated, discriminating, well-informed, unprejudiced, public-spirited, metropolitan-minded, broad-visioned and quietly liberal."[6] Copious enough to gather together a geographically dispersed community, *The New Yorker*'s definition of its readers nevertheless established a rigid code of conduct that shaped – and as we shall see, continues to shape – the sensibilities of its devout and aspirational readership. As John Leonard put it in a 1975 review of Brendan Gill's history of the magazine, *The New Yorker* "was as much a part of our class conditioning as clean fingernails, college, a checking account, and good intentions."[7] Furthermore, as the pamphlet makes clear, this class conditioning consisted of far more than dictating on matters of taste: *The New Yorker* fostered in its readers a like political mind.

This readership took shape and expanded rapidly in the postwar years thanks to unprecedented prosperity and the benefits of the GI Bill; its low-interest mortgages and free college tuition delivered the magazine new subscribers at an exponential rate.[8] But while scholars have focused on the role that *The New Yorker* fiction we identify with Cheever and Updike played in articulating, romanticizing, and compensating for the sense of compromised masculinity afflicting the commuting executives who took the magazine home with them on the train in the postwar years, we have paid scant attention to the ways that it has cultivated the sensibilities of the other half of its readers: by 1954, women accounted for 55 percent of the magazine's subscribers, owing in part to the fact that among all those new college graduates, an unprecedented number were female.[9] How does our understanding of *The New Yorker*'s aspirational suburbs change if, instead of defining them by the world conjured by Cheever, Updike, and other male writers we turn our attention to the work of iconic *New Yorker* contributors such as Mary McCarthy, Mavis Gallant, Alice Adams, and Ann Beattie and follow the trajectory of their stories to those of established and emerging writers such as A. M. Homes, Jhumpa Lahiri, and Sadia Shepard, who cover the same territory but from the perspective of suburban women rather than men?

Tom Wolfe offered an early idea. On the occasion of *The New Yorker*'s fortieth anniversary, in 1965, he wrote a two-part, take-no-prisoners takedown of the magazine and its editor Shawn in the fledgling competition, *New York Magazine*, insisting, among other things, that "the short stories in *The New Yorker* have been the laughingstock of the New York literary community for years" due to the proliferation of stories aimed to please women, and in particular, suburban "educated women with large homes and solid hubbies and the taste to . . . *buy expensive things.*" To be sure, he continued, as the only magazine "they heard their professors mention in . . . a good cultural way," *The New Yorker* had become "a totem for these women. Just having it in their home is, well, it is . . . a *symbol*, a kind of *cachet*."[10] Wolfe's assessment is flagrantly misogynistic and depressingly familiar in its determination that fiction written by and about women is not to be taken seriously, but the portrait he draws of the typical upper-middle-class college-educated suburban woman reader's relationship to the magazine is not entirely wrong. Yagoda makes a similar observation when he observes that women belonging to this demographic, finding themselves "at home with more babies than ever before, flocked to *The New Yorker* because it represented one of the few ways they could exercise – and in some cases advertise – their learning and culture." Responses to Yagoda's query to longtime *New Yorker* readers further indicate that female readers in particular felt a "pedagogical" connection to the magazine that they often articulated in concrete ways, by saving old issues for "decorative purposes," whether displaying back issues on the coffee table or using them to wallpaper entire rooms.[11]

That is to say, if *The New Yorker* offered male readers a way to distinguish themselves from their purportedly less-educated and -cultured neighbors by teaching them to position themselves as spiritually homeless, the magazine provided women with a way to distinguish themselves, too, but as *homemakers*. Mary McCarthy's story, "A Charmed Life" (1954), for instance, centers on Martha, a young playwright with a PhD who has returned to the artsy town she had originally fled with the man who is now her second husband. And while it is he and not she who had wanted to return in the first place, she actively works to make a home for both of them with elegant competence, sewing curtains, growing fresh herbs in a window box, and serving up cocktails and simply prepared meals in their "pale-yellow eighteenth century cottage" as he bumbles and grumbles about, nursing a cut finger and a bad case of self-pity.[12]

In contrast to the male-centered suburban fiction which suggests that upper-middle-class identification inheres in disorientation and isolation, *New Yorker* fiction centering on suburban women's experience advances protagonists who advertise their education and class privilege through hospitality. Take Anna Tracy, the homemaker at the center of Mavis Gallant's story, "Madeline's Birthday" (1951), who, much like Martha, runs her "eighteenth century Connecticut farmhouse" with gracious command. Having inherited her childhood home, she looks upon her summers there "as a therapy to be shared with the world": accordingly, there was "the summer of the Polish war orphans, [. . .] the summer of the unmarried mother, the summer of the Friends of France, and the summer of the Bundles for Britain," and now, the summer of Madeline, the daughter of a divorcee friend who has absconded to Europe for the summer, leaving Madeline in Anna's care.[13] While the story pokes fun at her serial altruism, it also offers Anna, ensconced in her antique, breeze- and book-filled house, as a model for aspirational readers: "fair-haired and unhurried," she not only inhabits but also shapes her world with the sheer force of her "good will and optimism,"[14] a legacy she has inherited as surely as her stately home. Indeed, unlike Cheever's and Updike's fiction, which is fueled by the twin dramas of adultery and unhappy marriages, both McCarthy's and Gallant's stories move past such tawdry details to fashionably domesticate divorce and second marriage. As we'll see, *The New Yorker* not only helped college-educated white women assimilate to their new suburban surroundings, the magazine also guided them in accommodating and domesticating the social changes happening within and beyond their borders by literally welcoming them into their homes.

Certainly, even just flipping through groundbreaking articles such as John Hersey's "Hiroshima" (1946), James Baldwin's "Letter from a Region in My Mind" (1962), Rachel Carson's "Silent Spring" (1962), Hannah Arendt's "Eichmann in Jerusalem" (1963), Renata Adler's "The Selma March" (1965), and Jonathan Schell's dispatches from the frontlines of the Vietnam War (beginning with "The Village of Ben-Suc" in 1967), would have given postwar suburban women a sense of the events and issues shaping the world beyond their cloistered communities. But it was by way of the short stories they encountered that they learned to craft their identities in relation to the issues these articles raised. To consider *The New Yorker*'s suburban fiction through the eyes of its female readers is to divine a composite portrait of a demographic that has confounded (and in many cases infuriated) pundits and politicians alike over the past several election cycles, and certainly in the 2016 and 2018 elections: the white suburban college-educated liberal female voter, coveted because she is "swingable."[15] Make no mistake, though: far from being submissive, the women who preside over their homes in these stories, like the editor Shawn himself, may be discreet in their authority, but they make and enforce the house rules.

McCarthy's and Gallant's stories further suggest that the contours of this identity were forged early on. Both Martha and Anna serve as correctives to a nasty inversion of the type, the young housewife, Eloise, who spends the day drinking and gossiping with her former college roommate in J. D. Salinger's "Uncle Wiggily in Connecticut" (1948). For one thing, Eloise is only partially college-educated, having been expelled her second year for being caught with a man. She's also an indifferent hostess, a bitter wife, and a negligent mother. We might overlook these flaws in light of the dead soldier for whom she still pines, but the casual racism and blithe cruelty with which she treats her housekeeper make her irredeemable. When her maid, Grace, who has quietly attended to Eloise's needs throughout the story, asks if her husband could possibly stay the night in her room because the roads have become dangerously icy, Eloise haughtily refuses her request, sneering, "I'm not running a hotel." We thus immediately recognize Eloise's concluding question – "I was a nice girl, wasn't I?" – as rhetorical: she's monstrous.[16]

"Uncle Wiggily" assumes the same ostensibly antiracist stance the magazine had held since mid-century. But Salinger's Eloise is a rare depiction of a northern racist. As Mary Corey explains, in the wake of World War II, the magazine, newly sensitive to the racial and ethnic stereotypes to be found in its own pages, attempted to excise them by banishing "mammies and shoeshine boys and even many black domestics" from its stories and sketches. Nevertheless, the anxieties and perquisites associated with having domestic help continued to interest what Corey calls its "precariously upper-middle-class" readers, who strove to emulate the egalitarian principles espoused by the intelligentsia but who also simply strove.[17] Consequently, and in contrast to actuality, stories set in the Northeast most often depicted domestic help as white. There were, however, plenty of stories set in the American South that served to flatter "enlightened" northeastern readers with damning portraits of unreconstructed southern bigots – "Elmer Gantry types, Southern Bumpkins, and perhaps worst of all, *The New Yorker* readers' Southern counterparts, white upper-middle-class *educated* professionals who incomprehensibly indulged in the kind of wrong thinking commonly held south of the Mason-Dixon line."[18] Such stories castigate their white female protagonists for their personal and offensive bigotry not to challenge their privilege, per se, but only the abuse of that privilege by way of their bad manners. Eloise and her southern counterparts are mere straw men against which self-congratulatory suburban women could position themselves. These stories are not concerned with remediating systemic racism or inequality, nor are they concerned with the inner lives of their African American characters or the vicissitudes of domestic work. They merely establish the attitudes and mores that write the code for belonging among the magazine's community of female readers.

In fact, *New Yorker* stories about white suburban women consistently advance liberal causes and ideals as means for enhancing their characters' own standing at home and in their community. In "Marching through Boston" (1966), Updike deviates from the thrill of extramarital sex to contemplate instead how alluring the protagonist, Richard, suddenly finds his wife, Joan (a Radcliffe graduate), now that she has become involved in the Civil Rights Movement. Remarking somewhat jealously on her attending nonviolence classes in Roxbury and making phone calls in support of fair housing in her town, Richard can't help but notice that Joan's "posture was improving, her figure filling out, her skin growing lustrous, her very hair gaining body and sheen. Though he had resigned himself, through twelve years of marriage, to a rhythm of apathy and renewal, this raw burst of beauty took him unawares."[19] Told from a male perspective, "Marching through Boston" makes the case that championing racial equality not only distinguished white affluent suburbanites such as Joan from their less-enlightened neighbors, it also bathed them in the residual glow of the youth movements taking place across the country, giving suburbanites access to an aura of cool with which they were not usually associated.

Michael Szalay counts Updike among the authors whose fiction sought to reinvent and expand the Democratic Party across race lines and around the issues of civil rights and sexual freedom by adopting a hip aesthetic of surfaces – music, fashion, popular culture, sex, and slang – that invited

professional white male readers to imaginatively and temporarily try blackness on for themselves as a "cost-free means" of bringing together "otherwise multicolored bodies possessed of different economic interests."[20] As if
on cue, in the story's conclusion, Richard attempts to gain his wife's
attention by talking in a dialect meant to sound like a southern black
man, thereby symbolically bridging the racial divide via a shared interest in
his wife's body. In depicting civil rights as sexy, "Marching Through
Boston" makes seductive use of the rhetoric of equal opportunity that
operatives likewise used to lure northern US white upper-middle-class
professionals – once squarely aligned with the GOP – over to the
Democratic Party after effectively ceding the South with Harry
Truman's 1948 convention speech demanding civil rights legislation.[21] In
the decades following World War II, Democrats could thank widespread
prosperity and anticommunist sentiment for helping them build a broad
coalition of African Americans, white professionals, and members of the
white working class, all of whom saw the practical appeal of a platform
based on the causes of "human dignity" and civil rights over the apparently
moot (and politically dangerous) goal of economic redistribution.[22]

The New Yorker's female-authored short fiction likewise aligns the
emancipatory ideals of a new Democratic Party with the class prerogatives
of affluent suburbanites, although not by figuratively gathering diverse
bodies but instead by uniting the like minds of similar bodies. In Alice
Adams's "Gift of Grass" (1969), which takes place outside San Francisco,
a slightly rebellious teenager, Cathy, and her seemingly out-of-step step-
father, Bill, surprisingly connect over their mutual disdain for the "coarse
and unintelligent" deer hunters that spoil their family trips to Lake Tahoe.
More importantly, though, they discover that they intensely dislike the
"hostile" psychiatrist they both see, who talks incessantly about his
"finances" and whose name never appears on the antiwar petitions circulated by the area's doctors because "he probably owns stock in Dow
Chemical."[23] Such fellow feeling spurs Cathy to give Bill two nicely rolled
joints. From the confines of his well-appointed study, and with tears in his
eyes, he ponders the gift's meaning before falling contentedly to sleep.

This story, too, hinges on a female protagonist's act of kindness within
her own home (or, in the case of "Uncle Wiggily," lack thereof). In the
same generous spirit, we might credit it for suggesting that the status quo
can be changed from within by way of antiwar petitions and bridging the
generation gap. In truth, however, "Gift of Grass" does not encourage
political activism. Instead, it merely builds solidarity among New Yorker
readers by uniting them in direct opposition to the reactionary Republican

suburbanites that Lisa McGirr discusses in *Suburban Warriors: The Origins of the New Right* (2001). In her account of the rise of the conservative movement in 1960s Orange County that would eventually lead to Ronald Reagan's election, she notes that the bulk of its members were not working-class people with financial struggles; they were successful business people and entrepreneurs whose politics were an odd amalgam of Christian fundamentalism, xenophobic nationalism, and western-US libertarianism.

Lily Geismer offers a portrait of their ostensible opposite in her book, *Don't Blame Us: Suburban Liberals and the Transformation of the Democratic Party.* Geismer's case study focuses on the suburbs north of Boston which, thanks to massive government spending in science-based university research and the concomitant arrival of high-tech industries in the postwar era, filled up with engineers, scientists, academics, and other professionals drawn to the prerevolutionary history and architecture that distinguished them from newer and nondescript suburban developments. In successive years, Geismer notes, the residents themselves lent this group of suburbs the "cultural, social, and political markers of open-mindedness and a commitment to education" that made them "ever more attractive to a particular type of liberal homebuyer" who took pride in the "wall-to-wall Ph.D.s" that made for such "nice, sensitive, caring communit[ies]."[24]

Geismer argues that these suburbs are representative of postindustrial enclaves across the country whose political priorities since the postwar years have proudly embraced liberal causes such as civil rights, feminism, environmentalism, and peace. Significantly, however, these causes were translated in such a way that they "required limited financial sacrifice, and offered tangible quality-of-life benefits."[25] Then as now, suburbanites sought social solutions that would not raise taxes, lower property values, or compromise their children's education and safety. Residents organized around the issue of fair housing in the late 1950s and 1960s, for instance, on the principles of equal opportunity and meritocratic individualism: an African American professor "of means" should not face discrimination when buying a home.[26] Along similar lines, liberal-minded suburbanites met the demand for school integration by implementing a private, voluntary and one-way busing program. Since it was largely subsidized by the state, it cost residents of these affluent communities almost nothing, and provided the perceived social benefit of enriching their own children's education in an increasingly diverse world.[27]

This is not to suggest that white, female-authored *New Yorker* fiction revolving around suburban hospitality has not occasionally welcomed and even promoted genuine social transformation. At their best, these stories evince a spirit of inclusion that imaginatively opens a space for people previously excluded because they were perceived as threatening the suburban status quo. Ann Beattie's "Cinderella Waltz" (1979) was ahead of its time in its depiction of a love triangle between a suburban housewife, her husband, and another man. When her husband, Milo, leaves her for a man, the unnamed narrator learns to accommodate his partner, Bradley, for the sake of their daughter, Louise, although at first, she "was actually afraid of him." She eventually musters the courage to invite him into the house; the two become comfortable friends, and their blended family a happy one. "Cinderella Waltz" thus normalizes same-sex partnership well before the marriage equality debate had gotten traction (and in advance of the AIDS crisis). But it is not just that the narrator is a welcoming host. Bradley is also a good guest; "gentle and low-key," he brings lovely gifts and helps the narrator find freelance work in advertising.[28] Furthermore, he provides a loving, secure home for Louise on the weekends. Bradley may be non-conforming in his sexuality, but he abides perfectly the house rules of *The New Yorker* suburban housewife, and he in no way challenges the individualist, meritocratic, and consumerist ethos undergirding suburban liberalism.

Whatever the issue, the free-market discourse animating the suburban conservative and liberal worldviews alike has conveniently aligned with suburbanites' self-interest and preserved their class privilege. Adams's "Waiting for Stella" (1983) illustrates well the limits of a suburban liberal agenda predicated on individual rights rather than social justice. The story concerns a group of friends now in their seventies and eighties living in the same "small enclave" south of San Francisco, gathered for lunch around their friend's pool to commemorate the recent death of their friend Stella. Reflecting on the basis of their friendship over the past several decades, the hostess, Rachel, herself a "professor of medicine, rather distinguished," notes that it is no accident that this group has settled in "somewhat similar houses" given how alike they all are: in addition to all being "mildly intellectual" professionals, they were also "'liberals.'" The scare quotes around the word perhaps connote that while the group may share similar political beliefs, their strictly abstract and consequence-free expression actually binds them together. As we saw, Salinger's racist Eloise represents one extreme against which readers might identify themselves. Rachel offers readers another in her description of Stella, noting that she and her friends "have generally been united in opposition to whatever [Stella] was doing." It's not that they don't share her views, but that "Stella always, somehow, went too far. Wonderful of her to march in Selma at already sixty-odd, but did she have to get arrested, so purposefully, and spend a week in that jail?"[29] To their minds, Stella's tendency to put her body on the line for her political beliefs is unseemly, of a piece with the fact that she drank too much, talked too much, and slept around too much.

Even still, Rachel admits that "everyone is a little mad at Stella for dying."[30] Given that the story is told from the vantage point of the 1980s when the radical possibilities that Stella embodied have been thoroughly subsumed by the conservative Reagan Revolution, we might conclude that the group has gathered not only to mourn her passing but also their own failure to bring about real social change. Then again, Rachel also admits that it is "rather a relief not to have Stella around, loudly splashing in the pool, and always urging them all to exceed themselves somehow."[31] Stella perhaps reminds Rachel and her friends of their own willingness to abandon the lofty goals of social justice and economic populism in the wake of George McGovern's resounding defeat in 1972, when a "neoliberal" party arose from the ashes with a social and economic agenda tailor-made for people just like Rachel and her friends: upper-middle-class and entrepreneurial types with money to donate.[32] Stella's passing and these characters' willingness to subject themselves to mild self-scrutiny effectively absolve them not only of their past mistakes but of any obligation to the present or future. It is not only that it is too late for these aging "liberals" to combat the rise of Reaganism they helped foment; it is that Reagan's triumph has proven as inevitable as death itself.

It is the abdication of responsibility to anything other than oneself that A. M. Homes sends up in "Music for Torching" (1995). Set in Westchester County, New York, and revolving around alienated suburbanites playing their respective parts in an unhappy marriage, the story takes up the precise territory that preoccupied Cheever. Yet it's perhaps more revealing to read the story alongside Adams's "Waiting for Stella." "Torching," which begins in the aftermath of a dinner party, likewise dwells on the regrets of its hostess, Elaine, who, like Adams's Rachel, admits that she and her husband, Paul, are just like their friends and their friends are just like them because they "like it that way."[33] Unlike Rachel's, however, Elaine's regrets are not remotely concerned with her failure to make good on her political ideals. Motivated by only the vaguest of "good intentions," overcome by sheer boredom, she regrets only "having cooked the dinner, having made the enormous effort to make everything good again," since those efforts are for naught; her husband's complaints about the meal pique her enough that she takes a knife to his throat.[34]

Published during the boom years of the Clinton administration, in the midst of Tina Brown's glamorous turn at *The New Yorker* (1992–98), and in the wake of what Francis Fukuyama infamously declared the "end of history as such" with "the universalization of Western liberal democracy,"[35] the lily-white community the story describes has no connection whatsoever to life beyond its borders; as yet another hostess at yet another dinner party happily chirps, "House, house, house, as though nothing else mattered, as though that's all there was in the world."[36] The vacuous fetishization of her house inadvertently bespeaks the very real advantages of home ownership, whose value not only defines the suburban "good life," but also secures it at the expense of those outside its tax base.[37] It is tempting, therefore, to read Elaine and Paul's impulsive decision to burn their own house down by dousing it with lighter fluid and flipping over the barbecue as a bold move to overturn a system whose very foundations are unfair. But they retreat only as far as the local motel, where, tucked safely under a "fortress" of covers meant to "protect [them] from the world," Elaine admits that *they* are the problem, and resolves to be "nicer" going forward.[38] Once again, the story fails to challenge the systemic injustice that such communities ignore and perpetuate. Instead, the story reassures readers that all that is called for is an attitude adjustment, the goal being not to improve conditions outside but only within, since what distinguishes affluent suburban liberals are the "nice, sensitive, caring communit[ies]" they form.

Elaine, like Eloise, is too self-absorbed and entitled to adequately fulfill her obligation as a suburban hostess. In contrast, the discreetly generous, highly educated first- and second-generation Bengali American characters who populate Jhumpa Lahiri's *New Yorker* fiction appear to represent the model toward which suburban women readers should strive. "Once in a Lifetime" (2006), for instance, set in the Boston suburbs that concern Geismer, is indeed a story that features hospitality graciously given and received. Furthermore, revolving as it does around fully integrated people of color, the story should confirm the realization of suburban liberal ideals. But while Lahiri's story narrates the twin processes of assimilation and accommodation that have perhaps made these communities more welcoming to an ethnically and racially diverse population, it also suggests that the very foundations upon which suburbia has been built – consumer-driven individualism and the primacy of home ownership – preclude even the possibility of forming a truly caring community.

The story looks backward to center on two Bengali American families who first met not long after they'd moved from Calcutta to Cambridge in the 1960s to attend MIT. Brand new to the country and financially strapped, the adults formed an intimate network among themselves and other recent Bengali immigrants, handing down their few possessions to one another and sharing in the shopping, cooking, childcare, and upkeep of their respective, growing families. This early experience of mutual care starkly differs from their experience several years later, in the suburbs in the early 1980s, when the Choudhuris, who had moved back to Bombay, return to the United States and stay temporarily with the narrator, Hema, and her parents, as they search for a house of their own. Steeped in the advice that comes with her subscription to *Good Housekeeping*, Hema's mother prepares for her guests' arrival by sprucing up the house with new furnishings, cooking and cleaning for days on end, reconfiguring sleeping arrangements to guarantee her guests' privacy, and generally doing all that she can to be a perfect suburban hostess. Even so, the two families fail to connect. The Choudhuris are polite but distant. For her part, Hema's mother is jealously resentful of the Choudhuris' clearly elevated economic status: they arrive with stories to tell of first-class flights and vacations in Rome, and spend their evenings looking at houses in leafier neighborhoods where the houses are bigger and the schools are the "best."[39] When the Choudhuris move into one of these enviable homes issuing vague promises of future invitations to swim in their pool, the friendship effectively ends. It is only because of a conversation between Kaushik, the Choudhuris' son, and Hema, that we learn that Mrs. Choudhuri has terminal cancer, and has returned to the United States not to live but to die. In Bombay, Kaushik explains, her friends and family would have gathered around her, "trying to shield her from something she could not escape"; barricaded in her secluded suburban home, she knows she will "be left alone."[40] Cheever's fiction is rife with characters who step outside the bounds of suburban propriety, as, say, Neddy Merrill, the protagonist of "The Swimmer," whose profligate ways leave him broken, homeless, and utterly alone. Lahiri's story, on the other hand, offers a fairly damning assessment of what happens not when characters fail, but instead when they succeed in mastering the behavior and attitudes modeled for them by *New Yorker* suburban stories: profound isolation and death.

To be sure, unlike "Music For Torching," which savagely flouts the conventions of *New Yorker* fiction in order to assure its predominantly white readers that they are better than the odious people it portrays, "Lifetime" and the characters within fully adhere to the unspoken but rigid house rules of the white suburban hostess in order to offer a subtle but scathing critique of the world *The New Yorker* has made. In fact, Lahiri's story operates in a similar fashion to Ann Petry's "Has Anybody Seen Dora

Dean?" published almost half a century earlier in 1958, told from the perspective of an African American domestic worker in the Northeast, and so an exception that proves the rule. Sinead Moynihan calls the story a "literary version of the cakewalk," noting that "by mimicking and reproducing the tone of typical *New Yorker* 'help' stories, which were, up to that point, composed exclusively by white writers, Petry subtly comments on the world of white privilege depicted in the pages of the magazine and *The New Yorker*'s often problematic assumptions regarding race and class differences."[41] "Once in a Lifetime" likewise assumes the tone and style of *New Yorker* fiction in its portrayal of women of color thoroughly assimilated to a brand of hospitality that is anything but welcoming.

But parody and critique only work if they're recognized as such. Considering the reception of "Dora Dean," Moynihan argues that the magazine itself has trained its readers to be "attuned and receptive to irony and self-satire."[42] But as Aubry points out, *New Yorker* fiction cultivates self-irony only as far as it is "salutary." Sadia Shepard's 2018 story, "Foreign-Returned," and the ensuing controversy after its publication, illustrate the limits of white liberal female readers' willingness to cede their authority in the name of self-scrutiny. The story relates the experience of a Pakistani couple, Sara and Hassan, who have come to the United States with high hopes of achieving the American Dream but find their prospects diminished when Hassan loses his job at a big New York bank and finds lower-paying work as a junior analyst at a bank in the Connecticut suburbs. It is with aggrieved superiority that he regards his new desk-mate, a young Pakistani American woman, Hina, an observant Muslim who is earnest, hard-working, and ambitious. His stance changes toward her, however, when he and his wife discover that she is the protégé of Mona, a wealthy Pakistani American woman who presides over the social circle of which they desperately want to be a part.

Mona is just the sort of homemaker that Sara aspires to be, graciously entertaining large crowds every weekend in her "big white Colonial with green shutters" in the tony suburb of Darien, Connecticut. Mona is indeed an excellent hostess, showering each of her guests with attention and compliments, while also, Sara senses, subjecting them to a "kind of audition."[43] But even as Sara lies and ingratiates herself in hopes of making the cut, Hina rejects Mona's invitation of belonging out of hand. Finding herself surrounded by semi-drunk women who cajole her into shedding her headscarf so that they can take her photo for a dating website, Hina flees the party in disgust. Finally, however, it is not Hina who fulfills the prophesy of the story's title, but Hassan and Sara, who return to Karachi after Hassan is let go by the bank. For her part, Hina is promoted, and is thus one step closer to realizing her own version of the American Dream, which emphatically does not involve marriage but does involve earning enough so that she can afford to make a home for her younger siblings. Like "Once in a Lifetime," "Foreign-Returned" depicts immigrants who have adopted the role of homemaker outlined for them by the white liberal suburban women who have benignly ruled the leafy, privileged world conjured by *The New Yorker*. Unlike Lahiri's story, however, Shepard's story extends beyond parody and critique to reimagine this terrain and its inhabitants. Comfortably repatriated in Pakistan, Hassan envisions the white clapboard Colonial that was the object of his wife's most fervent desire. "But he doesn't see Sara in the house, nor the children they plan to have. Rather, he sees another man's children, Hina's siblings: three girls and a boy. [...] They look content in their kingdom, padding around the carpets in their socks." In place of a story organized around motherhood and the white heteronormative nuclear family, Shepard offers an extended, brown, and possibly queer household in which responsibility and privileges are evenly dispersed – it's all of "their kingdom," after all.[44]

It might come as a surprise that the brouhaha that erupted after the story's publication was not provoked by its quietly radical conclusion but, instead, its strict adherence to the established style and tone of *New Yorker* fiction. The author Francine Prose took to her Facebook page to accuse the story of being nothing more than a "copy" of Mavis Gallant's 1963 *New Yorker* story, "The Ice Wagon Going Down the Street," with "the only major difference being that the main characters here are Pakistanis in Connecticut during the Trump era instead of Canadians in post-WW II Geneva."[45] Never mind that Shepard acknowledged her indebtedness to Gallant's story in an accompanying interview with *The New Yorker*'s fiction editor, Deborah Treisman, who was herself clearly aware of the similarities between the two stories.[46] Never mind that Shepard is hardly the first writer to reimagine a story with new characters and in a new time and place, and never mind that the very act of imagining a happily settled, queer, brown family in a predominantly white suburb in Trump's America fundamentally imbues the bones of Gallant's story with new meaning. Prose's predominantly white, *New Yorker*-reading followers chimed in to express their outrage, with a few writers, among them Jess Row, Alexander Chee, and Porochista Khakpour, vociferously defending Shepard and noting that what was really at stake was the role that race and power play both in the story and in the discussion about it. When Shepard herself entered the Facebook fray to politely thank Prose for eliciting thoughtful discussion, Prose accused her of being "disingenuous," and wondered, "as to why you'd want to do this, it's still a bit of a mystery, since presumably you have stories of your own to tell."[47] For his part, Row found this particular comment so offensive that he sent a letter to *The New Yorker*, asserting "the real scandal here is the proprietary rage of Shepard's critics, who insist that she has no right to this material. As if they were the ones in charge."[48]

My aim is not to relitigate the debate over whether Shepard's story is homage or plagiarism (it is an homage). I call attention to the turf war Prose initiated because even as Shepard's story offers a new vision for the suburban female liberal homemaker – one that is principled, caring, inclusive, truly democratic – Prose unwittingly demonstrates how fiercely the established model for this character continues to guard the door. A tour through Prose's Facebook timeline indicates that she is deeply invested in the requisite liberal causes; that she has a keen sense of the events and issues shaping the world-at-large; and that she welcomes a variety of voices in the discussions she initiates on her page. Nevertheless, her reaction to Shepard's story makes clear that her brand of liberalism is soaked in the language and ethos of ownership and entitlement. In short, Prose's behavior fits to a T that of the white suburban woman that *The New Yorker* has shaped, encouraged, and occasionally critiqued over the years. Very much like the protagonist of another Gallant story, Anna Tracy, Prose's largesse toward others is a means for securing her own authority rather than actually lifting others up.

Given the complex dynamics and challenges redefining the suburban environment, why should we care about the petty concerns of a middle-aged white woman? Primarily because her ilk is prized by political operatives and candidates, not only because she shows up at the polls, but because she has a voice and money, and she uses both. Fairfield County, where Shepard's story is set, for instance, voted overwhelmingly Democratic in the 2016 and 2018 elections. But the county is hardly a beacon of equal opportunity. In the predominantly white, wealthy town of Fairfield, 94 percent of its high-school students graduate. Just next door in Bridgeport, one of the state's poorest cities, only 63 percent graduate. This is because school funding is determined not by need but by local property taxes (yet another way home ownership secures the "good life") and by the clout of individual legislators, which derives from the power of their purses, which are filled on the condition that they benefit white suburban donors and their families. This is just one unfortunate consequence of the power that white suburban female voters continue to wield. Redirected, that power could contribute to something more equitable and just than merely serving its own selfish interests. With Shepard's story, *The New Yorker* has taken a step toward unmaking the world it has made and offering its aspirational suburban female readers a new path they might follow in order to help remake it.

Notes

1. Shawn Bucholtz and Jed Kolko, "America Really Is a Nation of Suburbs," *CityLab* 14 (November 2018), www.citylab.com/life/2018/11/data-most-american-neighborhoods-suburban/575602/.
2. Richard Florida, "The New Suburban Crisis," *CityLab* 2 (May 2, 2017), www.citylab.com/equity/2017/05/the-new-suburban-crisis/521709/.
3. For all their increasing diversity, the majority of suburban residents are still white in 90 percent of suburbs and small metro counties. See Kim Parker et al., "Demographic and Economic Trends in Urban, Suburban, and Rural Communities," Pew Research Center, May 22, 2018, www.pewsocialtrends.org/2018/05/22/demographic-and-economic-trends-in-urban-suburban-and-rural-communities/. That said, however, the suburbs, once a landscape associated with prosperity and upward mobility, now account for the largest and fastest-growing poor population in the country and more than half of the metropolitan poor. See Elizabeth Kneebone and Michael Bérubé, *Confronting Suburban Poverty in America* (Washington, DC: Brookings Institution Press, 2014), p. 141.
4. Catherine Jurca, *White Diaspora: The Suburb and the Twentieth Century American Novel* (Princeton, NJ: Princeton University Press, 2001), p. 7.
5. Timothy Aubry, "Cheever and the Management of Middlebrow Misery," *Iowa Journal of Cultural Studies* 3 (2003), www.uiowa.edu/~ijc/suburbia/aubry.htm.
6. Mary F. Corey, *The World through a Monocle*: The New Yorker *at Midcentury* (Cambridge, MA: Harvard University Press, 1999), p. 10.
7. John Leonard, "Fifty Years Old and All Grown Up," *New York Times*, February 16, 1975, www.nytimes.com/1975/02/16/archives/fifty-years-old-and-all-grownup.html.
8. Ben Yagoda, *About Town: The New Yorker and the World It Made* (New York: Da Capo, 2000), p. 59.
9. Ibid., p. 311.
10. Tom Wolfe, "Lost in the Whichy Thickets: *The New Yorker*" (1965), in *Hooking Up* (New York: FSG, 2000), p. 281; Wolfe's ellipses and italics.
11. Yagoda, *About Town*, pp. 311, 13, 13.
12. Mary McCarthy, "A Charmed Life," *The New Yorker*, October 9, 1954, 41.
13. Mavis Gallant, "Madeline's Birthday," *The New Yorker*, September 1, 1951, 22.
14. Ibid., 21.

15. Danielle Kurtzleben, "What We Mean When We Talk about 'Suburban Women Voters,'" *NPR Weekend Edition*, April 7, 2018, www.npr.org/2018/04/07/599573817/what-we-mean-when-we-talk-about-suburban-women-voters.
16. J. D. Salinger, "Uncle Wiggily in Connecticut," *The New Yorker*, March 20, 1948, 36.
17. Corey, *World through a Monocle*, pp. 42, 136.
18. Ibid., 92.
19. John Updike, "Marching through Boston," *The New Yorker*, January 22, 1966, p. 34.
20. Michael Szalay, *Hip Figures: A Literary History of the Democratic Party* (Palo Alto, CA: Stanford University Press, 2012), p. 4.
21. Vance Packard noted that affiliation with the Republican Party increased as one climbed the socioeconomic ladder, with the vast majority of white-collar, professional, small-and large-business people identifying with the GOP. However, during the period from 1950 to 1958, "the proportion of college-educated Americans who considered themselves Republicans dropped 8 per cent. [...] Other studies show the shift away from the GOP reached into both well-to-do and poor neighborhoods" (Packard, *The Status Seekers* [New York: David McKay, 1959], p. 210).
22. More than prosperity and anticommunist sentiment, it was the Taft–Hartley Act of 1947 that seriously curtailed (and continues to curtail) the right to strike, that robbed organized labor of much of its political power. Thus, union heads increasingly adopted the language of civil rights, as for example, United Auto Workers president Walter P. Reuther, who, in his address before the 48th annual NAACP Convention in 1957, asserted, "I believe that the question of civil rights must be made the top priority item on American Democracy's unfinished business in the 20th Century," Walter P. Reuther Library, Archives of Labor and Urban Affairs, http://reuther100.wayne.edu/pdf/NAACP_1957.pdf.
23. Alice Adams, "Gift of Grass," *The New Yorker*, November 8, 1969, 62.
24. Lily Geismer, *Don't Blame Us: Suburban Liberals and the Transformation of the Democratic Party* (Princeton, NJ: Princeton University Press, 2017), p. 4.
25. Ibid., p. 6.
26. Ibid., p. 50.
27. Ibid., pp. 72–95.
28. Ann Beattie, "Cinderella Waltz," *The New Yorker*, January 29, 1979, 29.
29. Alice Adams, "Waiting for Stella," *The New Yorker*, May 2, 1983, 36.
30. Ibid., 42.
31. Ibid., 38.
32. Joshua Mound, "What Democrats Still Don't Get about George McGovern," *The New Republic*, February 29, 2016, http://newrepublic.com/article/130737/democrats-still-dont-get-george-mcgovern.
33. A. M. Homes, "Music for Torching," *The New Yorker*, February 6, 1995, 79.
34. Ibid., 78.

35. Francis Fukuyama, "The End of History?," *The National Interest* 16 (Summer 1989), 4.
36. Homes, "Music for Torching," 80.
37. For a discussion of the way that homeownership has unjustly benefited white Americans, see George Lipsitz, *The Possessive Investment in Whiteness: How White People Profit from Identity Politics* (Philadelphia: Temple University Press, 2006).
38. Homes, "Music for Torching," 83.
39. Jhumpa Lahiri, "Once in a Lifetime," *The New Yorker*, May 8, 2006, 70.
40. Ibid., 73.
41. Sinead Moynihan, "Ann Petry's Cakewalk: Domestic Workers and *The New Yorker* at Midcentury," *MELUS* 44:1 (Spring 2019), 5, 2.
42. Ibid., 6.
43. Sadia Shepard, "Foreign-Returned," *The New Yorker*, January 8, 2018, 60, 61.
44. Ibid., 66.
45. Francine Prose, Discussion of Mavis Gallant's influence on Sadia Shepard's story, "Foreign-Returned," *Facebook*, January 8, 2018, 3:35 p.m., www .facebook.com/francine.prose/timeline?lst=1667515534%3A505900066% 3A1553115513.
46. Deborah Treisman, "Sadia Shepard on the Nuances of Immigration and Cultural Identity," *The New Yorker*, January 1, 2019, www.newyorker.com/ books/this-week-in-fiction/fiction-this-week-sadia-shepard-2018-01-08.
47. Ibid.
48. Jess Row, letter to *The New Yorker*, January 22, 2018, 5.

CHAPTER 8

Transnational American Cities
Camilo Mejía's ar Ramadi, Iraq, and Jason Hall's Topeka, Kansas

John Carlos Rowe

Thank You for Your Service
>   prescribed greeting for members of the US Armed Forces

The city has a venerable place in American studies, because urban centers are keys to national cohesion in the regionally and ethnically diverse United States. In addition, American studies has long focused on the modernization process as a measure of democratic progress, and urbanization is an important measure of the success or failure of various forms of modernization. With its foundational interest in westward expansion and Frederick Jackson Turner's "frontier thesis," American studies has studied the growth of the American city, especially because of settler-colonial migration, as a key index of US nationalism. The Puritan ideal of a "city on a hill" is more than just a crucial colonial mythology; that divinely ordained and aspiring city is part of the mythopoeia of American studies as a discipline.[1]

Today's American studies scholars will claim correctly that all the preceding scholarly interests in the city belong to traditional American studies. With its emphasis on American exceptionalism, technological progress, the imperial march of Manifest Destiny, and consensus history, traditional American studies remained firmly focused on *US* cities to the neglect of the powerful influence of cities outside the boundaries of the geopolitical nation. There have been some studies of the influence of foreign cities on US national identity, but most deal with transcultural influences of such global metropolitan centers as Paris, London, Rome, and Berlin, often reinforcing the superiority of Western Civilization and its imperial heritage.

Paul Jay argues in *Global Matters: The Transnational Turn in Literary Studies* (2010) that much contemporary literature published in the United

States ought to be interpreted as global rather than "American" literature.[2] The transnational social and personal conditions represented in such novels often express the urban conditions of such US metropolitan centers of finance and trade as New York, San Francisco, and Los Angeles. Previously understood rather generally as "cosmopolitan" sites, these American cities are today the intersections of significant immigration patterns and changes in US demographics that extend and revise US immigration history, in part because the same technologies that supply the global economy's infrastructure also permit migrants to remain intimately connected to their homelands. In short, the transnational turn to which Jay refers is not just a phenomenon of literary studies; transnationalism is the defining social condition of contemporary US urban life in cities across the nation.

This transnational approach is evident in a host of different novels published at the turn of the last century and proliferating in the wake of 9/11 in the broad cultural responses to global terrorism. When published in 1997, Karen Tei Yamashita's *Tropic of Orange* seemed to mark a radical departure from previous urban novels, insofar as it deconstructed the usual boundaries separating Los Angeles, Mexico, and Singapore. Apparently jumbling together different social and linguistic realities, the novel represents the cultural differences in which most people today live. Anticipating 9/11, Salman Rushdie's *Fury* (2001) interprets these multicultural conflicts as potentially informing the violence we associate with global terrorism, but internalized by Rushdie in the psychological anxieties of Malik Solanka, a South Asian-English immigrant to New York, who fears he may have committed the murders about which he reads every morning in the newspaper.

Other transnational novels may distribute such violence to different locations, producing more recognizable narratives of US assimilation and redemption. Khaled Hosseini's *The Kite Runner* (2003) is a good example of this pattern, in which the Taliban's cruel regime in Afghanistan and neighboring Pakistan can only be overcome by the characters who escape to the relative safety of Fremont, California. In Karan Mahajan's *The Association of Small Bombs* (2016), Delhi in 1996 is a city shattered by terrorist bombs, disrupting everyday life and ordinary people in profound and unpredictable ways. As in Hosseini's *The Kite Runner*, the United States offers an escape to one of the characters, Mansoor, who attends Santa Clara University to study computer science and leave behind the violence in his hometown. Yet shortly after his arrival in California, he learns that planes had crashed into the World Trade Center. 9/11 brings global terrorism to the United States.

Paul Jay is thus right to focus on a transnational turn in literary studies that requires a more global perspective. Yet in the novels I have mentioned, global terrorism is the principal cause of urban violence at home and abroad. To be sure, Rushdie and Mahajan argue convincingly that Americans have contributed to the global terrorism that eventually finds its way to their homes. Unlike Hosseini, both authors remain vigorous critics of US neoimperialism that has helped fuel violent dissident groups in the Middle East, Afghanistan, India, Pakistan, Indonesia, and Africa. Often identified with the loose category of "post-9/11 literature," such novels offer various arguments about the consequences of the so-called War on Terror.

The direct costs of US military support for neoimperialist foreign policies are less frequently assessed in terms of social and urban life in the United States, especially after 9/11. Yet if US militarism since the First Gulf War, perhaps even dating back to the Vietnam War, is considered a major cause, rather than simply an effect, of such problems, then we ought to look directly at its consequences for American democracy. In what follows, I hope to offer a transnational perspective on the city in American literary and cultural studies by offering a brief comparative analysis of two cities ravaged by US warfare: al Ramadi, Iraq, and Topeka, Kansas. Both cities have been transformed by US neoimperial ventures in Afghanistan and Iraq, especially after 9/11, but also dating back to the First Gulf War in 1991, arguably the prelude to the US military occupation of Afghanistan since 2001 and of Iraq between 2001 and 2011. Al Ramadi, the capital of al Anbar Province, is today a ruined city, which in 2001 boasted a population of 375,000 but by the time of its liberation by the Iraqi army in 2011 counted only 1,000 civilians. With a population of more than 125,000, Topeka, the state capital of Kansas, is located only sixty-five miles from Fort Riley, a US Army base in the north-central part of the state. Although dramatically affected by the physical and psychological wounds of soldiers returning to Fort Riley from Iraq and Afghanistan, as well as by the economic recession of 2008, Topeka is by no means a ruined city. With its domed, neoclassical state capitol building, memorial to the 1954 *Brown v. Board of Education* decision ending segregation, and its numerous monuments to Kansas history, Topeka is outwardly a prosperous Midwestern city exemplifying middle-class, middle-American family values.

Shortly before al Ramadi became the military flashpoint for battles between Coalition and Iraqi forces versus various insurrectionary groups, ranging from al-Q'aeda to ISIS, Staff Sergeant Camilo Mejía went on an approved military leave from his post in the Iraqi city and never returned.

Acknowledged as the first US soldier to refuse service in the Second Gulf War, Mejía tells his story in *Road from ar Ramadi: The Private Rebellion of Staff Sergeant Camilo Mejía* (2007). Court martialed and convicted for his desertion, Mejía served nine months of a one-year sentence and was "discharged from the service with a bad conduct discharge."[3] When he refused to return following his approved leave, Mejía had served a total of eight years in the US military, initially joining the Florida National Guard and then being called to active duty during the US troop buildup in Iraq following 9/11. A non-US citizen living in Florida as a permanent resident, Mejía had exceeded the military service limits in the US Army by more than a year. Only the fact that he had been recently "reupped" for additional military service in Iraq, despite the illegality of this extension of his deployment, prevented him from being routinely discharged from military service. Although the legal technicalities that kept a soldier enlisted beyond his voluntary term and then prevented him from leaving service are part of Mejía's story, the main reason for his refusal to return to al Ramadi and to US military service in Iraq was his strong opposition to the war.

When Mejía left al Ramadi in 2003, the city still existed and functioned as a city, even if just barely. Water and electrical services were intermittent, and traffic was interrupted at regular intervals by US and Iraqi military checkpoints. Access to the hospital, schools, markets, and government offices was limited by these checkpoints, most of which became regular sites of combat between rebel groups and the US-Iraqi forces. With a significant Sunni majority and many members of Saddam Hussein's Ba'ath political party, al Ramadi was home to many soldiers from the Iraqi army that had been disbanded shortly after the US-led Coalition toppled Saddam Hussein's government. Those well-trained military personnel had not disappeared; they had simply joined the various insurrections fighting what they perceived to be the US imperial occupation of their country. Despite propaganda in the US news and governmental media that the Iraqis generally welcomed the US invasion and occupation, most Iraqis deeply resented the US presence.

Between 2003 and 2016, al Ramadi would be the site of 100 separate battles, involving a long list of combatants, including US Coalition forces working with the Iraqi military to defeat such insurgent groups as al-Q'aeda and ISIS. As al Anbar Province became one of the major regions of Iraq and the greater Middle East to be contested, its capital, al Ramadi, became the center of fierce fighting and military destruction that would transform a dysfunctional city into a virtual ruin. Two major battles in this period define both the struggle for al Anbar Province and the changing US foreign policy in Iraq. The First Battle of Ramadi in April 2004 coincided with the First Battle of Fallujah, resulting in massive urban destruction and numerous civilian casualties. In the effort to control the city of Fallujah, US Coalition and Iraqi military forces surrounded the city but were unable control the numerous insurgent groups within the city. In an effort to escape the US-Iraqi siege, many insurgents fled to nearby al Ramadi, where they cut the main road and the supply line from Baghdad to al Anbar Province to create a new combat front.

The First Battle of Fallujah was highly publicized in 2004 because of two key events. On March 31, 2004, four Blackwater Security contractors were killed by insurgents who dragged the bodies from the burning SUV and strung the corpses from a railroad bridge spanning the Euphrates. The photograph circulated widely in the international press, most journalistic accounts concluding that the image represented the brutality of the insurgents. Indeed, much of the US Coalition's violence toward civilians in this battle was attributed to revenge for the public display of the corpses. Second, this was the historical moment in which Abu Musab al-Zarqawi (1966–2006) became a recognized insurgent leader in Iraq. As the organizer of al-Q'aeda in Iraq (AQI), the Jordanian developed a foreign insurgency within Iraq, attracting fighters trained in other Middle Eastern countries and Afghanistan. Emerging as a leading insurgency among the many competitive rebel groups, AQI and al-Zarqawi gave a name and a face to the otherwise diffuse anticolonial guerilla struggles in occupied Iraq.

The Second Battle of al Ramadi began on April 17 and lasted until November 15, 2006, when US and Iraqi security forces succeeded in driving insurgents from the city, especially the Ramadi Government Center, where most of the Coalition troops were garrisoned, and from the Ramadi General Hospital. Despite broad publicity, especially in the US press, regarding the successful Anbar Awakening during which Sunni sheiks organized resistance to the insurgents, the Coalition's victory in the Second Battle of al Ramadi could not hide the fact that most of Anbar Province had been lost to insurgents, especially ISIS as it emerged from AQI. In August 2006, the Chief Intelligence Officer for the Marines, Colonel Pete Devlin, issued a classified report declaring that the US and Iraqi militaries were unable to quell the insurgencies in Western Iraq, especially Anbar Province. The much-touted Anbar Awakening Council turned out to be little more than propaganda. Although the US and Iraqi armies controlled al Ramadi, the rest of Anbar Province, including Fallujah, was controlled largely by AQI and the emerging ISIS.

Continuously contested between 2006 and 2015, al Ramadi was invaded by ISIS on May 15, 2015, Iraqi security forces infamously abandoning their US-supplied weaponry and vehicles as they retreated from the city. In a much-publicized blockade and subsequent invasion, the Iraqi military would retake the city between November and December of 2015. The "liberated" city was filled with IEDs, booby-trapped houses, and massive destruction from the numerous battles waged in the past decade. By the end of 2015, the population had dwindled to 1,000 civilians.

Camilo Mejía escaped Ramadi just months before the First Battle, but he certainly saw the signs of the future in the region. Beginning with his unwilling participation in the torture of Iraqi detainees by US Special Forces at the al Assad prisoner-of-war camp near Baghdad International Airport, Mejía witnessed firsthand the US military's destruction of civil society. Distrustful and paranoid, especially in situations where they understood neither the Arabic language nor Islamic religious practices, US military interrogators tried to root out "terrorists" by torturing detainees with sleep deprivation, verbal threats, and physical abuse.

In walking away from Ramadi, Camilo Mejía repudiated an imperial project that lacked a legitimate purpose. During his court-martial, Mejía writes, "I declared myself a conscientious objector, and said that the war in Iraq was oil-motivated, that I was not a mercenary."[4] Yet the United States and its fabricated coalition invaded Iraq neither for oil nor to eliminate "weapons of mass destruction," which US officials already knew Saddam Hussein did not possess. Whether or not Mejía understood that the invasion and occupation were utterly quixotic, futile efforts to respond to the 9/11 attacks planned and organized by the Saudi Osama bin Laden from distant Afghanistan, Mejía certainly did understand that the US military operations in which he participated had produced the anarchy they were intended to overcome.

When Mejía returned to the United States, he found cities physically intact with fully operating infrastructures. Deployed originally to Iraq as part of a Florida National Guard unit called for active service, he learned in Iraq that as a non-US citizen he had already completed his service and could not be extended unless offered US citizenship. Yet once his commanding officer made the decision to extend Mejía's service, no one seemed able to rescind an order that violated Army regulations. As Mejía contested the unfairness of this decision, his opposition to the US military presence in Iraq grew even stronger. Aided by the activist group, Citizen Soldier, and eventually used as a test case in the US antiwar movement, Mejía traveled from Miami to New York City and Boston to meet with

activists and lawyers in preparation for his decision to refuse to return to
military duty and his expected court-martial.

Amid the psychological and public conflicts he faced as he moved
toward his decisions not to return to active duty in Iraq and to surrender
voluntarily to military authorities for trial, Mejía traveled frequently up the
Eastern Corridor of the United States. The normal operations of the cities
he visits barely deserved his notice, except when his own financial and legal
circumstances required him to accept help from lawyers and other activists,
many operating in a well-known underground of antiwar protesters. The
contrast is great between the diverse, functioning US cities of Miami,
New York, and Boston, each containing large military and antiwar organizations, and Ramadi, Iraq, in which multiple insurgencies fight daily with
US and Iraqi military. Iraq is shattered by sectarian and political differences
simply pushed to the point of collapse by the US military invasion and
occupation, whereas urban life in the United States proceeds normally.

Mejía's status as a permanent resident in the United States was the result
of his mother's emigration from Nicaragua and Costa Rica to join her
mother in the relative safety of the United States. Mejía's mother and
father were both members of the Sandinista revolution against Nicaraguan
dictator Anastasio Somoza. Camilo Ernesto Mejía was born in Managua
on August 28, 1975, and named for Camilo Torres, the "Colombian
Catholic priest who died in combat; and Ernesto for Ernesto Che
Guevara."[5] Although his mother and father separated when Camilo was
a child, both parents continued to work actively for the Sandinistas,
operating from urban undergrounds in Managua, Nicaragua, and San
José, Costa Rica, before his mother emigrated with Camilo to the United
States in 1994, as her role as a revolutionary became increasingly dangerous
to her and her children. Counterintuitive as it was for Mejía to decide to
join the Florida National Guard at the age of nineteen, not long after the
family's arrival in Miami, his decision was largely practical – Florida guard
members gain educational benefits from their service.

In *War Echoes*, Arianna E. Vigil connects Mejía's refusal to return to
active duty in Iraq in 2003 with US intervention in Central America in the
1980s, but there is little evidence in Mejía's memoir that he himself made
these connections.[6] Vigil is of course right that US foreign policies in Latin
America and the Middle East are related, even if individuals like Mejía may
not recognize these geographically remote connections. Such geopolitical
links are also evident in transnational urban relations, if one looks just
beneath the surface of everyday experience. In the current news cycle,
immigrants from Central America desperate to escape gang violence arising

from the collapse of local police and military authorities have traveled in highly publicized "caravans" to assemble at the southern border of the United States. Despite their legal right to apply for political asylum in the United States, most of these immigrants have not even been processed. Trump administration efforts to frustrate them from even applying for asylum include separating children from their parents, extensive detentions in overcrowded, inhumane conditions, judicial backlogs and slowdowns, and changes in the rules defining asylum. As human-rights activists have argued, the urban conditions in Central America forcing such immigrants to flee for their lives often have their roots in US carceral and immigration policies. Trump's frequent references to "criminal gangs," such as MS-13, during his political rallies fail to acknowledge that MS-13 originated as an urban gang in Los Angeles and then in US prisons where gang members were sentenced before being deported. The export of US urban gang violence to Central American cities is well known, and immigrants' appeals for political asylum has considerable legal standing.

Like the Trump administration, the George W. Bush and Barack Obama administrations pursued foreign policies that alienated Central American governments from their people by aligning those governments with the US pursuit of its "War on Drugs" of the 1980s. Often deploying US military and other foreign aid primarily in pursuit of the larger drug cartels, as well as appropriating such funds for their own personal uses, political leaders in Panama, Honduras, El Salvador, Costa Rica, and Nicaragua neglected poor residents in both the countryside and the cities, allowing local gangs to take control as Central American governments pursued, often half-heartedly, organized transnational drug cartels whose operations ranged from Colombia through Central America and Mexico to the United States.

Consequently, many Central American cities in the past twenty-five years have become ungovernable, divided into poor neighborhoods controlled by gangs and rich enclaves protected by armed militias. From the outside, such cities appear to represent the worst excesses of "banana republics" run by corrupt dictators or revolutionaries. Mejía points out in his memoir that after the Sandinistas overthrew the Somoza regime, many Sandinistas "became multimillionaires" profiting from Nicaragua's "new economy."[7] The "Drug Wars" initiated by the Reagan administration provide a convenient cover story for US aid to friendly, anti-Socialist regimes in the region. Like the "war on gangs" in the United States, the "war on drugs" in Mexico and Central America has become a self-defeating prophecy, in which drug cartels have become even more powerful, transnational in scope, and militarized. In 2018, the number of murders in Mexico attributable to the drug wars is the highest in the last decade, and the continuing erosion of civil society in Panama, Honduras, Guatemala, El Salvador, and Nicaragua is attributable at least in part to the US-led militarization of the region in the interest of suppressing the drug trade.[8]

US neoimperial policies have not only destabilized cities in Central America, Mexico, Iraq, and Afghanistan; such foreign policies and military occupations have also had profound effects on US cities. Mejía takes little notice of these negative consequences on Baltimore, Miami, New York, and Boston, despite his participation in their antiwar undergrounds. Yet, the returns of hundreds of thousands of military personnel from long-term military operations in the Middle East and Afghanistan have had devastating effects on many communities, especially those closely tied to large military bases. Elsewhere I have discussed how post-9/11 US cultural representations of these neocolonial wars have tended to nationalize the international, restaging foreign political and military crises, especially terrorist acts, in US domestic contexts.[9] A variation on this theme is the representation of returning veterans and their failures to readjust as a consequence of physical injuries and psychological traumas, including posttraumatic stress disorder (PTSD).

Jason Hall wrote the script for Clint Eastwood's *American Sniper* (Clint Eastwood, 2014), a film that fits this argument about the US cultural trend to domesticate international conflicts in the post-9/11 era. Although much of the film's action takes place in Iraq, the psychological focus is on Chris Kyle (Bradley Cooper) growing up and returning to Texas from his numerous tours of duty during which he achieves the record of US military "kills" of the enemy at 225. Kyle first learns his skills with a rifle hunting deer with his father, and he was killed at a shooting range by a troubled veteran he was attempting to help. The film makes no argument for gun control in the United States, emphasizing how Kyle's tragic death at home is a consequence of another veteran's instability, not the failure to control weapons in civil society. After all, hunting and target shooting are legitimate sports in the film; PTSD is the problem we have not addressed adequately. Although Kyle suffers from some combat trauma, he seeks and obtains help, even if the advice of his military psychiatrist to help other veterans ends up contributing to his death. In the final scene of the film, Kyle's funeral procession is met by hundreds of citizens lining the highway to honor his military heroism. Nominated for six Oscars and winning one for sound editing at the 2015

Academy Awards, *American Sniper* was a box-office hit, earning $350 million in 2014, the highest gross earnings of any film released that year.

Three years later, Jason Hall would have his directorial debut with *Thank You for Your Service* (2017), a film that takes seriously the consequences of traumatic brain injuries and PTSD not only for military veterans but for the cities and military bases they inhabit. The film is based on *Washington Post* reporter David Fink's 2013 nonfiction book of the same title about three soldiers of the Second Battalion, Sixteenth Infantry Regiment, returning in 2007 to Fort Riley and Topeka, Kansas after a fifteen-month deployment in Iraq. The book and film tell the stories of Staff Sergeant Adam Schumann, Tausolo "Solo" Aeiti, and Billy Waller. The three soldiers share the general trauma of combat as well as a specific event for which two of them feel personally responsible: the combat death of Sergeant First Class James Doster. In many respects, the film is a conventional "coming-home" war movie of the post–Vietnam War era, familiar for its treatment of how veterans are not understood by civilians and deal with their alienation by refusing to talk about their traumatic experiences in combat, except among themselves.

Badgered by Doster's wife, Amanda (Amy Shumer), who demands to know how her husband died, Adam Schumann (Miles Teller) refuses to tell her the true story until close to the end of the film. The film opens with a combat episode in a suburb of Baghdad, near the soldiers' base at Rustamiyah, the venerable Iraqi military academy turned into US military outpost. Schumann directs their convoy of Humvees on an alternate route to avoid anticipated IEDs, but they drive instead into a snipers' ambush. Taking cover in an abandoned, war-torn building, the soldiers take up positions on the rooftop to return fire when Michael Emory (Scott Haze) is shot in the head. As Schumann struggles to carry the wounded Emory down the stairs, he drops him, further injuring him. The combat scene is typical of post-Vietnam War movies, from its setting amid urban ruins, the chaos of combat in the middle of civilian life, and the general aura of US soldiers fighting invisible insurgents in foreign settings. Although the war films of this era often treat inevitable mistakes made by US military personnel in the fog of war, *Thank You for Your Service* bases its Iraqi combat episodes on a series of errors made by multiple soldiers, which coincide to produce wide-ranging consequences back home in Kansas.

Near the end of the film, Schumann tells Amy Doster the story of how her husband recognized Schumann's trauma for having dropped the wounded Michael Emory and insisted on taking Schumann's place on the next patrol. When their Humvee is struck by an IED, Solo saves everyone in the vehicle, except for Doster, who is burned fatally. Schumann's job on such patrols was to identify IEDs, which is what Doster fails to do. All three soldiers share some of the responsibility for Doster's death: Schumann for not going on the patrol; Doster for lacking Schumann's skills at identifying IEDs; Solo for forgetting Doster was in the vehicle. As it turns out back in Kansas, Solo is suffering from a traumatic brain injury, which has "scrambled" his brains, causing him to forget important details. No individual is exclusively responsible for Doster's death, of course, but the two surviving soldiers feel profound guilt for its occurrence.

In cinematic terms, the two battle scenes in Baghdad frame the entire film, suggesting that Topeka and Fort Riley are contained within the military destruction of the Second Gulf War. On the surface, civil life in Kansas seems largely unchanged by the war, but small touches from the beginning of the film suggest how both Topeka and Fort Riley have been affected. On their drive home from the veterans' welcome at the airport, Schumann and his wife, Saskia (Haley Bennett), and their two children drive past their former home, now rented, which they lost in a foreclosure. Although Saskia breezily blames their financial problems on a pool Adam added to the house, it is clear that his military service has affected their earning power back home. Their more modest rental home is a source of humiliation to Adam, who plans to buy back their lost home, and even sneaks out at night to water its neglected lawn.

Billy Waller returns to his house to find that his fiancée, Tracey (Erin Darke), has moved out, taking with her all the furniture, shutting off the utilities, and leaving him only his dress military uniform. Consoled by Adam and Solo, Billy spends a night on Adam and Saskia's living-room sofa, but is gone the next morning, leaving behind neatly folded bedding. Having announced that he has "got to make some money," Billy next appears putting his service revolver in his waistband as he gets out of his car in front of the Bank of Topeka. Expecting Billy to rob the bank, viewers are surprised when he confronts Tracey, one of the tellers, who insists that their relationship is "over," even threatening to call security if Billy does not leave. Pulling out his revolver, Billy shoots himself in the head in front of Tracey. In the next scene, we see EMTs removing his body to a waiting ambulance.

Veterans' financial and psychological problems do not shatter the quotidian realities of Topeka or even compare with the destruction of war-torn Baghdad, but they do suggest that years of foreign wars have changed US cities, especially those close to, and economically dependent on, large military bases. These social, economic, and psychological realities become clearer as Adam and Solo decide to seek help from the Department of Veterans Affairs (VA) in Topeka. The Topeka VA is located in a large, modern government building whose cleanliness and tidy landscaping belie what the two veterans find inside the waiting room. The enormous room is crowded with several hundred veterans watching the digital number display for their turns, in the meantime tending prosthetic limbs, emptying medical bags of urine, and otherwise displaying the physical consequences of warfare. The scenes embody in graphic ways frequent news stories about overcrowding and long delays for medical and psychological treatment by the VA. Panning shots of the VA waiting room give viewers the impression not only of the large numbers of veterans involved but also of a battlefield littered with wounded.

Just as in Camilo Mejía's memoir, the film shows how problems with the military bureaucracy prevent these veterans from getting the attention and justice they deserve. Because Solo cannot document the fact his brain injury was the result of combat, he is sent to Fort Riley to request a letter from a commanding officer. Both Adam and Solo are also given long questionnaires to complete, full of questions that often provoke traumatic memories and flashbacks or seem irrelevant to the help they are requesting. Several earnest officials at the VA confirm the long delays for psychological counseling and medical treatment. Commanding officers at Fort Riley seem more interested in protecting their reputations and careers than in helping the veterans they commanded. Without job skills to qualify them for civilian jobs, both Adam and Solo struggle to readjust to life at home. Adam wants to get his job back as a greenskeeper at the local golf course, and Solo wants to reenlist for another tour in Iraq. Adam's wife, Saskia, makes it clear that Adam's former job is "for a boy," not someone who led twelve men in battle, and that it would not pay enough for them to survive. Solo is rejected in his effort to reenlist, because of his brain injury, despite the fact that the Army cannot confirm that his injury is a consequence of his military service.

Such bureaucratic Catch-22s are typical of the "coming-home" war film in the post-Vietnam era, but *Thank You for Your Service* argues that such problems affect not only veterans and their immediate families, but have consequences for broader civilian lives. Long after John Sayles emphasized in *Lone Star* (1996) how racial minorities enter US military service because they have few other options, Hall's film shows the legacy of racial discrimination in the military in the criminal underworld of Topeka.[10] Tausolo "Solo" Aeiti is an American Samoan, and he is asked by an officer at Fort

Riley, "American Samoa, where's that?" and "Are Samoans even citizens?" Solo answers patiently that he was able to apply for US citizenship after completing basic training, but this exchange and Solo's role in the film remind us of the many American Samoans, Chamorros from Guam, and other residents of US territories in the Pacific who enlist in the US military. American Samoa is an unincorporated territory of the United States, and people born on the island are "nationals," not "citizens."[11] American Samoans and Chamorros have among the highest percentage by population of US military service of any demographic group, in large part because both American Samoa and Guam house large US naval bases.

Solo's role in the film and David Fink's book reminds us that US long-term wars in the Middle East and Afghanistan have had consequences that reach far beyond their regions and even the continental United States to include the US Pacific. In the film, Solo is often identified as an African American, reinforcing the systemic racism in the United States. Having failed to obtain satisfactory medical treatment for his "scrambled brains," including flashbacks that lead to violent episodes at home with his pregnant wife, Alea (Keisha Castle-Hughes), Solo looks for the drug ecstasy in the criminal underworld of Topeka. Although known as a party drug, ecstasy has therapeutic effects for traumatic brain injuries like Solo's. His quest for the drug leads him to the African American drug dealer, Dante (Omar J. Dorsey), a veteran of the First Gulf War, in 1991, who knows how little Solo can expect from the VA. Dante's cynicism about the US military and its use of people of color to fight its wars against other people of color is conventional for the post–Vietnam War film. Nevertheless, it helps Dante establish a bond with the disillusioned and medically desperate Solo, who soon agrees to serve as a runner for Dante in exchange for the drug.

As it turns out, Solo is delivering weapons not drugs to one of Dante's customers. Called urgently to the hospital to visit Alea during her delivery of their son, then rushing late to the meeting point for the delivery of the military-style weapons, Solo gets lost, his traumatic brain injury contributing to his confusion in the unfamiliar world of criminal arms deals. Dante has warned Solo of the importance of being on time; when Solo misses the delivery time, Dante and his gang members seek to kill him in punishment for the botched deal. The film's climactic scenes revolve around Solo trying to hide from Dante and his gang, who shoot at him in the dark, rainy parking lot of a mall. Suggesting nightmare versions of daylight battles in Iraq, these urban action scenes represent how the war has come home as social, economic, racial, gender/sexual, and colonial problems the United States has failed to address.[12]

Thank You for Your Service transforms the "coming home" theme and the domestication of international issues in the era of the Iraq-Afghanistan wars in related, interesting ways. Popular television series like *24* and *Homeland* treated global terrorism as a US domestic issue, rationalizing foreign military exploits as legitimate defenses of national security. Of course, no national security interest has been served by either the two invasions of Iraq or the continuing occupation of Afghanistan. Neither Afghanistan nor Iraq ever had the capability to strike the US nation in any military way that would threaten its domestic security. On the other hand, the nation's wars in the Middle East since 1991 – more than a quarter of a century of warfare – and US military presence in Afghanistan since 2001 – the longest continuous war in US history – have certainly destabilized the US nation. Although these long-term consequences are often discussed, they are treated most often in relation to the federal government, specifically the Departments of State and Defense. The real, lasting, negative consequences are local, dispersed throughout the United States in ways often difficult to trace and understand.

In cities and towns across the United States, police departments are increasingly militarized, often with war surplus vehicles and armaments decommissioned from use in foreign wars. Systemic racism and economic inequalities have grown as the United States has focused so much of its attention on foreign conflicts in which it must devote significant military personnel and resources. Urban cores have crumbled further since dein-dustrialization as a consequence of the 2008 financial crisis or "Great Recession," causing veterans to return home to impossible economic conditions. The news cycle is full of stories and images about "ruined" cities like Detroit, Pittsburgh, and Buffalo, some of which are making today miraculous economic recoveries. Less attention is paid to those cities like Topeka, operating in the shadow of large military bases, like Fort Riley, Kansas, and enduring the social, economic, and personal conse-quences of returning veterans trying to adapt to an urban world of the past.

Cities remain, then, indices of national coherence or dysfunction, much as they were once studied by traditional American studies scholars as central to the discipline. Yet the conditions shaping these cities, contribut-ing to their failures to enable their citizens simply to live productive, healthy lives have changed dramatically with the ongoing militarism of US society. Today more than ever, the US city is a war zone, only superficially different from the ruined cities of Baghdad, al Ramadi, Fallujah, and Managua that Americans see on the news and consider distant from and alien to them. The United States have not only occupied them; they are its new, terrifying neighborhoods.

Notes

1. Lewis Mumford's work in the 1930s and 1940s on the city is foundational to American Studies as a discipline, as represented well by his tetralogy – *Technics and Civilization* (1934), *The Culture of Cities* (1938), *The Condition of Man* (1944), and *The Conduct of Life* (1941) – and *The City in History* (1961). Post–World War II scholarship on the city, such as James L. Machor's *Pastoral Cities: Urban Ideals and the Symbolic Landscape of America* (Madison: University of Wisconsin Press, 1987), Kevin R. McNamara's *Urban Verbs: Arts and Discourses of American Cities* (Palo Alto, CA: Stanford University Press, 1996), and Justin T. Clark's *The City of Second Sight: Nineteenth-Century Boston and the Making of American Visual Culture* (Chapel Hill: University of North Carolina Press, 2018), has extended this work on the American city as central to the field.

2. Paul Jay, *Global Matters: The Transnational Turn in Literary Studies* (Ithaca, NY: Cornell University Press, 2010), pp. 1–5.

3. Camilo Mejía, *Road from ar Ramadi: The Private Rebellion of Staff Sergeant Camilo Mejía* (New York: New Press, 2007), p. 298. The correct name of the city is "al Ramadi," but the publisher notes on the copyright page that "ar Ramadi was chosen over the more properly transliterated al Ramadi in order to emphasize the proper pronunciation."

4. Ibid., p. 240.

5. Ibid., p. 6.

6. Arianna E. Vigil, *War Echoes* (New Brunswick, NJ: Rutgers University Press, 2014), p. 5.

7. Mejía, p. 12.

8. Nicola Chávez Courtright, "Green for Blue in the Mexican Security State," *NACLA* [North American Congress on Latin America], February 15, 2018, http://nacla.org/news/2018/02/15/green-blue-mexican-security-state.

9. John Carlos Rowe, *The Cultural Politics of the New American Studies* (Ann Arbor: Open Humanities Press, 2012), pp. 105–30.

10. John Sayles, *Lone Star* (Castle Rock Entertainment, 1996). *Thank You for Your Service* is full of allusions to Vietnam War films, including Hal Ashby's *Coming Home* (1978), Michael Cimino's *The Deer Hunter* (1978), and Oliver Stone's *Platoon* (1986). Hall's frequent references to these films seems to underscore what I have termed the "Vietnam Effect" in the cultural representations of the Iraq and Afghanistan wars in Rowe, *The Cultural Politics of the New American Studies*, pp. 51–77.

11. For a fuller discussion of the neocolonial relationship of US "unincorporated territories" to the US nation, see Rowe, "'Shades of Paradise': Craig Santos Perez's Transpacific Voyages," in Brian Roberts and Michelle Stephens, eds., *Archipelagic American Studies* (Durham, NC: Duke University Press, 2017), pp. 213–31.

12. See Rowe, *The New American Studies* (Minneapolis: University of Minnesota Press, 2002), pp. 173–93.

CHAPTER 9

The Poetics of Rims
New Orleans

Ruth Salvaggio

Cities on the rims of great oceans and seas and gulfs of water. Historic port cities. Cities of exile and refuge. Global market cities where big bucks are made from international trade. Cities of toxic waters and trash piles of plastics. Cities of enslaved laborers, curious migrants, desperate immigrants, natives and strangers and strangers who beget natives. Cities increasingly rimmed in by water. Cities infused with water, cities that need, fear, and desire water all at once. Cities on the verge of submersion, on the verge of a nervous breakdown. And one city in particular, nested in an alluvial bowl, that "rises on a shot of sloe gin," whose music and lyric voice mix a certain sweetness with its waters of sorrow and "honeys yet this cup of woe."[1]

Situated along an edge of water, rim cities are typically defined by a crossing of cultures – variously tumultuous, festive, and troubled – at the intersections of shared regional geographies. Consider the more famous North American examples of Los Angeles and its "geopolitical preeminence via-á-vis the Pacific Rim and Mesoamerica," or Miami's location on the strategic edge of the Caribbean.[2] On such sites, both cities have emerged as centers of multicultural convergence, especially during their economic expansions in the late nineteenth and twentieth centuries. At the core of such geopolitical placement are the dynamics of trade and tariffs, imports, exports, the calculation of tonnage and the gleaning of profits. Yet it is water that inevitably facilitates convergence in rim cities, especially those that claim great port status. New Orleans is positioned prominently here. The Port of South Louisiana is the largest port by volume of trade exchange in the Western Hemisphere and the largest bulk cargo port in the world. Before being claimed by the French in 1718, indigenous people lived and traded along its Mississippi River levees. Today, three centuries later, you can watch massive ocean liners and strings of barges glide on the murky river waters between these levees. You can walk sections of its two miles of docks – the longest wharf area on the globe. Profits from the trade in oil and petrochemicals alone are staggering, even as they are shipped into the hands of oil barons and wealthy financiers. And there are also the major products of coffee and metals and natural rubber to be unloaded at its docks. Global investment firms are amok in money made here from the export of plastic resins, as if hydrocarbon man set up his doomsday kingdom along the river.

Yet in this watery city, old shotgun houses lean uneasily to one side or another – at least in neighborhoods where gentrification has yet to straighten them out. Its poorest people hardly reap the monetary benefits of a great port city, most working in a plethora of jobs that support fun-loving tourism. Older than and unlike most modern US rim cities, New Orleans remains impoverished. Three colonial powers – France, Spain, and the United States – loom over the multilingual and multicultural confluence that has shaped the city's culture: a history of indigenous deltaic peoples, enslaved Africans and free people of color, and waves upon waves of migrants from the Caribbean and Atlantic rims and beyond, most seeking refuge from their own troubled homes – San Domingue and postrevolutionary Haiti, Sicily, Ireland, Canary Islands, Central America, Vietnam, Mexico, to name only some of the most prominent. Multilingual from the start, people called the eighteenth-century city a modern Babylon. Today it remains culturally saturated with diverse people and languages. Secondary to English, Spanish has replaced the once dominant French language and its Creole fusions, while the New Orleans brogue has expanded its intonations to include East Indian and Vietnamese sounds, with African and indigenous chants still heard in ritual street performance.

The very concept of the city as a rim – one situated on and also within rims of water, calls out for understanding its cultural melding as insepar-able from its saturated topography. Water, of course, has always served as a driving force in both ecology and human culture. But in our own age of global warming, apprehending the mutual embeddedness of human bodies and bodies of water within a shared hydrosphere becomes a vital undertak-ing. Our bodies are mainly composed of water, fluid pumping through our veins as within rivers and watersheds, liquid facilitating how we swallow and speak, infusing our intestinal and neurological geographies. And our shared wet geographies mark our mutual fate. Surrounded by swamps and wetlands that are fast dissolving, New Orleans now sits precariously on the edge, or edges, of the Gulf of Mexico as its waters consume the deltas in lower Louisiana. Shouldered by saltwater lakes, sliced through by natural bayous and man-made canals, and cupped in by a huge crescent curve in the Mississippi River, the city forms a hydrosphere all its own – a cup that at once seems to beckon everyone down for a drink, but also a "cup of woe" as the recurring sorrows of hurricanes and surges and tropical rains and the intense warming of Gulf waters take their toll. This cup rims the city, often described as a bowl, one that is sinking more and more every day.

It is precisely here, at the intersection of human and hydraulic forces, that poems offer a means to navigate troubled yet metamorphic waters. I want to suggest that New Orleans – the US city most likely to go under, sooner rather than later, in our times of climate crisis – also calls out to be understood, read, and heard as poetic ecosphere. In its poems and in poems about the city, we encounter saturated, tangible images, the wave-like rhythms of jazz and the myriad musical forms from which this lyrical calling has emerged within the Afro-Caribbean rim, and a buzzing convergence of human vocalization, animal sounds, botanical profusion, and environmental wetness. The city's poetry seems always a tenuous, damp embrace. *Everything is in touch.*

Poems allow us to enter this rim, this embrace that can be variously enticing, soothing, and scary. Poems also inform a paradoxical poetics because desire drives everything here – ecology, economy, erotics. *Everything wants.* Desire shapes watery stirrings that are manifold, and that unfold well beyond "the name of that rattle-trap streetcar that bangs through the Quarter," as Blanche DuBois brashly described its meanderings in Tennessee Williams's *A Streetcar Named Desire* (1947).[3] But there may be some logic to Williams setting his play by the city's river wharves on Elysian Fields Avenue, echoing Plutarch's description of the Elysian Fields as islands floating on water. Dig only a few feet in most areas of the city and you will hit water. The city practically floats on water. Water moves everything here – boats and barges, bodies and passions. A poetics of place emerges in the city as a moist, damp haunt that is itself a desired abode, and is haunted by myriad currents and subtle undercurrents. In my own writings on the city and its poetry, writings that were themselves urged on by the floodwaters of Katrina, I have turned to ancient concepts of *eros* – the desire for someone or something missing, and to contemporary accounts of longing – as in jazz musician Sidney Bechet's notion of a "long song," "something you gotta hear starting way behind you," to describe the complex vigor of desire as it links past and present, and keeps fixing a beat to our passions.[4]

Desire here, especially within the specific circumference of modern empire, flows within water, joining the haunts of such lyrical traditions as the Portuguese Fado steeped in the waters of seafaring, or African

American blues immersed in the flow of the Mississippi River – or the kinds of longing for place that are captured in the Spanish word *querencia* – from the Latin root *to want*.[5] Because longing in New Orleans possesses and is possessed by a long history yet a decidedly uncertain future, the imaginative and metamorphic work of poetry calls out to be taken dead seriously. Poems here are not simply packed with rhythms and images, but become reservoirs for the currents of desire and imagination. Imagining the city as a desire-infused haunt may not promise salvation from submersion. But it arouses. Even in this sinking rim of a city, even amid all the damage that has and continues to be wrought, one never quite knows the fate of desire.

Not far from Elysian Fields Avenue, we enter such a haunt in a bar, and in a poem. Here, on Decatur Street in the French Quarter, Katherine Soniat builds her poem on especially intense sensory, tangible, water-infused images that culminate with a question about the sea. It is at once a poem and a bar and a haunt filled with desire, a place that allows us to sip slowly on the question of what the sea means, to feel and smell the humid night air and sour breath, to encounter the sailors arriving at the dock and the women who wait here to serve them. Here,

> . . . bars exude a sorry music,
> so homesick it drags the fog
> for Greeks,
> draws them to the late-faced women,
> lips fluent with ouzo, bouzouke [. . .]

Through the bar's window, we encounter "a woman with a swollen arm" who waves in the sailors, and a place where everyone becomes fused in fog and fluent lips – "all the exiled loose in a broth of fast and glut, / of garlic and magnolia mixed in the same sour breath." A neon sign, hanging above the bar, shows ancient Greek columns toppling as the "blue sky of Plato hangs adrift / in a city that rises on a shot of sloe gin." As we descend from Plato's blue sky, we encounter Greek sailors roaming Decatur Street, their "pockets full from the sea, / heavy with what the sea comes to mean."[6]

In one sense, this poem relates a story as old as Odysseus and his sailors as they pass the haunting, seductive song of the Sirens. But something is different here. Instead of some epic tale about a hero ultimately resisting the forces of seduction, everything here seems fused, "all the exiled" caught up in the same "sour breath." Having surrendered Plato's blue sky for the dingy bar, the poem wants to know what the sea means, and what the sea can come to mean. It *wants* us to ask the question. Its images and metaphors, its fog and swollen reach, are at once infused with desire and desire something of us.

On foggy Decatur Street, we are dragged into the "sorry music" that the Acropolis Bar exudes, and into a poem, caught up in some question about the sea's meaning. Entering the bar, we become "homesick" for a place where sirens do not beckon some epic hero beyond his quests. This city is the remaining evidence and damage of those quests – all the trade and traffic, exports and imports and labor and longing. The poem stirs us to ponder a question about the meanings of the sea – here in the city and on a shot of sloe gin that remains inseparable from sunrise and all that the day opens to.

What the sea "comes to mean" therefore remains an open question, and a port of entry into poems that we are urged to enter in this rim city as one might enter a place, an ecosphere. Within such haunts, we continue to encounter women who inhabit the vortex of desire. Contemporary poet Sybil Kein casts her as the Yoruban deity Erzuli. Her poem unwinds through a sea-like metamorphosis of the female deity and a human woman, making her way to the port, her haunt on the rims of cities throughout the Caribbean and Gulf waters:

> She is singing as she glides towards the azure port,
> past all sorrow, past the weeping willow;
> she is walking on stepping-stones of green moss
> towards the sea, towards the sea.[7]

The meaning of the sea here is part and parcel of the material waters of the "azure port" itself – the gliding female body, the "stepping-stones of green moss," the beckoning "sea." Yet these are hardly the waters of seduction and repression. As if stepping out of the Acropolis Bar on Decatur Street, this woman "glides" directly toward port and rim, "past all sorrow" and "towards the sea." Here, she undergoes metamorphosis yet again, emerging under the name Ezili:

> Ezili,
> Her bare feet on heated ground
> make a whispering sound
> which joins the soft wind,
> which joins the soft wind.
>
> She is carrying the moon, carrying the moon
> to dip it in the sea, in the silken sea.
> For the old women of the village, she is singing,
> To heal; to heal.
> Ezili.[8]

The "same sour breath" circulating in the Acropolis Bar now becomes transformed into "a whispering sound," a "soft wind" – and calls out to be heard well beyond the poem, perhaps reaching those "late-faced women" waiting for the sailors at the Acropolis Bar. As Ezili carries the moon, "to dip it in the sea, in the silken sea," the poem itself indulges a dramatic leap, from ground to sky to sea, joining all three in "silken" waters. No one is fearing seduction as submersion. The waters here are infused with moonlight, serene and silken. The "old women of the village" are calmed. The sea absorbs the moon as readily as it absorbs the sound of bare feet on heated ground, and the sound of soft wind. Everything becomes infused with and immersed within the rim of a poetic ecosphere. And precisely here, within the poem, there is healing. There is a silken healing for something the old women are old enough to remember – maybe too many proverbial nights at an Acropolis Bar, or three centuries of sexual ravishment.

What the sea can come to mean becomes saturated in a poem where everything in its abundant ecology – ground, wind, sea, moon, sound – comingles, and where we are urged to find meanings within this haunt. Such a dense poetic haunt has long flourished in New Orleans, on and within its rims, fed by water, water everywhere. The "whispering sound" in Kein's poem echoes the omnipresence of water, where sound resonates and enfolds all that reside in its auditory sphere. A jazz musician once claimed that the river and its curve carry the circulations of sound in the city. Within this crescent, a trumpet played in one part of town can often be heard far off in another. Louis Armstrong famously described this aural ecosphere: "Yeah, music all around you."[9] Poems emerge on the river's mouth and from its echoing sounds. The "heated ground" is made up of sediment-rich alluvial deposits that have formed the deltas on which the city sits, and that nourish its willows and green moss. The Gulf, which ultimately absorbs the river, remains inseparable from the river waters, its load of sediment, the rains, the humidity of the city's ecology. Nor can it be separated from the city's poetry, the very language that absorbs sounds and messages. This rim city becomes a saturated port of call, and a call for healing.

The very concept of Creole itself nods to the importance of such fluid edges, and unfolds not so much as a mixture of distinctive races, ethnicities, languages, sounds, but a melding and comingling. In language, Creole imbues words with sounds elided and transformed from distinct and dominant languages, producing what some have called a soft, melodious poetics. Lafcadio Hearn claimed that the Creole sounds he heard in the city were "Frenchy in construction" but African in "intonation."[10] More recently, critic Wai Chi Dimock suggests that the fusion of languages instigated by

Creole link us with our "prehistories and pregeographies," and describes this confluence of languages as "oceanic and drifting" rather than "land-based, patrilinear, and clannish."[11] Dipping into and mingling with "pregeographies," Creole can also be understood as the melding, over time, of physical matter and lifeforms that shape both an ecology and an ecopoetics – water, moss, wind, trees, fog, sediment. Caribbean poet Édouard Glissant describes a "poetics of relation" that derives from the Caribbean Sea and its arc of islands, a poetics embedded in water, land, and history, and layered through a process of "sedimentation" linking people over time.[12] In New Orleans, its alluvial landmass the very product of centuries of Mississippi River sedimentation, such a poetics of relation would also become creolized, a poetic hydrosphere saturated with the comingling of people, dampness, tropical growth and tropical storms, incessant rainwaters, hurricanes and floods, and the wave-like rhythms of sound.

Going back three centuries in the city's literary history, we encounter some especially intriguing and elusive lyrics that might well account for the long legacy of such a poetic ecosphere in the city. George Washington Cable described them as simply words in "some African tongue" in his essay "Creole Slave Songs."[13] He printed them as follows:

> Day zab, day zab, day koo-noo wi wi,
> Day zab, day zab, day koo-noo-wi wi,
> Koo-noo wi wi wi wi,
> Koo-noo wi wi wi wi,
> Koo-noo wi wi wi mom-zah ......
> Mom-zah, mom-zah, mom-zah, mom-zah,
> Ro-zah, ro-zah, ro-zah a-a mom-zah.[14]

But he was unsure of their meaning. Cable claims that he consulted "the negroes themselves" for an explanation, and that they related this translation: "Out from under the trees our boat moves into the open water – bring us large game and small game!" Historian Gwendolyn Midlo Hall writes that these words were possibly part of "a ritual to control the *nyama* from the slain animals," given that the Bambara, the largest group of Africans who arrived in the city during the early years of the French slave trade, believed that plants and animals and humans possess souls, as she explains, "a belief that probably derives from their descent from Moussa Koroni, the first woman, who gave birth to all forms of life."[15] Hall's extraordinary insight into the Africanized culture of the early city helps inform the equally extraordinary origins and legacy of the city's poetic ecosphere – its trees and open waters, its ritual poetic calls to animals who possess souls, the comingling of human and animal sounds in rhythmic repetition, the interweaving of lifeforms – human, animal, botanical, watery – through which everything thrives. Here, where all descends from a first woman, we have abandoned "patrilinear" languages and cultures, and are "drifting" within open waters and their incantations.

And here, the meaning of the sea also drifts through the Acropolis Bar on Decatur Street, because we can never quite leave behind the "late-faced women" who stir on questions about the sea – and because what the sea can come to mean is suspended in alluvium and over three centuries of modern empire's wreckage. Meaning is not an answer. It may circle within waters where fish and animals possess souls, where boats glide on bayous that nourish humans, reptiles, the very sounds of song itself. Meaning may arise from a sea infused with the moon, carried to its waters by a Yoruban deity, carried also to old women, and for healing some sorrow that they carry with them. Meaning may descend from the transformed "sorry music" in a bar on a foggy street near the river. What the sea means may be carried by a "long song" that today remains inseparable from the songs of slaves who long ago sang on the river and waterways: "you gotta hear it starting way behind you." And you have got to give it a hearing – as in a court of poetic justice – if there is ever to be any healing.

What the sea means may also rise from a sea turtle in an old Creole lullaby, "Gae, Gae Soulangae." To give this lyrical poem a hearing, we must also go back in time and sweep a dreamlike path in the fog, in the night. This song poem is dateless because it seems to be deeply sedimented in time for as long as any of its singers can remember. As one woman who passed on this lullaby said, she heard such songs sung on plantations throughout New Orleans and Louisiana, where they "had always existed." She cites the elderly African woman who sung these songs, who explained that "her mother's mother had taught them to her as she had been taught before."[16] Here is the first stanza of three, each asking that we "listen" to the message of a certain animal: a tortoise, a crocodile, a wildcat – all creatures who inhabit a poetic ecosphere situated within a natural ecology. We encounter the lullaby here in English, translated by Mina Monroe from the African-French patios:

> Dreamland opens here, sweep the dream path clear!
> Listen, chile, listen well,
> What the tortoise may have to tell.[17]

Sybil Kein offers a slightly altered translation, maintaining the original language of the first line:

Gae, gae soulangae,
Sweep the road.
I tell her, yes,
I tell her,
The turtle knows how to talk,
The little turtle knows how to talk.[18]

The sea and its meanings become transformed yet again as we enter the haunt of dark wetlands. Within this poetic ecosphere, yet other rims emerge, embodied on the very sea turtle of this lullaby – the round, ovular shell, the creature of oceanic expanse, the sea turtle who survived past mass extinctions, the turtle whose shell once formed the ancient lyre, the same shell worn in Indian shaker dances, the long-lived turtle resembling the old women of the village, the turtle who appears in folktales and who looks up women's skirts to ponder the mysteries of sexuality and birth, the epochal turtle who comes back to life after having been beaten to death.[19] Turtle has a powerful message in this lullaby, a message about surviving all the beatings and abuses that have unfolded in this troubled historic rim. Again, the poem wants something of us. It wants us to listen to a turtle who has "something to tell," a creature of the sea who, in this lyric, hovers a thin line between waking consciousness and its metamorphic wanderings in sleep.

"Listen." We are drawn into the haunt of animals and messages, dream-like states of mind and body that proffer insights beyond reasoned conclusions. We are drawn into a poem that arouses within hazy spaces, and especially here, through messages delivered by creatures who *animate* – from the Latin, *anima*, feminine gender, meaning soul, spirit, breath, air, wind. Again, we desire meanings imbued in the sea where turtle swims, in layers of sedimentation where turtle burrows and survives great extinctions. The lullaby looks back to the waters of *De Zab, De Zab* and the *nyama* of animals. Yet it also looks forward, as if in prophetic insight, to Deepwater Horizon, when an oil well erupts in the depths of the Gulf, and sea turtles are among the oil-drenched carcasses left floating on its waters. Entering this all too real ecology – through a dateless poem and an environmental tragedy dated barely a decade ago – our talking turtle possesses some crucial messages to deliver about fossil fuels embedded in the Gulf's sedimentary deposits – deadly serious poetic messages about the atmospheric heat these extracted fuels are now generating, about extinctions that this talking turtle has survived and a great extinction unfolding in our own midst.

And that is why the women who pass on songs about talking turtles, or who wait for sailors in bars, or who carry the moon to the sea, urge us to ponder questions fueled by desire all along – something we want to know

about each other and our habitations, something beyond the rapacious
quests of the past and exploitive economies of the present. They ask that we
enter a comingled sea-like haunt of words and sounds, humans and
animals, moss and sediment and layered messages. Contemporary Creek
poet Joy Harjo, in her poem "New Orleans" (1983), embarks on such an
inquiry as she tries to uncover evidence her own Creek history in the city.
She discovers this evidence in the river bottom, where memory surfaces in
the very "delta" of her skin and blood. The waters that rim the city reside in
embodied memory, but are also comingled in mud. And here, in another
bar in the Quarter and within a wild leap of imagination, she sees the
colonizer De Soto having a drink and dancing with a woman whose skin is
"as gold as the river bottom."[20]

Don't we all want to have this drink within a dramatic collapse of history
on Bourbon Street. Because here, and maybe, too, in the nearby Acropolis
Bar, sipping on that shot of sloe gin, embedded memory surfaces. We hear
a beat, a dance rhythm, that rises and rouses from the past, from a tragic
mingling of water and mud and skin and blood – all metamorphosed in
a poem. Harjo's poem gets to the indecipherable bottom of things – the
alluvium with no firm bottom, the query that can never offer a full answer,
and the poem that keeps dragging us in and through the fog.

In her poem "Mother Catherine" (1986), New Orleans poet Brenda
Marie Osbey gives over her voice to a small, poor devotional figure, but also
a figure who steps out of history, as Osbey describes in her Glossary, "a
healer and saint of the Spiritual church of New Orleans." Written before
Katrina, yet ending with a glance to the flooded lower ninth ward after the
hurricane, Mother Catherine becomes spirit-refuge for her impoverished
followers, and like Ezili, she seeks to heal. The poem, like many of Osbey's
African chant-like poems, is long and complex. Yet in what remains for me
its most memorable stanza, we hear the voices of those who would have
Mother Catherine banished:

> carry off this woman
> this negress
> from this blessèd congress.
> . . . .
> we cannot have her followers
> forever banging at the gates of heaven crying for justice.[21]

Yet the poem desires a hearing. In the "quiet" and "hush" that follows this
outburst, Mother Catherine offers her final blessing – the blessing of water,
"and so you find me," she says,

they used to have me drawing up their holy water.
but now i am a common lavatrice.
i wash their robes.
and that is why
whenever it rains and thunders and pours there in the lower
      nine and floods the levees
my followers
those who remember me can be heard saying:
"it is mother catherine
washing the robes of the blessèd congress of saints
and showering down her blessings on her people."[22]

When the waters of the Industrial Canal – a thin chain linking the river to the lake and the Gulf – flooded this old neighborhood during Katrina, the blessings of this poor saint seemed stretched to their limit. What are the limits of water's floods and messages that the city's poetry keeps dragging us through?

Two nineteenth-century poets composed elegies that circulated within this question. Creole poet Camille Thierry – whose work appeared in *Les Cenelles*, the first African American literary anthology – offers a poem entitled simply "You" (1845), addressed to a child who died. Yet it seems almost to be calling out to the city now, as "You" becomes the "name" of something that lingers after death, a memory inseparable from what is gone:

> That name! It honeys yet this cup of woe
> That I, alas, drink dry.[23]

Near the end of that century, Léona Queyrouze pens her elegy, "For Magda" (1891), addressing a child who died and also, in another dramatic leap of poetic expression, recalling a group of innocent Italians murdered by a vigilante mob:

> Dashed hopes, reality, phantasmal quest –
> No more shall these feed on your sleeping heart;
> Nor will you sip life's goblet, woe-possessed. [. . .][24]

This cup and this goblet rim the poet's drink of sorrow and ouzo, sloe gin and holy water. They shape a vortex of waters that flow within the same poetic haunt where turtle swims, where women wait and sailors roam the fog, where animals possess spirits, and where a poor saint showers down her blessings. Like the rims of water on which New Orleans resides, they present perplexing questions about the sea that we *want to ponder*. What happens when everything that is in touch begins to dissolve? Can a poetics of desire cohere on and within such rims?

A century later, contemporary poet Gina Ferrara writes of the watery space "Where A Great Heron Wades."

> In this basin, this point beyond confluence,
> the earth indents and deepens like a baritone.

We are called back into the depths of a long song. Remarking on how "Wood drifts with gargantuan obsessions," she describes "a decade of desire," and

> what you always wanted,
> what is unintelligible and hushed,
> last night's indiscretion,
> the unreported and denied,
> sink into the concave
> giving source to what flows.[25]

A poetics of the rim, where some great heron wades, sustains here. Desire gives force to what flows. We are at once wading in a place – an indentation in the "earth," and called into a sinking, poetic "concave" of baritone sounds and gargantuan obsessions.

In our scary new century, we do not know what will continue to flow in New Orleans – in this city on a precarious rim, within its confluence of voices and cultures, sounds and sedimentation. The fate of this watery rim city remains a question that keeps circulating within poems. It is a question about longing beyond "a decade of desire" and forever steeped in "what you always wanted." Poems flow here as intractable currents and incomprehensible blessings. They *want us* to listen, they fuel a desire that takes us to the limits of loss and imagination, where the moon gets dipped into the sea or where bodies surface in the golden mud of the river. They want to know what talking turtles have to say in a lullaby or on the edge of extinction. They want to ask what the sea can come to mean in this old yet distinctly modern rim city where the rim is giving way, in a bar and in a "broth of fast and glut," before the day is done.

Notes

1. Katherine Soniat, "Toppled Columns, Blue Sky and Sea," in *Alluvial* (Lewisburg, PA: Bucknell University Press, 2001), p. 99; Camille Thierry, "You," in *Creole Echoes: The Francophone Poetry of Nineteenth-Century Louisiana*, trans. Norman R. Shapiro, intro. M. Lynn Weiss (Urbana: University of Illinois Press, 2004), p. 219.

2. See Vincent Brooks, *Land of Smoke and Mirrors: A Cultural History of Los Angeles* (New Brunswick, NJ: Rutgers University Press, 2013), p. 18, and Anthony Maingot, *Miami: A Cultural History* (Northampton, UK: Interlink Books, 2015). Brooks offers an insightful way to "read" Los Angeles as a "palimpsest," a city written into being and continually rewritten as if a script in the many Hollywood films he discusses.

3. Tennessee Williams, *A Streetcar Named Desire* (New York: New Directions, 2004), p. 81.

4. Ruth Salvaggio, *Hearing Sappho in New Orleans: The Call of Poetry from Congo Square to the Ninth Ward* (Baton Rouge: Louisiana State University Press, 2012), p. ix.

5. Sylvia Rodriguez, "History, Memory, and *Querencia*," in Barbara Mills and Severin Fowles, eds., *The Oxford Handbook of Southwest Archaeology* (New York: Oxford University Press, 2017), pp. 196–207, studies *Querencia* in terms of the complex workings of memory, imagination, and water, informing an emergent field of US Southwest studies that is also complexly relevant to the poetic intensities of New Orleans.

6. Soniat, "Toppled Columns, Blue Sky and Sea," p. 99.

7. Sybil Kein, *Gumbo People* (New Orleans: Margaret Media, 1999), p. 92. Kein presents the poem in four languages: French, Spanish, Haitian Creole, and English.

8. Ibid.

9. Louis Armstrong, "Growing Up in New Orleans," in John Miller and Genevieve Anderson, eds., *New Orleans Stories: Great Writers on the City* (San Francisco: Chronicle, 1922), p. 26.

10. See Henry Krehbiel, *Afro-American Folk Songs: A Study in Racial and National Music* (New York: Shirmer, 1914), pp. 133–35.

11. Wai Chee Dimock, *Through Other Continents: American Literature across Deep Time* (Princeton, NJ: Princeton University Press, 2006), pp. 144–45.

12. Édouard Glissant, *Poetics of Relation*, trans. Betsy Wing (Ann Arbor: University of Michigan Press, 1997), pp. 33–34.

13. George Washington Cable, "Creole Slave Songs," *Century Magazine*, February 1886, 823.

14. Ibid., pp. 827–28.

15. Gwendolyn Midlo Hall, *Africans in Colonial Louisiana: The Development of Afro-Creole Culture in the Eighteenth Century* (Baton Rouge: Louisiana State University Press, 1992), pp. 196–97.

16. Mina Monroe, *Bayou Ballads: Twelve Folk Songs from Louisiana* (New York: Shirmer, 1921), p. 6.

17. Ibid., p. 6.

18. Sybil Kein, ed., *Creole: The History and Legacy of Louisiana's Free People of Color* (Baton Rouge: Louisiana State University Press, 2000), p. 117.

19. Keith Cartwright, *Sacral Grooves, Limbo Gateways: Travels in Deep Southern Time, Circum-Caribbean Space, Afro-creole Authority* (Athens: University of

Georgia Press, 2013). Citations to the literary and folkloric messages of turtle run through Cartwright's study.

20. Joy Harjo, "New Orleans," in *How We Became Human: New and Selected Poems: 1975–2001* (New York: Norton, 2002), pp. 44, 46.

21. Brenda Marie Osbey, "Mother Catherine," in *All Saints: New and Selected Poems* (Baton Rouge: Louisiana State University Press, 1997), p. 83.

22. Ibid., pp. 83–84.

23. Thierry, "You," pp. 217–19.

24. Léona Queyrouze, "For Magda," in *Creole Echoes*, pp. 143–46.

25. Gina Ferrara, "Where a Great Heron Wades," in *Amber Porch Light* (Cincinnati, OH: CW Books, 2013), p. 17.

City Lives

CHAPTER 10

American Vertigo
The Metropolis and the New Biopolitical Order
William Boelhower[*]

It is a telling fact that not only artists and writers returning to New York City from "exile" in Paris or London in the threshold decades of the early twentieth century but also immigrants from eastern and southern Europe (above all, Russian Jews and southern Italians) arriving there in the same period reacted in remarkably similar ways to the brutal dynamism of the quintessential US metropolis. This somewhat astonishing and unacknowledged corroboration, which this chapter will document primarily through the genre of autobiographies and memoirs, offers concerted testimony to what was experienced as a major anthropological shift in the normative conditions of life peculiar to the American metropolis of 1900. Although there are certainly a host of factors contributing to this shift, the most conspicuous ones might be fruitfully convened under the metaphor of vertigo.[1] The rise of avant-garde movements in the arts, the critical formation of modernism as a radical break from earlier literary and artistic traditions, the unprecedented movement of people across the Atlantic, rapid urbanization, and the new technological and industrial regimes shaping metropolitan identity found their ideal manifestation in such big cities as Chicago and New York. There in particular, evidence of an emerging global capitalism and its new biopolitical accommodations (ethnic enclaves, neighborhood police, public schools, sanitation, housing plans, rent control, and immigration restriction laws) led American enthusiasts to announce the dawning of a new stage of civilization.

In 1907 Henry Adams pondered, "Images are not arguments, rarely even lead to proof, but the mind craves them."[2] While the dynamo led Adams to posit the need of a "dynamometer" to measure the effects of this new force on history, the poet Ezra Pound, after being exposed to the Italian Futurists, overhauled the age-old notion of the poetic image. Captivated

[*] I am grateful to Kevin McNamara for his superb editorial work and many suggestions.

by the same dynamic forces that stunned Adams, Pound wrote in 1914, "The image is not an idea. It is a radiant node or cluster [...] a VORTEX, from which, and through which, and into which, ideas are constantly rushing."[3] Indeed, New York City, the modern metropolis par excellence, had by 1900 become a civilizational epitome of James Clerk Maxwell's electromagnetic force-field, a vast grid-like vortex generating new forms of human exertion. "All New York was demanding new men, and all the new forces, condensed into corporations, were demanding a new type of man, – a man with ten times the endurance, energy, will and mind of the old type," Adams reckoned, adding further, "the city had the air and move-ment of hysteria. [...] Prosperity never before imagined, power never before wielded by man, speed never reached by anything but a meteor, had made the world irritable, nervous, querulous, unreasonable and afraid."[4]

The effects of New York's techno-industrial exuberance on its popula-tion (as both cause and issue of the city's biopolitical distress) converged in the anthropological crisis of vertigo.[5] The city's writers and artists repre-sented this crisis in dramatic and often belligerent ways, as they themselves embraced it, became unanchored by it, and ended up having to settle for Rimbaud's "*Je est un autre*" (I is somebody else).[6] Malcolm Cowley described his generation's sense of intersubjective alienation upon return-ing to New York from Paris in these terms: "Crowds, whistles, skidding taxicabs, all the discomforts of the city were a personal affront. In my uneasy sleep I trembled when a subway local passed underneath me, gathering speed as it left the Canal Street station." Such everlasting commotion chased his avant-garde group off to farms in Connecticut and New Jersey for a spell before they found the courage to return to a "subterranean life and began to rebel once again."[7]

One evening when Marsden Hartley and William Carlos Williams were waiting on the Erie Platform, "an express train roared by right before our faces," prompting Hartley to say, "That's what we all want to be, isn't it, Bill?" To which Williams cheerlessly replied, "Yes, I suppose so."[8] Perhaps they had Frederick Winslow Taylor's time-study method for improving the efficiency of industrial workers in the back of their mind. Impressed by Taylor's stopwatch measures, Henry Ford developed his infamous assem-bly line, by which the workers themselves were compelled to follow machinelike motions. In his *Quaderni del carcere* from the early 1930s, Antonio Gramsci mused that the new techniques developed by Taylor and Ford "[have] created a new and original psycho-technical condition." In Gramsci's opinion, Ford's assembly line produced "a new type of worker and man [...], a new psycho-physical connection [...], and muscular-nervous efficiency."[9] Although he had not read Henry Adams's *Education*, the Italian Marxist saw in this anthropological transfer the dawning of a new, specifically American civilization.

Earlier in his autobiography Williams recounted another New York happening that uses the *Stimmung* of vertigo to cast direct light on processual poems such as "Overture to a Dance of Locomotives" and "The Great Figure." About the latter he wrote:

> I heard a great clatter of bells and the roar of a fire engine passing the end of the street down North Avenue. I turned just in time to see a golden figure 5 on a red background flash by. The impression was so sudden and forceful that I took a piece of paper out of my pocket and wrote a short poem about it.

In his attempt to render the immediacy and clamor of this image-event, Williams, perhaps unwittingly, also illustrated Pound's definition of vorticism to perfection. The poem's chief purpose is to capture the flash and sequence of sound, color, and moving image: "it comes, it is there, and it vanishes. But I have seen it, clearly."[10] The poem reads rapidly, in one swift vertical sweep:

Among the rain
and lights
I saw the figure 5
in gold
on a red
firetruck
moving
tense
unheeded
to gong clangs
siren howls
and wheels rumbling
through the dark city.[11]

"The Great Figure" (1921) delivers a brute staccato perception of violent motion, perhaps calling into question "the very continuity of the [persona's] self."[12] Did the poet mean it to be a provocation, an example of Walter Benjamin's discussion of Baudelaire's poetics of urban shock?[13] There is no attempt here to surround the event with some mitigating comment, no effort by the persona to take over at the end. The words of the poem seem to function as a sort of nerve language, as if jotted down

reflexively rather than reflectively. But this is precisely the kind of stimula-
tion the big city has to offer. As the Swiss-French architect Le Corbusier
observed while riding the commuter train from New Haven to New York
City, "We are in a whirlwind, we are the whirlwind, we do not have good
judgment about anything that is outside of the whirlwind." His visit to the
United States led him to concur with the reckonings of Adams and
Gramsci. In a section titled "Fairy Catastrophe" in his memoir *When the
Cathedrals Were White* (1937 in French), Le Corbusier wrote, "New York is
an event of worldwide importance. I have called it the first place in the
world on the scale of the new times, the work yard of our era."[14]

Commenting on Manhattan's "intensely metropolitan character and
electrifying tempo," Matthew Josephson in his memoir *Life among the
Surrealists* (1962) recalled of his group of writers associated with the avant-
garde journal *Broom* (1921–24), "we ourselves, in effect, were being flung to
the machines."[15] Among these writers was Hart Crane, then in the throes of
composing his epic poem *The Bridge* (1930), in which he sought to extend
the symbol of the bridge across the continent. As Josephson pointed out,
Crane's poetics of ecstasy and synthesis is both willful and woeful: "We had
the effect of a few people firing off peashooters at the unbreakable plate
glass-and-steel facade of our civilization." Regarding himself Josephson
confessed, "In truth I was living my life as a schizoid personality."[16] Trying
to write poetry at night while working on Wall Street during the day led to
a breakdown. He clearly suffered from what T. S. Eliot, who endured
a similar fate while working at Lloyd's Bank, later diagnosed as a defining
malaise of the modern condition. As Josephson tried to hold down his job
and still fire his poetic pea shooter against New York's skyscrapers, he
experienced a split between thought and emotion, mind and sensation. In
short, he suffered from "a dissociated sensibility."[17]

Not all the returning exiles were unnerved by the city. Some were even
quickened by it. A representative figure of his generation, the millionaire
aesthete Harold Crosby declared, "I love New York, a madhouse full of
explosions with foghorns screaming out on the river and policemen with
shrill whistles to regulate traffic and the iron thunder of the Elevated and
green searchlights stabbing the night."[18] While Josephson and others
initially chose to withdraw from the city and cultivated a hyperaesthetic
stance, people such as Crosby and F. Scott Fitzgerald embraced it in search
of Dionysian sensations. Rather than suffering disconnection, they surrendered to the city's rhythms, dancing to jazz and drinking themselves silly.
Their unspoken wish was to achieve permanent wakefulness.[19] Quoting
Charles Olson on Projective poetics, William Carlos Williams found

a confirmation of his own urban vision: "get on with it, keep moving, keep in, speed, the nerves, their speed, the perceptions, theirs, the acts, the split-second acts, the whole business, keep it moving as fast as you can, citizen."[20]

As we might expect, the notion of vertigo has an allusive genealogy.[21] Long before this semantically rich label was used to designate the anthropological shift manifested in turn-of-the-century New York, medical doctors, philosophers, and scientists had labored over centuries to conjugate its psychological and biopolitical import. Erasmus Darwin in *Zoonomia or the Laws of Organic Life* (1794) was among the first to study the effects of drinking and dancing on people. In Section XXI of his book, "of Drunkenness," he noted:

> For though in the vertigo from intoxication the irritative ideas of the apparent motions of objects are indistinct from their decrease in energy: yet in the vertigo occasioned by rocking or swinging the irritative ideas of the apparent motions of objects are increased in energy, and hence they induce pleasure into the system, but are equally indistinct, and in consequence equally unfit to balance ourselves by.

In his exhaustive review of all imaginable kinds of vertigo, Darwin also described the dizzying sensation caused by seasickness or by spinning in a circle: "After revolving with your eyes open till you become vertiginous, as soon as you cease to revolve, not only the circum-ambient objects appear to circulate around you in a direction contrary to that, in which you have been turning, but you are liable to roll your eyes backwards and forwards."[22]

Applying vertigo to matters related to civil governance, the physician Joseph Mason Cox in his book *Practical Observations on Insanity* (1804) recounted his experiments on deranged people while in residence at the Lunatic Asylum of Cork, Ireland. In the early 1800s, Cox was famous throughout Europe for having developed an idea of Erasmus Darwin's for curing the mentally disturbed. The device he built and applied to his patients was called the circulating chair. The patient was tied in a chair suspended from a cable, which was then made to rotate as much as one hundred times a minute. Some of those treated actually enjoyed the ride while others passed out. But there was no cure. In another episode of vertigo's often gruesome history, the Italian scholar Andrea Cavalletti mentions an important medical doctor who attributed the social upheavals of the French Revolution to mass vertigo.[23]

Challenged by an equally broad social problem, the American physician George Beard in 1915 wrote *American Nervousness*, a widely read diagnosis of the mental strains of living in a metropolis like New York City or for that matter anywhere in the new US civilization. As this distinguished member of the New York Neurological Society noted at the outset of his book, "The chief and primary cause of this development and very rapid increase of nervousness is modern civilization, which is distinguished from the ancient by these characteristics: steam power, the periodical press, the telegraph, the sciences, and the mental activity of women."[24] Not surprisingly, Beard found much to rail against: the assembly line ("this exclusive concentration of mind and muscle to one mode of action, through months and years"), the effect of Edison's electric light, the invention of watches ("they compel us to be on time, and excite the habit of looking to see the exact moment"), modern noise (caused by "the tramping and shuffling of vast multitudes in our crowded streets"), omnibuses and "elevated railway trains in New York City" (their harsh, jarring sounds "cause severe molecular disturbance"), "business trans-actions due to inventions," buying on a margin, and the rapid development of ideas. Surveying the country's politics, business, and entertainment sectors as a whole, Beard concluded that Americans have a lot of "nerve-force" com-pared to other peoples, although the excesses of American liberty tend to produce a peculiar "American nervousness."[25]

American physical and social mobility, factory work, pleasure-seeking, and other Beardsian determinants like crowds and electrical effects imme-diately caught the attention of the Italian immigrant artist Joseph Stella, who experimented with Futurist techniques in his stunning painting *Battle of Lights, Coney Island, Mardi Gras* (1913–14), an epitome of his vision of New York City's flagrant energy (Illustration 10.1). Having come to his adopted city in his teens, he reminisced, "Steel and electricity had created a new world," and with his own New York-themed oeuvre in mind: "A new drama had surged from the unmerciful violation of darkness at night, by the violent blaze of electricity, and a new polyphony was ringing all around with the scintillating, brightly colored lights. The steel had leaped hyperbolic altitudes and expanded to vast latitudes with the skyscrapers and with bridges made for the conjunction of worlds."[26] At the other end of the representational spectrum from Alfred Stieglitz's signature photo *The Hand of Man* (1902, printed 1910), which features a charging locomo-tive spewing a dark cloud of steam as it barrels out of the railway yard, Stella's *Battle of Lights* celebrates urban electrification and the city's famous amusement park with a pied swirl of floating signifiers. These are set in motion by such novel rides as the Ferris wheel (its steel spokes visible) and

10.1 Joseph Stella, *Battle of Lights, Coney Island, Mardi Gras* (1913–14). Oil on canvas 77 × 84 ¾ in.; 195.6 × 215.3 cm. Courtesy Yale University Art Gallery.

the roller coaster, which stir the crowd to screams in the face of safe danger. The painting is Stella's enervated rendering of metropolitan vertigo.

While artists and poets sought new ways to express the city's inflamed life and its ceaseless motion, inventors were beginning to make photographs move in rapid sequence. In short, they began to make moving pictures, which successfully substituted life itself with a vertiginous, hypnotizing phantasmagoria. To launch their new gimmick in the penny arcades, early directors often celebrated the speed and force of a charging locomotive or, less recklessly, a train ride offering a roving view of the landscape. As one scholar put it, "Cinema can be imagined as a hybrid of railroad and photography, an outgrowth of those two definitive nineteenth-century inventions."[27] Stephen Kern added a further distinction in *The Culture of Time and Space, 1880–1918* (1983): "The message of the railroad lay not in anything it transported but in the acceleration of movement and the dimensions and structures of the cities it created."[28]

It is hardly surprising that the subject of one of Louis Lumière's very first films is *Arrival of a Train at La Ciotat* (1896). In an even more spectacular vein, Thomas Edison in 1904 made the short film *Smashup*, which features a mesmerizing collision between two locomotives. As Siegfried Kracauer argued in his important study *Theory of Film: The Redemption of Physical Reality*, among the various media only cinema was invented to produce visual overload or mental vertigo.[29] In effect, the new art form developed a range of dizzying techniques: the close-up, the zoom, cross-cutting, panning, fade in/out, aerial shot, dissolve, tilting, ellipsis, and so forth. But these techniques did not drop from the sky. In his arcades project, Walter Benjamin suggested their likely source: "film: the unfolding [. . .] of all the forms of perception, the tempos and rhythms, which lie preformed in today's machines."[30] As anyone familiar with early silent films knows quite well, the seventh muse put all of Coney Island, the Ferris wheel and the roller coaster to boot, on screen by the first decade of the new century.

The factory, mass transportation, moving pictures, and the quickened pace of daily life helped to shape the new anthropological order on display in the nation's big cities. The dawn of a *Neuzeit* also signaled a species-transformation. Due to the influence of books like Charles Darwin's *The Descent of Man* (1871), people came to believe that the human species had evolved over time and presumably would continue to do so in the future. While elite intellectuals from Henry Adams to Antonio Gramsci identified what they deemed a basic anthropological turn in American life, due above all to a concert of techno-scientific and urban-industrial innovations, waves of immigrants came to New York and other industrial centers, hoping to start a new life and share in the legendary advantages of US civilization. During the period from 1880 to 1924, the nation's cities became big thanks to the immense influx of immigrant laborers who were needed in the factories and the building trades, the mines, and myriad unskilled jobs. As their autobiographies unfailingly bear out, these new-comers were awestruck by the dimensions and antics of New York City's energetic masses.

Quite frankly, these urban crowds and the city's unprecedented mosaic of ethnic enclaves were largely due to successive waves of immigration. As Richard Sennett has noted, turn-of-the-century New York was home to significant communities of Jews, Italians, Irish, Germans, Slovaks, Greeks, and Hungarians – in short, "a city collecting its population from all over the world."[31] As these immigrants threw themselves into the crucible in order to become "American," they would indeed be made over – but not without a civilizational twist of their own.

In his influential book *Man, His Nature and Place in the World* (1940 in German), Arnold Gehlen remarked that human beings as a species are not genetically tied to a specific environment the way animals tend to be.[32] Humans do not have a prescribed ecological niche but instead are open to the world in ways that are species-specific. This defining flexibility and openness is evident in the fact that humans have built an endless variety of ecological habitats over time and space, such as the metropolis of New York City. To be sure, this incredible gift of freedom is accompanied by an equal amount of ontological contingency, resulting in a constitutive ambiguity in human nature. For as the writers and artists quoted above have indicated, this transformative burden of freedom, of having to create one's own milieu, has produced the psychosocial and urban-industrial effects of vertigo peculiar to the US metropolis.

Moreover, these big-city effects were often perceived as a destabilizing menace or, in Beard's biopolitical diagnosis, multiple forms of neurasthenia. In Joseph Stella's *Battle of Lights*, for example, New Yorkers seem to have lost anchorage in space or more remarkably, to have liberated themselves from geography entirely. It is worth recalling that in foundational terms, the British colonists of North America initially inscribed their stunning world-openness in a political manifesto based on a set of self-evident truths, namely, the right to life, liberty, and the pursuit of happiness. But to defend these truths, a governing apparatus was needed to provide security and protection. As we shall see in the chapter's conclusion, this was the central problem of political theory: how should the people and their so-called inalienable rights be defined? The parameters for this discussion were ultimately anthropological, world-openness versus the need for protection and security. With the dawning of the metropolis, this political problem flamed forth as never before.

The right to life and the pursuit of happiness, which the nation's founders had the gumption to qualify as inalienable, not only led to political independence and a unique sense of individual freedom, but also attracted millions of Europe's oppressed masses to New York, Chicago, and other cities in the 1890s–1920s. Indeed, the mere thought of this political paradise – the chance to live freely, as one chooses, and to be able to pursue happiness as a personal goal – was enough to make any Jewish or Italian immigrant dizzy with hope. And so, multitudes of downtrodden foreigners poured into New York until the east coast political and intellectual elite began to call for legislative protection against these now stigmatized invading "hordes." In terms of political economy, the metropolis was caught in a double bind; the foreigners were needed as a work force but their presence was transforming the city into an unexampled linguistic and civic Babel.

In effect, the immigrants initially were not part of the people (Hobbes's *populus*) but were a mere unhinged multitude (again, Hobbes's *multitudo*).[33] The biopolitical concept of *people* ("we the people") made political representation and an ordered, superintended civil society possible.[34] Its freedom was consensually shielded and governed at the municipal, state, and federal levels. Hobbes's concept of the multitude accurately describes the city's millions of foreign-born crowded into the cheap real-estate zones of the Lower East Side and East Harlem, where by 1930 approximately 80,000 southern Italians were packed into dense rows of tenements.[35] Thus a reputed population threat to the stable order of New York's already vertiginous society was spatially quarantined through the formation of a mosaic of Chinatowns, Little Italys, Little Polands, and so forth – all of them offering a semblance of communal solidarity outside the city's official purview. In the meantime, as Goldie Stone's autobiography, *My Caravan of Years* (1945), recounts, "Wheels within wheels moved about them [. . .] in the great swarming population of the ghetto."[36]

Singularly exemplifying Gehlen's world-openness, the immigrants from the city's enclaves aggressively pursued the same inalienable (biopolitical) right to happiness that underpins their host country's civic culture. But the first time they set foot in Manhattan and faced a city in endless motion, these mostly agrarian and small-town legions came up against a hypermodern civilization and its radical, unbounded contingency. "The first sight of New York lifted me out of myself. The skyline [. . .] was impressive enough to stir one's emotions and make one feel strange powers," Rebekah Kohut confessed in *My Portion: An Autobiography* (1925).[37] Often these powers were incarnated in speeding strident steel. Thus, Yuri Suhl recounts in *One Foot in America* (1950), "I was never prepared for anything like a train that [. . .] ran one minute underneath the ground and the next minute shot out into the open." While tearing along in a car of the elevated – "I felt eyes creeping all over me. I was lousy with eyes" – Yuri steals a glance through the car window: "I saw myself crashing through the roof into the kitchen of total strangers, just as supper was being served, and I said, 'Pardon me for barging in on you this way, but, really, it's not my fault – the train – ' 'Oh, that's nothing,' a very kind old lady said. 'You must have just come off the boat from Europe, so you don't know. In America this happens every day.'"[38] In a dormitory in Antwerp, Yuri's father had already warned, "In America it will be different."[39] If only they could have imagined just how much.

On the whole, immigrant autobiographers tell of their memorable first encounter with Manhattan in ways remarkably similar to the views expressed by writers and artists returning to the city during the same period. Describing New York as "brutal, ferocious, stark," Ludwig Lewisohn in *Up Stream, An American Chronicle* (1922) reveals his sense of mental dissociation as he sits alone in his hall bedroom in East Harlem: "I heard the far away roar of New York like the roar of a sinister and soulless machine that drags men in and crunches them between its implacable wheels. It seemed to me that I would never be able to face it." In effect, he was still trying to recover from his ride on the Ninth Avenue El, a tale of urban initiation that he, too, felt compelled to chronicle:

> We climbed the iron staircase, scrambled for tickets and were jammed into a car. It was the evening rush hour and we had barely standing room. The train rattled on its way to Harlem. At One Hundred and Sixteenth Street we slid down in the elevator to the street, frantically dodged people and vehicles across Eighth Avenue, turned south and west and stood presently before one of a row of three story houses wedged in between huge, dark buildings.[40]

Lewisohn's experience was more than a twice-told tale. For George Beard this too-familiar immigrant script illuminated the city's very soul: "This elevated railroad, it may be observed, has been a convenient means of illustrating all the principles here brought forward in regard to the relation of noise to nerves." Beard contrasts the soothing sounds of nature with the city's "unrhythmical, unmelodious and therefore annoying, if not injurious" noises heard night and day without pause. In effect, "they cause severe molecular disturbance." What particularly got on Beard's nerves were "the rumble of omnibuses, the jangling of car-bells, and the clatter of many carriages, with the trampling and shuffling of vast multitudes in our crowded streets."[41]

But it wasn't just the noise. In these crucial decades the metropolis continued to shoot upward and expand outward because of its transportation and communication systems. And these systems helped to produce the "chaos of visual sensations" that assaulted newcomers like Louis Adamic when he arrived in 1913. In his words, "The sensation of being in New York, in the midst of America's tallest buildings, with trains thundering under my feet, was so overwhelming."[42] The psycho-physical phenomenon of feeling topsy-turvy (the sense of the Middle English root, *whelmen*) suggests that Adamic had momentarily lost his hold on himself due to an overload of impressions. He was literally mastered by them.

On the other hand, in the metropolis vertigo was no longer merely a subjective experience. Now space itself – objects, signs, lights, people – darted and whirled around the urban dweller. This all-encompassing speed-up signals a major anthropological change in the urban habitat ("its sharp, mechanical tempo, its ceaseless drive and hustle and noise") which demanded an equal change in the inhabitants. Indeed, when at leisure both citizens and the foreign-born thronged to the cinema, where they were treated with the same whirl of visual images. Adamic recounts that "the motion pictures," which he frequented once or twice a week, gave him "frequent brain-whirls."[43] As they submitted to the trials of Americanization, tyros like Adamic, Marcus Ravage and countless others were inevitably sucked into a thousand such vertigos, leaving them temporarily "unattached, drifting nobodies." One day an elderly peddler took Ravage into his confidence and divulged the secret to success: "Don't be timid. America likes the nervy ones."[44]

New York City's physical growth was accompanied by an equal increase in population, as workers were needed to meet the demands of industrial expansion. No script more than that dealing with work conveys the new impositions on the swelling army of immigrant workers. Ground down by the crucible of work, the young Constantine Panunzio noted with rue, "I too had been caught in the whirlwind."[45] Never quite accustomed to riding the elevated train to work, Pascal D'Angelo conceded, "I felt as if those unseen wheels above were grinding paths through my body." New York remained for him a "vast dream whirling around me." And not without reason: "What confusion greeted us at the station! We hurried through a vast turning crowd and dashed down toward a train. Almost before realizing it, we were speeding toward our destination."[46] The point is, everybody in New York was always in a hurry, both on and off the job. Having found work in a railroad yard cleaning up after collisions, D'Angelo ends up living there, in a boxcar. "At times," he reminisced, "I would stand in front of the boxcar on a clear night. Around would be the confusion, whistles, flashes and grinding sounds of the never-ending movement in the yard."[47]

The new work rhythms and vertigo of everyday life also spread to the burgeoning garment industry around the Lower East Side, on which the Jewish population held a monopoly. Himself a skilled sleeve-maker, Ravage provided an inside view of the kinesthesia of a typical sweatshop: "men and women they were, collarless, disheveled, bent into irregular curves; palpitating, twitching, as if they were so many pistons and levelers in some huge, monstrous engine."[48] As for the southern Italians, the great majority of them had to settle for unskilled, low-paying jobs – pick-and-shovel work in and around New York City. A representative of his class, D'Angelo summed up his life on the job in a riveting catalog:

> Everywhere was toil – endless, continuous toil, in the flooding blaze of the sun, or in the slashing rain – toil. In Hillsdale, Poughkeepsie, Spring Valley, New York, Falling Water, Virginia, Westwood, Remsey, New Jersey, Williamsport, Maryland, where the winding Potomac flows, Utica, New York, White Lake Corner, Otterlake, Tappan, Statsburg, Oneanta, Glen Falls, and many other places where we could find work, always as a pick and shovel man – that's what I was able to do, and that is what I work at even now.[49]

Although not William Carlos Williams's citizen, D'Angelo certainly kept moving.

The immigrant masses invariably responded to the urban whirlwind and American Anglo-Saxonism by retreating to one of the city's many ethnic enclaves. In Arnold Gehlen's terms, they were both fully open to the new-world metropolis and, at the same time, sought protection from its breathtaking contingencies. "We formed our own little world," D'Angelo recalled, adding, "we fellow townsmen in this strange land clung desperately to one another."[50] The United States advertised itself to the world as the great melting pot, but in those early decades it was not. As Goldie Stone's cousin explains in *My Caravan of Years*, "The East Side is all the countries of Europe in miniature – little colonies of Irish, Italian, French, German, and Russian citizens. Your immigrant is afraid to lose himself in the melting pot and so he runs to his own where he can hear his own language, his own music, and eat his own particular dishes."[51] Many of the colonies, including the African American enclave of West Harlem, were of significant size; the Jews and Italians alone occupied several electoral districts and added significantly to the city's ethnic politics.

The anthropological ambiguity mentioned at the outset – according to which the human species is inherently open to the world but at the same time seeks to create its own protective niches – heavily shaped the spatial and cultural boundaries of the nation's metropolises. In 1916, as Adamic found himself without a job and alone in New York City, a friend told him that he "should mix with Americans and become American."[52] But as Goldie Stone argued, "Americanism is an idea. That's all it is – the idea that men have the right to be different and must respect that right in others." Ahead of her time, she added, "I clenched my hands and vowed that America – my America – should learn to value the cultures brought from many lands. We did not all have to be alike."[53]

Recounting his initiation experience in a chapter titled "The Tragedy of Readjustment," Marcus Ravage noted, "I myself was in the meantime moving in two separate worlds." But later in his autobiography he says, "I had become one of them. [...] I was an American."[54] In truth, most second- and third-generation immigrants of this period remained vertically split; they undoubtedly sought to profit by the fast-paced economy of the metropolis, but they also remained deeply committed to their ethnic niche. In short, like their foreign-born parents they expressed both world-openness and the desire for a highly segmented form of ethnic security based on Old-World values and customs. By the 1920s, New York City had to be governed by what Robert Dahl called a "majority of minorities" or a process of overlapping consensus.[55]

If indeed the United States represented a new civilization and New York City a new image of the human condition, it was above all due to a diffused form of dissociated sensibility. This psychosocial splitting created and demanded a double trust: on one hand, full participation in free-market capitalism's vertiginous energies and on the other, allegiance to a compensatory ethnic niche. Among the city's immigrant masses, American vertigo found biopolitical relief in American multiculturalism. This *Spaltung* (or split), which Goldie Stone would have called cultural democracy, was the necessary consequence of being swept up in the city's whirlwind. While American vertigo undoubtedly helped to create New York City's spatial mosaic of ethnic neighborhoods, it is equally true that the city's immigrant millions added further spin to its accelerated image.

A final dimension of vertigo emerges from the biopolitical blur among the overlapping and often indistinct categories of people, multitude, and population. Toward the end of his autobiography Henry Adams sought to apply the concepts of mass and energy to history, but he left it up to Henry James to identify their applicability to New York City's animated gusts of Croatians, Hungarians, Russian Jews, and southern Italians. While visiting the so-called ghetto of the Lower East Side ("in the very heart of the New York whirlpool"), James noticed "a great swarming [...] where multiplication, multiplication of everything, was the dominant note" and "overflow [...] the main fact of life."[56] For the occasion James had adopted a distinctly ethnographic approach, but in point of fact, "getting away from one's subject by plunging into it, for sweet truth's sake, still deeper" was merely a roundabout label for ethnic slumming.[57] As a result of his investigative forays, James evoked what was for New England's elites an all-consuming obsession: "Which is the American [. . .]? – which is *not* the alien, over a large part of the country at least, and where does one put a finger on the dividing line, or, for that matter, 'spot' and identify any particular phase of the conversion?"[58]

A decade later, Madison Grant, president of the New York Zoological Society, added a more markedly racist twist to James's East Side worries. In his influential book *The Passing of the Great Race* (1916), Grant suggested that American Nordics risked being mongrelized into "a walking chaos."[59] Fixing on New York City's largest ethnic enclave in *The Conquest of a Continent*, he notes, "In the Negro section of Harlem a further problem is arising from crosses between Negroes and Jews and Italians," observing further that these mixed breeds "are showing a tendency toward Communism."[60] But what both James and Grant ignored is the fact that the simmering energy of Harlem and the Lower East Side was really no different from that of a typical rush-hour crowd caught in the swirl of metropolitan vertigo – involving the speed-up and noise of daily life, the new transportation and communication systems, the many forms of American neurasthenia, the behavioral modifications brought on by industrial capitalism, delight in moving pictures and the delirium of Coney Island's roller coaster ride.

Whether in East Harlem, the Lower East Side, or downtown on Wall Street, the big-city crowd appeared opaque, dense, open, and unbounded[61] – in short, a vertigo inflected by often baffling markers of class, gender, race, age, costume, accent, and shifting sexual preferences, all accompanied by countless covert desires. To be sure, the scare of this intersectional tangle historically gave birth to a variety of social sciences launched to regulate the urban crowd's basic needs and often disruptive agency, from ethnography, anthropology, eugenics, sociology, and psychoanalysis, to political economy, criminology, and urban planning. The challenge of governance lay in the very nature of the object, for the crowd is more of a happening than an object, an always idiosyncratic instance of a more stable conceptual entity, the people, whose historical genealogy helps to clarify the anthropological shift hosted by turn-of-the-century New York City.

Historically, the concept of people has been read in terms of three sequential stages that are actually morphological and overlapping. In other words, the three strata exist simultaneously as imbricated categories. To be sure, this collective subject first took form in the political idea "we the people," invested with those inalienable rights set forth in the Declaration of Independence. But this political fiction harbored a darker side which the philosopher Thomas Hobbes called the multitude. Since Hobbes, people and multitude are considered two faces of the same coin. In US history, the people as a social category emerged during the destructive excesses of Jacksonian egalitarianism along the nation's frontier, where unrestrained individuals demanded as little government as possible.[62] As the Bill of Rights attached to the Constitution confirmed, the pursuit of happiness and the right to liberty are birth rights, and Jacksonians translated these rights as guarantees of little or no state regulation.

The third concept came to the fore with the birth of big cities such as New York and Chicago, where the explosive influx of millions of immigrants over a few decades radically changed the nature of urban life. Not yet citizens or recognized members of "we the people," these foreign-born huddled into ethnic enclaves as a work force, mere population requiring a sustained biopolitical approach to the city's cumulus of problems. The overcrowded enclaves presented dire sanitation and housing problems, lacked schools and playgrounds for children, and harbored dens of vice. If the fictional unity of people as a political entity melts away under the centrifugal force of the people as a social and then a biopolitical entity, the further addition of ethnic strife and distress would seem to make the study of metropolitan vertigo all the more challenging. In effect, the population of New York City embraced masses of people constantly in motion, presumably in pursuit of life, liberty, and the pursuit of happiness. But who knew what that actually meant on the streets?

Indeed, most of the descriptive observations on metropolitan vertigo so acutely cataloged by both avant-garde and immigrant writers indicate that as an intersectional phenomenon it is best studied as an effect rather than an entity, a metaphor rather than a concept. When happenings, new habits, or even fads – such as protesting the execution of Sacco and Vanzetti, marching for the right of women to vote, taking the elevated train during the rush hour, or more banally, joining the craze over Coney Island's Ferris wheel – become significant collective events forming a powerfully condensed cultural site, then we have what Krzysztof Pomian calls a semiophor.[63] The stunning anthropological experience of vertigo characterizing life in early twentieth-century New York City, with its dizzying commotion of all kinds of signs and marks, is one such semiophor and epoch-making at that.

Notes

1. For the general framework of this essay, I am indebted to Andrea Cavalletti, *Vertigine: La tentazione dell'identità* (Turin: Bollati Boringhieri, 2019), and *La città biopolitica, mitologie della sicurezza* (Milan: Mondadori, 2005); Louis A. Sass, *Madness and Modernism: Insanity in the Light of Modern Art, Literature, and Thought* (Cambridge, MA: Harvard University Press, 1995); Stephen Kern, *The Culture of Time and Space 1880–1918* (Cambridge, MA: Harvard University Press, 1983). This essay also builds on Boelhower, "Avant-Garde Autobiography: Deconstructing the Modernist Habitat," in Fernando Poyatos, ed., *Literary Anthropology: A New Interdisciplinary Approach to People, Signs and Literature* (Amsterdam: John Benjamins, 1988), pp. 273–303.
2. Henry Adams, *The Education of Henry Adams*, in Adams, *Democracy, Esther, Mont Saint Michel and Chartres, The Education* (New York: Library of America, 1983), p. 1167.
3. Ezra Pound, "Vorticism," in *Gaudier-Brzeska: A Memoir* (Hessle: Marvell Press, 1960), p. 92. For further discussion of vorticism, see Peter Nicholls, *Modernism: A Literary Guide* (London: Macmillan, 1995), pp. 172–74.
4. Adams, *The Education*, p. 1176.
5. This biopolitical distress took many forms: the creation of ethnic ghettos, the neurasthenic issues analyzed by George Beard, the density of the crowds, the exhausting pace of metropolitan life, the pervasive presence of machines, and so forth.
6. Artur Rimbaud to Georges Izambard, May 13, 1871, http://fr.wikisource.org /wiki/Lettre_de_Rimbaud_à_Georges_Izambard_-_13_mai_1871.
7. Malcolm Cowley, *Exile's Return: A Literary Odyssey of the 1920s* (New York: Viking, 1951), pp. 190, 204.
8. William Carlos Williams, *The Autobiography of William Carlos Williams* (New York: New Directions, 1948), p. 172. As Rebecca Solnit notes, "the railroad had in so many ways changed the real landscape and the human experience of it, had changed the perception of time and space and the nature of vision and embodiment"; see her book *River of Shadows: Eadweard Muybridge and the Technological Wild West* (New York: Viking, 2003), p. 219.
9. Antonio Gramsci, *Quaderni del carcere*, 4 vols., ed. Valentino Gerratana (Turin: Einaudi, 1975); Q 2 § 138, 274; Q 4, § 52, 489–90; Q 22 § 11, 2164. English translations are mine.
10. Williams, *The Autobiography*, pp. 172, 289.
11. Williams, "The Great Figure," in *Collected Poems*, 2 vols., ed. A. Walton Litz and Christopher MacGowan (New York: New Directions, 1986–91), 1:174.
12. See Robert Alter, *Imagined Cities: Urban Experience and the Language of the Novel* (New Haven, CT: Yale University Press, 2005), p. 98. Later, in a tribute to Williams, Charles Demuth painted the scene described in the poem. The result was *The Figure 5 in Gold*. See Paul Mariani, *William Carlos Williams: A New World Naked* (New York: McGraw-Hill, 1981), p. 273.

13. Walter Benjamin, "On Some Motifs in Baudelaire," in *Illuminations*, trans. Harry Zohn (London: Fontana, 1973), pp. 157–202.

14. Le Corbusier [Charles-Édouard Jeanneret], *When the Cathedrals Were White*, trans. Francis E. Hyslop Jr. (1947; New York: McGraw-Hill, 1964), pp. 82, 83.

15. Matthew Josephson, *Life among the Surrealists: A Memoir* (New York: Holt, Rinehart, and Winston, 1962), pp. 26, 261.

16. Ibid., pp. 261, 289.

17. Sass, *Madness and Modernism*, p. 357.

18. Crosby, quoted in Cowley, *Exile's Return*, p. 274.

19. On the relation between modernist writers and schizoid hyperaesthesia, see Sass, *Madness and Modernism*, pp. 80–85, 100–103; on Dionysianism, pp. 2, 4–5, 8; on permanent wakefulness, p. 38. In the 1930s, Fitzgerald wrote his famous essay "The Crack-Up" (1936), a confession about living a vertiginous life in 1920s New York.

20. Williams, *The Autobiography*, p. 330.

21. See Cavalletti, *Vertigine*, and his rich bibliography covering medico-scientific and philosophical texts.

22. Erasmus Darwin, *Zoonomia or the Laws of Organic Life*, 2 vols. (London: J. Johnson, 1794–96), vol. 1, section XXI, "Of Drunkenness," n. 3, http://gutenberg.org/files/15707/15707-h/15707-h.htm#sect_XXI_3; and vol. 1, Section XX, "Of Vertigo," n. 6, http://gutenberg.org/files/15707/15707-h/15707-h.htm#sect_XX_6.

23. Cavalletti, *Vertigo*, p. 27.

24. George Beard , *American Nervousness, Its Causes and Consequences* (New York: G. P. Putnam's Sons, 1881), p. vi. Beard does not expatiate on the mental activity of women. Instead, he discusses female beauty, problems of parturition, and the fact that their brains are in constant motion. See pp. 65–75, 137, 233.

25. Ibid., pp. 101, 103, 106, 108, 116, 118, 123, 122.

26. Joseph Stella, "Discovery of America: Autobiographical Notes," *ARTnews* 59 (November 1960), 64. For a review of other immigrant artists who painted the cityscape of New York, see Cynthia Jaffee-McCabe, ed., *The Golden Door: Artist-Immigrants of America* (Washington, DC: Smithsonian Institution Press, 1976).

27. Solnit, *River of Shadows*, p. 219.

28. Kern, *The Culture of Time and Space*, p. 229.

29. Siegfried Kracauer, *Theory of Film: The Redemption of Physical Reality* (New York: Oxford University Press, 1960), p. 252. Commenting on silent film comedy, Kracauer wrote, "It [cinema] was as if you sat in a roller coaster driving ahead at full blast, with your stomach all upside down. The dizziness happily added to the shock effects from disasters and seeming collisions" (Kracauer, *Siegfried Kracauer's American Writings*, ed. Johannes von Moltke and Kristy Rawson [Berkeley: University of California Press, 2012], p. 214).

30. Walter Benjamin, *The Arcades Project*, trans. Howard Eliland and Kevin McLaughlin (Cambridge, MA: Harvard University Press, 1999), p. 394.

31. Richard Sennett, *The Conscience of the Eye: The Design and Social Life of Cities* (New York: Norton, 1992), p. 126; by 1900 the German population in New York was around 324,224; the African American population, 60,666; the Jewish population, 290,000; the Italian population, 250,000; and by 1890, there was a Chinese population of 2,048; see Edwin G. Burrows and Mike Wallace, *Gotham: A History of New York City to 1898* (New York: Oxford University Press, 1999), pp. 1111–31.

32. Arnold Gehlen, *Man, His Nature and Place in the World*, trans. Clare McMillan and Karl Pillemer (New York: Columbia University Press, 1988), pp. 3–13, 24–31; see also Massimo De Carolis, *Il paradosso antropologico: Nicchie, micromondi e dissociazione psichica* (Macerata: Quodlibet, 2018), pp. 41–90.

33. Thomas Hobbes, *Leviathan* (1651; Oxford: James Thornton, 1881), pp. 124–28; see also Quentin Skinner, "Hobbes on Representation," *European Journal of Philosophy* 13.2 (2005), 155–84.

34. Here the two seminars of Michel Foucault are essential reading: *Naissance de la biopolitique* (2004) and *Sécurité, territoire, population* (2004).

35. See Robert A. Orsi, *The Madonna of 115th Street* (New Haven, CT: Yale University Press, 1985), pp. 14–22.

36. Goldie Stone, *My Caravan of Years* (New York: Block, 1945), p. 122.

37. Rebekah Kohut, *My Portion: An Autobiography* (New York: Thomas Seltzer, 1925), pp. 94–95.

38. Yuri Suhl, *One Foot in America* (New York: Macmillan, 1951), pp. 18, 19.

39. Ibid., p. 19.

40. Ludwig Lewisohn, *Up Stream: An American Chronicle* (New York: Modern Library, 1926), p. 121.

41. Beard, *American Nervousness*, pp. 110, 106, 107, 108–9.

42. Louis Adamic, *Laughing in the Jungle: The Autobiography of an Immigrant in America* (New York: Harper, 1932), pp. 40, 62–63.

43. Ibid., pp. 71, 76.

44. M. E. Ravage, *An American in the Making: The Life Story of an Immigrant* (1917; New York: Dover, 1971), pp. 82, 98.

45. Constantine M. Panunzio, *The Soul of an Immigrant* (1928; New York: Arno Press, 1969), p. 188.

46. Pascal D'Angelo, *Son of Italy* (1924; New York: Arno Press, 1975), pp. 60, 161, 61.

47. Ibid., p. 148.

48. Ravage, *An American in the Making*, p. 141.

49. D'Angelo, *Son of Italy*, p. 74; the misspellings are his.

50. Ibid., pp. 188, 183.

51. Stone, *My Caravan*, pp. 105–6.

52. Adamic, *Laughing in the Jungle*, p. 113.

53. Stone, *My Caravan*, pp. 106, 108.

54. Ravage, *An American in the Making*, pp. 160, 266.

55. Quoted in De Carolis, *Il paradosso antropologico*, p. 14.

56. Henry James, *The American Scene* (1907; Bloomington: Indiana University Press, 1968), pp. 134, 131.

57. Ibid., p. 126.

58. Ibid., p. 124.

59. Quoted in John Higham, *Strangers in the Land* (New York: Athenaeum, 1978), p. 272.

60. Madison Grant, *The Conquest of a Continent* (New York: Charles Scribner's Sons, 1933), p. 283.

61. See Elias Canetti, *Crowds and Power*, trans. Carol Stewart (New York: Continuum, 1973), pp. 16–22.

62. Greg Grandin, *The End of the Myth* (New York: Metropolitan Books, 2019), pp. 50–61, 72–85.

63. Krzysztof Pomian, *Che cos'è la storia* (Milan: Mondadori, 2001), pp. 113–14, 129–45. A semiophor can be an object, an image, a scene, an event, or a person. What marks them as semiophors is the fact that they become central sites of cultural signification at a diachronic and synchronic level. When studied, semiophors reveal complex stories.

CHAPTER 11

Labor's City

Joseph Entin

For laboring people, US cities have long held an ambiguous promise. In the eyes of many workers, particularly immigrants and migrants, cities have offered new hope and horizons: economic opportunity and a chance to leave behind more traditional, rural worlds and enter the heart of industrial and commercial modernity. During the nineteenth and twentieth centuries, cities were often home to large manufacturing plants and dense neighborhoods, and they have long been crucial sites of working-class connection and solidarity. As a result, cities have facilitated many of the US labor movement's most notable organizing efforts: among garment workers in New York, packinghouse workers in Chicago, autoworkers in Detroit, dockworkers in San Francisco, and janitors in Los Angeles. At the same time, however, cities embody the uneven geography of capitalist accumulation and have historically been structured to reinforce class divisions and the subordination of working people. As nodes of what Fredrich Engels described as "the concentration of capital in the hands of a few," marked by residential, social, and economic segregation, cities embody the structural inequalities that shape capitalist society and facilitate labor's exploitation.[1]

This chapter argues that urban labor literature depicts cities as sites of geographic, social and political struggle. Working-class literature frequently aspires to limn what Marx called "living labor," or "labor as subjectivity," focused more on the lives of laboring people beyond the job – in their families, neighborhoods, and social relationships – than on labor per se.[2] Labor literatures of the city, often focused on the dilapidated, segregated districts to which urban workers have frequently been relegated, underscore both the power of capitalist interests to control urban space, and the efforts of working peoples to remake city spaces – from factory floors, to streets and stoops, to tenement hallways and kitchens – to advance their own interests and aspirations. Labor geographer Andrew Herod argues that workers are spatial as well as historical agents who shape the landscapes they inhabit, although always within limits set by dominant cultural, political, and economic forces. "Workers make their own geographies," Herod asserts, riffing on Marx, but "not under the conditions of their own choosing."[3] Urban labor literature depicts the city as a deeply uneven space that is not merely an arena of conflict between labor and capital, but is itself one of the stakes of that conflict.

As places where heterogeneous working populations converged in a landscape of highly uneven power, cities have been laboratories for class formation and labor activism. Labor literature, too, became a testing ground for imaginatively exploring relations between social space and economic power, and among workers themselves. A central question these texts ask is: Can diverse populations of workers (including the unemployed and those laboring in informal positions and in reproductive work) find common cause across the city's often sharp social, economic and spatial divisions? These literary depictions of the city, often rendered through a social-realist or naturalist lens, tend to emphasize the restrictive and exploitative qualities of urban space for working people, but a vital thread in many of these works, especially in more experimental forms of poetry and fiction, points to the potential of urban workers' solidarity. Urban labor literature not only testifies to capitalism's power to structure the city, but also projects labor's power to occupy and reshape neighborhoods, streets, and workplaces through collective action.

This chapter focuses on three key historical periods: first, the early twentieth century, when the surge in immigration from southern and eastern Europe transformed the ethnic, labor and linguistic landscapes of several northeastern US cities, especially New York; second, the long 1930s, when economic collapse, internal migrations, and the rise of new levels of union power recast labor's possibilities; and third, the post-1970s era, when globalization, deindustrialization, and a rise in immigration from Latin America and Asia dismantled the industrial working class and created new terms on which to imagine labor's claim to the United States' increasingly transnational cities. This essay examines only a fragment of the literature relevant to its topic, but these texts underscore the heterogeneity of the urban working classes – fragmented, racially and ethnically mixed, "multiple in [their] aims and needs, more often itinerant, disorganized and fluid rather than solidly implanted," in the words of David Harvey – and the diversity of genres and modes that artists have used to imagine the city from labor's perspective.[4] Cutting across the antinomies of division and solidarity, alienation and belonging, work and its absence, labor literatures of the city – realist, modernist, and more speculative modes – depict the deeply contradictory nature of urban space for working people, who are the source of so much of the city's social and economic wealth, yet can win their share of it only through collective, creative struggle.

"Electric currents of life"

At the turn of the twentieth century, the US urban working classes were transformed by waves of immigration, precipitous growth in the scale and power of industrial capitalism, and the emergence of the modern, commercial city. The period from 1880 to 1920 witnessed unprecedented immigration; millions of newcomers, especially Jews and Catholics from eastern and southern Europe, entered the United States seeking opportunity and fleeing persecution. Overwhelmingly laboring people, they entered sweatshops, mills, factories, packing houses, and homes in cities throughout the Northeast and Midwest. In this era before the passage of comprehensive federal labor law in the 1930s, hours were long and working conditions often quite dangerous. The new urban immigrants were no strangers to labor struggle, however, and many brought socialist, syndicalist and anarchist ideas from the Old World. Their encounters with the US industrial capitalist system were frequently explosive.

A series of actions across the clothing industry demonstrated the resolve and collective power of urban immigrant workers. In 1909 in New York, 20,000 shirtwaist producers, mostly young Jewish and Italian women, walked out. Their strike spread to Philadelphia, where the International Ladies Garment Workers Union negotiated improved pay and reduced hours, which inspired a strike of 60,000 mostly male cloak makers in New York. In Chicago, 40,000 garment workers struck, sparked by fourteen women who walked out over a cut in the piece rate at one of the city's prestigious apparel firms. In 1912, 20,000 workers – the majority of them foreign born or the children of immigrants, hailing from fifty-one different nations – struck the textile mills in Lawrence, Massachusetts, demanding not only a rollback of cuts to already starvation-level wages, but also an eight-hour working day and improved living conditions. Led by organizers from the Industrial Workers of the World (IWW), the Lawrence strikers, half of whom were women between the ages of fourteen and eighteen, held out for two months, and they finally won raises and overtime pay, despite the imposition of martial law by state authorities who intervened on the side of the mill owners.[5]

The emergent presence of new immigrants in US cities was rendered potently in works of experimental art, as the avant-garde and labor converged and tried to challenge the spatial, affective and ideological divisions that structured the capitalist metropolis, and often were reinforced by realists and reformers like Upton Sinclair, who famously referred to Chicago's working-class ethnic enclaves as "jungle[s]," and Jacob Riis, who cast New York City's immigrant precincts as a dark, foreign country inhabited by the "Other Half." By contrast, Lola Ridge's 1918 poem "The Ghetto" aimed to pierce the chasm separating the slum from the rest of the city (and from middle-class readers), even while acknowledging the barriers that made such experiments in seeing difficult. "The Ghetto," portions of which were published in *The New Republic*, is a bold attempt to blend modernism's collage aesthetics and spirited commitment to make it new with the social concerns of the labor left and a burgeoning women's movement. The poem's nine sections present "imagist snapshots" of life, labor, commerce, and tradition among the Jewish immigrant community of the Lower East Side.[6]

At the heart of the poem are young women who recall labor activist Clara Lemlich and other immigrant "new women" who led the era's daring shirtwaist strikes. The poet rents a room from a family whose daughter, Sadie, "dresses in black" and works in a garment factory, where she "quivers like a rod [. . .] / A thin black piston flying, / One with her machine." An icon of modern, urban, working-class womanhood, Sadie reads "books that have most unset thought, / new poured and malleable," and has "thought / [that] Leaps" "at a protest on the Square." But, as the poem makes clear, her restless energy and searching intelligence are kept in check by the economic forces bearing down on her: "She – a fiery static atom, / Held in place by the pressure all about – / Speeds up the driven wheels / And biting steel – that twice / Has nipped her to the bone."[7]

Ridge's ghetto is cramped and dark, a confining space, but also bursting with energy that the poet frames in a modernist language of electric desire: "Electric currents of life, / Throwing off thoughts like sparks, / [. . .] Making unknown circuits."[8] Although as a Dublin-born, Australia and New Zealand-raised gentile bohemian, Ridge was an outsider to the community she depicts, the poem is an exercise in creative solidarity that forges "unknown circuits" of connection. Rather than reduce the ghetto to a single or representative figure, Ridge renders it as heterogeneous and heteroglossic – a mix of ages, voices and languages, and attitudes toward Judaism. Indeed, the poem foregrounds the conflicts *within* the community, as well as between insiders and outsiders; ghetto life is in continual formation and flux, fusing tradition and modernity to remake the streets and workplaces from the bottom up.

Perhaps the most audacious effort to use art to support early twentieth-century urban labor was the Paterson Strike Pageant. Paterson, New Jersey, was the nation's Silk City; by 1910, its mills produced more silk drapes, ribbons, and clothes than anywhere else in the United States. In January 1913, 800 workers of the Doherty Silk Mill walked out when the owners proposed to double the weavers' workload. The Doherty operators were joined in February by 5,000 mostly Jewish weavers who marched off the job and invited the participation of the IWW, which was fresh off its victory in Lawrence, Massachusetts. By early spring, workers at over 300 Paterson mills were on strike.

To raise money for the strikers, the IWW, in cooperation with Greenwich Village intellectuals and their patron Mabel Dodge Luhan, organized a pageant at Madison Square Garden. The IWW believed that rank-and-file workers should play an active role in directing both the strike and the pageant, and journalist and writer John Reed visited Paterson to collaborate with strikers on the script. On June 7, over 1,000 strikers marched up Fifth Avenue in Manhattan and into a packed Madison Square Garden to reenact notable moments from the work stoppage, including picketing and conflicts with police, rousing speeches by IWW organizers Elizabeth Gurley Flynn and Bill Haywood, and the death and funeral of a bystander, Valentino Modestino. The strikers sang "The Internationale" and "The Marseillaise," and invited the 15,000 audience members to become participants rather than observers. In the end, the pageant cost more money than it raised, and the strike itself ended without winning its demands. Nevertheless, in casting strikers to play themselves, and in breaking the fourth wall between actors and viewers, the pageant dissolved the boundaries between representation and reality, creating an engaged, activist art in which workers and their allies transformed Manhattan's premier site for popular entertainments into a space for mass demonstration. Robert Edmund Jones's cover for the pageant's program depicts a male striker, a silhouette of mills behind him, climbing out of the frame toward the viewer with his hand up (Illustration 11.1), raising the specter of working-class power that the pageant, like the strike, suggested might transform urban life.

11.1 Robert Edmund Jones, program cover for *The Pageant of the Paterson Strike*
(1913). Courtesy of the American Labor Museum.

"We Live Here and They Live There"

The Great Depression was not only a national trauma, it was a devastating
period for working-class Americans, as tens of millions went unemployed.
Yet the 1930s also saw an upswing in industrial unionism, as the passage of
the National Labor Relations Act in 1935 opened the door to new labor
struggles. Strikes across the mining, auto, steel, and rubber industries

consolidated the Congress of Industrial Organizations, which split from the more craft-oriented American Federation of Labor, inaugurating the Age of the CIO, a prolonged period of increased labor influence in the United States. Union membership swelled from 3 million in 1933 to 10 million by the start of World War II, and continued to rise into the 1970s.[9]

During the 1930s, labor literature, too, was consolidated in a new form, proletarian literature, which enfranchised a generation of ethnic and African American writers, who found support in the capacious left-wing Cultural Front. The 1930s is often remembered via Farm Security Administration photographs of dust bowl refugees and impoverished farmers as a rural decade. But proletarian literature, produced by the children of immigrants and migrants raised in the ghettos and slums of the nation's cities, was very much an urban affair, as many of its most celebrated novels – Mike Gold's *Jews Without Money* (1930), Henry Roth's *Call it Sleep* (1935), Pietro di Donato's *Christ in Concrete* (1939), among others – represented "tenement pastorals."[10] In photography, Depression-era urban culture was given compelling graphic form in the chiaroscuro images of Weegee's *Naked City* (1944), which cast the complex world of New York's multiethnic working class in the emerging genre of noir, and in the lyrical, often off-beat street shots of Helen Levitt, who "decided [she] should take pictures of working-class people and contribute to [. . . w]hatever movements there were – Socialism, Communism, whatever was happening."[11]

Yet the surge in union strength did not always produce a more optimistic literature. In fact, the period's literature written by and about working people frequently underscored the determinative, alienating power of the modern cityscape. For instance, the work of one of the era's most acclaimed working-class writers, Richard Wright, offers a sophisticated, materialist analysis of the ways that urban space is deliberately designed to perpetuate economic and racial disparities. Wright's bestselling novel, *Native Son* (1940), is structured by a network of spaces, from Chicago's Black Belt, to the white suburbs, to the prison cell where the novel ends, that frame and enclose Bigger's life. The novel opens in the cramped apartment Bigger shares with his mother and sister; an alarm clock clangs as sunlight "flooded the room to reveal a black boy standing in a narrow space between two iron beds."[12] This image underscores Bigger's confinement in spatial terms, suggesting the "iron" constrictions that shape his life. Bigger descends to the streets, "sick of his life at home," but as he looks around, the city literally speaks to him, reinforcing his feelings of internment: a "huge colored signboard" of a candidate for State's Attorney looms overhead; the candidate's "index finger pointed straight [. . .] at each passer-by." Its message is inscribed clearly in "tall red letters: YOU CAN'T WIN!"[13]

Talking to his friend Gus, Bigger lucidly explains that Chicago's spatial design turns the city into a virtual prison for poor blacks: "We live here and they live there. We black and they white. They got things and we ain't. They do things and we can't. It's just like living in jail. Half the time I feel like I'm on the outside of the world peeping in through a knot-hole in the fence." The links between urban space and racial-economic power are further underscored by the fact that Bigger's wealthy white employer, Henry Dalton, is also the CEO of the company that owns Bigger's tenement building. In the end, Bigger's journey though Chicago's deeply variegated spaces leads him to prison, convicted of the murder of Dalton's daughter Mary, whom Bigger, the family chauffer, accidentally smothers after returning her home drunk late one night when he fears any noise she made would lead to him being accused of rape. From his cell, Bigger can see the "sun-drenched buildings in the Loop."[14] The paradox of physical distance and visual proximity between the cell and the downtown sky-scrapers, which serve as physical embodiments of white financial rule, highlights the novel's emphasis on the spatialized dimensions of capitalist, racialized power in the industrial city.

If *Native Son*'s literary naturalism is organized around our sense that, from the opening pages, the socio-spatial forces molding Bigger's life are destined to defeat him, Wright's documentary photobook *12 Million Black Voices* (1941) offers a more ambivalent depiction of working-class urban possibility. This lyrical history of black American life from slavery into industrial modernity is narrated in the voice of a poetic, collective "we." The heart of the book examines the Great Migration, and the transition from rural, folk life, as Wright terms it, to modern, urban existence. Accompanied by powerful photographs drawn from the Farm Security Administration archive by his collaborator, Edwin Rosskam, Wright shows that the layout of cities is not a result of rational forces or democratic planning, but of white, capitalist interests conspiring to contain and diminish black life. This exclusion is spatially enforced by "restrictive covenants" that lock "hundreds of thousands of us black folk in single, constricted areas." At a more granular level, African American city dwellers are confined to kitchenette apartments leased by the "Bosses of the Buildings" at exorbitant rates. The kitchenette, Wright proclaims, "is our prison, our death sentence without a trial, the new form of mob violence that assaults [. . .] all of us in its ceaseless attacks."¹⁵

Yet the final chapter offers a more sanguine view of the industrial city as a space of intersectional possibilities – a crossroads where cooperation across racial lines can occur. "We are crossing the lines you dared us to cross," Wright insists. "The differences between black folk and white folk are not blood or color, and the ties that bind us are deeper than those that separate us. The common road of hope we have all traveled has brought us into a stronger kinship than any words, laws, or legal claims." The city becomes the site where antinomies of time, space, and race – and opposi- tions between ancient and modern, folk and industrial, and black and white – converge to produce new working-class unities in what Wright calls "the sphere of conscious history."¹⁶

Wright's double-edged rendering of the city is echoed in Meridel Le Sueur's novel *The Girl* (1939), about the eponymous, unnamed young woman, who works as barmaid in Depression-era St. Paul, Minnesota. Stitching together short stories she wrote during the 1930s drawing on ethnographic interviews she had conducted with impoverished Midwestern women, Le Sueur's socialist-feminist rendering of the city underscores the highly precarious position of women within its economic, social, and physical infrastructures. The protagonist learns how to navigate the streets and the speakeasy where she works from Clara, her fellow waitress and roommate. Admitting that she was fortunate "to get the job after all the hunting and waiting Clara and I had been doing," the Girl stresses the scrutiny that working-class women face: "I was lucky to have Clara showing me how to wander on the street and not be picked up by plainclothesmen and police matrons," who could "give you tests and sterilize you or send you to the women's prison."¹⁷ The Girl does in fact end up in a state-run maternity home after she becomes pregnant and the staff at the local relief office describe her as "maladjusted, emotionally unstable," and conclude that "sterilization would be advisable."¹⁸

If the novel offers a robust critique of the state's policing of women's sexuality, it also depicts the city as a harsh, competitive preserve of desper- ate, abusive men, who are continually compared to wolves, snakes, and foxes. Men in the bar where the Girl works "tried to make a home run or a strike, with their too-free paws," and the Girl is eventually raped by a local gangster, Ganz, who ropes her boyfriend Butch into attempting a bank robbery. While the Girl explains that she wants "to be [. . .] to feel good," Butch aims "to beat everyone in the world, to rob them of their faith and not give them anything." He warns the Girl that survival calls for one "to be tough and strong alone," but she counters with a vision of collective sociality: "I don't want to be alone. I want to be with others."[19]

The instrumentalism that the men pursue leads to their demise, as the central male characters in the novel are killed during the bank robbery – a pulpy, noir-ish plot that comes to a bullet-riddled conclusion two-thirds of the way through the book. But the female characters persist. When the Girl returns from burying Butch, she finds new resonance to her voice, a deeper connection to other women, and in the process, a new understanding of the city. The Girl brims with what she calls "hankering" – an unquenchable desire for ways of being and relating that exist beyond the patriarchal culture of acquisitive capitalism. "I was full but I was hungry," she insists. "Nobody can shut me up, I'm not going to be good, be happy, make plans, act like nothing has happened." Her resolve and the newfound knowledge of her own desires lends her a new perspective on the city as a site of collective, feminist possibility: "Now I know the whole city and the way it is and the way those in it can be together."[20]

This vision of collective togetherness is realized during the novel's final segment, when the women in the novel occupy an abandoned warehouse. They organize a demonstration to demand milk and iron pills for Clara, who suffers the aftereffects of the electric shock treatments she was forced to undergo at a state mental hospital, and the Girl gives birth, in what she calls "the realest dream," surrounded by other women "who seem to breathe with [her]."[21] Clara dies, but the Girl names her baby Clara, and the book ends on a hopeful note of feminist, working-class struggle. The novel's image of an alternative mode of cooperative city life runs hand-in-hand with Le Sueur's experimental mode of writing, keyed to women's desire. She crafts a feminist, proletarian modernism inspired by the real-world voices of impoverished women that defies realism's pretensions of transparency and legibility, and naturalism's focus on the overwhelming power of determinative forces. In the process, both literature and the city are "occupied" and transformed into creative, collaborative spaces.

"The Great Flow of Humanity"

US workers greeted the end of World War II with the largest strike wave in the nation's history. In the following two decades, organized labor remained robust, and workers in several major industries, including auto and steel, negotiated contracts that kept incomes and living conditions relatively high. Between 1946 and 1960, workers' inflation-adjusted annual earnings rose by one-third, and they continued to increase through the early 1970s. Rising incomes allowed many workers, especially whites, who also were the beneficiaries of New Deal programs such as the GI Bill and home loan guarantees that were not equally extended to nonwhite workers, to purchase homes and cars, move to the expanding suburbs, and achieve unprecedented levels of prosperity. But capital, aided by the ascendance of Reaganomics and neoliberal policies that dismantled the New Deal welfare state, was on the move, too: it responded to the power of organized labor by starting to relocate production in search of a cheaper workforce – out of the heavily unionized Midwest and Northeast to the South, the Sun Belt, and, eventually, overseas.

This outsourcing and deindustrialization – globalization – alongside significant social and demographic shifts, reshaped US cities and the working class. Increasingly, steady blue-collar work was replaced by contingent, low-paid, service sector jobs, as life and labor for working people became more precarious. Unionization rates declined, from 33 percent in the private sector in 1955 to under 9 percent in 2009. Jobs in the auto industry were cut almost in half between 1978 and 1982 alone; manufacturing workers dropped from 30 percent of the nonfarm workforce in 1960 to less than 10 percent in 2009; wages stagnated, losing power against rising inflation.[22] At the same time, accelerating rates of female participation in the workforce and a post-1965 surge in immigration, primarily from Latin America, Asia, and the Caribbean, rather than Europe, brought new levels of diversity to the US working population. As the authors of *Who Built America?* explain, these transformations forged a new social, economic, and political landscape: "The wave of suburbanization during the 1950s and 1960s, followed by significant loss of millions of factory jobs, [. . .] eroded the nation's old industrial base and virtually destroyed traditional urban working-class neighborhoods," which created a "new geography of racial, ethnic, and economic stratification" across the nation.[23]

One of the most ambitious literary works to chart the fate of laboring people across this new geography is Russell Banks's novel *Continental Drift* (1985), which narrates the intersecting migrations of two workers who collide off the coast of Miami, Bob DuBois, an oil furnace repair man who moves his family from New Hampshire to the Sunshine State in search of economic opportunity, and Vanise Dorsinville, who flees Haiti with her infant son and nephew Claude in search of personal, political, and economic freedom. Together, the narrative threads allegorize the demise of the white industrial proletariat and the emergence of a new, precarious, immigrant working class. Bob's narrative takes its place in a post–Vietnam War canon, alongside the film *Falling Down* (Joel Schumacher, 1993) and such television series as *Hung* (2009–11) and *Breaking Bad* (2008–13), which chronicle the travails of white working men coming to grips with their economic vulnerability, even obsolescence, in a deindustrializing world.

Appropriately, Bob's story is a tale of decline as he moves from a position of relative economic stability (a steady job, ownership of a house, car and boat) to a state of accelerating insecurity, destitution, and desperation (living in a trailer at the end of a dirt road, turning to smuggling in a doomed effort to improve his economic lot). While Bob had previously imagined himself as a member of the blue-collar middle class, he eventually comes to see himself, like millions of other laborers roaming the planet, as a poor person who "has as much chance of becoming rich as he had of becoming [baseball star] Ted Williams."[24]

The novel devotes fewer pages to Vanise and Claude, but they, too, are working people – neoslaves, in fact, whose jagged, desperate journey to reach the United States is a figurative, and almost literal, death. "They had come," the narrator explains, "over three hundred miles as if chained in darkness, a middle passage." During one stretch in the hold of boat, they are "surrounded by darkness, as if buried" and raped repeatedly, reduced to a state akin to what Giorgio Agamben calls bare life, although here it is not a state of exception but rather a form of terror and exploitation internal to, and constitutive of, contemporary racial capitalism.[25]

The novel ends in Miami, but its geographic gaze is focused primarily on the Florida exurbs and the way the state's integration into a burgeoning Sun Belt economy shaped its physical landscape. Driving into Florida, Bob's family is surrounded by "a long, straight tunnel of [fast food] franchises broken intermittently by storefront loan companies and paved lots crammed with glistening Corvettes, T-Birds, Camaros and Trans Ams" and "miles of trailer parks laid out in grids, like the orange groves beyond them, with a geometric precision determined by the logic of ledgers instead of the logic of land, water, and sky." After the trailer parks, the DuBois family passes "tracts of pastel-colored cinderblock bungalows, [. . .] instant, isolated neighborhoods, suburbs of the suburbs, reflecting not the inhabitants' needs so much as the builders' and landowners' greed."[26] This prefabricated landscape bluntly expresses the economic forces that drive Sun Belt economies and their resultant geometries of sprawl.

Continental Drift might be considered a transnational proletarian novel of the Caribbean Rim, but it lacks the revolutionary possibility of many radical texts from 1930s. In its most imaginatively and politically ambitious moment, when Bob, Vanise and Claude meet off the coast of Miami, Bob, the bearer of US labor and racial privilege, senses that his existence can only be grasped through the lives of these black refugees, who appear to know something about him that, he realizes, "I don't know myself, something crucial, something that basically defines me," something that "will make [Bob's] mere survival more than possible."[27] But disaster ensues, and the possibility of an emergent post-Fordist, hemispheric working class finding common ground lingers as a missed opportunity that the characters do not even recognize as such.

In *Tropic of Orange* (1997), Karen Tei Yamashita attempts a similar mapping of labor, depicting post-NAFTA Los Angeles as a Pacific Rim city. Yamashita's novel is a dizzying blend of postmodern metafiction and magical realism that draws inspiration from film noir and reality television to narrate an apocalyptic story about transnational, migratory workers like Bobby Ngu, who is "Chinese from Singapore with a Vietnam name speaking like a Mexican living in Koreatown," flowing into and reshaping California's largest city during the mid-1990s.[28]

The similarities between labor precarity at this and the previous turn of the century are evident in *La Ciudad/ The City* (1998), directed by David Riker, which tells four stories about immigrant workers from Latin America in New York City. In the first, "Ladrillos" (Bricks), a group of day laborers cleans bricks on the lot of an abandoned, crumbling building; while they work, one of them is crushed by a collapsing wall and dies. In "Casa" (Home), two young people from the same Mexican town meet by chance at a quinceañera and start to fall in love, only to lose contact as the man, who had arrived the day before, gets lost in the labyrinthine housing development where the woman lives. In "El Titeretero" (The Puppeteer), a homeless, tubercular puppeteer tries to enroll his young daughter in public school but is denied because he has no rent or utility receipts to prove residency. In the final story, "Costurera" (Seamstress), a woman working in a sweatshop where she has not been paid in four weeks tries to raise $400 to send to Mexico for her ill daughter. Made in the neorealist tradition, the film was shot on location in black and white, and it features nonprofessional actors – migrant workers who helped Riker develop the stories during five years of research and filming when the Latin American, especially Mexican, population of New York grew rapidly, forming a key segment of the city's new, transnational labor force.[29]

The film opens and closes with a bleak, hazy view of the New York City skyline as an elevated train moves slowly across the gritty, gray urban landscape. These shots are echoed by other shots of large-scale apartment houses, skyscrapers, and factories that punctuate the film and underscore the city as a force over the lives of characters who, like the snaking train, work their way laboriously through the cityscape. In commencing and closing the film this way, Riker emphasizes the necessity of thinking about the materiality of migrant life and putting individual stories in a larger field of forces, flows, and structures. This tension between individual predicaments and structural conditions is echoed by another uneasy dialectic at the center of the film: the friction between isolation and collectivity, especially in cities, which bring workers together, but at the same time often serve to divide them against one another, as competitors in the labor market. These tensions pervade the film's content and its form – a collection of separate stories, featuring singular characters and situations, that asks viewers to search for common threads to weave together the otherwise independent tales.

In a dynamic that recalls the suppressed film *Salt of the Earth* (Herbert J. Biberman, 1954), in which women take over a picket line during a miners' strike, Riker framed *La Ciudad* as a call-and-response format in which the mostly female sweatshop workers in the fourth and final story answer the lamentable lack of unity displayed by the male day laborers in the film's opening segment. In the concluding scene, the protagonist, Ana, stops sewing, and when the boss approaches, says she needs to be paid to help her daughter. He yells at her to leave, pushing and then yanking her, but she refuses and wraps her arms around her machine. Slowly, the other workers halt their labors, and the shop falls still. The manager and his wife survey the room as the camera cuts to individual shots of the sewers and pressers, whose expressions seem to convey a mix of emotions: fatigue, despair, sadness, anger, resolve.

The narrative ends abruptly, *in medias res*, without indicating whether the workers' momentary pause translates into collective protest and resistance. The camera pans out to the exterior of the building containing the sweatshop, and then to the city skyline beyond. Can the urgency of the scene unfolding in the life of this one worker, and this one sweatshop, translate to a broader horizon? While the silence that prevails as the camera recedes from shop to building to cityscape suggests that such a possibility is doubtful (the mass garment strikes that shook New York City in the early twentieth century are distant memories), the film's final shots ask us to consider how the city might be transformed if these most precarious of workers and others in similar circumstances stand together.

La Ciudad reminds us that as we enter the third decade of the twenty-first century, cities continue to be hot spots for labor struggles, as automation, deindustrialization, and globalization reshape what work is. Jobs are declining in traditional sectors such as manufacturing and construction, but growing in the service industry, where the Bureau of Labor Statistics predicts 81 percent of all US jobs will be by 2026. While this includes white-collar and professional occupations, almost one-third of US jobs in 2016 were in retail, health care and social assistance, and hospitality services.[30] The plight of urban workers in the precarious service industries are taken up in a range of recent films, including *Bread and Roses* (Ken Loach, 2000), about the Justice for Janitors campaign among undocumented workers in Los Angeles, *Man Push Cart* (Ramin Bahrani, 2007), about a Pakistani immigrant running a coffee cart in midtown Manhattan, and *Sorry to Bother You* (Boots Riley, 2018), about an African American telemarketer caught up in a strike in Oakland, California. As urban workers continue to organize both inside and outside the workplace, linking economic concerns to issues such as gentrification, immigration, transportation, and climate policy, literature and culture will no doubt provide crucial insight into the challenges and possibilities facing laboring people in the American city, and beyond.

Notes

1. Friedrich Engels, *The Condition of the Working Class in England* (London: Penguin, 1987), p. 36.
2. Karl Marx, *Grundrisse*, trans. Martin Nicolaus (London: Penguin, 1973), p. 272.
3. Andrew Herod, "Workers, Space, and Labor Geography," *International Labor and Working-Class History* 64 (2003), 113.
4. David Harvey, *Rebel Cities: From the Right to the City to the Urban Revolution* (London: Verso, 2012), p. xiii.
5. See Bruce Watson, *Bread and Roses: Mills, Migrants, and the Struggle for the American Dream* (New York: Penguin, 2006).
6. Nancy Berke, "Ethnicity, Class, and Gender in Lola Ridge's 'The Ghetto,'" *Legacy* 16.1 (Fall 1999), 72.
7. Lola Ridge, *The Ghetto and Other Poems* (New York: Huebsch, 1918), pp. 6, 7, 6.
8. Ibid., p. 25.
9. On the "Age of the CIO," see Michael Denning, *The Cultural Front: The Laboring of American Culture in the Twentieth Century* (London: Verso, 1997), pp. 21–38.
10. Ibid., p. 132.
11. Melissa Block and Helen Levitt, "Helen Levitt's Indelible Eye: Photographer Captures the Lost Outdoor Life of New York City," National Public Radio,

January 17, 2002, www.npr.org/programs/atc/features/2002/jan/levitt/020117
.levitt.html.

12. Richard Wright, *Native Son* (New York: Harper Perennial, 1998), p. 3.

13. Ibid., p. 13.

14. Ibid., pp. 20, 426.

15. Ibid., pp. 113, 133, 106, 106.

16. Ibid., pp. 146, 147.

17. Meridel Le Sueur, *The Girl* (Albuquerque, NM: West End Press, 1995), p. 1.

18. Ibid., p. 114.

19. Ibid., pp. 1, 24, 15.

20. Ibid., pp. 101, 102.

21. Ibid., p. 131.

22. Dan La Botz, "What Happened to the American Working Class," *New Politics* 12.4 (Winter 2010), http://newpol.org/content/what-happened-american-working-class.

23. The American Social History Project, *Who Built America: Working People and the Nation's Politics, Culture and Society; Volume Two: From the Gilded Age to the Present* (New York: Pantheon, 1992), p. 481.

24. Russell Banks, *Continental Drift* (New York: Harper Perennial, 1994), p. 342.

25. Ibid., pp. 207, 197.

26. Ibid., pp. 59–60.

27. Ibid., pp. 345, 343.

28. Karen Tei Yamashita, *Tropic of Orange* (Minneapolis, MN: Coffee House Press, 1997), p. 15.

29. New York's Mexican population increased from approximately 40,000 in 1980 to almost 300,000 by 2000, the fastest growth of ethnic group in the city; see Robert Smith, *Mexican New York: Transnational Lives of New Immigrants* (Berkeley: University of California Press, 2005), p. 19.

30. US Department of Labor, Bureau of Labor Statistics, "Employment by Major Industry Sector," www.bls.gov/emp/tables/employment-by-major-industry-sector.htm.

CHAPTER 12

White Immigrant Trajectories in US Urban Literature

The Italian American Case

Fred L. Gardaphé

The immigrant to the United States, whose immediate experience of the city William Boelhower examines in Chapter 10, faces many ways to deal with the pressures of acculturation and assimilation. One could simply refuse to connect to the new world and live inside the Old World culture, protected by a language not English, do work that could be done with little or no adaptation, wear unfashionable clothes, eat strange foods, and maintain attitudes about life consistent with the way things were in old country. This path was easy if one lived in any of the ethnic enclaves formed in urban centers in the late nineteenth and early twentieth centuries. One could acculturate by accommodating the demands of the new country's ways but without sacrificing one's inherited traditions and values, and therefore not assimilate. Or, one could abandon the old ways for the new: struggle with the new language and give children up to the new ways through schooling.

The choice of trajectory would be recorded as conflicts in early US immigrant fiction. In his 1977 study, *The City, The Immigrant and American Fiction, 1880–1920*, David M. Fine writes that the heart of "urban immigrant fiction is the clash between two distinct cultural groups and the results of that clash." However the sides are represented, the literature's recurrent "issues [are] intermarriage and the survival of racial, ethnic, and religious ties in the face of the collision of cultures – one basically northwestern European and largely Protestant, the other southern and eastern Europe and overwhelmingly Jewish or Catholic." What Fine identifies as central in the next generations of Jewish American writers – "the emancipated second- or third-generation Jew's traumatic recognition of his past, usually objectified in the form of an Old World father-figure who appears to suddenly haunt the American Jew" and produces "a fiction of nostalgia" – holds equally for John Fante's *Wait Until Spring Bandini*

(1938), Pietro di Donato's *Christ in Concrete* (1939), and Mario Puzo's *The Fortunate Pilgrim* (1964).[1]

A political twist on such generational conflict erupted with Philip Roth's *Goodbye, Columbus* (1959), which Irving Howe initially thought "signifies the end of a tradition, the closing of an arc of American Jewish experience." If his elegiac reaction seems kind in comparison to some epithets thrown at Roth by other Jewish American readers, in a 1973 reconsideration, Howe added his own curse, accusing Roth of disrespecting the Jewish American tradition by drawing "not upon a fresh encounter with the postwar experience of suburban Jews but upon literary hand-me-downs of American-Jewish fiction, popularizing styles of rebellion from an earlier moment and thereby draining them of their rebellious content." This difference may be attributed – as Howe explicitly did – to suburban migration and to a lack of what Edward Alexander calls "imaginative sympathy," which in Howe's account leads to a failed satire that lacks "comedy" and has "no moral standard."[2] In effect, Roth was cursed for returning to the city as a deracinated, middle-class American with no love for, or loyalty to, traditional Jewish cultural identity. This chapter examines that generational and geographical shift, the literature it generated, and the ways that the process of becoming was tied to changes in cultural identity and attitudes toward it that also shape political outlooks. Since it cannot possibly be all inclusive, it primarily focuses on Italian American writers, who lacked the close critical attention of an Irving Howe to critique their relationship to, and representations of, Italian immigrant culture in the United States.

Living in and Leaving Little Italys

The legal definition of an American rests on citizenship. Beyond that formal criterion, immigrants and old stock have grappled with the contention that there is a mainstream American culture that contains, but is different from, the many cultures have found homes in the United States and what, if any, obligation that culture imposes on new arrivals. Fine argues that while "Immigrant writers differed as to what form assimilation would or should take, [...] they never seriously questioned the virtue of assimilation." Only later, "with the upsurge of white ethnicity in America – with what Professor Michael Novak has called 'the rise of the umeltable ethnics'" does debate arise.[3] What this reclaiming and preserving of ethnic identity too often misses, for Italian Americans as much as Jewish Americans like Howe's Roth, is the radical labor tradition that these immigrants brought with them, that shaped collective life in in the ethnic enclaves of US cities, and that provided an avenue for engagement with the broader urban society. The earliest voices of Italian Americans heard publicly were those of political and labor activists such as poet/organizer Arturo Giovannitti, novelist, biographer, and journalist Frances Winwar (born Francesca Vinceguerra), and labor organizers Carlo Tresca and Luigi Fraina, who was among the first to publish Marxist literary and cultural criticism in the United States.

Pietro di Donato, Mari Tomasi, Angelo Pellegrini, Carl Marzani, Vincent Ferrini, and Diane di Prima are a half-dozen of the many Italian American intellectuals whose careers both included critical examination of the consequences of economic class and ethnic identity on urban politics and culture and continued a radical tradition of thinking that encourages us to join them in challenging the social and economic status quo. Rather than abandon their working-class origins, they focused their life energies on understanding their own class origins and working for social change. Unlike the few Italian immigrant writers who preceded them, whose work essentially argued for acceptance as human beings and pleas for recognition as Americans, these children and grandchildren of Italian immigrants used their writing to document and explore the conditions under which they were born and raised.

We can see in the shift from earlier Italian American writers who created origin narratives featuring struggles with the host culture, alienation from the ancestral culture, and the price paid for integration, to the inward turn of later writers what Richard Lehan identifies as in *The City in Literature: An Intellectual and Cultural History* (1998) as the passage of the literary city from realist to modernist narrative. Yet that inward turn toward loss in later generations is not merely formal; it measures the distance between a vibrant ethnic urban world commonly founded on regional identities (often called *campanilismo*) to the shards of memory, the ancestral ghosts that survive in recreated Italian American identities, and it poses the aesthetic and existential question of what to make of it.

Felix Stefanile's poem "The Americanization of the Immigrant" (1995) speaks this sense of loss:

> Like Dante
> I have pondered and pondered
> the speech I was born with,
> lost now, mother gone,
> the whole neighborhood bulldozed
> and no one to say it on the TV,
> that words are dreams.[4]

Similarly elegiac but more politically pointed, his "The Bocce Court on
Lewis Avenue" (1995) recounts the history of his boyhood neighborhood of
Corona, Queens, through a meditation on a photograph that appeared in
the *New York Times*. The seven-part poem is composed of stanzas that
describe fragments of the photo, suggesting the very fragmentation that
occurs as Italian immigrants begin the process of acculturation. The
opening section, "The center of the shot," describes a man playing
bocce, a game in the heart of a Little Italy that has been in Corona for
nearly a century, and contrasts the outcomes of a similar strategy in the
game and the politics of urban renewal:

> Displacement is the dearest thing in bocce;
> not dump-shot, not home run, it can reverse a point,
> turn losers into winners. This leads to drinking.
> Here, as displacement, it is kinder than
> the one the mayor plans, our suave John Lindsay,
> who has ordered the demolition of this street,
> this bocce course four generations old,
> to make room for a high school playing-field

as age gives way to youth.[5] Displacement in bocce is celebrated commu-
nally, the mayor's shot shatters the community. After taking us through
"The left border of the photograph," "The right border of the photograph," and "Foreground," the poet takes us behind the scenes by creating
a section entitled "The frame to hold the photograph," which presents how
the city's machinations result in "maiming" if not destroying Italian
Corona Heights. The poet knows that it will not be long before what
remains of this Little Italy is a memory and a photograph, the point
a young woman makes as she confronts the newspaper's photographer, "I
told that man to come/ and see my fig-tree, take a picture maybe. / The one
my father planted. I told him, / these are my memories, this house, that
tree. / How do you pay for memories, I said."[6]

   From another perspective, the key to assimilation is not what one loses,
but what one acquires by becoming available to influences outside one's
home culture, even as it may lead one to abandon Corona or another Little
Italy for new opportunities. For Gilbert Sorrentino and many American
writers of his generation, moving outside the "old neighborhood" meant
encounters with social and cultural influences of the world beyond the
family. These encounters not only enabled them to explore exciting directions as artists, but also challenged them to establish an awareness of how
their backgrounds differed from other writers and artists. Without any sort

of unifying cultural spirit, such as that fostered by Jewish critics like Howe, Lionel Trilling, Cynthia Ozick, Norman Podhoretz, Alfred Kazin and others, Italian American writers were not challenged to nurture a sense of obligation to the connection to any group history and, so freed, soon launched into independent discoveries of America.

In *Steelwork* (1970), Sorrentino created a series of prose fragments of people who populate a single Brooklyn neighborhood, some of them obviously Italian. Refusing sustained narrative, he re-creates the past without the sentimentality and nostalgia of earlier writers, even as the fragments reflect the sense of disintegration of the world as it had been known. Of *Steelwork*, Sorrentino has said, "If there is tragedy, it is the tragedy of trying to live as a human being in this kind of milieu, which is not particularly degrading, but which is deadening."[7] Through Sorrentino's Artie Salvo (Art Savior or a salvo at art), we see the frustration of the immigrant's son, a "born ballplayer" wounded by the streets, who has no way of connecting to the world outside the neighborhood once his athletic dream is destroyed. Too proud or ignorant to get the "Special Training" the city offers people with physical handicaps, he is doomed to wander the neighborhood limping in and out of people's lives. The most sustained Italian presence in the novel, Salvo is a "dark kid" who must fight to enter the world of the street kids who define their world by ethnicity. In "Shining Green Coupe – 1938," Artie sits on the car of a "hero [...] fair of hair, blue of eye," who regards it as a "symbol of home and regeneration, a sock full of golden eagles sewn into the mattress" and must throw Artie off it because, "no greasy-haired Dago was going to sully that."[8] Similar consciousness of Italian/American otherness plays out ironically as Americanness is lost in the web of ethnic and religious differences that pulse through the neighborhood like blood:

> Dago, he said to Gibby, you're a Protestant Dago. Not, Gibby said, looking at Pat, bigger, older by three or four years. And he was born on this block. His block. Not? Pat said, not a wop? Not a Protestant, Gibby said. But a wop, Pat said. An American, Gibby said, he fumbled, American, like you. I'm Irish, Pat said. My mother's Irish, Gibby said.

This familiar Irish/Italian conflict echoes with the typical wise guy, Fredo, a street-tough who "never went to school" and "never went home." He steals merchandise from boxcars, change from newsstands, and beats up Red Mulvaney because he hates the Irish whom he equates with cops. To Eddie Beshary, a "Joo bastid" who is the closest thing in the neighborhood to a philosopher, Sorrentino assigns a wisdom that challenge these teen dreams of success:

menkind must get out of that basement to be happy, get away from these menial tasks he thinks are okay. [...] The improvement of the mind, the richness of reading the dictionary to express yourself. [...] All these things are the key to get you out of the basement and up to the higher floors – to the roof, the penthouse! Money is nothing without culture and learning, who cares about a new suit on a stupid back?[9]

If escape is the only recourse, what remains of the enclave is the shell, Little Italy as a gentrified hot spot with an honorary street sign or a wall plaque signifying what was. To read the Little Italys of such Italian American writers is to look at maps leading to a past that disintegrates as it recedes in memory, to recall and perhaps to reclaim what was lost, and to discover what Italian Americans have become.

Tina DeRosa's stylistically modernist novel *Paper Fish* (1980) depicts the disintegration of one of Chicago's largest Italian neighborhoods in the 1960s along with the journey of Carmolina, its protagonist, from family and neighborhood outward to the creation of a self. The novel ends with an "Epilogue" divided into six segments that illustrate from different angles the neighborhood's demise. Rather than describe its destruction, DeRosa recreates the experience through imagistic language:

> Underneath, the street is brick, brick that is no longer whole and red, but chipped and gray like the faces of dead people trapped under lava. The street heaves up bricks, the guts of the street spit up brick. The face of the street cracks open and reveals its belly of brick, the gray faces. Squads of men in white t-shirts and hard hats with pickaxes in their hands chew into the street's cement face and the face cracks and there is no body under the bricks, only the cracked cement face. [...]
>
> The people of the neighborhood sit on wooden benches, eat lemon ice in fluted cups, their lips are wet from the ice. They look at the clean steel bones of the tracks.[10]

The excavation of the city streets, like the archeological diggings of historical sites, might reveal layers of past life, but for the observer of this scene, there is nothing beneath the surface. What made this site sacred is not the life that came before, but the living that are being displaced as the workers remove the streetcar line. What remains is for the observer/writer to transplant this all into memory where the loss and displacement can live forever.

What's missing in *Paper Fish* is the full story of this urban migration. DeRosa and Stefanile wrap the movement in the logic of urban renewal – new schools, new streets – and DeRosa, like Sorrentino, recounts a story of growing up and out. Yet if we want to call this demise of the old place the price of success, we may invoke James Baldwin, from "The Language of the Streets" (1981), to remind us of the political and racial attitudes, far from the historical labor radicalism of the Italian "other," that also figure into the price of that transit:

> The European immigrants coming through Ellis Island is a very important matter. They had gone to the city before I did; and once they had become white Americans, part of their function, part of their action was to keep me out of the city. [...] The price of the ticket was to become white. Americans failed to realize they were not white before they got here. [...] They were be[com]ing white because they had to keep me black; and there are economic reasons for that, and the economic reasons have more repercussions and moral results.[11]

Later writings of Italian Americans reveal this shift of priorities that accompanied passage into the mainstream US culture.

Emilio DeGrazia's swan song for a disintegrating Little Italy that looms large in the mind as it shrinks on the streets of St. Paul, Minnesota, comes in his novel *A Canticle for Bread and Stones* (1997), which confronts the racist turn in Italian immigrant culture. Drawn to Minnesota to build a cathedral, Raphael Amato, the stone artist great-grandfather of protagonist Salvatore Amato, runs into trouble caused by an American philanthropist who can change minds and neighborhoods with a wave of his cash-filled hand. Salvatore searches for meaningful work in 1970s America, as he tries to find out why his great-grandfather was fired from the job of building the great cathedral. This quest turns into a mystery that Salvatore must solve before he can go on with his life. The mystery takes the protagonist to several storytellers who ultimately teach him that the country he has inherited is not the America that drew his immigrant ancestors from the poverty of the old country.

DeGrazia presents a Little Italy that was once a dream world for immigrants and has become a nightmare for subsequent generations. Salvatore's college degree never helped him find that white-collar job his parents believed would be his by rite of passage. While they see him as the fulfillment of their American Dream, Salvatore recognizes it as the nightmare it is. Anchored to working-class culture, Salvatore, unlike his father, understands the economic system, wants more than a job, and is left to philosophize on the demise of Little Italy:

> Once upon a time my kind of neighborhood, full of people strolling by, shopkeepers standing in doorways when business was slow, mothers walking

hand-in-hand with children distracted by some new things in a store window, old men on street corners arguing about the weather, baseball and politics and boys weaving in and out of the sidewalk traffic so girls would see how wonderful they were. All that noise and activity gone now, nothing left but empty sidewalks and stores, here and there a yellow light shining dimly through drawn shades in an upstairs' windows and the slogans of sex and disgust tainted on walls. At the end of the block a black woman sat head-in-hands on the curb. "Loro," Guido called them. Them. Beware of Them, the blacks moving in with their ragged mattresses and box springs and stares, this sullen people from a time so lost in space our Old World seemed new.[12]

The post-immigrant paradigm presented in DeGrazia's novel is one in which the Italian American must confront not only the silence of the past but the silent lessons of racism that have been instilled as the immigrants learned to become white in the United States; the lesson learned was "They" are what we were, and if we no longer want to be like that, we need to distance ourselves from "Loro," Them. The changing economic and social status of Italian immigrants and their children, attributed to the process of pursuing the American Dream of upward mobility in a tough economic system, found Italians heading to the suburbs at a time when the political climate began to listen to voices of the minorities through mass media outlets, news, and music. The suburbs, on the contrary, became the place for white ethnics to acculturate, and often to assimilate, as they lacked the concentration of multigeneration families, the vital street life (indeed, the street-ward orientation of houses), the institutions and spaces to support the uprooted culture.

Carol Maso's *Ghost Dance* tells this story through a third-generation suburban ethnic who has the option of choosing among the traditions that make up American culture. Like DeRosa's *Paper Fish*, *Ghost Dance* records a young woman's efforts to achieve her identity amidst the chaos of her family's disintegration as she comes of age. Vanessa Turin is the grand-daughter of Italian immigrants on her father's side, and of Armenian and German ancestors on her mother's side. Throughout the novel, she examines the constraints that ethnic identities created. Her parents remain very distant from their immigrant parents. After what he believes is a failure to achieve the American Dream, Vanessa's Armenian grandfather changes his name back to Sarkis Wingarian from Frank Wing, leaves his college-aged daughters, and returns to the old country where, Vanessa imagines, he might say he is "worth his weight in gold": "In America I would look like an old man, but here old men are respected. Old age means wisdom."[13] Her

Italian grandfather, determined to make himself American, attempts to erase all his Italianita and replace it with normative American beliefs.

The novel is composed of narrative fragments, some only a single sentence, in no chronological order. Most of them present what Vanessa imagines might have happened in the past. To find the sources of those myths, Vanessa and her brother, Fletcher, turn first to their parents, Michael, a father who doesn't say much, and Christine Wing, a mother whose "mind could not be trusted completely."[14] To get their father to speak, they invent a homework assignment of writing their family history, but their father tells them to make up anything they like and goes for a walk. Denied their father's story, they study a mail-order family tree. The names only bring questions; Vanessa fabricates the answers.

Eventually, the siblings learn about their ancestry and the reason their father won't discuss his past through their immigrant grandparents, Angelo and Maria. Without a sense of how the narrator acquired this story (whether someone told her or she made it up), Vanessa presents a scene in which her father watches his father destroy the garden of tomatoes, peppers, and eggplants, "insisting that they are Americans now, not Italians." This destruction of Italian signifiers leads Vanessa to question:

> Is this what my father means when he says there are things it is better to forget? Is this what he is forgetting – his own father out in the garden chopping the tomato plants into pieces. [. . .] Did his father announce that there will be no more Italian spoken in his house? No more wine drunk with lunch [. . .]? Did he tell his wife there would be no more sad songs from the old country? How much she must have wept, hugging her small son to her breast![15]

Vanessa imagines that this experience terrorized her father, creating a fear of being the unaccepted ethnic; his story piques her curiosity and leads her into a search for ancestral roots.

During a family visit to 1964 New York World's Fair, Vanessa's father spends nearly the entire time viewing Michelangelo's *Pieta* in the Vatican Pavilion. Her mother walks the Fair alone. While Vanessa does not know what her grandmother did, she does know that her grandfather and Fletcher get arrested in a civil rights sit-in outside Ford's "Progressland" exhibit. After bailing them out, the family returns to the Fair, and Vanessa imagines, "My grandfather thought, looking at this exquisite show, that we had traded something important for all this. Primitive man was better." When they leave, she thinks, "My grandfather turned his back on the lights finally and shook his head with the tremendous sorrow of someone who has been betrayed at the core." He then journeys back into the past, "to a simpler place, where he would live the last years of his life."[16] Here we see Angelo fighting against America racism, refusing to accept it as the cost of becoming American despite what he earlier sacrificed.

In Part Four, Vanessa lives with her grandmother on the farm. With Angelo gone, Maria attempts to pass on her knowledge as a legacy, "repeat-[ing] things she thinks [Vanessa] should know – useful things like when to sow vegetables. [...] Life is understandable was what my grandmother was trying to say. You can understand your life." Later, Christine attempts to rearrange the garden but inadvertently kills everything: "'Let's clear out the roots, honey. Let's start over. [...] We'll get rid of the roots, it's the only way.' 'It's the only way,' she kept saying. 'We'll get rid of the roots.'"[17] This scene becomes a metaphor for the way Christine has dealt with her own past. Ethnicity serves no role in the creation of her art; "the roots" only get in the way of the new. But the price paid for this disconnection is loss of knowledge of how to live. Such rootlessness inverts what Lehan sees as signaling the breakdown of a culture when, speaking of Nick Carraway's disgust with the ethnic city, he writes, "With the rise of ethnic diversity, what is organic and homogenous to a culture breaks down. As these factors drive the move from Culture to Civilization, a process of decline begins. The modern city thus has a shell that promises great vitality while an inner reality works destructively and pushes us toward death."[18] Quite the opposite, Maso implies that the *loss* of ethnicity in the imperative to Americanization leaves only a brittle husk of existence.

Our final novels, Frank Lentricchia's *The Music of the Inferno* (1999) and Don DeLillo's *Cosmopolis* (2003) take us squarely into the politics of postwar assimilation and white ethnic identity. *The Music of the Inferno* expresses the futility of maintaining a subculture in a society that rewards individualism and demands separation from subcultures as the price of success. The Italians of Utica, New York, who bought into the deal, doffed ethnic identity as soon as they could be seen as white, as soon as they could afford middle-class lives. We see the conservative drift accompanying assimilation as they begin to wield political power. The protagonist, Robert Tagliaferro is an orphan of unknown racial background, adopted and raised by a black couple, Morris and Melvina Reed, and an Italian couple, Gregorio and Caterina Spina; he is a "man [...] made of words," self-taught through a lifetime of reading in the New York City bookstore that became his home after he left Utica at eighteen.[19] As he traces the etymology of his surname, he finds that Tagliaferro (Iron cutter) was a name often given to African American slaves (Booker T. Washington bore the phonetic spelling), and so begins his questioning the differences between Italian Americans and African Americans. With his knowledge and his reading of all nine books on Utica's history, he exacts his vengeance on the city's Italian Americans, whom he sees as hopelessly corrupted, each deserving a place in a contemporary Inferno of Robert's making.

Through a series of revelations at three dinners, the first appropriately held on the Fourth of July, Tagliaferro slowly and deliberately destroys the Italian hold on the city by speaking publicly the secrets protected by the city's racist powerbrokers, such men as Albert Cesso, Professor Louis Ayoub, and Sebastiano Spina, all descendants of Utica's first immigrants. The intended victim is Spina, a mayoral candidate with a dark past that Robert will expose after the election because "the ascension of Spina will trigger epic Italian American self-cleansing. They will loathe their ethnicity. They will want to change their surnames to Windsor, Spencer or Bowles." Robert attributes the conservative turn of Italian Americans to an exaggerated ethnic pride enabled only by their acceptance as white Americans. It requires forgetting parts of their ancestral history, like "the southern side of Sicily, where they had a considerable amount of warm interaction with the people of Africa," and offers no alternative sense of authentic community. Here Lentricchia rails against the public display of what Herbert Gans calls "symbolic ethnicity," which is more about business and branding than any internal and ethical sense of what it means to be Italian American; they have become, Robert says, "people who wear buttons saying Kiss Me, I'm Italian" on Columbus Day.[20] Lentricchia's later urban tales recount the end of a world in which ethnic and religious identities matter and are replaced through racial and class identifications – key factors in expediting the assimilation of European immigrants whose tribal behavior in ethnic neighborhoods and religious loyalties were seen as obstacles to a strong national identification.

From Polis to *Cosmopolis*

From his earliest short stories to his most recent novels, Don DeLillo has become one of the great contemporary urban writers. While much of his earlier fiction shows a more nostalgic version of the city, *Cosmopolis* presents a dystopian view of contemporary US urban culture focalized through young hedge-fund star Eric Packer. DeLillo dramatizes Packer's quest to get a haircut, but not get from just any place because "a haircut has what. Associations. Calendar on the wall. Mirrors everywhere."[21] So he heads to the old neighborhood, to Anthony Adubato, the Italian American barber who cut his father's hair and his own when he was young. The conversation associated with this particular haircut give us a sense of Packer's search for a past. While we never get a gloss on the surname Packer – has it been Anglicized, shortened in the process of acculturation? – we cannot help but read Eric's quest as one for some part of his identity that has been lost. The movement of the entire novel is toward this single act, a journey not out of a "longing or yearning of sense of the past. He was too young to feel such things, and anyways unsuited, and this had never been his home or street. He was feeling what his father would feel, standing in this place." Anthony reconnects Eric to his father by retelling the story of how he died. When he finds out that Eric is being hunted but is unarmed because he threw his gun away, Anthony gives him an old pistol and exclaims, "I thought you had a reputation. Destroy a man in the blink of an eye. But you sound pretty iffy to me. This is Mike Packer's kid? That had a gun and threw it away? What is that?" At this point, it's someone uncertain about himself, recalling times when he and his mother went to the movies, where "we were cold and lost and my father's soul was trying to find us to settle itself into our bodies." Now, he loses his financial acumen because, he reflects, "Power works best when there is no memory attached."[22] This humanizing experience infiltrates the psychic fortress Eric created by his market savvy, a fortress represented by his custom limousine – a moving office where he takes reports from his advisors, makes his financial plays, and gets a checkup from his doctor as he moves through the city. DeLillo's narrative instances what Lehan sees as the deep theme of modernist city literature; "We have changed how we measure humanity, from relying on the rhythms of the land to using urban mechanisms. Behind such mechanics lies the destructive desire to conquer nature in the name of money."[23]

For Lehan the urban terminus is entropy, which DeLillo represents with Packer stuck in traffic. Caught at Times Square in a march against capitalism, he finds protesters swinging live rats by the tails and flinging them at suspected capitalist leaders, scribbling graffiti on financial centers, and turning his custom limo into a demolition derby loser. Yet the posthuman terminus of these historical developments as charted by *Cosmopolis* is articulated by Vija Kinski, Packer's "chief of theory," who explains that "clock time accelerated the rise of capitalism. People stopped thinking about eternity. They began to concentrate on hours, measurable hours, man-hours, using labor more efficiently." The new structure and rhythm of "time is a corporate asset now. It belongs to the free market system" that

Packer, the market whiz, seems to have mastered. Yet, racked by memory that eddies a human past out of the data flow and creeping doubt about finding in the market's activity "an affinity between market movements and the natural world," Packer loses control, squandering billions of dollars in a frenzied attempt to push the currency market in his direction and shore up his sense of self.[24] Being unmoored also leads him to meet his nemesis, a former employee and would-be assassin, Benno Levin. Levin, whose real name is Richard Straights, is a loner who lives much like Lentricchia's Tagliaferro; he squats in an abandoned building where he nurtures his single desire of killing Eric Michael Packer in retribution for the way he and his work were dehumanized by the young, de-ethnicized mogul.

Thinking of market mastery, Kinski points to something that might have served as a way for Packer to right his wrongs: "'We used to know the past but not the future. Time is changed,' she said. 'We need a new theory of time.'"[25] Instead of looking for how patterns from the past produce the present and might predict the future, Packer might have focused on how his actions in the present shape the future and reinterpret the past, which is also Lentricchia's theme. Similarly, for urban immigrants, ethnic memory ought to focus on the future, as Michael M. J. Fischer suggested. Ethnic reinvention, he tells us, is accomplished through a narrative's "inter-references between two or more cultural traditions" which "create reservoirs for renewing humane values." By identifying and reading these interreferences we will be able to see that, as Fischer concludes, "Ethnic memory is [. . .] or ought to be future, not past oriented." This is an idea that needs to be developed as we begin looking for ways to present ethnic American cultures, especially as ethnic identification and representation has become a matter of choice, a prerogative in the postmodern world. Human values can be renewed if usable pasts are recovered and reworked to guide people away from reactionary politics based on forgotten discriminated pasts that separate and divide and toward the type of revolutionary politics that unite. A hopeful possibility for this was advanced by Patrick Gallo in his 1974 study, *Ethnic Alienation: The Italian-Americans*. Gallo saw enough similarities between Italian and African Americans to suggest the creation of an alliance of, in his words, "whites and Blacks, white-collar and blue-collar workers, based on mutual need and interdependence. [. . .] Italian-Americans may prove to be a vital ingredient in not only forging that alliance but in serving as the cement that will hold urban centers together."[26] Gallo's idea, while never formally acted upon, was echoed in Michael Parenti's more recent call for new bases for the construction of Italian American identities:

Ethnic identity is not only reactive but proactive, not only a defense against stereotypes, not only a compensatory assurance of group work, but a positive enjoyment, a celebration of our history and culture in this country and in Italy. It is a way of connecting with others in what too often is a friendless and ruthless market society, a nurturing identity that is larger than the self yet smaller than the nation. [. . .]

To frame the Italian-American experience within a context of struggle for social justice and economic survival is to give it a dimension that goes beyond nostalgia and sentimentality and flies in the face of the stereotypes that weigh down upon us Italians.[27]

The illumination of the consciousness of new generations of immigrants and their descendants through education in the arts and humanities can help us renew hopes of rehumanizing our urban cultures and help us to redefine and refine our ideas of what cities can and should do for all of us.

Notes

1. David M. Fine, *The City, The Immigrant and American Fiction, 1880–1920* (Metuchen, NJ: Scarecrow Press, 1977), pp. 143, 22, vi.
2. Irving Howe, "Suburbs of Babylon," in *Celebrations and Attacks* (New York: Horizon Press, 1979), p. 39; Howe, "Philip Roth Reconsidered," in *The Critical Point* (New York: Horizon Press, 1973), p. 141; Edward Alexander, *Irving Howe – Socialist, Critic, Jew* (Bloomington: Indiana University Press, 1998), p. 168.
3. Fine, *The City*, p. 146, citing the title of Novak's 1971 book.
4. Felix Stefanile, "The Americanization of the Immigrant," in *Songs of the Sparrow: The Poetry of Felix Stefanile* (New York: Bordighera Press, 2015), p. 274.
5. Stefanile, "The Bocce Court on Lewis Avenue," ibid., p. 304.
6. Ibid., p. 308.
7. John O'Brien, "A Conversation with Gilbert Sorrentino," *Review of Contemporary Fiction* 1.1 (1981), 13.
8. Gilbert Sorrentino, *Steelwork* (Elmwood Park, IL: Dalkey Archive Press, 1992), pp. 120–21, 53.
9. Ibid., pp. 94, 99–100, 172–73.
10. Tina DeRosa, *Paper Fish* (Chicago: Wine Press, 1980), p. 133.
11. James Baldwin, "The Language of the Streets," in Michael C. Jay and Ann Chalmers Watts, eds., *Literature and the Urban Experience: Essays on the City and Literature* (New Brunswick, NJ: Rutgers University Press, 1981), p. 135.
12. Emilio DeGrazia, *A Canticle for Bread and Stones* (Rochester, MN: Lone Oak Press, 1997), p. 43.
13. Carole Maso, *Ghost Dance* (San Francisco: North Point Press, 1986), p. 212.

14. Ibid., p. 37.
15. Ibid., p. 74.
16. Ibid., pp. 129, 130, 130.
17. Ibid., pp. 175, 217.
18. Richard Lehan, *The City in Literature: An Intellectual and Cultural History* (Berkeley: University of California Press, 1998), p. 220.
19. Frank Lentricchia, *The Music of the Inferno* (Albany: SUNY Press, 1999), p. 27.
20. Ibid., pp. 164, 105, 136; see Herbert Gans, "Symbolic Ethnicity: The Future of Ethnic Groups and Cultures in America," *Ethnic and Racial Studies*, 2.1 (1979), 1–20.
21. Don DeLillo, *Cosmopolis* (New York: Scribner, 2003), p. 15.
22. Ibid., pp. 159, 167, 185, 184.
23. Lehan, *The City in Literature*, p. 135.
24. Ibid., pp. 79, 86.
25. Ibid., p. 86.
26. Michael M. J. Fischer, "Ethnicity and the Post-Modern Arts of Memory," in James Clifford and George E. Marcus, eds., *Writing Culture: The Poetics and Politics of Ethnography* (Berkeley: University of California Press, 1986), p. 201; Patrick J. Gallo, *Ethnic Alienation: The Italian-American* (Rutherford, NJ: Fairleigh Dickinson University Press, 1974), p. 209.
27. Michael Parenti, "Italian American Identity: To Be or Not to Be," *Common Dreams*, August 27, 2009, www.commondreams.org/views/2009/08/27/ital ian-american-identity-be-or-not-be.

CHAPTER 13

Crime and Violence; or, Hard-boiled Chronicles of Mean Streets and Their Hidden Truths

Brian Tochterman

Emergency calls, crime statistics, and talk-radio commentary about Chicago, "the city of death," overlay a shot of a patrol car speeding along the edge of the Loop. It carries a wounded cop whose ultimate end is called by Dr. Paul Kersey. Saddened, resentful, and frustrated, the departed's partner utters a rhetorical quip about Kersey getting "the animal that shot him." Thus commences the consummate urban revenge fantasy of our time, *Death Wish* (Eli Roth, 2018), a film that marks the triumph of the political narrative of urban violence and depravity that Donald Trump sold throughout his first campaign and presidency. Trump's rhetoric recalls another time and place and another *Death Wish* (Michael Winner, 1974), which depicts New York City overrun by a criminal underclass acting at random and with unprecedented violence during the years of Trump's rise as a developer. Trump's effective signaling on inner-city crime during a period of relative urban tranquility speaks to the lasting political power of narratives of violence in fiction and fantasy.[1]

Each generation has its own version of the death-wish city. While fiction writers and other cultural producers often fabricate urban settings for lurid tales, discursive power lies when they map realist representations of crime and violence onto actual US cities. In the aftermath of World War II, crime narratives and concern about the fate of cities intensified in tandem. The postwar disruption of urban political economy, combined with structural changes across the media landscape and shifting public norms, created a provocative and persistent narrative of urban violence. Older cities in the Northeast and Midwest seen as problematic by political leaders and master planners swiftly underwent slum clearance and purported renewal that failed to address systemic urban problems. "Slum," "urban crisis," and other such labels refracted increasingly diverse urban citizenries through associations with crime and violence. Literary representations of violence served as commentaries on the causes of, and solutions to, the social problem of crime; they fed off and informed the era's political culture, characterized by white backlash, fear, exodus, and lasting resentment. Initially, cultural producers conjured masculine fantasies of the white vigilante. As the urban crime problem evolved coinciding fictional narratives probed the human condition, exploring the sources of persistent violence and exposing the limits of political responses like the wars on crime and drugs. These competing sensibilities borrowed from prewar antecedents.

Amid the rapid urbanization of the nineteenth century gothic authors took advantage of the emergent penny press to serialize and sensationalize urban crime for political ends. Ned Buntline's *Mysteries and Miseries of New York* (1848) deployed nativist codes to condemn the city, creating a lasting association between immigrants and crime, violence, and debauchery that was immediately capitalized on by George Foster's gothic tales, *New York by Gaslight* (1850). George Lippard had commenced the US urban gothic vogue with *The Quaker City; or, the Monks of Monk-Hall* (1845), a novel written in service to a radical agenda; Lippard sought to address the growing economic polarization of the modern city and the exploitation – including sexual exploitation – of its lower classes. Gothic tropes informed later works of reformist nonfiction including Jacob Riis's *How the Other Half Lives* (1890), which laces reportage with gothic tropes that at once shocked audiences and solidified the image of the city as a den of violence and criminality.

By the 1920s, crime fiction acquired legitimacy and a home in bound books. In 1944, Raymond Chandler celebrated the emergent "hard-boiled" genre in "The Simple Art of Murder" (1944), presenting a treatise on the realism in Dashiell Hammett's protagonists, the Continental Op and Sam Spade. Central to that realism is the art of detection, the learned but logical process for solving crime. City streets have their problems but they harbor truths, Chandler suggested, and via the detective's brain – the supreme tool for justice in these works – a man might come "down these mean streets" to address those problems, particularly crime. These were the qualities that Hammett and Chandler carried through in their "hard-boiled chronicles" of prewar San Francisco and Los Angeles.[2]

Those conventions changed after the war, as the fate of major cities found its way into the spotlight and paperbacks expanded hard-boiled readership. In several bestselling novellas set in New York City, Mike Hammer represented Mickey Spillane's fantasy of a final solution to urban violence and disorder. Hammer is a private investigator by trade, but within the novels' narratives he never operates for hire. Motivated in most cases by revenge, Hammer instead functions as a vigilante out to clean up the city. In *I, the Jury* (1947), he returns from the war "anxious to get some of the rats that make up the section of humanity that prey on people."[3] Depicted by Spillane as a good guy with a gun, Hammer circumvents established law and due process, as the title of the first novel suggests. Within popular culture, Hammer proved a lasting model for both persecution and prosecution of criminals going forward.

In Spillane's imagination, the city's declining physical plant and shifting racial and ethnic demographics posed the most significant problems. This volatile combination wrought the city's "monster," a permanent underclass of criminals that terrorize the city and its inhabitants with abandon and at random. Hammer narrates a section on Harlem as "that strange no-man's-land where the white mixed with the black and the languages overflowed into each other like that of the horde around the Tower of Babel," while tenements overflowed with "strange, foreign smells of cooking and too many people in too few rooms."[4] In more than one novel Hammer notes his unease within the geography of the city he knows well, seeking to get back to "[his] kind of people"[5] – white working-class ethnics then crossing the bridges en masse into the suburban hinterland of New Jersey and Long Island. Scholar Sean McCann suggests that Spillane's racial politics "echoed features of [Ku Klux] Klan fantasy" found in pulp fiction and the pages of *Black Mask* magazine during the 1920s.[6]

The well-chronicled origins of the urban crisis lay in the policies, migrations, and mobilizations of Spillane's era, but its public image was slow to emerge. In the 1960s, local incidents of racial brutality, discrimination, and injustice as well as nationally broadcast events like the frequent assassination of civil rights leaders provided the spark that ignited black communities, unleashing a wave of uprisings in cities across the country. Kathryn Bigelow's film *Detroit* (2017), set during the city's 1967 uprising, offers a precise context in a series of prologue titles:

> The Great Migration set in motion before World War I would spur some 6 million African Americans to leave the cotton fields of the South for the lure of factory jobs and civil rights in the North. After World War II, white Americans began their own migration to the suburbs, drawing money and jobs away from increasingly segregated urban neighborhoods. By the 60's, racial tensions had reached a boiling point. Rebellions erupted in Harlem, Philadelphia, Watts, and Newark. In Detroit, African Americans were restricted to a few overcrowded neighborhoods, patrolled by a mostly white police force known for its aggression. The promise of equal

opportunity for all turned out to be an illusion. Change was inevitable. It was only a matter of how, and when.

News coverage and investigative reports of seemingly disintegrating cities and contemporary texts on crime, violence, and culture, such as *The Negro Family: A Case for National Action* ("The Moynihan Report," 1965) and the *Report of the National Advisory Commission on Civil Disorders* ("The Kerner Report," 1968) provided a framework and vocabulary for the era's policies. President Johnson declared a War on Crime in concert with his War on Poverty and the war in Vietnam, as did his successor, Richard Nixon. An insurgent right-wing called for "law and order" and Hollywood fleshed out public options. As producer Dino De Laurentiis put it, the original *Death Wish* was "an open invitation to the authorities to come up with remedies to the problem of urban violence, and fast."[7]

As the success of *Death Wish* illustrates, the heroic vigilantism of Mike Hammer and the image of the violent city that Spillane presented transferred easily to film by the 1970s, with filmmakers seeking a heroic salve to the most visible symptoms of the urban crisis. Rising crime rates and fears in New York made for a fertile climate for the film, which both harkened back to Spillane and foreshadowed the preemptive violence of Bernhard Goetz, the so-called Subway Vigilante, who shot four black teenagers on December 22, 1984. The shooting, which left one victim paralyzed and brain damaged, mimicked a scene from *Death Wish* where Paul Kersey hides behind a newspaper allowing two would-be subway muggers to approach before firing on them. While Goetz boasted of wanting to murder his victims and "gouge one of the guy's eyes out with my keys afterward," he managed to walk away from assault and attempted murder charges, much like the fictional vigilantes he imitated.[8]

Clint Eastwood's "Dirty Harry" Callahan, perhaps Mike Hammer's most faithful torchbearer patrolling the streets of San Francisco killing crazed hippies and begging crooks to make his day, offered Goetz another critical reference. Don Siegel's infamous *Dirty Harry* (1971) sprang from the era's "law-and-order" political culture and the transformative success of Arthur Penn's shockingly violent *Bonnie and Clyde* (1967). In contrast to the dreadful representation of the NYPD in *Death Wish*, the honor and duty of police work, and its inherent risks, are signaled in *Dirty Harry's* opening shot, a scan of local officers killed in the line of duty, four from 1970 alone. The camera suggests a hidden truth: San Francisco is a war zone where even cops are unsuspecting casualties. That war erupts in the subsequent scene as a rooftop sniper fires across the downtown canyon to kill an unsuspecting woman in the swimming pool of another skyscraper. The crime shocks with its brutal randomness – the film's antagonist, "Scorpio," was modeled on Northern California's concurrent "Zodiac" serial killer – and its rendering of the private as now public. The victim's right to residential privacy has been deposed by weapons technology and the mad citizen's pathological urge to kill.

Dirty Harry exhibited a new ideology of policing inspired by contemporary appeals for criminal retribution. Callahan routinely brings arms and gunfire into the public sphere. When a daytime bank heist interrupts lunch, he gleefully fires and wounds the black thief across a crowded block while breaking out his trademark "do you feel lucky?" tag line. Callahan's penchant for public shootouts is part of the film's engagement with the cultural tension between victims' rights and the rights of the accused. The state prosecutes Callahan for violating Fourth and Fifth Amendment protections, in which activity he echoes Mike Hammer's disdain for due process. In contrast with police procedurals of the *film noir* era – some of them produced in cooperation with local and federal law enforcement agencies – such as *The Naked City* (Jules Dassin, 1948), *The Street with No Name* (William Keighley, 1948), and *Detective Story* (William Wyler, 1951), vigilantes from Hammer to Harry argue that police work is outdated in the face of urban crisis, providing fodder for both right-wing talking points and proactive crime-fighting strategies. Administrators up the chain of command loathe Callahan, but he is a hero to the audience nonetheless. *Dirty Harry's* immediate sequel (of four), *Magnum Force* (Ted Post, 1973), plays on that positionality. The film centers on four rookie cops inspired by Callahan's actions and reputation – members of "the first generation that learned how to fight" – who form a secret death squad to murder San Francisco's public enemies. The prodigal sons are doomed, but their actions require some soul-searching. "I hate the system," Harry admits in *Magnum Force*. "But until someone comes up with a better one," he adds even as he overstretches the Constitution to resolve San Francisco's new violent scourge, "I'm sticking with it."

Vigilante cop and citizen fantasies were not spectacular enough to bring order to the violent city by the 1980s. Disruptions in the national political economy made deindustrialization and population decline watchwords for urban crime, and cities of the so-called Rust Belt emerged as critical places of fear. Popular culture, seeking to repair the trauma of Vietnam, transplanted the vigilante from the urban jungle into the literal jungles of Central America and East Asia, resulting in a series of paramilitary and sometimes cyborg commando fantasies starring a stable of hypermasculine actors including Sylvester Stallone, Arnold Schwarzenegger, Chuck Norris, and Steven Seagal. Paul Verhoeven's *Robocop* (1987), set in Detroit (by then labeled "Murder City") four years into the future, melded the traditional police procedural with the growing obsession with paramilitary cyborg technology.

Robocop drew on ascendant neoliberal strategies for bringing order to urban life, notably in the realms of privatization and partnered redevelopment. The film is prophetic and prescient, foretelling the expansion of private military outfits like Blackwater, the growth of the prison–industrial complex, and the incessant armoring of the police and their hardware. Omni Consumer Products (OCP), private manager of the police force, achieved financial success within the once public security market, overseeing prison development and supplying the military. Their ED (Enforcement Droid) 209 marks the logical conclusion of this fusion of roles; OCP's fully automated, 24-hour police robot is "programmed for urban pacification." Order imposed by ED 209 should ensure OCP's renewal plans for Delta City, the rebranded Old Detroit. Its CEO lifts the rationale for redevelopment from the vocabulary of postwar master planners who engaged private developers in partnerships to clear slums and construct housing and cultural amenities. *Robocop* imagines the neoliberal next step, a wholesale takeover of municipal governance by corporations and private firms, allowing them to orchestrate slum clearance and redevelopment without electoral accountability. Despite the film's critique of power and techno-policing, *Robocop*'s foresight extends not only to Detroit's recent bankruptcy, but also to Michigan's emergency manager model of governance, a strategy informed by neoliberalism and immune to community resistance.

Robocop's futurism and politics evolved from Ridley Scott's *Blade Runner* (1982), which projected a schizophrenic third-world Los Angeles of 2019. *Blade Runner* centers on the Tyrell Corporation's mutinous and increasingly self-aware bioengineered androids, called replicants, who have been enslaved in extractive work "off-world." Their fast-growing revolt results in ever more restrictive policies on mobility. Treated as "illegal aliens" with purported violent tendencies, the replicants are an implicit allegory for the criminal pathology linked to urban populations of color by mass media and a fearful white public, an allegory of particular relevance given Anglo Ange-lenos' fears about immigration in the 1980s. "Blade runners" are instructed to kill replicants on sight regardless of guilt and due process; as a result, shoot-outs on congested streets become common and desensitize human citizens to violence. Yet the film's development of emotional depths in the replicants and the flat affect of the putatively human blade runner, Rick Deckard (Harrison Ford), push back against that framing. In hindsight, *Blade Runner* offers some of the most prescient mise-en-scène in the futurist catalog, with Los Angeles sunshine replaced by omnipresent rain, smog, and darkness, gas flares from Wilmington and the bulwarks of the Tyrell Corporation's pyramids. Projection screens and drones cycle digital messages, distracting from the harsh reality of earth-bound life for those citizens unable to migrate to the off-world colonies that promise the "opportunity to begin again" and "live clean."

In the actual 1980s and 1990s, Los Angeles confronted its image as the new national posterchild for urban violence: crack and gang wars, drive-by shootings, and police corruption. The Crips and Bloods, among other gangs, entered the white consciousness in part through films like Dennis Hopper's *Colors* (1988). While earlier organized-crime narratives kept violence within the family so-to-speak, Los Angeles gang culture swiftly became associated with violent hazing rituals and shootings that killed innocent citizens. Boosters and political leaders sought to control the problem by subscribing to a fortress brand of architecture – Mike Davis famously linked Frank Gehry's aesthetic to *Dirty Harry* – enhancing the surveillance infrastructure, and creating alternative faux-urban spaces like CityWalk, a simulacrum of an ideal Los Angeles on the Universal Studios lot.[9] Non-gang-related violence further compounded the city's image, most notably the videotaped beating of Rodney King by four Los Angeles policemen and the wave of violence and destruction, unseen since the Watts Uprising of 1965, that met the not-guilty verdict. Joel Schumacher's timely *Falling Down* (1992), which chronicles one aggrieved white man's ill-fated march of vengeance across the city's multicultural landscape, seems born of the resentment and violence percolating in Los Angeles. In contrast to previous vigilantes, however, Michael Douglas's William Foster turns out to be the antagonist. "I'm the bad guy?" he asks, "How did that happen?" Films like *Colors*, *Falling Down*, and Lawrence Kasdan's *Grand Canyon* (1991) investigated the white psyche when confronted with the new demographics of Los Angeles, which became a majority-minority city by 1980. But the era also saw the rise of the New Black Cinema grounded in realist narratives, and a cycle of films that questioned the goals and outcomes of policing black communities.

Starting in the 1960s, independent production companies took advantage of the waning of the studio system and its prohibitive Production Code. Low-budget, improvised, loosely assembled productions resulted in a cinema-verité style that inadvertently injected realism into the films. One such genre of films starring and primarily directed by African Americans thrived alongside vigilante crime dramas. Commencing with Melvin Van Peebles's *Sweet Sweetback's Baadasssss Song* (1971), so-called Blaxploitation productions shot mostly on the streets of New York and Los Angeles entered the filmic conversation on urban violence. Blaxploitation examined the complicated structural relationship between police and criminals in black ghettos in a way that contested the racist subtext of the white vigilante genre. In addition to lionizing detectives like John Shaft (Richard Roundtree) and vigilantes like the eponymous Friday Foster, Coffy, and Foxy Brown (all Pam Grier), Blaxploitation also created sympathetic characters out of pimps, prostitutes, drug dealers, and gangsters, in other words, the anonymous faces Paul Kersey and Harry Callahan eliminated with ease and without consequence. *Super Fly* (Gordon Parks, Jr., 1972) follows the quest for freedom and justice of a Harlem coke-dealing hustler (Youngblood Priest played by Ron O'Neal) via one last score. At a time when white audiences saw the police as infallible (e.g., the concurrent Frank Sinatra vehicle *The Detective* [Gordon Douglas, 1968] and television fare like the second run of *Dragnet* [1967–70] and *Adam-12* [1968–75]), black audiences celebrated Priest's escape and particularly his outwitting double-cross of corrupt, racist cops. To credit *Super Fly's* prescience: Hollywood tales of NYPD corruption would soon follow, most notably Sidney Lumet's *Serpico* (1973) and *Prince of the City* (1981), in the wake of the *Knapp Commission Report on Police Corruption* (1973) and other exposés.

Black cinema proved a critical venue for challenging the narratives of police efficacy and benevolence. A decade after Blaxploitation cooled and the budgets and markets for African American films expanded, Spike Lee's masterpiece, *Do the Right Thing* (1989), brought contemporary conflicts around urban space and race into the canon. A brutally hot day on single block in Bedford-Stuyvesant, a largely black neighborhood in Brooklyn, is the setting. Racial and ethnic tensions rise along with the mercury, and by the end, the NYPD crosses the thin blue line into chaos. When a cop strangles Radio Raheem, the corner pizza shop erupts in flames and the thin bonds of trust between the longtime Italian American proprietors and Mookie, the local delivery man, are severed, seemingly forever. Drawing upon concurrent episodes involving racist terror in Howard Beach, Queens, and the strangulation-by-cop of graffiti artist Michael Stewart (later replicated in the strangulation of Eric Garner in 2014), Lee highlighted the fragility of perceived structural harmony in the post-crisis city.

The New Black Cinema that Lee ushered in forged a productive alliance with the changing landscape of hip-hop music. Lee's film centers Public Enemy's racial justice anthem "Fight the Power" as its musical theme. Public Enemy's critique of the urban power structure was a consistent echo across songs and artists in the black cinema milieu. Mario Van Peebles's directorial debut, *New Jack City* (1991), reimagined the classic crime formula of kingpin versus cop with a mostly black ensemble. Set in New York City and starring West-Coast hip-hop artist Ice-T, Van Peebles's film transformed the crime genre by interweaving the new style of gangster rap, whose graphic content was swiftly attacked by politicians and media. NWA's *Straight Outta Compton* (1988) brought the subgenre into the mainstream with hits such as the title track and "Fuck tha Police." Their anthems exuded a hypermasculine swagger, inviting and welcoming conflict with gangsters, rappers, women, and police officers both black and white. The unambiguous realist narratives explored in rhyme by Ice Cube and Eazy-E, along with gratuitous glorification of sex, drugs, and urban violence, sent shivers down the spines of culture warriors increasingly fearful of the gangland threat.

In John Singleton's *Boyz n the Hood* (1991) and, later, the Hughes Brothers' *Menace II Society* (1993), the culture's chief urban fear and battlefront merged on the filmic streets of Los Angeles. *Menace* is notable for its bleak commentary on the dead-end cycle of African American life; it follows friends O-Dog (Larenz Tate) and Caine (Tyrin Turner) who avenge insults and macho posturing with high-powered weaponry. The film concludes with the brutal drive-by murder of Caine on the verge of escape. *Boyz* presents an even deeper meditation on the complexities of ghetto and gang life in Los Angeles. Set in the Crenshaw neighborhood of South Central, it tracks the orbit of three friends playing to type: a star athlete with an escape route (Morris Chestnut), his gang-member brother (Ice Cube of NWA), and Tre Styles (Cuba Gooding, Jr.) who could go either way. Despite their divergent paths, the brothers meet the same fate, pushing Tre to escape, but not before contemplating a life on the street and witnessing Ricky's death by drive-by. *Boyz* marked Crenshaw as a liminal, ambiguous space, at once a dead end and a site of rare escape.

Menace and *Boyz* share a theme of vigilante films of the past. New York was once portrayed as a place devoid of opportunity for the white middle class. However, the narratives offered options for impending victims: escape to the suburbs or Sun Belt, or awaiting a white knight delivering order to the city. By the 1990s, crime fears only intensified as realist depictions of violence were exploited and perfected, and sensational stories of random criminality dominated the news cycle. In this context, films by Lee, Singleton, and the Hughes Brothers posed the question, what awaits citizens of color without such options? Productive answers did not lie in what critic Vincent Canby called the "simple-minded remedies" of regeneration through violence proposed by reactionary filmmakers of the 1970s.[10]

At the time, simplified answers arguably defined the political response to the complex problem of urban crime and violence. The policies that emerged from the War on Crime beginning in the 1960s laid the foundation for the uniquely American phenomenon of mass incarceration, perhaps most famously a series of drug laws pursued by Governor Nelson Rockefeller of New York. By the early 1990s, and fed by narratives of cities such as Detroit and Los Angeles, political leaders suggested that the wars on crime and drugs did not go far enough. Even self-identifying liberal politicians outmuscled one another to demonstrate their toughness on crime. The rhetorical posturing that produced the ripped-from-Hollywood super-predator scare resulted in the Violent Crime Control and Law Enforcement Act of 1994, signed by President Bill Clinton, that added thousands of new police officers to the streets and entrenched what legal scholar Michelle Alexander has termed *The New Jim Crow* (2012). California, responding to the specter of Los Angeles, instituted a "three strikes" law that lacked conscious deliberation and failed to account for the severity of each crime and the lasting consequences of the policy, much less the accused person's motivation for criminal activity. The crime politics of the 1990s, and the fear that fed it, resulted in part from an expanding market for sensational television news, a production philosophy of "if it bleeds it leads," and the popularity of ride-along shows beginning with *COPS* (1989–2020), which focuses primarily on nonwhite and poor communities. And yet, television became the venue for complex deliberation on the problem of crime and failure of such policies.

For its first fifty years American television storytelling avoided risky content, pursuing instead a formulaic path of clarity and resolution in thirty- to sixty-minute increments. By the 1970s and coinciding with the crime dilemma, police stories supplanted the Western as the preeminent television genre by transplanting its tropes to the metropolis. In the spirit of vigilante films, but far more benignly, shows focused on a lone crime fighter outsmarting crooks and, sometimes, cops in order to solve the day's mystery. The solo crime-fighting authority shone through in series titles of the era: *Colombo* (1968–78), *Kojak* (1973–78), *Quincy M.E.* (1976–83); *Baretta* (1975–78), a toned-down reboot of *Toma* (1973–74), based on the life of Newark detective David Toma, was an exception to the benign crime fighter image. Each episode of these shows was a self-contained unit – crimes were committed, investigated, and solved and the personal lives of crime-fighters explored within a safe, family-friendly forty-two minutes plus commercials. Episodic police procedurals lacked the authenticity and complexity of real urban crime detection and prevention, and perhaps offered viewers false hope that crime solving was easy and inevitable. Steven Bochco's *Hill Street Blues* (1981–87), however, successfully challenged the formula through serial story lines involving primary players, and it borrowed realist techniques like hand-held cinematography and location shooting from film. In 1993, Bochco challenged the network television establishment with *NYPD Blue* (1993–2005), adding realistic representations of sex, violence, and language in tangible urban locations, as well as cameos by local officials.

By the end of the century, cable television networks emerged as venues for bold content. Television and the crime story were revolutionized simultaneously in 1997 with HBO's *Oz* (1997–2003), a series that offered a window onto the interior landscape of the new Jim Crow. Set within a fictional federal penitentiary and featuring a diverse cast of actors and characters, *Oz* perfected a multitiered narrative about the intersecting lives of the incarcerated and their overseers. The serial format's success, grounded in a new television realism, encouraged HBO to further invest in innovative dramas. Its follow-up, *The Sopranos* (1999–2007), extended Hollywood's love affair with the mafia while expanding the geography of crime and violence to the suburbs from Newark, where Tony Soprano's roots remain in his social club and childhood home. In contrast to the cultural obsession with urban gang activity, *The Sopranos'* dark representation of the American Dream is a family drama in two senses; it follows the domestic life of an upper-middle-class family whose father was in therapy from the occupational stress of being capo of a North Jersey crime family. This splicing of genres, the repeated focus on Tony's psychic vulnerability behind his mask of ruthless violence and the show's occasional comic plot lines that play alongside stark violence, add complexity to the received narrative formulas of violence and crime.

The most significant innovation in early twenty-first-century crime drama occurred in Baltimore, where former *Sun* reporter David Simon molded television series out of reportage written with former homicide detective Ed Burns. After *Homicide: Life on the Street* (1993–99) and *The Corner* (2000), *The Wire* (2002–8) earned its lasting reputation in significant part through its sharp critique of the wars on crime and drugs. *The*

Wire surpassed narrative conventions by deploying city-specific slang, filming on location in impoverished and "vacant" neighborhoods, and employing local nonactors. It resists the episode as self-contained-unit structure more so that its contemporaries, relying on season-long arcs structured around an aspect of urban political economy and grounded in the relationship between the police and the organized heroin trade. New characters appear without introduction, much less fanfare, while some disappear for a season or two before reemerging. This tactic enhanced *The Wire*'s sense of realism by alluding to the vastness of the American city and its diversity of types. Employing writers drawn from law enforcement and crime fiction, Simon challenged the genre. A vigilante was one of the show's most popular characters, but in contrast to the hypermasculine white knight, Omar Little is black and queer; he kills drug dealers, yet he steals dope. Diversity within police ranks transcended tokenism, lending verisimilitude, depth, and authenticity to its representation.

Across the arc of the series, institutions wrestle with broader forces of structural change in the neoliberal era, including the West Baltimore drug gangs. Avon Barksdale and Stringer Bell are a study of contrasts. As a violent, methodical leader, Avon would not be out of place in the gangland genre of the 1980s and 1990s. Stringer is a reformer, as symbolized by his attempt to impose parliamentary order on family meetings. Via night school he acquires the skills to streamline the drug business, and he launders heroin profits into real estate development in Baltimore's gentrifying neighborhoods, hoping thereby to legitimize the Barksdale family. Reforms proved short-lived, however, as Stringer meets a deadly end. Barksdale's power wanes and Marlo Stanfield assumes control of "the corners," combining traditional unrelenting violence with innovative technology and inscrutable communication techniques.

The "good police" assembled and tasked with controlling the West-Side trade signify resistance to the department's prevailing order and theories of policing that the showrunners subject to critique. The force demotes its most skilled detective, Lester Freamon, for insubordination. Homicide detectives Jimmy McNulty and Bunk Moreland face pressure to improve "clearance rates" on their cases. Department administrators confront their quantitative performance through monthly Comstat (a play on Compstat and Citistat) meetings, using a Broken Windows Theory approach to preemptive policing developed in New York by Bill Bratton. "Quality-of-life" policing or "juking the stats" take precedence over fighting crime at the roots, and the commander's self-interest or self-preservation supersedes the community ethic. As Omar liked to say, "[it's] all in the game, yo."

The show's representation of crime and policing intersecting in the neoliberal urban environment was poignant, but the location choice was also pertinent. In the wake of failed urban renewal strategies, James Rouse pioneered in Baltimore's Inner Harbor his signature redevelopment of disused industrial spaces into retail- and entertainment-focused destinations, a pattern followed by HOK architects' incorporation of a former Baltimore & Ohio railroad warehouse into the Oriole Park at Camden Yards stadium complex. More recently, the suspicious death of Freddie Gray while in Baltimore police custody marked one of several acts of police and vigilante violence – an abbreviated roll call of victims include Trayvon Martin, Michael Brown, Sandra Bland, Oscar Grant, Breonna Taylor – that gave rise to Black Lives Matter, a movement that indicts racism in police practice and challenges entrenched narratives about black citizens.

Body cameras emerged as a popular political response to the recent wave of police violence, a practice that renders cops cinema-verité documentarians of alleged mean streets. Cameras are said to add objectivity, realism, and equity to the narratives that emerge from confrontations between cops and citizens, despite the fact that from Rodney King to Eric Garner to Philando Castile potentially to George Floyd videotaped police violence has not offered enough truth for juries to convict officers of wrongdoing. The body camera builds off the familiarity of *COPS*, but the perspective invokes another venue of contemporary crime storytelling, "first-person shooter" video games that combine vigilante and police role-playing fantasies with public collateral damage. For all its purported realism, a body camera cannot probe the mind of the officer – Chandler's supreme tool for justice – nor the psyche of the suspect, whose mutual perceptions, as well as jurors' perceptions, have been shaped in part by narratives and images of violent behavior. Much of the truth about urban crime, then, remains hidden.

Notes

1. See Tochterman, "Why Donald Trump (Wrongly) Thinks Chicago Resembles a War-Torn Country," *Washington Post*, March 16, 2018, https://www.washingtonpost.com/news/made-by-history/wp/2018/03/16/why-donald-trump-wrongly-thinks-chicago-resembles-a-war-torn-country/. This chapter's discussions of Mickey Spillane and *Death Wish* are expanded in Tochterman, *The Dying City: Postwar New York and the Ideology of Fear* (Chapel Hill: University of North Carolina Press, 2017).
2. Raymond Chandler, "The Simple Art of Murder: An Essay," in *The Simple Art of Murder* (New York: Vintage Crime, 1988), pp. 16, 18.

3. Mickey Spillane, *I, the Jury*, in *The Mike Hammer Collection*, 2 vols. (New York: New American Library, 2001), 1:14.

4. Mickey Spillane, *One Lonely Night*, in *The Mike Hammer Collection*, 2:133.

5. Mickey Spillane, *Kiss Me, Deadly*, in *The Mike Hammer Collection*, 2:418.

6. Sean McCann, *Gumshoe America: Hard-boiled Crime Fiction and the Rise and Fall of New Deal Liberalism* (Durham, NC: Duke University Press, 2000), p. 84.

7. Judy Klemestrud, "What Do They See in 'Death Wish'?," *New York Times*, September 1, 1974, 2:9.

8. Margot Hornblower, "Intended to Gouge Eye of Teen, Goetz Tape Says," *Washington Post*, May 14, 1987, A3.

9. Mike Davis, *City of Quartz: Excavating the Future in Los Angeles* (London: Verso, 1990), p. 236.

10. Vincent Canby, "'Death Wish' Exploits Fear Irresponsibly," *New York Times*, August 4, 1974, 2:4.

CHAPTER 14

Disaster, Apocalypse, and After

Sean Grattan

Colson Whitehead's *The Intuitionist* ends with a dream of an apocalypse. Lila Mae Watson, stopped at a red light, contemplates the elevator – and with it the city – to come. She realizes the breadth of destruction and rebuilding that will go into remaking the city:

> What need shaped this building, now husk. Its desiccated skin has been sooted by decades of automotive bile. Hard to see beneath it. Warehouse, office building, sweatshop. Obsolete and doomed, soon to be replaced by one of those new steel and glass numbers. [. . .] They will have to destroy this city once we deliver the black box. The current bones will not accommodate the marrow of the device. They will have to raze the city and cart off the rubble to less popular boroughs and start anew. What will it look like. The shining city will possess untold arms and a thousand eyes, mutability itself, constructed of yet-unconjured plastics. It will float, fly, fall, have no need of steel armature, have a liquid spine, no spine at all.[1]

This might not be the most obvious place to start with Whitehead and urban apocalypse, but unlike *Zone One* (2011), which seems to be about reproducing forms of neoliberalism in the wake of a zombie infection, *The Intuitionist* concerns a world that might radically change. As a genre, the apocalyptic is concerned with what comes after the apocalypse, James Berger argues in *After the End: Representations of Post-Apocalypse* (1999). The end never actually occurs; instead, there is a persistence and an attempt to usher something new into the world. So, too, Evan Calder Williams notes that "apocalypse is the coming-apart of the rules of the game, and in the ruined wake of this, the task isn't one of rebuilding, of mourning, or of moving on."[2]

This chapter looks at narrative forms of apocalypse and the city that try out different ways of being in the world after the world has lost the rules. Cities are often the sites of these apocalyptic ruptures, and more often than not, urban locations operate as spaces to flee after everything has gone sideways. Octavia Butler's burned out Los Angeles in *Parable of the Sower*

(1993) offers a particularly robust vision of the city as degraded space that must be fled, and films in the mode of Roland Emmerich's *2012* (2009) and *The Day After Tomorrow* (2004) depict the post-disaster city as an impossible space. Yet the city is more than a place to flee; the city – in its pre-disaster moment – already offers innovative and creative forms of community in everyday life that speak to a potential for radically different modes for living.

Although under tattered trappings, the apocalyptic contains a kernel of utopianism; it insists that, even if tomorrow is going to be at first much worse than today, perhaps there is the chance for something better to rise from the catastrophic rubble. Visions of the end of the world most often either leave the social relations of that world intact or evoke a nostalgia for them. In Emily St. John Mandel's *Station Eleven* (2014), one set of characters travels around performing Shakespeare plays, and while they sometimes flirt with performing original works, those works go over poorly enough that they abandon any newness for a repetition of the known, friendly, "cultured" Shakespeare. Another set of characters sets up a museum of lost technology – a hodgepodge collection of credit cards, cell phones, and other detritus from a past that haunts seemingly every moment of their lives. These acts emanate, if not a desire for a return to normalcy, then at least a hope that the world of Wi-Fi might restart sooner rather than later. This tension between the apocalyptic as a stage for imagining a future world that reproduces more of the same and the apocalyptic that opens up a space for *actually* reimagining the future is crucial to Kim Stanley Robinson's *New York 2140* (2017), which is this chapter's focus.

For the apocalyptic novel to be about more than a restaging and reaffirmation of the past, it must present a form of living entanglements that are no longer connected to a teleological narrative of industrial progress, or even to what Anna Tsing describes as "salvage rhythms," and the "adventure" of "precarious living."[3] For Tsing, the salvage rhythm exists adjacent to capital accumulation and is made up of the ways not only people, but other animals and plants find ways to survive in the destructive ruins wrought by capital accumulation. The question is, then, what remains. Whether zombies, roving nomads, or scrabbling city dwellers survive the bomb, virus, comet, or environmental cataclysm, the detritus of the end seems to stick around. The creative destruction of accelerationist capitalism lends itself to narratives of apocalyptic destruction that lead to getting things done or getting back to work, but what these things look like is often more of the same – just fancier, glossier, and less available to large swaths of the population. It suggests, as Williams notes, that "we don't believe that 'another world is possible,' because we know that things superseded still stick around and stink, unwelcome remainders with which we have to deal. Another world is necessary, but only built from the gutted hull of this one." What this gutted hull might look like is the crucial question. As Fredric Jameson famously said, "It's easier to imagine the end of the world than the end of capitalism."[4] The persistent ghost, the thing that haunts apocalyptic novels, is capitalism. And in the case of *New York 2140*, this haunting takes the form of a focus on the neoliberal individual as the problematic locus of action to repair climate change rather than imagining forms of systemic alterations in social structures.

Robinson uses New York City as a privileged site for understanding the interlocking communities and histories put at risk by ecological disaster. *New York 2140* imagines a flooded New York that has turned into a "super-Venice" and become a new kind of frontier financially and socially. This mammoth novel serves as both a gentle reminder of the remainders of disaster and an attempt to fashion the possibility of a utopian future out of the long rubble of the 2008 financial collapse and the omen of Hurricane Sandy in late October 2012. Crucially, rather than depicting the immediate aftermath of a disaster, Robinson describes a tenuous survival strategy where, at first, late capitalism still reigns, even if the United States' financial capital has been relocated to Denver. Speculation in New York real estate continues unabated, derivatives trading is still going strong, and hedge fund managers still dine at exclusive restaurants. In other words, although patches have been applied to the immediate ecological situation, very little has been done to alter the underlying reasons for the ecological disasters in the first place.

The story follows a motley crew of characters: a vlog star, two hackers, a hedge fund manager, a building superintendent, a police detective, a city organizer, two scrappy kids, and an unnamed narrator called The Citizen. They are brought together because they live in the Met Life Tower (also a setting in W. E. B. Du Bois's postapocalyptic short story, "The Comet" [1920]), which sits squarely in the flooded tidal zone. These characters are primarily represented through their occupations, which confirms Ted Martin's claim that postapocalyptic fiction forges an "*occupational aesthetic*"; the postapocalyptic novel is not so secretly a genre about work, he observes in *Contemporary Drift*, because the "entwined logics of survival and work afford us a glimpse not of a post-capitalist future but of a contemporary moment shaped by a constant yet precarious labor."[5]

Robinson demonstrates the varied skills that characters bring from their occupations to the work of changing the world, although they represent a range of ideological positions, and some are much less interested in changing the world than others.

Initially, *New York 2140* is very interested in how the two hackers, Mutt and Jeff, might destroy the thing that has remained after the apocalypse: late-late capitalism. In classic cyberpunk style, Jeff proclaims, "Whoever writes the code creates the value," before explaining to his friend Mutt that because of computational financialization, money can be rerouted, taxes changed, and so on. Jeff introduces several changes into this financial system that include eliminating tax havens, introducing a progressive tax structure, and rerouting money from a derivatives company to the SEC as a form of whistleblowing. His recoding ends on a note of ambiguous optimism. The banks have not been bailed out, and the possibility of something like communism has come into being. However, "the citizen" cuts in to remind us, "there are no happy endings! Because there are no endings! And possibly there is no happiness either!"[6]

Indeed, Robinson's use of New York City as the novel's predominant setting helps to illustrate multiple histories – both human and nonhuman – at work in the flood zone. For instance, one way the drama of extinction is played out in *New York 2140* is through Amelia's vlog as she travels the skies in her dirigible, *Assisted Migration*. Even after it has become abundantly clear that humans are not capable of looking after themselves, let alone the rest of the planet, people still tune in to Amelia's dramatic rescue attempts to save certain species from extinction. It is not a stretch, then, to see Amelia's almost slapstick attempt at polar bear salvation as a critique of anthropocentric extinction tales when she somehow contrives to get herself locked in a tool closet while the polar bears rampage around the cockpit. In a book that drastically shifts its tone from character to character, Amelia's slapdash attempt to take control of a situation while simultaneously playing up both her conservationist ideals and the radical contingency of her actual ability to produce change illustrates an anthropocentric desire to conserve, while simultaneously highlighting a misguided sense of ecological mastery. Although the tone is quite different, the narration of the Citizen is similarly focused on human actions as he intones from on high, "History is humankind trying to get a grip. Obviously not easy. But it could go better if you would pay a little more attention to certain details, like for instance your planet."[7] And yet, the Citizen is often narrating a story that has at least a multigenerational arc that lies somewhere between merely human time and something slightly longer.

Riffing on Walter Benjamin, Gerry Canavan describes Robinson's project as an "attempt to seize hold of the *future* as it flashes up at a moment of danger."[8] Surveying a post-2008, post–Hurricane Sandy United States that seems more interested in papering over the cracks than in enacting any sort of preventive action, *New York 2140* insistently describes and articulates the failure to anticipate and to react to the clear danger of the present. The disaster that floods the novel's New York consists of two "pulses" that produce dramatic rises in water because of melting icecaps. Even considering the acceleration of climate change because of human actions, the time when the disaster could have been prevented is already well in the past when the first pulse occurs. The distance between cause and effect reminds us that one of the more compelling arguments about the Anthropocene is the way that thinking about climate forces a massive reconceptualization of temporality and periodization; gauged against the slow time of melting ice caps or plastic's decomposition, a periodization of decades – or even human lives – seems paltry. While describing the actions humans took after the pulses, The Citizen snarkily remarks on this failure to scale up, "closing the barn door after the horses have escaped: of course. That's what people do. In this case the horses in question happened to be the Four Horsemen of the Apocalypse, traditionally named Conquest, War, Famine, and Death. So the closing of the barn door was particularly emphatic. Although naturally even this instinctive and useless reaction was contested, as many pointed out it was indeed too late."[9] The narrativization of this temporality illustrates that the long time of disaster is always playing a game of catch up. In other words, it is always already too late; the disaster has happened, but the symptoms have not necessarily appeared. Mark Anderson notes that the "process of narrating the disaster mobilizes existing social and political power relations at the same time it renegotiates them."[10] While Robinson insists on narrating the future in a moment of danger, he also attends to the ways that future is deeply encoded in the present. Not that this is a particularly shocking revelation about temporality, but in the face of suicidal inaction around climate change, *New York 2140* maps how the temporal drag of indecision, of pretending the disaster is not already here, significantly determines the shape of the future. One way of combating this inaction is by narrating the multiple temporal and geographic scales of climate disaster.

As Kate Marshall argues in "What are the Novels of the Anthropocene? American Fiction in Geological Time," the contemporary novel responds to the "anthropocenic imagination by staging its own temporality within increasing time scales and geologies." For Marshall this occurs along both temporal and spatial axes as "the turn toward epochal time also points at the way that contemporary fiction participates in the larger set of scalar moves within art and theory."[11] To wit, *New York 2140* presents both large-scale temporal logics – global warming, floods, and superstorms, often through aerial views that take in large swaths of land at once – and smaller scale descriptions of ecological disaster such as Stefan and Roberto's description of a myriad of animals converging on them while they all wait out the superstorm. Amelia, the popular vlogger who navigates her dirigible, *Animal Migration*, across the globe, stares down at a New York City that is "in every direction a great sheet of water, with some giant sticklebacked sea serpents eeling around the bay: Manhattan, Hoboken, Brooklyn Heights, Staten Island. Land lay in the distance everywhere, green and flat, except in the south, where the Atlantic gleamed like a dull old mirror." From this vantage point she, her passengers, and her viewers on the cloud take in nonhuman views of both the destruction and the teeming life below; people "looked like ants" going forth.[12] For Marshall this sort of self-awareness of the scalar particularities of the contemporary marks an important shift in contemporary aesthetics.[13] In the middle of the revolutionary utopian possibility rearing up in the middle of *New York 2140*, Robinson offers the reminder that there is always a futural storm surge out there; he writes, "now, recall, and this you should be capable of as it is the overriding omnipresent fact of life on Earth today, that sea level is already fifty feet higher than it was pre-pulse. Add a storm surge to this preexisting condition, and what do you get?

"You'll only find out when it happens."[14] And, of course, when the storm surge arrives, it results in catastrophic destruction that lays bare economic iniquities like the giant luxury apartment buildings in northern Manhattan sitting empty – their hyperrich residents use them merely as investments – while thousands of now-homeless refugees flood Central Park. This moment is the impetus for the Met Life gang to start their economic restructuring plan, which points to a potential utopian redemption. Yet the text ends with ambivalence because it is impossible to provide a stable fix for the ongoing disasters. James Berger articulates the paradox inherent in any postapocalyptic text as the fact that "the end is never the end" because "in nearly every apocalyptic presentation, something remains *after the end*."[15] Robinson insists on how a reckoning of the end will involve multiple moments and temporalities rather than one seismic collapse. The end inches along. *New York 2140* narrates more than a century of economic collapse and storm surges, along with massive animal extinctions. All of it is punctuated by the largest storm surge in New York history.

Despite the challenge of imagining a postcapitalist future, Jameson has argued that the apocalyptic always carries a kernel of utopian potential because there is the possibility of, if not starting completely again, at least having an opening to assemble a "new community of readers and believers around [the apocalypse] itself."[16] There are perhaps two utopian moments nestled into *New York 2140*. The first of them happens before the beginning of the text's action. In the wake of the second pulse, with capital fleeing New York and other coastal cities, they become home to "squatters. The dispossessed. The water rats. Denizens of the deep, citizens of the shallows" who experiment with new kinds of living in the postapocalyptic. There was a "proliferation of cooperatives, neighborhood associations, communes, squats, barter, alternative currencies, gift economies, solar usufruct, fishing village cultures, mondragons, unions, Davy's locker free-masonries, anarchist blather, and submarine technoculture."[17] By the time the text begins, many of these economic forms have shrunk, replaced by investment capital and gentrification, but the ethos still holds in certain quarters, including – to some extent – the Met Life Tower, where the main characters live. The second utopian moment occurs after the disastrous hurricane and storm surge. In this moment, all the Met Life gang's creative potential comes together and their disparate jobs, resources, and abilities map (with perhaps a little too much narrative perfection) onto a group collectively capable of restructuring the US economic system.

Two particular attributes make *New York 2140* a crucial text in the postapocalyptic genre, its dismissal of nostalgia for the pre-apocalyptic world and its thinking at multiple scales. Robinson clearly articulates a shift from a form of global capitalism that does not reckon with the disasters that the vicissitudes of global capital produces. For the novel's first half, the hedge fund manager, Franklin – who would comfortably sit alongside *Wall Street*'s (Oliver Stone, 1987) Gordon Gecko – surveys from his corner office "all the parts of the global mind most concerned with drowned coastlines," which is his particular area of expertise. Staring at a series of graphs, charts, and trees, Franklin remarks,

> one can glance at the totality, sure, but then it's important to slow down and take in the data part by part. That required a lot of shifting of gears these days, because my screen was a veritable anthology of narratives, and in many different genres. I had to shift between haiku and epics, personal essays and mathematical equations, Bildungsroman and Götterdämmerung, statistics and gossip, all telling me in their different ways the tragedies and comedies

of creative destruction and destructive creation, also the much more common but less remarked-upon creative creation and destructive destruction.[18]

At this moment in the text Franklin – whose next narrative contribution will be to almost kill two children, and then, uninterestedly and grumblingly, to save them – embodies the rush and thrill of abstractly trading on the economic potentialities of flooded tidal zones. In a chat with another finance guy, Franklin explains that the trading algorithm he has created takes into account the fact that in the intertidal zones the structural instability of the buildings makes continued ownership uncertain. Properties might just slide into the water; the human lives lost lie outside this accounting. Yet Franklin's character changes drastically throughout the novel, even though this shift happens in what might be the most finance-bro way possible: to attract a woman who is disgusted by his "old school" approach to finance, in which money is abstract, not a resource with which to create better modes of living.[19] His shift's significance is illustrated by the radical social transformation that takes place using tools he created to pop the intertidal real estate bubble and thus to collapse the world economy in the hope that US banks will subsequently be nationalized. In other words, *New York 2140* pushes against the nostalgia and describes a moment of crisis wherein a diehard capitalist transforms into a Benjaminian historical materialist seizing the world in a time of danger.[20]

Perhaps, in part, the push against nostalgia illustrates what happens (finally) when very real extinction seems no longer a vague possibility but, instead, becomes very real. Even in moments that appear to summon nostalgia, Robinson quickly pulls the rug from under any *utopian* nostalgia. When the two hackers, Mutt and Jeff, are captured for trying to start a revolution through recoding tax laws, Jeff becomes very sick and Mutt tells him a story about New York when it was first colonized. As Jeff lies in bed, Mutt tells of a harmonious relationship between the settlers of New York and the natural world; the indigenous people who survived their own apocalyptic encounter with settlers

> joined this community and taught the newcomers how to take care of the land so that it would stay healthy forever. That's the story I'm telling you now. It took knowing every rock and plant and animal and fish and bird, that was the way they did it. You had to love the land the way you loved your mother, or in case you didn't love your mother, the way you loved your child, or yourself. Because it was you anyway. It took knowing all the other parts of your self so well that nothing was misunderstood or exploited, and everything was treated respectfully. Every single element of this land, right down to the bedrock, was a citizen of the community they all made together,

and they all had legal standing, and they all made a good living, and they all had everything it took for total well-being and everything.

During the telling of this story Jeff falls asleep; Mutt realizes he has told his friend a "tale for children," and he puts his "face in his hands and cries."[21] Just as when he takes a dig at Amelia's preservation podcast by making her look foolish, so Robinson also denies Mutt's childish fantasy of a utopian New York City where everyone lives equally and in common with the world around them. It seems that Robinson is also openly mocking the settler-colonial fantasies of a lot of US dystopian fiction (notably Cormac McCarthy's *The Road*). While in other parts of the book Robinson plays up the utopian and creative potential of cities, here, when an agrarian utopian fantasy emerges – it reads a bit like William Morris's *News From Nowhere* (1890) – it is quickly shattered, but not with humor this time; he shatters it with the poignant image of Mutt crying next to his friend because the fantasy he weaved is brutally distant from the wretched present they live in.

Franklin also illustrates the other way that *New York 2140* articulates a descriptive (and proscriptive) mode of postapocalyptic fiction. When Franklin reads the information flashing along his screen, he produces a narrative of a totality, one he thinks he can "glance at," but also a totality that cannot be held for long. The glance is always a passing one. He shifts gears, slows down, and tarries over details – seeing how these descriptive moments fold into a larger financial narrative. The tension between these two reading practices is also played out in responses to the ecological disaster in the text. There are multiple scales of distance operating in the text. On the one hand, the large-scale totality works on the level of the forced collapse of the banks through the housing bubble's collapse; on the other hand, small-scale reclamation projects are enacted by Stefan and Roberto, who attempt to bring wildlife back to the city. Robinson gestures to the failure of either of these modes to operate individually, climate change, for instance, will not be reversed by picking up seaside litter, but it will also not be reversed through an entirely top-down model. The postapocalyptic novel – and literature of the Anthropocene more generally – is often invested in a large-scale ruse that imagines, even if in failure, the ability to do more than glance at the totality. While Robinson does not entirely avoid this trap, *New York 2140* does map the contours of the multiple scales that must be attended to when thinking about the Anthropocene. Thus, in showing the entanglements between small, medium, and large-scale fixes, Robinson produces a figuration or representation of possible methods for engaging with the apocalyptic present.

In *The Mushroom at the End of the World,* Anna Tsing addresses a related form of thinking about scale through a lengthy meditation on matsutake mushrooms. Tsing sets out to produce a mode of reading illustrative of scalar thinking that decenters human actors but keeps them alive as part of a larger biosphere. Her questions are: How do we describe what remains, and how are our analytic tools compromised by the anthropocentrism of the Anthropocene? She articulates the need to turn away from narratives of progress and to look, instead, at what falls out of these histories. "Precarity" she writes "is the condition of being vulnerable to others. Unpredictable encounters transform us; we are not in control, even of ourselves. [. . .] Thinking through precarity changes social analysis. A precarious world is a world without teleology. Indeterminacy, the unplanned nature of time, is frightening, but thinking through precarity makes it evident that indeterminacy also makes life possible."[22]

Following the commodity chain of the matsutake, Tsing shows how the world exists in disturbed times and how "salvage rhythms" become a crucial element for understanding the ruinous depredations of global capitalism and the potential for not only surviving but even thriving within these conditions. "People and trees," she writes, "are caught in irreversible histories of disturbance." She continues,

> Peasant oak-pine forests have been eddies of stability and cohabitation. Yet they are often put into motion by great cataclysms, such as the deforestation that accompanies national industrialization. Small eddies of interlocking lives within great rivers of disturbance: these are surely sites for thinking about human talents for remediation. But there is also the forest's point of view. Despite all the insults, resurgence has not yet ceased.[23]

Here, she is not flattening out all disturbances, nor is she reveling in the apocalyptic voyeuristic dreams of books like Alan Weisman's *The World Without Us* (2007) and subsequent videos that depict the world without people in a documentary style. Like Robinson, Tsing does not give up the disturbance of human actors, but she also imagines the moments after disturbance as offering the potential for creating assemblages that *might* radically alter social relations. These social relations are based around a salvage aesthetics, or what Evan Calder Williams has called "salvagepunk,"[24] which is rooted in what is cobbled together in times of crisis, in how precariousness forces, foregrounds, and describes human innovation, discerns surprising or forgotten connections between humans and their environments, and, perhaps most importantly, how it clarifies the links between different nonhuman actors. Salvagepunk, therefore, looks more than a little like the struggle between Roberto, Stefan, and a group of hungry displaced muskrats during the hurricane and storm surge near the end of *New York 2140*. There are also resonant echoes in the Citizen's curse that humans oversimplify the world to create a narrative they can understand, but in the end "Life! Life! Life! Life is going to kick your ass."[25]

By no means does all apocalyptic literature operate along the lines here described; one way to conceive the importance of *New York 2140* is to think about what is missing in the desire to recuperate the past that caused the disaster. Claire Colebrook puts it well when she declares, "what we should *not* do is try to retrieve or repair a proper human vision; nor should we think, too easily, that we have abandoned human myopia once and for all." Kim Stanley Robinson makes clear that a novel that takes in the multiple spatial and temporal scales of disaster might at least cognitively map how the contemporary anthropocenic novel operates. What the novel does is describe a more-than-possible future and articulate ways that both nostalgia and too-easy scalar fixes foreclose the openings that postapocalyptic literature might generate. Indeed, as Colebrook notes, "two of the senses of the post-apocalyptic lie in this indication that there will not be a complete annihilation but the gradual witnessing of a slow end, and that we are already at that moment of witness, living on after the end. Indeed, this is what an ethics of extinction requires: not an apocalyptic thought of the 'beyond the human' as a radical break or dissolution, but a slow, dim, barely discerned and yet violently effective destruction."[26] In *New York 2140*'s penultimate chapter, the Citizen declares "there are no happy endings." The openness of this ending resists what Colebrook describes as the desire for postapocalyptic narratives to find redemptive endings "in which the seemingly senseless destruction of existence is given redemptive form. The unacceptable is rendered acceptable, not just in the sense of what is socially frowned upon being presented as more palatable, but in a more radical sense in which something like *the social* is formed. Narrative creates the lure of a world in common, an order of sense and humanity, in which otherness is personalized and rendered familial and familiar."[27] At first glance, Robinson cleaves closely to this model as all the characters have come together to work for a more just world in common, but the penultimate chapter undercuts this dream in the same manner that Robinson has undercut previous strains of utopian narrative in this novel. Novels such as *New York 2140* clearly demonstrate how apocalypse might not look like the shock of a mushroom cloud on the horizon; instead – and much more likely – catastrophic climate change has already happened and we are just waiting for the bruise to appear.

Notes

1. Colson Whitehead, *The Intuitionist* (New York: Anchor Books, 1999), pp. 198–99. For a more in-depth discussion of utopian potential in *The Intuitionist*, see Grattan, *Hope Isn't Stupid: Utopian Affects in Contemporary American Literature* (Iowa City: University of Iowa Press, 2017), pp. 100–121.
2. Evan Calder Williams, *Combined and Uneven Apocalypse* (London: Zero Books, 2011), p. 8.
3. Anna Lowenhaupt Tsing, *The Mushroom at the End of the World: On the Possibility of Life in Capitalist Ruins* (Princeton, NJ: Princeton University Press, 2017), pp. 132, 163.
4. Williams, *Combined and Uneven*, p. 13; Fredric Jameson, *The Seeds of Time* (New York: Columbia University Press, 1996), p. xii.
5. Theodore Martin, *Contemporary Drift: Genre, Historicism, and the Problem of the Present* (New York: Columbia University Press, 2017), pp. 164, 162.
6. Kim Stanley Robinson, *New York 2140* (London: Orbit, 2017), pp. 3, 604.
7. Ibid., p. 145.
8. Gerry Canavan, "Utopia in the Time of Trump," *Los Angeles Review of Books*, March 11, 2017, http://lareviewofbooks.org/article/utopia-in-the-time-of-trump/.
9. Robinson, *New York 2140*, p. 377.
10. Mark D. Anderson, *Disaster Writing: The Cultural Politics of Catastrophe in Latin America* (Charlottesville: University of Virginia Press, 2011), pp. 6–7.
11. Kate Marshall, "What Are the Novels of the Anthropocene? American Fiction in Geological Time," *American Literary History* 27 (2015), 523–24, 524.
12. Robinson, *New York 2140*, pp. 595, 596.
13. While it might seem too pat, I would add to Sianne Ngai's taxonomy enumerated in *Our Aesthetic Categories: Zany, Cute, Interesting* (2012) the category of *fucked*. More than anything, this is an attempt to build an aesthetic and affective category that describes a damning temporality that darts ahead of our lagging abilities to conceive of where we are actually positioned. I am attempting to dishevel the aesthetic categories we have at our disposal to speak about a moment that is not just destructive but is actually in the temporal lag of already destroyed – a proleptic representation of a destruction that has already happened, but one that perhaps we need to be shocked into recognizing. And, if we are to trace the line out further, dialectically, this is an aesthetics that has at its core an attempt to create space for belonging, care, and utopian moments in the face of a present that seemingly stands in stark contrast to these possibilities. As a genre the post-apocalyptic novel hums at this affective and aesthetic pace; its large scale spatial and temporal views illustrate the long durée of ecological disaster, but also decenter spatial relations around an individual human scale; instead, the human species have been translated into ants moving – at least from this vantage point – as one seething mass. In "Learning How to Die in the Anthropocene," Roy Scranton argues that, as a species, it is crucial that we

adapt "with mortal humility, to our new reality" (*New York Times*, November 10, 2013, http://opinionator.blogs.nytimes.com/2013/11/10/learn ing-how-to-die-in-the-anthropocene). While the scalar is not always the fucked, it seems that the contemporary moment needs an aesthetic category that describes the temporal lag of climate change and human response. Texts such as Robinson's narrate a small group of people dragging the rest of humanity toward something that might offer a utopian possibility in a world at, or over, the brink of apocalypse.

14. Robinson, *New York 2140*, p. 441.
15. James Berger, *After the End: Representations of Post-Apocalypse* (Minneapolis: University of Minnesota Press, 1999), pp. 5–6.
16. Fredric Jameson, *Archaeologies of the Future: The Desire Called Utopia and Other Science Fictions* (London: Verso, 2007), p. 199.
17. Robinson, *New York 2140*, p. 209.
18. Ibid., p. 18.
19. Ibid., p. 219.
20. The shift in his personality is also illustrated by a repetition of the earlier scene where he almost runs over Stefan and Roberto in his boat. In the second moment he goes out in the aftermath of a horrible hurricane to rescue them.
21. Robinson, *New York 2140*, pp. 296–97, 297.
22. Tsing, *Mushroom at the End*, p. 20.
23. Ibid., p. 190.
24. Williams, *Combined and Uneven*, p. 19.
25. Robinson, *New York 2140*, p. 320.
26. Claire Colebrook, *Death of the PostHuman: Essays on Extinction, Vol. 1* (London: Open Humanities Press, 2015), pp. 24, 40.
27. Ibid., pp. 193–94.

CHAPTER 15

Bohemia

Erik Mortenson

The term *bohemian* has fallen out of favor. While it used to be a common stand-in for *nonconformist* and still enjoys currency in academic studies, now it appears only sporadically in popular culture. There is *La Bohème* (Giacomo Puccini, 1895), of course, along with its modernized version, *Rent* (Jonathan Larson, 1996), and the Dandy Warhols' ironic song "Bohemian Like You" (2000), which pokes fun at hipsters waiting tables, playing in bands, and trying to be casual about casual sex. And in Paris, *New York Times* columnist David Brooks coined the term *bobo* to designate well-off professionals who embrace what he identifies as a bohemian outlook. Nevertheless, it is difficult to imagine anyone actually self-identifying as a bohemian these days; if the term is used at all it is uttered either in jest or by city officials describing their latest scheme to create urban amenities that will fuel a real estate boomlet and raise the urban tax base. For these boosters, bohemians may be either amenities or the target audience, the creative class. If the bohemian is out of fashion, there are always people who desire to challenge the status quo by choosing lifestyles at variance with accepted norms. Indeed, the desire to experiment and to explore outside the confines of acceptability is one of the major desires that propels Americans to the city, so bohemia has perhaps never left us, even if the term has. This chapter explores the reasons for bohemia's demise, makes an honest assessment of its shortcomings, and attempts to redeem what is worthwhile from the concept. At its best, the bohemian ideal of living an inwardly meaningful life outside society's margins functions as a utopian gesture that challenges our media-obsessed culture with a focus on the personal and inner-directed.

To say *bohemia* is an overloaded term is an understatement, and its overdetermined nature is in part responsible for its neglect. The one certainty is that it was coined in Paris in the 1830s. The first chronicler of bohemia, Henry Murger, plays on the old French word for Roma (or Gypsy) in his *La Vie de Bohème* (1851), linking the bohemian to the

245

marginalized ethnic group once thought to have originated in what is now the Czech Republic. This etymology highlights the antibourgeois nature of bohemian life that remains its major defining feature. Drawing on the image of the Gypsy as one who wanders unencumbered, from the very start bohemianism was conceived as an antidote to middle-class conformism. As with any concept defined through opposition, its meaning is inextricably intertwined with the object of its scorn. The term's other important chronicler, Jerrold Siegel, notes that "people were or were not Bohemian to the degree that parts of their lives dramatized these tensions and conflicts" through eccentric behavior, sexual exploration, the consumption of drink and drugs, and a focus on art rather than work. There are, however, no attributes exclusive to bohemianism; on the contrary, the term depends on situation, context, intent, and reception for its meaning because, as Siegel continues, "there is no action or gesture capable of being identified as Bohemian that cannot also be – or has not been – undertaken outside Bohemia."[1] The only constant feature of bohemia is the desire to get "outside" the system by challenging accepted practices and norms. In today's academic parlance, bohemianism is performative.

Instantiations of bohemia in the United States have been likewise varied. The first self-proclaimed American bohemia was located in New York at Pfaff's cellar, a rathskeller located on Broadway near Bleeker Street in Greenwich Village. Joanna Levin and Edward Whitley argue in *Whitman among the Bohemians* (2014) that Pfaff's was the epicenter for a group of mid-nineteenth-century writers, artists, musicians, actors, intellectuals, and radicals. As their book's title implies, bohemia has often been seen as the domain of the artistic class, but San Francisco's Bohemian Club (founded in 1872) included prominent doctors, lawyers, and businessmen, as well as writers like Frank Norris, Bret Harte, and Jack London. Members of the club would spend three weeks at their rural "Bohemian Grove" in the "hope of a personal and collective transformation"[2] (though today the Club has degenerated into little more than a private club of the rich and powerful). The New Bohemians of turn-of-the-century Greenwich Village were an even more diverse group. A mixture of artists, feminists, political activists, and general eccentrics like Joe Gould (renowned for his "seagull act" and his claim to have written the world's longest book, whose existence is disputed by Joseph Mitchell in *Joe Gould's Secret* [1965] but circumstantially substantiated half a century later by Jill Lepore in *Joe Gould's Teeth* [2015]), these bohemians "created the first full-bodied alternative to an established cultural elite, [. . .] developed an unrivaled vision of feminism [. . . and] injected into the politics of the left a new cultural dimension," according to Christine Stansell.[3] Despite differences in location, membership, and perspective, these bohemias were nevertheless united in a shared desire to explore alternative lifestyles that offered participants the chance to examine new configurations of the self that challenged mainstream social expectations.

Given the amorphous nature of bohemianism, this chapter will focus on a particular example, the Beat Generation writers and the culture of nonconformity their work both reflected and produced. There are numerous reasons why they are useful for such an inquiry. The Beats were, in many ways, both the last gasp of a more "traditional" bohemia that harkened back to Pfaff's cellar and The Bohemian Club, but they were also the beginning of a 1960s counterculture that still shapes the ways we conceive, experience, and theorize nonconformism. The Beats thus occupy a pivotal moment in American (counter)cultural history, offering valuable insights into the forms and functions of urban bohemian enclaves that reference earlier bohemias while prefiguring present-day configurations. Most importantly, Beat bohemia exemplifies the idea of using lifestyle as a form of politics. Like many bohemias before them, the Beat approach eschews direct political engagement in favor of changing attitudes and opinions by presenting lived life as an opportunity to interrogate social models on offer in the culture at large. For the Beats, this turn to "cultural politics" was in large part due to Cold War realities – the more traditional Left had been undermined by the failures of Joseph Stalin and rampant anticommunist hysteria – but this rejecting of accepted modes of life not only allows for the exploration and development of the self, but likewise offers the possibility of a freer, less alienated world in general.

The Hip and the Paid

Fundamentally, bohemia is a state of mind, an approach to life, a way of being in the city. For the postwar Beats, that way of being, and the catalyst for an art meant to challenge the stifling cultural climate of the 1950s, was spontaneity. As Daniel Belgrad notes in *The Culture of Spontaneity* (1998), the idea that uninhibited personal expression should form the basis for both art and life permeated music, dance, painting, theater, sculpture, as well as literature. Against conformism, consensus, and blind faith in a culture of expertise, the Beats posed the idiosyncrasy, irrationality, and authenticity that spontaneity was thought to deliver. Bohemians live as though they are in the world they want to see exist, and for the Beats, as well as for those in the "underground" subculture their writing both captured and spawned, living life spontaneously allowed chance for thoughts, feelings, and desires that normally had to be stifled in postwar America to emerge. In the process of that unfolding, latent fears and inhibitions on the personal and social levels could be vented and addressed. As in earlier bohemias, the ultimate goal was a freer world where personal growth trumped social expectation.

Bohemia sets itself against bourgeois culture, but in practice, such distinctions are fluid and fraught. The Beats were opposed to the imagined oppressiveness of bourgeois life, but an easy dichotomy between "hip" and "square" was difficult to maintain. Anticipating Brooks, Delmore Schwartz pointed out by 1958 that the Beats' attack on corporate man was "a form of shadow boxing because the Man in the Brooks Brothers suit is himself, in his own home, very often what [Bertrand] Russell has called an upper Bohemian. His conformism is limited to the office day and business hours: in private life – and at heart – he is as Bohemian as anyone else."[4] The boundaries between bohemian and bourgeois are far more porous than was often admitted, for not only was the bourgeois in many ways a nascent bohemian, but the Beats themselves were implicated in the culture they critiqued. Brooks cites Paul Goodman's assessment of the Beats, "though they were dissidents and though they rejected affluence and all that, the Beats actually lived pretty well. It was their spirit of pleasure that made them so attractive."[5] They may have celebrated the city's down-and-out, but their poverty, such as it was, was voluntary and did not stop them from going to bars, buying jazz records, and taking exciting cross-country road trips. Despite being painted by influential magazines like *Life* and *Time* as dirty and depressed, the Beat lifestyle attracted its substantial following in large part because their desire for personal exploration was generated by a wide range of consumable experiences; smoking marijuana while listening to the latest jazz on hi-fi was both transcendent and, well, fun.

This allure is precisely what makes bohemia exploitable. Given the Beats' insistence on living unencumbered and maximizing the intensity of each passing moment, it is unsurprising that Beat rebellion soon flowered into the full-scale youth movement that was the 1960s counter-culture. But Beat bohemia also represents the beginning of the trend of commodifying rebellion. Bohemias from 1830s Paris to 1920s Greenwich Village always drew curiosity seekers. But with the advent of mass media, bohemia could be commodified faster than ever. As early as 1976, Daniel Bell observed that "the impulse to rebellion has been institutionalized by the 'cultural mass' and its experimental forms have become the syntax and semiotics of advertising and haute couture."[6] The commodification of dissent allows consumers to participate vicariously in the transgressions of bohemian life without risking their secure places in mainstream society. Bohemia becomes an enjoyable spectacle to be sampled at leisure. Thomas Frank traces the frustrations with today's consumer capitalism to precisely this postwar moment, arguing that it saw the "consolidation of a new species of hip consumerism, a cultural perpetual motion machine in which disgust with the falseness, shoddiness, and everyday oppressions of consumer society could be enlisted to drive the ever-accelerating wheels of consumption."[7] Frank thus deflates the idea that the postwar counterculture was somehow purely authentic and revolutionary; just as the counterculture consumed in an act of rebellion, advertising professionals harnessed rebellion to fuel consumption.

Not only does capitalism's ability to co-opt bohemian style deprive the aesthetic of its revolutionary potential, it also directly influences bohemian communities in disruptive ways. There has always been a tension in bohemia between staying true to the underground ideals of the community and the desire to profit from the cultural cachet of the bohemian scene. The opportunity to turn bohemian experience into cash is ever present, which is precisely why so many bohemian enclaves are infatuated with the idea of authenticity and policing the boundaries of who is "in" and who has "sold out." Honoré de Balzac, in *A Prince of Bohemia* (1840), observed early on that "The *bohème* consists of young people, who are still unknown, but who will be well known and famous one day."[8] Following Balzac's cue, successive commentators have cast bohemia as a land of youth, where aspiring artists, thinkers, eccentrics, and radicals go to hone their craft, express their views, or simply live as they see fit. The assumption is that sojourns in bohemia will eventually come to an end, either through a "growing up" and moving on to a more socially acceptable existence, or through a "siphoning off" of talented individuals as mainstream society comes to value their abilities. This creates a paradox. The more visible bohemia, its lifestyles, and its aesthetic products become, the greater chance they have to make an impact in the culture. Yet the more visible they are in the culture, the more open they are to cooptation. Although some try to straddle this divide in an attempt to make a living while staying true to the ideals of the bohemian community, this balance is difficult to achieve and always under scrutiny.

Even when the bohemian stays "true" to her calling, her marginal social status and capitalism's ability to commodify all elements of the aesthetic means that she often ends up exploited in any case. Indeed, in his much-discussed treatise on the postindustrial urban economy, Richard Florida posits a "Bohemian Index" that seeks to establish a correlation between the incidence of artists and a city's economic viability to test his assumption that "the presence and concentration of bohemians [...] creates an environment or milieu that attracts other types of talented or high-capital individuals."[9] Thus, Florida asserts, cities should attract artists and other marginal-but-creative groups to spur development. Not only do such changes put pressure on bohemian communities through rising rents and more expensive amenities, but they often dissolve camaraderie and collaboration by incentivizing artistic endeavor. Richard Lloyd observes that in Chicago's once-bohemian Wicker Park neighborhood, "as in many other post-Fordist workplaces, the individual creativity of employees is a thing to exploit, not to suppress."[10] Capitalism inverts the bohemian bond between art and life by commoditizing creativity to produce a marketable "style" or "look." Florida, Lloyd, and other commentators further claim that such cooptation represents the present state of most contemporary workers in the information economy, which capitalizes on individual creativity through fast-paced, never-ending disruption. Ironically, the bohemian lifestyle characterized by contingency and adaptability is perfectly suited to work in present-day capitalism, even as the cost of survival in today's cities makes *l'art pour l'art*, the rallying cry of earlier generations of bohemian artists like Charles Baudelaire, James McNeill Whistler, and Oscar Wilde, nearly untenable. Bohemianism as a refuge from capitalism becomes increasingly impossible to realize.

As clear lines between rebel and philistine have blurred, the bohemian lifestyle and the art it engenders appear under threat of absorption into the mainstream. But the struggle to negotiate that line is itself illuminating and productive. In a world where every worker has taken on "bohemian" attributes and all bohemians without trust funds need to sell themselves, perhaps the term now denotes those who have given some thought to where their allegiances lie and the true price of bohemian pursuits. Playing with the line between "selling out" and staying alive, *Village Voice* photographer Fred McDarrah and Afrobeat musician/poet Ted Joans offered a "rent a beatnik" service for upscale New Yorkers looking to spice up their cocktail parties. Their enterprise, while pecuniary, was mainly playful (it started as a joke), but it reminds us that the bohemian of today cannot avoid engagements with capitalism.[11] The whole point of social media, for instance, is to be seen, and often to capitalize on this visibility. In such a climate, the idea of bohemia as purposely marginalized, a world apart, seems misguided, counterproductive, or simply unnecessary, an echo of a time chronicled in works like Douglas Coupland's *Generation X* (1991) or

Richard Linklater's film *Slacker* (1991), when someone could still afford, in the myriad senses of the word, to drop out of sight.

A Gentler Gentrification

As the mentions of Richard Florida suggest, bohemia has also become intimately related to capitalism, particularly in urban settings, because of its revitalizing effects on economically depressed neighborhoods. Spaces that capitalism has let become derelict or underutilized are brought back into cultural circulation by bohemians who repurpose the cast-off and neglected, proving the validity of Jane Jacobs's endlessly quoted chestnut, "new ideas must use old buildings."[12] In his classic study of Venice Beach, *The Holy Barbarians* (1959), Lawrence Lipton explains the Beat phenomenon in these terms: "An unrentable store, with its show windows curtained or painted opaque, becomes a studio. A loft behind a lunchroom or over a liquor store becomes an ideal 'pad.'"[13] On the other hand, it is difficult to imagine a bohemia being created from scratch, which is why attempts by planners to build bohemia inevitably fall flat. Bohemia seems to happen almost spontaneously, as a critical mass of like-minded people descend on an area of low rents and substantial vacancies, repurposing it to fit their own creative needs. Always emplaced and yet always displaced by the city's cycle of creative destruction, a stable or permanent bohemia would be a contradiction in terms.

The bohemian reclamation of space intends to open up new ways of living in, and responding to, the city. It seeks to be the place where things happen, the creative congregate, and art is made. As Jacobs suggests, old buildings mean cheaper rents, and cheaper rents divert less time and resources from other pursuits. Members of what Gilbert Millstein called the "Loft Generation" (1962) paid from $35 to $300 a month to rent industrial spaces that were "bare, filthy shell[s]; cold, dank, fly-specked, peeling and unpainted." Although they earned "less than a thousand a year from painting and sculpture," the artists Millstein interviewed were happy with the choice.[14] These spaces provided substantial room for studios, their walls offered blank canvases for self-expression, and the industrial detritus of the warehouse district became material for art. Beat author Joyce Johnson describes an "apartment on 115th Street [as] an early prototype of what a later generation called a pad – a psychic way station [. . .] in the mental geography of those who came together there, lived there sporadically, made love, wrote, suffered, experimented with drugs."[15] While monetary pressures, their often-quasi-legal status, and the difficulties of communal living meant that such spaces rarely lasted for long, the Beat "pad" sited a close-knit if fluid community that drew on each other's strengths, resources, knowledge, and energy.

Jacobs and Milstein imply, and Joyce Johnson's siting of that apartment in Harlem makes clear, that the bohemian's pursuit of cheap rents that preserve time for personal pursuits most often leads to working-class districts or minority and immigrant communities. While bohemians themselves do not typically displace existing residents of these neighborhoods, they often do function as unwilling urban pioneers, followed later by more financially secure newcomers who mark the proper start of the gentrification process (discussed by James Peacock in Chapter 6) and bring with them the sort of values and orientations that bohemias would resist. First, those attracted to the bohemian lifestyle choose marginal districts for their cheap rents and go on to establish the coffee shops, galleries, book and record stores, and other venues for which bohemia has always been known. Then, the cachet of bohemian ambiance attracts others whose presence drives up rents and prices both bohemians and the local residents out of the market. This story is not new. Joanna Levin observes in *Bohemia in America* (2009) that, "just as low rent had once enabled the 'spiritual geography' of [1920s] Greenwich Village to materialize, so did high rent finally curtail this most famous of American Bohemias."[16] However, the rate of turnover has accelerated. Sharon Zukin notes that in New York annual rent increases averaged 4.9 percent from 1950 to 1970, but jumped to 11.4 percent between 1970 and 1975 as rent-control programs were dismantled.[17] In cities like New York, San Francisco, Seattle and Chicago, bohemia has been almost entirely priced out of the market, displaced to Philadelphia, the Rust Belt, or to southern cities like the always-bohemian New Orleans. Recently, however, even Detroit has seen rent increases that effectively foreclosed on bohemias, at least in the more central locations of the city. Given a new generation's interest in the urban, fueled by ideas of bohemian life, however they define it, these trends are likely to continue.

For those bohemians (who would never call themselves that) who remain, or attempt to remain, rising rents and other costs engender new tactics of survival and means of experiencing and experimenting with the city. Faced with high rents in the tech-boom 1990s, even the quasi-legal pads of the 1950s could be too expensive and were supplanted by "squats" – the reclamation of vacated property – as chronicled in Ash Thayer's photo-book *Kill City: Lower East Side Squatters 1992–2000* (2015). But if bohemia extracts its price, in comfort and convenience, these arrangements brought with them a far higher risk to safety than was the bohemian norm. For many, "edginess" is precisely the draw; bohemia is about giving oneself to the vicissitudes of urban life that spur creativity. Yet these forms of temporary housing can have a more troubling valence. John Rechy's *City of Night* (1963) and Tama Janowitz's *Slaves of New York* (1986) both describe in detail a bohemian underworld that requires sexual transactions to fund it.

Problems with Difference

The fact that bohemia sets itself against social conventions has made it attractive for some in marginalized social groups seeking to challenge various forms of oppression. Because bohemia tends to promote "gender trouble," it comes as no surprise that many women desiring gender equality found in bohemia what Levin, quoting the "Queen of Bohemia," Ada Clare, described as a space for the "emancipation of women from the mountain of custom and conventional rubbish that has been piled upon her."[18] Moving from South Carolina to New York City in 1854, Clare was a regular at Pfaff's while acting, writing, and bearing a child out of wedlock. The New Bohemians that congregated around Greenwich Village around the turn of the century pushed even further. Discussing women's role in New York's turn-of-the-century bohemia, Christine Stansell writes that while "most studies of bohemias have found that women were sidekicks – 'minor characters,' in Joyce Johnson's mordant description of the Beat Generation, [. . .] these New Yorkers turned out to be strikingly different, because they so often gave feminism pride of place in their longed-for democratic revival."[19] If women in Paris played a supporting role, and the circle at Pfaff's was mainly men, in Greenwich Village the New Woman directly questioned the dominant conceptions of marriage, family, and sexuality while becoming a rallying cry for artists like Sarah Bernhardt and Belle Livingstone, who embraced the term in defiance of cultural norms. Bohemia became less relevant as a cultural signifier in second-wave feminism, but it was an important early site for the development and promotion of feminist concerns.

As Julie Abraham convincingly shows throughout *Metropolitan Lovers: The Homosexuality of Cities* (2009), there has always been a strong connection between the city and homosexuality, and the same thing is true for bohemia, not only because it is notoriously open to experimentation but also because turning art into life and life into art is a necessity for people negotiating sexual identities at variance with traditional mores – with "camp" an obvious instance – as is creating spaces for them to flourish. Abraham remarks that "in the model of the city developing from Balzac to Simmel, the urban person must work to control his or her legibility." Given that bohemia has always embraced this model of life as theater, it is unsurprising that homosexuals organized their own balls in 1920s Greenwich Village or that the defining image of the Stonewall Riots that inaugurated the gay liberation movement is "a chorus line of black and Latino drag queens high-kicking their defiance of New York City's police, on the evening of Judy Garland's funeral, June 27, 1969."[20] While the urban personality type is associated with the mythos of individuals leaving the confines of the small-town in order to reinvent themselves, only in bohemian districts does this desire for expression easily find full vent. If James Baldwin in *Giovanni's Room* (1956) found that dominant social norms quickly reasserted themselves, for Samuel R. Delaney in *Dhalgren* (1975) the city continues to be a utopic space for sexual and personal exploration. In either case, for many decades it was in the bohemian quarters that homosexual desire could become most visible, celebrated, and explored.

Nevertheless, bohemia's embrace of gender equality and gay rights is decidedly mixed. Women found that bohemia was most often a "man's world" where sexual exploration was more conducive to the libertine and the rake than in the flapper and the New Woman. While Greenwich Village was a hotbed for feminist thought in the 1920s, only thirty years later, Beat women in the Village were relegated to subordinate positions. Diane di Prima, in *Dinners and Nightmares* (1961), describes an argument with her male lover over who should do the dishes. As di Prima reluctantly begins to do them (yet again), her lover calls out from the living room, "It says here Picasso produces fourteen hours a day."[21] Despite pretensions to social rebellion, then, Beat bohemianism more often reinscribed the dominant gender binaries at work in 1950s culture. The same was true of homosexuality. Stansell notes of the 1920s a frustration with the new generation of post–World War I bohemians in New York, "they were skittish of the gay newcomers flooding the neighborhood, especially the 'boys' who embodied both avant-garde sophistication and the ambiguous sexual identity they had worked so hard to banish from their bohemian manliness."[22] And even though many Beats were gay and Allen Ginsberg celebrated those "who let themselves be fucked in the ass by saintly motorcyclists, and screamed with joy" in *Howl*,[23] their attitudes toward homosexuality were not always what we would recognize as progressive. They were often on the "wrong" side of gay liberation, embracing more "masculine" notions of sexuality prevalent in mid-century America. Bohemia's unrecognized complicity with many of the problematic assumptions at work in the cultures they critiqued is undoubtedly one of the reasons for the gradual demise of the concept as a rubric for thinking dissent.

Bohemia's mixed record is likewise evident with regard to race. Bohemia could be accepting of racial difference, but it could also be selective about which groups it was willing to account as equal to its predominantly white core. Stansell celebrates turn-of-the-century bohemia's willingness to accept differences in ethnicity, especially its acceptance of Jews and other marginalized European ethnic groups that were congregating around the Lower East Side. But she also points out that "for anyone black who sought admission, bohemia offered scant hospitality. In the 1940s, Richard Wright encountered bare bigotry from neighbors when he moved into a town house on a now-chic street in Greenwich Village."[24] While James Weldon Johnson chronicled a "black Bohemia" located at the turn of the century in New York's Tenderloin and San Juan Hill districts, the bohemian concept was largely a white one; the term was adopted by some immigrant and white-ethnic communities, but it did not seem to migrate to Harlem during its Renaissance. African American artists had to forge relationships with a bohemia that was often at odds with their own concerns. This frustration with white bohemia sent LeRoi Jones (Amiri Baraka) uptown to Harlem. Although energized by the art and lifestyles of fellow Beats like Jack Kerouac and Ginsberg, Baraka ultimately felt that this bohemia did not engage social issues relevant to blacks at the height of the Civil Rights Movement, claiming that while the Beats were rebelling "against what is most crass and ugly in our society" their rebellion was "without the slightest thought of, say, any kind of direction and purpose."[25] This is not to say all bohemias are apolitical (see Joseph Entin's discussion of Lola Ridge and the Paterson Strike Pageant in Chapter 11), but the quest for artistic and personal freedom often precluded sustained, collective political engagement.

Bohemia's Uncertain Future

While they have always been a beacon for those outside the mainstream, bohemias are becoming harder to form and sustain. Identity politics have eroded the idea of bohemia as a refuge for a broad range of marginalized groups, many of whom feel that collective political projects make a more attractive rallying cry. Bohemias normally draw their energy from youth who see the city as a space for exploring self, art, and life. While Generations Y and Z are indeed more urban-inclined, they do not seem to be rushing to set up bohemias, preferring to pay a bit more for bohemian amenities like bars, art galleries, music spaces, and cafes in order to avoid the grit and danger of past enclaves. The realities of late capitalism in the United States have made forming and maintaining bohemian communities much more difficult, while in a country where many states have legalized recreational marijuana and anyone can express their lifestyle choice through purchases of free-trade coffee, PETA-approved products, and locally made craft beer in esoteric styles, rebellion is defined through consumption and "virtue signaling" rather than by location or participation. Could it be that the only real rebels left are those without a Facebook page or Twitter account, whose lives are themselves statements?

Or perhaps it is just that the city is no longer the best site for bohemia. Discussing William Dean Howells's *The Coast of Bohemia* (1893), where the author juxtaposes a flight to the city with small-town life, Levin explains how Howells represents *la vie bohème* as both a "potential threat to an Arcadian America and a means for its ongoing preservation."[26] Bohemia thrives on frugality, but with the rising costs of the American city a return to the land – the Jeffersonian nation of small landholdings – might be a roadmap for twenty-first-century bohemias. In *The New Geography* (2000), Joel Kotkin labels technologically driven elite rural towns as "Valhallas." But the homesteading movement, "agrihoods" and intentional communities like Agritopia in Phoenix, and even urban farming in cities like Detroit, all eschew the atavism of the 1960s commune without succumbing to the hyperinflation of Kotkin's Jackson Hole or Park City. As Alexis de Tocqueville recognized, being rural in America does not mean being cut off from urban influence. With the rise of the internet, on-demand streaming, and affordable online shopping, the distance between rural and urban is less than ever. From Brook Farm to Vermont's Ben and Jerry's Ice Cream, Americans have always been fascinated by ideas of pastoral self-sufficiency; urban bohemians might be the next wave to decamp to the country. It might even be the case that bohemian life is harder to spot simply because it has been woven into the texture of everyday life. Repetitive but meditative acts such as shoveling manure or chopping wood lack the representational value of more visible urban transgressions or repeatedly shared Tweets, but for that very reason, the rural could very well be the preferred site for a new, if dispersed, bohemianism whose focus is on personal growth rather than social signaling.

Despite its paradoxes and problems, there are good reasons to retain the bohemian ideal. While we tend to discuss bohemia in more conceptual terms, bohemia is inevitably a space for praxis where the contradictions in everyday life come into sharpest focus. The bohemian strives to live in ways that challenge the mainstream, but that challenge is continually undercut. Rather than seeing this struggle as a failure, perhaps we should view it as an opportunity for examining the difficulties of living life on one's own terms. In a media-saturated environment increasingly able to manipulate fears, hopes, and desires, bohemia provides one of the last spaces left to step outside the mainstream, even if only for a short while, and envision something different. Bohemia offers the chance, rarer and rarer in our society, to replace media-driven influence (and "influencers") with an idiosyncratic, personal exploration into the self. As a form of utopia, bohemia is never fully realizable. It's a gesture, a goal, a beckoning horizon. But as a real, if temporary, place meant to confront and challenge social norms, it allows for the chance to experiment with new modes of life that provide an opportunity to negotiate our relationship to a highly mediated consumer culture that relentlessly encroaches on private experience. In such a world, bohemia is as difficult to enact as it is necessary for those who want to define life and its possibilities for themselves.

Notes

1. Jerrold Seigel, *Bohemian Paris: Culture, Politics, and the Boundaries of Bourgeois Life, 1830–1930* (New York: Viking, 1986), pp. 11, 12.
2. Joanna Levin, *Bohemia in America, 1858–1920* (Stanford, CA: Stanford University Press, 2010), p. 6.
3. Christine Stansell, *American Moderns: Bohemian New York and the Creation of a New Century* (New York: Metropolitan Books, 2000), p. 3. Gould was profiled by Joseph Mitchell as "Professor Sea Gull" in *The New Yorker*, December 12, 1942, 28+, and his seagull act is mentioned in William Burroughs's *Naked Lunch* (1959).
4. Delmore Schwartz, "The Present State of Poetry," in Donald A. Dike and David H. Zucker, eds., *Selected Essays of Delmore Schwartz* (Chicago: University of Chicago Press, 1970), p. 45.
5. David Brooks, *Bobos in Paradise: The New Upper Class and How They Got There* (New York: Simon and Schuster, 2000), p. 76.
6. Daniel Bell, *The Cultural Contradictions of Capitalism* (New York: Basic Books, 1976), p. 20.
7. Thomas Frank, *The Conquest of Cool: Business Culture, Counterculture, and the Rise of Hip Consumerism* (Chicago: University of Chicago Press, 1997), p. 31.

8. Sharon Zukin, *Loft Living: Culture and Capital in Urban Change* (New Brunswick, NJ: Rutgers University Press, 2014), p. 97.

9. Richard Florida, *Cities and the Creative Class* (New York: Routledge, 2005), p. 114.

10. Richard Lloyd, *Neo-Bohemia: Art and Commerce in the Postindustrial City* (New York: Routledge, 2010), p. 184.

11. Dennis McLellan, "Ted Joans, 74; Beat Poet's Work Reflected Jazz and African Culture," *Los Angeles Times*, May 13, 2003, www.latimes.com/arch ives/la-xpm-2003-may-13-me-joans13-story.html.

12. Jane Jacobs, *The Death and Life of Great American Cities* (New York: Random House, 1961), p. 188.

13. Lawrence Lipton, *The Holy Barbarians* (New York: Julian Messner, 1959), p. 16.

14. Gilbert Millstein, "Portrait of the Loft Generation," *New York Times Magazine*, January 7, 1962, 28.

15. Heike Mlakar, "The Beat 'Pad,'" *CLCWeb: Comparative Literature and Culture* 18.5 (2016), 2, http://docs.lib.purdue.edu/clcweb/vol18/iss5/15/.

16. Levin, *Bohemia in America,* p. 385.

17. Zukin, *Loft Living*, p. 141.

18. Levin, *Bohemia in America*, p. 361.

19. Stansell, *American Moderns*, p. xi.

20. Jennifer Abraham, *Metropolitan Lovers: The Homosexuality of Cities* (Minneapolis: University of Minnesota Press, 2009), pp. 104, 230.

21. Diane DiPrima, *Dinners and Nightmares* (San Francisco: Last Gasp, 1998), p. 74.

22. Stansell, *American Moderns*, p. 336.

23. Allen Ginsberg, *Collected Poems 1947–1997* (New York: HarperPerennial, 2006), p. 136.

24. Stansell, *American Moderns*, p. 68.

25. Amiri Baraka, *Home: Social Essays* (New York: Morrow, 1966), p. 131.

26. Levin, *Bohemia in America*, p. 245.

Theory in the City

CHAPTER 16

The Spatial Turn and Critical Race Studies

Sophia Bamert and Hsuan L. Hsu

The spatial turn in literary and cultural studies has its origins in the 1980s and early 1990s, when the publication of groundbreaking works by cultural geographers energized critical conversations about both the social production of space and the spatial conditioning of social relations. This critical attention to space – which frequently foregrounds urban examples – can be traced from the 1980 English translation of Foucault's "Questions on Geography" (in which Foucault declares that "Geography must indeed lie at the heart of my concerns") to David Harvey's account of postmodernity as the effect of a shift from Fordism to post-Fordist flexible accumulation characterized by intensified "time-space compression," Neil Smith's theorization of capitalism's dependence on geographically uneven development, Edward Soja's wide-ranging discussion of "the reassertion of space in social theory," and Doreen Massey's delineation of the differential mobilities at play in capitalism's "power geometry."[1] These cultural geographers were strongly influenced by the French sociologist Henri Lefebvre's *The Production of Space* (1974) well before the publication of Donald Nicholson-Smith's English translation in 1992. Commenting on the radicalization of the discipline of geography during this period, Smith writes, "It is extraordinary [...] that in the reactionary 1980s of Thatcher and Reagan and Kohl, Marxist, feminist and broadly radical research (eventually including postmodern, poststructural, postcolonial, and many other kinds of progressive theory) pretty much defined the research frontier in human geography."[2]

Rather than providing a comprehensive overview of these widely acknowledged thinkers on space and place, this essay will put key concepts from cultural geography in conversation – and at times in productive tension – with scholarly and literary accounts of black, Chicanx, and indigenous geographies. Although the "spatial turn" began to inform literary and cultural studies around the same time that these fields were reckoning with key works in critical race studies and research on cultural imperialism – such as Toni Morrison's *Playing in the Dark* (1992), Paul Gilroy's *The Black Atlantic: Modernity and Double Consciousness* (1992), and Amy Kaplan and Donald Pease's seminal collection, *Cultures of United States Imperialism* (1993) – scholars have only recently begun to reckon with the mutually constitutive histories of capitalism's geographies and racial formation. Understanding narratives of contemporary American urban space requires not only the dialectical perspective offered by Marxist cultural geography, but also a theorization of the deep historical connections between race and space. This chapter will thus bring discussions of cultural geography and the geographies of racial capitalism to bear on comparative case studies from African American, Chicanx, and indigenous urban literatures.

Marxist Geography

The foundation for the spatial turn was laid by Lefebvre's dialectical theorization of social space in *The Production of Space*. As Smith notes, "Lefebvre's lifework involved the attempt to rethink the dialectic in terms of space" rather than exclusively in temporal terms.[3] Rather than taking space for granted as a fixed, homogeneous expanse, Lefebvre understands space as "a means of production, produced as such": "Though a product to be used, to be consumed, it is also a means of production; networks of exchange and flows of raw materials and energy fashion space and are determined by it." For Lefebvre, "urban centrality" organizes agriculture in the countryside and orchestrates capital accumulation across scales, "connect[ing] the punctual to the global."[4] The city thus serves as a key example for Lefebvre's argument about the contradictory and potentially revolutionary nature of capitalism's produced spaces: if the city "makes it possible in some degree to deflect class struggles" and "disperse dangerous 'elements,'" it can also "become the arena of kinds of action that can no longer be confined to the traditional locations of the factory or office floor. The city and the urban sphere are thus the setting of struggle; they are also, however, the stakes of that struggle."[5]

Beginning with *Social Justice and the City* (1973), cultural geographer David Harvey has developed an influential Marxist approach to understanding the production and reproduction of space. Across numerous books and articles investigating the "urbanisation of capital," Harvey underscores how urban planning endeavors to optimize the conditions for capital accumulation: for example, *Consciousness and the Urban Experience* (1985) documents how Haussmannization provided spatial conditions for capital accumulation by producing infrastructure, clearing slums, and constructing new amenities to support a speculative real estate market. Harvey's works illuminate how the urban process (a process whose transformations extend far beyond the physical boundaries of cities) has provided "a key means for the absorption of capital and labor surpluses throughout capitalism's history." Urbanization thus provides a "spatial fix" for capitalism's inherent tendency toward overaccumulation crises by offering differentiated sites of capital investment – even if "in the long term" the spatial fix is untenable and only leads to greater conditions of overaccumulation.[6]

Harvey's student Neil Smith expands on these arguments in *Uneven Development: Nature, Capital, and the Production of Space* (1984), a book that arose from his "fascination for North American cities" and his interest in the multiscalar forces that shaped urban gentrification in the mid-1970s.[7] Arguing that capitalism depends on the restructuring of space and scale as a spatial fix for its inherent crises, Smith draws attention to how post-Fordist deindustrialization shapes processes of gentrification that bring capital investments back into urban neighborhoods previously disinvested by processes of suburbanization: "Insofar as uneven development resulting from the seesaw movement of capital depends on the ready mobility of capital, we would expect to find the furthest development of this pattern where capital is most mobile – that is at the urban scale. And indeed the most developed pattern of uneven development does occur at the urban scale."[8] Movements for the redistribution of urban infrastructures and amenities – such as those documented in Harvey's *Rebel Cities: From the Right to the City to the Urban Revolution* (2012) and Edward Soja's *Seeking Spatial Justice* (2010) – are thus at the forefront of anticapitalist organizing. However, as Neil Brenner and Christian Schmid note in "Planetary Urbanization," the urban process is not confined to the boundaries of cities; rather, the turn to urbanization as a "spatial fix" for capital has transformative consequences at all scales: "In every region of the globe, erstwhile 'wilderness' spaces are being transformed and degraded through the cumulative socio-ecological consequences of unfettered worldwide urbanization. In this way, the world's oceans, alpine regions, the equatorial rainforests, major deserts, the arctic and polar zones and even the earth's atmosphere itself, are increasingly interconnected with the rhythms of planetary urbanization at every scale, from the local to the global."[9]

While Marxist geography offers important insights into the relations between power, capital, and the production of urban space, its focus on class conflict tends to downplay the constitutive role of race and racial geographies. Doreen Massey's work addresses this problem to an extent by introducing the concept of "power geometry" to nuance the differential effects of globalization: for subjects differentially positioned vis-à-vis gender, race, citizenship, ability, and geographical location, capitalism's mobility is alternately experienced as voluntary or constrained, as free travel or forced migration, as disinvestment and immobilization or as urban revitalization.[10] In her comparative study of the effects of global economic restructuring on children's futures in rural Sudan and working-class New York City, Cindi Katz coins the term *time-space expansion* to describe how shifting investments in infrastructure make everyday social reproduction and mobility more difficult and time-consuming for vulnerable populations.[11]

Attention to the effects of geographic restructuring on the everyday lives of racially and socio-economically differentiated populations raises critical questions about the ways in which the production of space reproduces and restructures racial difference. If deindustrialization precipitated intensified investments in urban infrastructure and real estate, how did this process differentially affect wealthy real-estate investors, middle-class renters and homeowners, and poor inner-city residents? How do racializing techniques such as residential redlining, predatory loans, profiling, police brutality, mass incarceration, infrastructural disparities, and a host of neighborly microaggressions produce racialized urban geographies that differentially distribute profits, environmental externalities, and access to public space? Addressing these questions requires not only an investigation of Marxist geographies and working-class resistance, but also an understanding of how the historically sedimented and continually restructured geographies of racial capitalism have shaped the everyday lives of poor, racialized populations. In the following sections, we will turn to research informed by critical race studies and black, Chicanx, and indigenous urban narratives that address these issues.

Urban Geographies in Critical Race Studies

Drawing on the Marxist geography of the spatial turn, critical race theorists emphasize the fundamental interrelations between imagined and material spaces, but with the important qualification that spatial constructions are always racialized. As Katherine McKittrick notes, "black matters are spatial matters," highlighting not only that spatial arrangements correspond to and reinforce racial hierarchies, but that race is itself produced through space. For Sylvia Wynter, Western epistemologies of difference have always been articulated through the imaginary of a "space of Otherness," which in the post–Civil War United States came to be expressed by the color line, the symbolic and physical boundary that W. E. B. Du Bois prophesied would be "the problem of the Twentieth Century."[12] Whereas state and extralegal actors have deployed spatial segregation and hierarchization to regulate black, Chicanx, and Asian American populations, indigenous populations have been targeted by settler colonialism's ongoing drives toward the acquisition of land and "the elimination of the Native."[13]

Frantz Fanon documented how Western geographical knowledge was created in and for the colonial encounter: "it is the settler who has brought the native" – and concomitantly himself – "into existence," which is why "in spite of his appropriation, the settler remains a foreigner."[14] By dividing the world "into compartments," the white Westerner simultaneously creates the other and consigns them to a segregated "native town" – "a hungry town, starved of bread, of meat, of shoes, of coal, of light."[15] In *The Wretched of the Earth* (1961), Fanon anticipates the insights of Marxist geography; like Smith's concept of uneven development, Fanon's "world cut in two" comprises "opposed" but "not complementary" zones, which is why decolonization "is no more and no less tha[n] the abolition of one zone."[16] Yet Fanon also already introduces a critique of orthodox Marxism for not dealing with race and colonialism, which was later theorized in depth by Cedric J. Robinson in *Black Marxism* (1983). Mary Pat Brady's study of critical geography in Chicana literature also adds nuance to Marxist geography by noting the racial and colonial implications of Lefebvre's "abstract space" (i.e., the conception of space as a homogeneous, isomorphic, and empty container) in territories acquired by the United States in the wake of the 1848 United States–Mexico War. The US administration, Brady writes, brought about an "abstraction in the service of capital flows [that] entailed a shift from the differentiated spaces conceptualized by Apaches, Yaquis, and Mexicanos [...] a shift from the lived and sacred to the measured and homogenized."[17]

Scholarship on race and space often catalogs the range of scales, from the individual body to the transnational territory, at which race gets located, such as "ghetto, suburb, barrio, reservation, prison, [and] occupied territory" or "seemingly predetermined stabilities, such as boundaries, colorlines, 'proper' places, fixed and settled infrastructures and streets, [and] oceanic containers."[18] But where early scholarship of the spatial turn tended to center cities as prime sites at which the "social geometry of power" can be disarticulated and perceived, scholars of black and Chicanx geography turn to urban space as the operative scale of racial confinement in the twentieth-century United States.[19] The racialized native/black body has always been "a being hemmed in," and this racialization through spatial control both enabled and was perpetuated by twentieth-century practices of redlining, urban renewal, welfare policy, and mass incarceration.[20] For Saidiya Hartman, the "emergent ghetto" was the "form of racial enclosure that succeeded the plantation": "The afterlife of slavery unfolded in a tenement hallway."[21] The spatial turn in critical race studies thus highlights the co-constitutive social production of race through the "territoriality of power" and material production of American cities' architectures and infrastructures.[22]

In particular, the racist lending practices and restrictive covenants of Great Depression-era cities combined with postwar urban renewal and public-housing projects to produce the image – and reality – of the inner city that in turn produced the social and spatial conditions for contemporary mass incarceration and police violence. Describing the geographies of black masculinity in *Spatializing Blackness* (2015), Rashad Shabazz supplements Foucault's "race-neutral examination" of carceral power with an analysis of the ways in which the police presence in the "Black Belt" institutionalized and materialized a racialized carceral power whose later manifestation became the public-housing projects, exposing US "domestic security" as always necessarily racist.[23] In his analysis of the Western high-rise housing project as a technology that paradoxically renders racialized populations "peripheral at the social centre," David Theo Goldberg similarly conceptualizes racial geography in terms of "a plan to place (a representative population) so that it protrudes or sticks out. [...] Its external visibility serves at once as a form of panoptical discipline, vigilant boundary constraints upon its effects that might spill over to threaten the social fabric."[24] Work by critical race scholars thus attends to physical architectures like high-rise housing projects through seminal geographic concepts like Foucault's, while exposing that exclusionary racist spaces are not mere outcomes of geographic power differentials or capitalist spatial fixes, but rather that that unevenness is from the outset a form of racial – not just spatial – discipline.

In post–World War II US cities, racist stereotypes and racialized spaces reinforce one another in a positive feedback loop, as the physical geography of the city provides material evidence for the conflation of racialized populations with poverty and criminality, which results in further disinvestment from the infrastructures and welfare of the black "inner city." Wynter singles out "the Investor/Breadwinners versus the criminalized jobless Poor (Nas's 'black and latino faces') and Welfare Moms antithesis" as the newest iteration of the "space of Otherness," where visible blackness is made to "coalesce with the inner-city status of poverty and joblessness, crime, and drugs."[25] If in previous eras the slave plantation and the segregated South were the principal geographies shaping US racism, their successor is the contemporary American city, with its direct institutional links to mass incarceration and police violence.

The city has similarly played an important role in federal efforts to terminate Native American sovereignty and identity. As Laura Furlan notes, federal relocation initiatives relocated more than 100,000 indigenous people from reservations to (increasingly disinvested) cities between 1951 and 1971 in an effort to propel assimilation.[26] Likewise, Libby Porter and Oren Yiftachel argue that urban space plays a vital legitimizing role in settler societies: "the racist imaginary deployed by colonizers of Indigenous peoples has worked to render the urban as a place *not Indigenous*, profoundly spatially and temporally disconnected from Indigenous histories and geographies, despite the obvious fact in settler-colonial societies that most cities and settlements sit on unceded territories."[27] Just as the urban spatial fix transforms space at all scales, the erasure of the indigenous from the urban is twinned with the conflation of blackness and inner city as part of the same process; both "the freed Negro" and "the Indians interned in reservations [. . .] will now be interned in the new institution of Poverty/ Joblessness."[28]

We must therefore look to urban spaces for the racial geographies that are, as McKittrick asserts, "also lived and right in the middle of our historically present landscape"; that is, critical race studies – like Marxist geography – shows us that institutionalized, hegemonic representations of space do not extinguish alternate, lived spatial realities. As Brady writes in her study of Chicanx literary geographies, "alternative conceptions of space continue to thrive alongside, if not dominate, the flow of capital." Raúl Homero Villa argues that *barrioization* – or a segregationist "complex of dominating social processes originating *outside* of the barrios" – gave rise to diverse practices of urban Chicano *barriology* which "reveal multiple possibilities for re-creating and re-imagining dominant urban *space* as community-enabling *place*."[29] George Lipsitz proposes that "a distinct Black spatial imaginary" exists in spite of and in opposition to the "hostile privatism and defensive localism" – and, we would add, the accompanying carceral practices – "of the white spatial imaginary." For Lipsitz, black geographies counter segregation and panoptical discipline by "burrowing in, building up, and branching out"; Hartman terms these alternative uses of space – "the ongoing and open-ended creation of new conditions of existence and the improvisation of life-enhancing and free association [...] in social clubs, tenements, taverns, dance halls, disorderly houses, and the streets" – the "mutual aid society."[30] Similarly, Furlan notes that indigenous relocation efforts had the unintended effect of producing a reinvigorated "contemporary tribal cosmopolitanism" as urban Indians developed intertribal social and political connections.[31]

Black, Latinx, and Indigenous Writers on Urban Racial Geographies

Attending to the uneven and historically shifting grounds of urban racial geographies draws attention to the heterogeneous modes of spatial violence that are too often suppressed by liberal depictions of urban multiculturalism. Whereas capitalist interests put "diversity" on display in their efforts to attract the so-called creative class, this drive toward gentrification only exacerbates racial inequities by prompting further waves of eviction and displacement. Urban writings by black, Latinx, and indigenous authors provide nuanced accounts of the ways in which suburbanization and urban disinvestment remade black and brown urban neighborhoods as spaces of captivity, as well as the practices of mutual care and support mobilized in the interest of community defense and survival. In their refusal to turn away from the urban structural violence visited upon communities of color, these texts do much more than document the uneven effects of planning, architecture, infrastructure, and "urban revitalization" – they also depict inventive modes of support and "survivance."[32]

Marita Bonner, who in the 1920s and 1930s wrote prize-winning stories and essays in the African American journals *The Crisis* and *Opportunity*, explored the urban environment of Chicago's Great Migration-era "Black Belt" in her fiction. Her short story "The Whipping," published in 1939 in *The Crisis*, maps out the racist spatial fix that generates profit for banks, prison investors, and real estate speculators by miring black communities in cycles of poverty, trauma, and confinement. It opens with a "matron" of Danish descent driving thirty-five miles back to her city apartment, which is defined by its "warmth of color and all the right uses of the best comforts," after having delivered Lizabeth, a black woman charged with murdering her son, to the "impersonal greyness" of the exurban Women's Reformatory. As the story demonstrates, however, the contrast between comfort and discomfort, sunshine and grayness, is not that of city versus suburb or the domestic versus the institutional: "Everything had been grey around Lizabeth most all of her life," starting with the Mississippi sharecropper's hut where she grew up – and where her father deserted the family, which was floundering in debt to the commissary. When Lizabeth and her mother and siblings arrive in Chicago, they find that "the houses on Federal Street were just as grey, just as bare of color and comfort as the hut they had left in Mississippi," highlighting that the supposedly contrasting spaces of the US North and South turn out to be corresponding parts of a single system of oppression.[33] Black women like Lizabeth are particularly vulnerable in the face of this system because of the ways in which they inhabit space; as Hartman notes, "the law designated as crime [...] the forms of life created by black women in the city," including wandering the streets, living in female-headed households, and engaging in extra- or nonmarital relationships.[34]

The narrator recounts the events that lead to Lizabeth's accidental killing of her son with a fine-grained attention to urban geography. Lizabeth must "walk[] fifteen blocks one winter day to a relief station," and then, falling over from exhaustion, she gets arrested for drunkenness and taken to the police station: "Home was thirty blocks away this time." Returning home to her hungry son, she "who had never struck Benny in her life, stood up and slapped him to the floor" and walked back out to the relief station. Only later, again in police custody, does Lizabeth learn that her slap, which made Benny's head strike the iron headboard, killed her son. The text's attention to Lizabeth's walks through the city highlights the multiple scales at which structural violence takes place. At the scale of the body, Lizabeth's poverty causes the hunger and weakness – and forces her to walk rather than pay for public transport – that allow relief workers and police officers to misread her as drunk and violent. Those misreadings are not individual errors: the relief worker's "books had all told her that colored women carried knives."[35] This systemic injustice is reinforced and reproduced through spatial means, such as the predatory rental practices that isolate the black population in kitchenette districts and make it impossible to escape poverty, just as sharecropping tethered the descendants of slaves to the same parcels of land through debt.

Whereas "The Whipping" maps out the geography of structural violence, contemporary queer black poet Danez Smith's "Dinosaurs in the Hood" suggests ways of seeing and celebrating alternate forms of life that persist within and despite those oppressive structures – in McKittrick's words, "across the logic of white and patriarchal maps."[36] The poem was first published in 2014 in *Poetry* magazine, and it appears in Smith's collection *Don't Call Us Dead* (2017), a National Book Award finalist. It imagines a genre-blending movie about "a neighborhood of royal folks – //

children of slaves & immigrants & addicts & exiles – saving their town / from real-ass dinosaurs," an invading force suggestive of the community destruction wrought by urban renewal and gentrification. The first stanza instructs that "there should be a scene where a little black boy is playing / with a toy dinosaur on the bus, and then looks out the window" to see a real dinosaur. This insistence on the realness of the dinosaurs, which offers the black kid "proof of magic or God or Santa," accompanies a disavowal of racist stereotypes. For, as the next stanza implores, "don't let Tarantino direct this. in his version, the boy plays / with a gun, the metaphor: black boys toy with their own lives, / the foreshadow to his end, the spitting image of his father."[37] Like the books that teach the relief worker of "The Whipping" that black women carry guns, Hollywood tropes predetermine the boy's future – that of violent black man – and deny him both the innocence of childhood and the potential to assume roles other than those prescribed for him.

The Hollywood spatial imaginary that Smith lays over the geography of the inner city brings into relief the entanglement of uneven development and racial segregation. Depictions of the ghetto turn real lives into metaphors and accumulate more capital in the already-rich film industry; hence "this is not a vehicle for Will Smith / & Sofia Vergara." By invoking and then renouncing the stereotypes that would typically generate profit at the expense of poor people of color – "I don't want any racist shit / about Asian people or overused Latino stereotypes" – the poem reveals the ways in which the hegemonic representation of the city is itself an imaginary. The incantations "this can't be a black movie" and "no one kills the black boy" attest to the power of those representations; just as in "The Whipping," stereotypes and segregation do indeed have material effects, not least of which is police violence. That the movie envisaged by the poem depicts "a neighborhood of royal folks [. . .] saving *their* town" signals a hoped-for transfer of ownership that would confer on the black community authority over its spaces and self-representations.[38] "Dinosaurs in the Hood" thereby distorts the dominant perceptions of racialized space reproduced in Hollywood movies, while nevertheless stressing the lived reality of their violent consequences. By its final stanza, the poem has carved out a space that highlights the not-just-imagined presence of real, dignified black lives "right there": "Besides, the only reason / I want to make this is for that first scene anyway: the little black boy / on the bus with a toy dinosaur, his eyes wide & endless // his dreams possible, pulsing, & right there."[39]

The racial violence underpinning the production of space is at the heart of Helena María Viramontes's *Their Dogs Came with Them* (2007), a novel that tracks an ensemble of young Chicanx characters growing up in East Los Angeles during the decades when the community's homes were torn down and its neighborhoods divided to make room for a massive freeway interchange that serves suburban white commuters. The novel details the various forms of constraint and harm – particularly for young women, an undocumented migrant, and the transgender character Turtle – that result from "this dysfunctional urban milieu – produced not only by freeway construction but by the range of infrastructural redevelopments that support the expressway world of Los Angeles."[40] Freeways suffuse the air with noise, ash, dust, and exhaust (whose physiological effects in the novel range from wheezing and stinging eyes to potential mental and emotional debilitation); they displace families from entire blocks and raze their homes; they "amputat[e]" the neighborhood's connecting streets into "stumped dead ends"; they transfer jobs and tax revenue to predominantly white suburbs while allowing suburban commuters to pass through East LA with minimal contact; and they affect collective memory, social life, and individual psychology in countless predictable and unpredictable ways.[41] If freeways further time-space compression for suburban residents and business interests, East Los Angeles residents experience them as agents of time-space expansion. Viramontes compounds – and allegorizes – the isolating effect of freeway construction by adding a magical realist element; in the novel, a Quarantine Authority patrols East Los Angeles under the pretext of controlling a rabies epidemic, imposing a curfew, controlling access, surveilling the streets, and shooting stray dogs.

These forms of harm and constraint inform all of the novel's interlocking plots as they intersect and diverge like street traffic: Ermila, an orphan subjected to domestic captivity by her overprotective grandfather and domestic harassment by her cousin Nacho, finds a degree of freedom in dating a gang member with a car and hanging out with her group of girlfriends; Ben, who suffers from migraines, chronic pain, and depression long after being struck by a car, leaves his apartment and disappears into the streets; Turtle, a transgender gang member, walks the streets and sleeps in the cemetery, vigilantly avoiding Quarantine roadblocks and members of a rival gang. As the plotlines converge, the novel ends with a series of tragedies that include Nacho being stabbed to death by Turtle and Turtle being shot like a dog by the Quarantine Authority. Before these tragedies unfold, however, Viramontes details the vital and inventive forms of mutual assistance and care by which characters support one another in the face of what Jina Kim has characterized as "a narrative world centrally defined by disabled embodiment." For Kim, *Their Dogs* is far more than a novel that protests the various forms of debilitation that result from the freeways, the Quarantine, and other forms of structural racism; it is "an account of human enmeshment within and dependency upon systems of social support." Drawing on Maria Lugones's discussion of "streetwalker theorizing," Paula Moya similarly details how, in the course of "hanging out," telling stories, and supporting each other in the streets, Ermila and her three girlfriends "practice a form of mutual acceptance and collectivity that is both discerning and loving."[42] The encounters and convergences of the characters' plots disclose a form of spatial collectivity, a network not obliterated by freeway construction, but aggregated in its wake.

Like *Their Dogs,* the Cheyenne and Arapaho author Tommy Orange's critically acclaimed novel *There There* (2018) follows an ensemble of Native American characters toward a tragic convergence, in this case a powwow at the Oakland Coliseum. If the terms *urban* and *inner city* are often used as racist euphemisms for *black* or *Latinx,* they also invoke the notion that the settler city is antithetical to indigeneity – the concept of *urbs nullius* that naturalizes colonial genocide by erasing indigenous presence.[43] Reframing Gertrude Stein's observation about Oakland, "There is no there there," which is often quoted to suggest that the city lacks a sense of place, Orange writes that "for Native people in this country, all over the Americas, it's been developed over, buried ancestral land, glass and concrete and wire and steel, unreturnable covered memory. There is no there there."[44] Making claims to both the city of Oakland and their partially deracinated indigenous identities, Orange's characters evoke the diverse ways in which "urban Indians" contend with the legacies of ongoing colonialism.

As they struggle with diverse forms of colonial violence – including fetal alcohol syndrome, domestic violence, unemployment, criminalization, substance addiction, homelessness, gentrification, suicide, and gun violence – Orange's young characters mobilize social relations and cultural forms from documentary video and Wikipedia entries to the powwow in the service of survivance, insistently reinventing their indigenous identities. As Orange puts it in the novel's stunning prologue:

> Getting us to cities was supposed to be the final, necessary step in our assimilation, absorption, erasure, the completion of a five-hundred-year-old genocidal campaign. But the city made us new, and we made it ours. We didn't get lost amid the sprawl of tall buildings, the stream of anonymous masses, the ceaseless din of traffic. We found one another, started up Indian Centers, brought out our families and powwows, our dances, our songs, our beadwork. [...] We did not move to cities to die. The sidewalks and streets, the concrete, absorbed our heaviness. The glass, metal, rubber, and wires, the speed, the hurtling masses – the city took us in.[45]

Orange invokes conventional literary tropes of urban modernity, anonymity, and hypermobility in order to undo the erasure of indigenous presence that underpins settler notions of the city. The radical transformation offered by the city has the effect of catalyzing new practices of trans-indigenous survivance – practices that directly oppose the city's functions as a space of assimilation and a monument to settler modernity. Like "Dinosaurs in the Hood" and *Their Dogs Came with Them, There There* blends a tragic depiction of racial capitalism's urban manipulations with a sense of the city's potential for social and cultural transformation, even for its decolonization, as Viramontes's and Orange's scenarios of mutual support suggest. Moreover, by formally centering character ensembles rather than individual protagonists, these novels underscore the collective networks that struggle to hold space despite the bulldozing and displacements that pave the way for urban renewal.

The literary and critical treatments of race and space considered in this chapter demonstrate both the insights and limitations opened up by the spatial turn. By staging the constitutive racial qualities of uneven geographical development – in particular, its dependence on antiblack inflections of Atlantic slavery and settler-colonial patterns of indigenous elimination – critical race studies and spatially oriented works of black, Latinx, and indigenous literature insist that race and colonialism have been crucial factors in both the history and geographies of capitalism. These works not only highlight possibilities for forging solidarities and oppositional spatial practices across locations and scales, as we gain a better understanding of both the commonalities and frictions between disparate formations of race and indigeneity, but also emphasize the need for spatial theory to address the ongoing imperatives of desegregation and decolonization in its visions of possible futures for the American city.

Notes

1. Michel Foucault, "Questions on Geography," in Colin Gordon, ed., *Power/Knowledge: Selected Interviews and Other Writings 1972–1977* (New York: Pantheon, 1980), p. 77; David Harvey, *The Condition of Postmodernity: An Enquiry into the Origins of Cultural Change* (1990); Neil Smith, *Uneven Development: Nature, Capital, and the Production of Space* (1984); Edward Soja, *Postmodern Geographies: The Reassertion of Space in Critical Social Theory* (2011); Doreen Massey, *Space, Place and Gender* (London: Polity, 1994), pp. 164–67.
2. Neil Smith, "Neo-Critical Geography, or, the Flat Pluralist World of Business Class," *Antipode* 37 (2005), 889.

3. Neil Smith, "Foreword," in Henri Lefebvre, *The Urban Revolution* (Minneapolis: University of Minnesota Press, 2003), p. ix.
4. Henri Lefebvre, *The Production of Space*, trans. Donald Nicholson-Smith (Oxford: Blackwell, 1991), pp. 85, 331, 332.
5. Ibid., p. 386.
6. David Harvey, *Rebel Cities: From the Right to the City to Urban Revolution* (London: Verso, 2012), p. 42.
7. Neil Smith, *Uneven Development: Nature, Capital, and the Production of Space* (London: Verso, 2010), pp. xv–xvi.
8. Ibid., pp. 199–200.
9. Neil Brenner and Christian Schmid, "Planetary Urbanization," in Neil Brenner, ed., *Implosions/Explosions: Towards a Study of Planetary Urbanization* (Berlin: Jovis, 2013), p. 162.
10. See Massey, *Space, Place*, pp. 146–56.
11. Cindi Katz, "On the Grounds of Globalization: A Topography for Feminist Political Engagement," *Signs* 26 (2001), 224.
12. Katherine McKittrick, *Demonic Grounds: Black Women and the Cartographies of Struggle* (Minneapolis: University of Minnesota Press, 2006), p. xiv; Sylvia Wynter, "Unsettling the Coloniality of Being/Power/Truth/ Freedom: Towards the Human, after Man, Its Overrepresentation – An Argument," *CR: The New Centennial Review* 3:3 (2003), 317; W. E. B. Du Bois, *The Souls of Black Folk* (1903; New Haven, CT: Yale University Press, 2015), p. 1.
13. Patrick Wolfe, "Settler Colonialism and the Elimination of the Native," *Journal of Genocide Research* 8 (2006), 387–409.
14. Frantz Fanon, *The Wretched of the Earth*, trans. Constance Farrington (New York: Grove Press, 1963), pp. 36, 40.
15. Ibid., pp. 37, 39.
16. Ibid., pp. 38, 41.
17. Mary Pat Brady, *Extinct Lands, Temporal Geographies: Chicana Literature and the Urgency of Space* (Durham, NC: Duke University Press, 2002), p. 4.
18. Wendy Cheng and Rashad Shabazz, "Introduction: Race, Space, and Scale in the Twenty-First Century," *Occasion* 8 (2015), 1; McKittrick, *Demonic Grounds*, p. xi.
19. Massey, *Space, Place*, p. 3.
20. Fanon, *Wretched of the Earth*, p. 52.
21. Saidiya Hartman, "The Anarchy of Colored Girls Assembled in a Riotous Manner," *South Atlantic Quarterly* 117 (2018), 470, 476.
22. Ruth Wilson Gilmore, "Fatal Couplings of Power and Difference: Notes on Racism and Geography," *Professional Geographer* 54:1 (2002), 22.
23. Rashad Shabazz, *Spatializing Blackness: Architectures of Confinement and Black Masculinities in Chicago* (Urbana: University of Illinois Press, 2015), pp. 7, 37.
24. David Theo Goldberg, *Racist Culture: Philosophy and the Politics of Meaning* (New York: Blackwell, 1993), p. 198.
25. Wynter, "Unsettling the Coloniality," 323, 325.

26. Laura Furlan, *Indigenous Cities: Urban Indian Fiction and the Histories of Relocation* (Lincoln: University of Nebraska Press, 2017), p. 15.
27. Libby Porter and Oren Yiftachel, "Urbanizing Settler-Colonial Studies: Introduction to the Special Issue," *Settler Colonial Studies* (2017), 1.
28. Wynter, "Unsettling the Coloniality," 321.
29. McKittrick, *Demonic Grounds*, p. 7; Brady, *Extinct Lands*, p. 5; Raúl Homero Villa, *Barrio-Logos: Space and Place in Urban Chicano Literature and Culture* (Austin: University of Texas Press, 2000), pp. 4, 6.
30. George Lipsitz, *How Racism Takes Place* (Philadelphia: Temple University Press, 2011), pp. 13, 13, 19; Hartman, "Anarchy of Colored Girls," 471.
31. Furlan, *Indigenous Cities*, p. 17.
32. On "survivance" as an indigenous practice that instantiates an "active presence," see Gerald Vizenor, "Aesthetics of Survivance: Literary Theory and Practice," in Vizenor, ed., *Survivance: Narratives of Native Presence* (Lincoln: University of Nebraska Press, 2008), p. 11.
33. Marita Bonner, "The Whipping," in Joyce Flynn and Joyce Occomy Stricklin, eds., *Frye Street & Environs: The Collected Works of Marita Bonner* (Boston: Beacon Press, 1987), pp. 185–86, 186, 188.
34. Hartman, "Anarchy of Colored Girls," 469.
35. Bonner, "The Whipping," pp. 191, 192, 192, 191.
36. McKittrick, *Demonic Grounds*, p. 62.
37. Danez Smith, "Dinosaurs in the Hood," in *Don't Call Us Dead* (Minneapolis, MN: Graywolf Press, 2017), p. 26.
38. Ibid., emphasis added.
39. Ibid., p. 27.
40. Villa, *Barrio-Logos*, p. 115.
41. Helena María Viramontes, *Their Dogs Came with Them* (New York: Washington Square Press, 2007), p. 33.
42. Jina B. Kim, "Cripping East Los Angeles: Enabling Environmental Justice in Helena María Viramontes's *Their Dogs Came with Them*," in Sarah Jaquette Ray, Jay Sibara, and Stacy Alaimo, eds., *Disability Studies and the Environmental Humanities: Toward an Eco-Crip Theory* (Lincoln: University of Nebraska Press, 2017), pp. 511, 503; Paula Moya, "'Against the Sorrowful and Infinite Solitude': Environmental Consciousness and Streetwalker Theorizing in Helena María Viramontes's *Their Dogs Came with Them*," in David J. Vásquez, Sarah Wald, Sarah Ray, and Priscilla Ybarra, eds., *Latinx Environmentalisms: Place, Justice, and the Decolonial* (Philadelphia: Temple University Press, 2019), p. 255.
43. See Glen Coulthard, *Red Skin, White Masks: Rejecting the Colonial Politics of Recognition* (Minneapolis: University of Minnesota Press, 2014), p. 176.
44. Tommy Orange, *There There* (New York: Penguin, 2018), p. 39.
45. Ibid., pp. 8–9.

CHAPTER 17

From Trauma Theory to Systemic Violence
Narratives of Post-Katrina New Orleans

Arin Keeble

Trauma and trauma theory, as interpretive frameworks in literary and cultural studies, have been the subject of increasing scrutiny and criticism over the last decade. One notable and influential instance of this question-oning is Lauren Berlant's *Cruel Optimism* (2011), which argues for "moving away from the discourse of trauma – from [Cathy] Caruth to [Giorgio] Agamben – when describing what happens to persons and populations as an effect of catastrophic impacts."[1] For Berlant and others, what needs urgent attention is "a notion of systemic crisis," or what Rob Nixon terms "slow violence," and the focus on trauma diverts attention away from these less visceral and immediate but equally pernicious phenomena.[2] In particular, the discourse of trauma does not adequately describe the incremental, unspectacular and sometimes difficult-to-see violence of neoliberal capitalism and climate change. One consequence of the prevalence of the rhetoric of trauma and disaster, Berlant argues, is that the contemporary moment is experienced as a perennial state of exception where people are waiting to resume "some ongoing, uneventful ordinary life" where they feel "solid and confident," but that does not actually exist.[3] There is no doubt that climate change-related disasters are increasing, and adjacently, there is a common feeling in Western democracies that the world is seeing unprecedented levels of terrorism and increasing financial precarity (or "volatile markets") resulting in what Hua Hsu calls a "new age of anxiety."[4] In these contexts it is certainly legitimate to question the extent to which trauma should remain a central interpretative framework. But equally, there can be no doubt that moments of extreme violence or experience which exceed individual and collective psychological limits and haunt us via traumatic memories or posttraumatic stress disorder (PTSD), still occur and perhaps what is truly pressing is an understanding of how such limit events play out in the context of this new age of anxiety or what Berlant calls "crisis ordinariness."

Well before the seminal works by Berlant and Nixon, theoreticians of trauma and memory, particularly in postcolonial studies, had expressed concerns about the tendency of trauma studies to exceptionalize, depoliticize, or decontextualize violent events. For instance, Michael Rothberg, writing about 9/11 in the midst of its fraught aftermath, pointed out that "a focus on trauma solely as a structure of reception might [. . .] actually end up unwittingly reinforcing the repressive liberal-conservative consensus in the United States that attempting to explain the events amounts to explaining them away or excusing them."[5] Rothberg's concern proved to be warranted, and even before his contention was published in 2003, the few critics and commentators who had dared to consider the roles that American foreign policy, long-standing structural realities, or world-systems dynamics played in precipitating 9/11 were castigated.[6] Eventually, though, these myopic discourses were eroded, and there are compelling links between Rothberg's early post-9/11 concerns and Berlant's more recent arguments. For example, it is undoubtedly the case that the exceptionalization of 9/11 played a part in escalating the scrutiny and criticism of trauma studies and in the shift in focus toward systemic and slow violence.

In this context, it is worth looking back to Naomi Klein's *The Shock Doctrine* (2007). Lauded for both its scholarly rigor and accessibility, Klein's book traces a history of neoliberal capitalism from Milton Friedman and the Chicago School of Economics in the 1940s to Hurricane Katrina and the Iraq War. She argues that it has been propelled by moments of shock or trauma, in which society is "psychologically unmoored and physically uprooted," which provides the ideologues "clean canvases."[7] Klein's narrative is trenchantly political, global in scope and historically rooted, yet its focus on moments of "shock" has also been critiqued in relation to the emergent interest in the systemic. For instance, in *After Katrina: Race, Neoliberalism and the End of the American Century* (2017), Anna Hartnell argues that Klein's emphasis on shock or trauma "neglects the role of consent" and "fails to track the progression of neoliberal policies as forms of 'slow violence' that had been in train for decades before the storm."[8] So while Klein and Hartnell are both fundamentally interested in critiquing neoliberal practices and ideology, for Hartnell, Klein's emphasis on shock and trauma has the effect of exceptionalizing these practices and thus disavowing the fact that they are politically, culturally and socially entrenched. Hartnell's criticism is a telling example of the wider emergent tension across the humanities between trauma studies, which remains prevalent despite these recent challenges, and newer analyses of systemic violence. In addition to an increasingly polarized debate about what kind of frameworks are appropriate to interpret and understand the impact of crisis in the early twenty-first century, trauma and systemic violence both pose well-known – and antithetical – representational challenges. As Anne Whitehead noted in her monograph *Trauma Fiction* (2004), "the term 'trauma fiction' represents a paradox or contradiction: if trauma comprises an event or experience which overwhelms the individual and resists language or representation, how then can it be narrativized in fiction?"[9] But while traumatic ruptures or moments of extreme violence may be impossible to fully apprehend and therefore a challenge to represent, they often have at least some kind of dramatic potential. The lack of such potential has proven to be the critical representational challenge for slow violence; as Rob Nixon notes, it is "neither spectacular nor instantaneous, but rather incremental and accretive, its calamitous repercussions playing out across a range of temporal scales."[10]

This chapter argues that two contemporary city narratives that are also trauma narratives offer useful ways of considering the tension or impasse described above. It examines two texts of post-Katrina New Orleans, Dave Eggers's work of narrative nonfiction, *Zeitoun* (2009) and David Simon and Eric Overmyer's television series *Treme* (2009–13). These texts do important work plotting the overlaps and intersections of systemic violence and traumatic rupture in their accounts of the human tragedies of the Katrina crisis; a traumatic event whose violence was made acute by a series of systemic failures, particularly that of New Orleans's neglected and poorly constructed levee system. In doing so, they offer artistic responses to Rothberg's call in the preface to *The Future of Trauma Theory: Contemporary Literary and Cultural Criticism* (2014), ten years after his initial response to the trauma of 9/11, to represent "two forms of violence."[11] Naming those forms, he points to the persistence of trauma and the enduring value of understanding the ways people and nations experience and respond to moments of sudden rupture or incomprehensible violence, but also to a kind of violence which is "neither sudden nor accidental: exploitation in an age of globalized neo-liberal capitalism."[12]

As key narratives of the Katrina crisis, *Treme* and *Zeitoun* are deeply invested in navigating the intersections of these "two forms of violence." They do this by dramatizing experiences of trauma in the context of ongoing systemic violence, and particularly the human suffering that occurs as they overlap. In both texts, the city of New Orleans is shown to be a site where these intersections are vivid – it is diverse, unpredictable, dynamic, and also generative. New Orleans has seen a succession of traumatic events or ruptures from nineteenth-century outbreaks of small-pox to Hurricane Betsy in September 1965, Katrina, and the explosion of the Deepwater Horizon oil-drilling platform in April 2010, and the subsequent spill of 4.9 million barrels of crude oil into the Gulf of Mexico. Equally, as a key port and marketplace in the slave trade, it has been a site where the United States' most brutal and violent institution was fostered and perpetuated over centuries; that legacy endures in national and local government institutions. Indeed, some of the United States' most violent systems can be traced back to slavery, and particularly US penal policy as an instrument of racist culture, which Michelle Alexander theorizes and describes as the "new Jim Crow." Alexander demonstrates in painful detail how a vast swath of American society still suffers radically curtailed and limited rights, and is "subject to legalized discrimination in employment, housing, education, public benefits and jury service, just as their parents, grandparents, and great-grandparents once were."[13] Even so, New Orleans – and other American cities – have staged the most vivid examples of institutional racism while simultaneously being sites of transcendence that have generated social, cultural, and political resistance to such practices. In New Orleans, the struggle for the right to the city can be traced back to the early slavery-era meetings of black Americans at what was then Congo Square, through to the birth of jazz, the Mardi Gras Indians, and many of the city's other cultural traditions. It has been a struggle "from the periphery," which has aimed to "empower outsiders to get inside," and to "live out the city as one's own, to live for the city."[14]

New Orleans and the United States

Partially because of its unique cultural traditions (whose roots in New Orleans's rim-city status are Ruth Salvaggio's subject in Chapter 9), New Orleans is also a city that is often seen as a kind of internal other in the American national imagination – in positive and negative ways. This positioning was acute after the Katrina crisis, and aided by President George W. Bush's speech of September 2, 2005, at Mobile Regional Airport in southern Alabama, which he closed by emphasizing the importance of giving "comfort to people in that part of the world."[15] Such rhetoric characterized New Orleans (and the wider Gulf Coast region) as other, somehow outside the homeland mainstream, and it built on existing notions of New Orleans as an exotic and dangerous place, ultimately characterizing post-Katrina New Orleans as "third world." As Julia Leyda notes:

The images of the extreme subtropical climate and the poverty, compounded by the already widespread cultural knowledge of the city's excesses
and history of corruption, contributed to the notion that New Orleans is
somehow not American; indeed, in many respects it is portrayed as a "third-
world" place. Conjuring the idea of New Orleans as part of the third world
reassured Americans that the rest of the United States was still in fact "first
world."[16]

Leyda's assessment has been echoed in a range of scholarly accounts of the
Katrina crisis, many of which also point to New Orleans's unique ability to
illuminate or to expose problems within American national culture.
Hartnell, who also discusses the ways that New Orleans has been othered,
singles out the city's role as a "whistleblower in relation to the larger
national imaginary."[17]

    She points out that New Orleans's cultural traditions "have mocked" the
hubris and narcissism of "U.S. political ideology," via their conspicuous
comfort with, and acceptance of, death and mortality.[18] The city's unique
position in American national culture is undoubted, but *Treme* and
Zeitoun both depict the city in ways that powerfully implicate national
issues. In these texts, New Orleans is positioned as an exemplar of the
progressive potential of American cities and the broader United States, but
also as a site where twenty-first-century American exceptionalism and the
melting pot myth are brought into acute focus. One of the most productive
consequences of these explorations is their sustained examination of intersections between traumatic and systemic crises.

    Both *Treme* and *Zeitoun* deploy specific formal and narrative devices to
explore these intersections. *Treme* is deeply preoccupied with its characters'
experiences of trauma and meaningfully attends to the traumatic and
systemic via its seriality. The program's slowly unfolding narrative,
which dramatizes a period from three months after the crisis in late 2005,
to the early days of the Obama presidency in 2008, allows time to explore
the way trauma haunts as well as the ways people work through trauma
while simultaneously mapping out complex webs of structural and institutional racism and inequality over thirty-six hours of narrative. Crucially,
Treme frequently explores the ways in which systemic malaise prohibits
recovery from trauma. With its interest in systems, *Treme* dedicates long
story strands to political and governmental systems including policing,
education, disaster relief, and rebuilding (with particular emphasis on the
neoliberal privatization of the latter three civic responsibilities) – it is
clearly linked to Simon's previous, celebrated TV drama, *The Wire*
(2002–9; which Brian Tochterman discusses in Chapter 13), which

examines structural racism, inequality and corruption in neoliberal Baltimore. But unlike *The Wire, Treme* depicts a city and community in the aftermath of a moment of collective trauma that revealed systemic and structural failures, which means that the "two forms of violence" converge or, at least, that the moment of rupture reveals existing systemic failures. *Zeitoun* is also deeply invested in attempting to represent and work through the trauma of the Katrina crisis, while also exposing and critiquing systemic and structural violence.

Zeitoun tells the true story of Abdulrahman Zeitoun's wrongful arrest as a terror suspect after he had rescued several imperiled citizens during the flooding of New Orleans. It addresses Abdulrahman and his wife Kathy Zeitoun's experience of trauma and the systemic malaise and the institutional prejudices that exacerbated it. To do so, *Zeitoun* adapts several ideologically loaded genre conceits; it features a marriage plot (in which it resembles any number of American television sitcoms), an immigrant's American Dream, a story of self-reliance, as well as classic conceits from frontier and adventure narratives.[19] These conceits ostensibly do two jobs. First, they assert the titular protagonist's and his family's Americanness in a climate when it was routinely questioned on account of their being an interethnic Muslim family. Second, the use of established narrative frameworks helps to manage and bring meaning, coherence, and familiarity to incomprehensible or traumatic events by inserting them within established narrative frameworks. As Kristiaan Versluys notes, "traumatic memory must be turned into narrative memory" in order to undo its "never-ending circularity."[20] However, these genre frameworks are subject to intense pressure by the introduction of a further genre frame, prison writing. A central episode in *Zeitoun* operates in this mode to depict one of the United States' most brutal systemic blights, its carceral culture. The presence of this sustained narrative segment means, of course, that what we are reading as a city narrative features an 84-page central episode of confinement. If this narrative of confinement might appear to challenge such a description, three features of this episode and the text more generally establish *Zeitoun* as an urban narrative. First, Abdulrahman's incarceration begins at Camp Greyhound, the Guantanamo-style prison camp erected at New Orleans's central bus station. Second, its sustained evocations of police brutality and aggressively punitive penal culture evoke an omnipresent anxiety of urban life for people of color. Finally, this episode is bookended by striking depictions of the potential of New Orleans and New Orleanians. *Treme* and *Zeitoun* thus depict the intersections of traumatic and systemic violence using different formal strategies but both texts explore the ways in which psychological traumas unfold in the context of systemic violence. Additionally, and crucially, both texts contain depictions of traumatic moments, that, while both thematically and formally painfully attentive to such extreme occurrences, consistently draw attention to their sources in systemic issues. In doing so they give representation to a pernicious form of violence that is nonspectacular and sometimes invisible.

Trauma in the Context of Systemic Failure in *Treme*

Named for the New Orleans district in which it is primarily set, *Treme* presents the Katrina crisis as a series of systemic failures from its first episode, "Do You Know What It Means." Following a stirring musical prologue, the episode opens with a scene featuring Tulane literature professor Creighton Bernette (John Goodman), who angrily tells a glib British reporter that "what hit the Mississippi Gulf Coast was a natural disaster, a hurricane pure and simple. The flooding of New Orleans was a man-made catastrophe, a federal fuck-up of epic proportions." However, despite his (and the program's) insistence on systemic failure, Bernette's story is an acute psychological trauma that affects his work, his family relationships, and ultimately precipitates an epistemological crisis. Season one's dramatic highpoint is Bernette's suicide, which, of course, emphasizes his inability to work through the trauma of Katrina, despite the privileges and advantages he enjoys as a white, middle-class man whose home and family are undamaged. While Bernette's searing opening lines resonate throughout the season and series, and while all of *Treme*'s story lines demand that we focus on long-standing, everyday effects of systemic failure, his story is motored by the advent of acute psychological trauma, and his experience is well described by canonical trauma theory as the experience of being irrevocably "possessed by an image or event."[21]

While Bernette's story, even more so his diatribes, gestures beyond trauma toward its intersections with systemic violence, the story of LaDonna Batiste (Khandi Alexander) most vividly illuminates these intersections. LaDonna's story harnesses the full narrative potential of *Treme*'s slow-burning seriality. It begins in season one as the story of her search for her brother Daymo, but it extends into a series-long narrative of multiple traumas and systemic failures in New Orleans. Daymo was in police custody when the storm struck, and like the titular protagonist in *Zeitoun*, he was lost in a militarized disaster-relief effort redolent of the Federal Emergency Management Agency's jurisdictional position within the Department of Homeland Security. Throughout the first season and into the second, LaDonna uncovers multiple instances of negligence, racism, and incompetence that extend from Daymo's wrongful arrest to his death. Stephen Shapiro names this storyline "*Treme*'s suturing link" because it connects all the characters thematically and harks back to *The Wire*'s critical project, which also addresses Bush-era social issues.[22] What is critically important, however, is the way LaDonna's story roots her experience of trauma in structural racism and systemic violence.

Determined to reopen her bar, GiGi's, after the Katrina crisis, LaDonna struggles first with the traumas of Daymo's disappearance and death. LaDonna then experiences further, severe trauma when she is brutally raped in the bar late one night. In the overlapping aftermaths of these events, she is repeatedly forced to relive them in meetings with lawyers, police officers, city officials, relatives, and reporters. She does so under oath in front of strangers in courtrooms and other public venues, all the while repressing these traumatic memories in front of her family. In both cases, LaDonna receives limited sympathy; in some instances, she is met with doubts that she is telling the truth. Moreover, because the rape occurred at her beloved New Orleans bar, in which she had invested so much effort to reopen after the storm, this individual trauma is linked to the collective trauma of the Katrina crisis, its destruction of social ties and institutions. After being raped, LaDonna does what many trauma victims are known to do – she turns inward, she self-medicates, she zones out, and she lashes out at her husband, Larry (Larry E. Nichols) and her children. While *Treme* faces the same challenges that any narrative text does in attempting to represent trauma – the challenge of representing phenomena so extreme that they resist comprehension, let alone representation – through narrative repetition the show is able to at least replicate the experience of reliving horrific moments over a long period of time, and of one's life being shaped and determined by the experience. Obviously, it is unlikely that audiences will fully relate to the specific set of experiences LaDonna undergoes, but this repetition forces us to imagine the experience of ongoing PTSD. Additionally, both the Daymo and rape storylines in *Treme* speak to traumatic repetition while highlighting them as instances of systemic failures: incompetent record keeping, ineffectual civil service, negligent prison management, police corruption and violence, and institutional racism. As individual incidents, these failures are significant and often malicious, but in aggregate they represent a powerful indictment of what we must consider to be systemic violence. Moreover, these systemic failures exacerbate the traumas that unfold around them and are shown to curb recovery. In the season two finale, "Do Whatcha Wanna," after finding out that one of her rapists was released because of a clerical error shortly after finally being caught, LaDonna unleashes an understandably furious and trenchant response to the Assistant District Attorney:

> What the fuck is wrong with you people? You lose my brother in the damn jail for months and then you let this vicious little motherfucker go first chance you get. We tryin' to live in this city. We tryin' to come back here [. . .] and live and all you manage to bring to that is nothin.' Rebuild the house? Hell no – fill out these forms and wait. Get your child back in school. Which one? You've got three different school systems. Two of them ain't teachin' shit and the third one can only open so many. Open the hospital back up? Hell no – let's tear down some more neighborhoods instead. Solve a crime or two? Oh, hell the fuck no.

The lawyer responds sympathetically, "I don't blame you for being upset," but LaDonna does not back down: "Upset? Bitch, I'm past upset. I'm all the way to lost my fuckin' mind." In this scene, the narrative urges us to understand what LaDonna has suffered as both traumatic and systemic violence.

This experience of two kinds of violence is (at least partially) made possible by the city, and the intersections between them are made vivid by the city. These intersections are illuminated by the city's capacity for institutional oppression and systemic failures. Cities rely on complex systems and are also sites of acute difference. Indeed, LaDonna's experience quite precisely dramatizes Gary Bridge and Sophie Watson's argument that "urban processes, particularly capitalist urban processes [. . .] inevitably involve socio-spatial inequality of some kind."[23] Cities rely on infrastructure whose resources *Treme* shows to be unevenly distributed among races and classes, and thrown into disarray by Katrina, which exacerbates these existing disparities.

Simultaneously, cities have unique, generative qualities that can articulate positions of resistance to systemic violence and offer healing or opportunities to work through trauma. As an example of an authentic New Orleans cultural hub, LaDonna's bar is such a place despite also being the site of one of her traumas. The city is also a place of complex formations of identity, community, and belonging that foster intense devotion and a kind of exceptionalism. Jennie Lightweis-Goff shows how the often-dogmatic devotion to New Orleans that its citizens espouse amounts to a kind of neutral exceptionalism that has both positive and negative effects. In many ways, *Treme* dramatizes what Lightweis-Goff describes as the "exceptionalist claims that have a long history of hazarding New Orleans even as they seek to defend it."²⁴ Further complicating this duality is the particular way in which the cultural diversity of New Orleans and American cities more generally is simultaneously held up as the embodiment of the melting pot myth and the most explicit example of its fallacy. In *Treme*, in the aftermath of Katrina, LaDonna has returned to live and work in New Orleans while her children and husband have resettled in Baton Rouge. She is a devoted New Orleanian; even as her personal traumas collide and aggregate with the collective trauma of Katrina, even as the corruption and racial prejudice become ever more vivid, her determination to stay only increases. For her husband this is stubbornness, but for LaDonna the city is home and its sense of community and tradition is the best chance for a fulfilling life.

There is another example in *Treme* of why New Orleans is a particularly revealing site of trauma overlapping slow violence, the way the rupture of Katrina appears to create opportunities for the corrosive forces of neoliberal capitalism. Indeed, the program in some ways replicates the logic that Klein describes in *The Shock Doctrine*. When the developer Nelson Hidalgo (John Seda) attempts to "monetize the culture" and says things like "never let a disaster go to waste," it might be an allusion to Rahm Emanuel's often-quoted argument that "you never want a serious crisis to go to waste," but it also very conspicuously evokes Klein's arguments about "disaster capitalism" and neoliberalism which clearly have influenced the series in many ways. Moreover, it initially appears to reinforce Anna Hartnell's argument (which draws on Henri Lefebvre's writings) that *The Shock Doctrine*'s "language of 'shock' masks a much longer running battle for the 'right to the city.'"²⁵ However, as the Hidalgo story develops, its response to long-standing systemic issues and the complicity of characters in sustaining them make clear that such practices are not exceptional; they are entrenched, and Hidalgo represents a particularly egregious enemy in this longer-running battle. Hidalgo is characterized as affable and appreciative of New Orleans's cultural traditions, so much so that viewers are invited to reflect on their own complicity in the practices he represents as his story intersects with some of *Treme*'s most sympathetic characters. Indeed, Hidalgo's cheerful demeanor exemplifies the way that even the most flagrantly violent forms of neoliberalism are "notoriously good at hiding behind a 'common sense' ethic of competition and individualism."²⁶ Moreover, as the extent of Hidalgo's operation is revealed – it is national and driven by the exploitation of political allegiances – it becomes impossible to see the neoliberalism he represents as being driven solely by disaster opportunism. Instead, what *Treme* powerfully captures is how trauma can reveal corruption, systemic violence, and the routine ruthlessness of neoliberalism. So while Hidalgo is introduced through the familiar rhetoric of disaster capitalism, the ways in which he operates are shown to represent the entrenched norms of the neoliberal city.

Zeitoun, Trauma, and Penal Systems Culture

Zeitoun also explores the overlapping impacts of traumatic rupture and systemic violence through its formal features, particularly genre structures that, as with the seriality of *Treme*, map these intersections and their implications. While this strategy is foundational to *Treme*, it creates tension at *Zeitoun*'s broadest formal level. The text is a work of lyrical nonfiction that functions partly as a very personal memoir and partly as political reportage. A note in the text's front matter states that it "does not attempt to be an all-encompassing book about New Orleans or Hurricane Katrina," but "only an account of one family's experiences before and after the storm." Yet in one of the book's blurbs, also in the front matter, Michael Eric Dyson tells us that it addresses the "swirling vortex of Hurricane Katrina and post-9/11 America," surely a highly politicized and capacious topic. Eggers has also stated in an interview in the *Observer* that the Zeitoun family's experience "seemed like the absolute nadir of all the Bush policies," so he clearly felt that their experience embodied a wide set of societal issues.[27] The text's broad aims are, then, somewhat conflicted, and this twoness is embodied by its formal and stylistic features. In some places, *Zeitoun* reads like a poetic memoir, particularly in the passages that recount Abdulrahman's past in Syria, his family history and ancestry, and his career as a traveling longshoreman. In other places, particularly the account of Abdulrahman's arrest, it is closer to reportage as the narrator carefully presents a timeline of events, corroborative sources, and contextual facts. This broad formal tension underpins its use of multiple, ideologically loaded genre frames, a device that makes its depiction of trauma amidst systemic failure and institutional racism particularly powerful. While this formal feature offers a narrative familiarity necessary for the textual representation of trauma and its working-through, one of the specific genre modes it adopts, the prison narrative, opens up a sustained critique of America's punitive culture and its structural inequalities, again bridging its discussion of traumatic and systemic violence.

    Zeitoun alludes to a range of American literary and cultural traditions, beginning with epigraphs that in and of themselves highlight the text's internal tensions: "in the history of the world it might even be that there was more punishment than crime," from Cormac McCarthy's *The Road* (2006), and the observation popularly attributed to Mark Twain that "to a man with a hammer, everything looks like a nail," foreshadow some of the text's sustained narrative preoccupations and nicely illustrate these tensions. The second quotation evokes a kind of myopia that Eggers is seeking to challenge here, but also Abdulrahman's work ethic, which the text presents as his defining characteristic. It is linked to his proud family history, his successful integration as an immigrant, his roles as a breadwinner, family man and businessman, and to his heroic acts during the Katrina crisis. Clearly, this emphasis is made to position this – in the eyes of many post-9/11 Americans – "other" Muslim man, as archetypally American, as does the text's rhetoric of self-reliance, the heteronormative family unit, and the immigrant who achieves the American Dream. A crucial section of *Zeitoun* even appropriates the frontier/exploration narrative of American pioneers, which remains an important and vivid feature of the white American imaginary. In scenes describing Abdulrahman's heroic rescues in flooded New Orleans, he is depicted as purposeful and in tune with the newly rugged and hostile urban environment. The narrator describes how he "woke with the sun and crawled out of his tent" before he "scanned the horizon." As he paddles through New Orleans's apocalyptically flooded boulevards and avenues, he is "at peace" and inspired: "this was a new world, uncharted. He could be an explorer. He could see things first."[28] This adoption of stock ideas and archetypes is also clearly designed to assert the protagonist's Americanness. However, Cynthia G. Franklin argues that the accumulation of archetypes, genre tropes, and stock characteristics erodes his characterization and individuality because even as the narrative "challenges the dehumanization [he] underwent during Katrina, its mobilization of generic conventions and dominant narratives reveals the dehumanization inherent in these hegemonic constructions" even if the intent is to challenge Islamophobia and racism.[29]

For this chapter's purposes, it is enough to note that literary allusion and genre are more central than characterization in building meaning in *Zeitoun*. It is also important to note that Eggers's use of ideologically loaded American genre archetypes also reinforces neoliberal ideals of self-sufficiency and individualism that were at the heart of some of the particularly toxic rhetoric that blamed Katrina's victims for their plight. As Diane Negra shows, conservative politicians and media outlets immediately focused criticism on poor, mostly black, New Orleanians who stayed in the city during the mandatory evacuation. This criticism invariably relied on "a set of pre-existing stereotypes about the idle urban poor in a city where 'black gangsterism' was understood to thrive."[30] *Zeitoun*'s emphatic portrayal of hard work and self-reliance aligns with such views even though it is at odds with the text's critique of systemic or structural problems that have severely limited opportunities for huge swaths of the population regardless of their work ethic.

The text concludes with an assertion of progress couched in construction metaphors that articulate Abdulrahman's belief that, three years after the flooding of New Orleans, the city has "removed the rot" and is "strengthening the foundations." Hartnell contends that this passage serves to reinforce neoliberal ideology. For her, "the reference to 'weeding out the rot' no doubt inadvertently but unavoidably points us toward the 'disposable' elements of a neoliberal society," the unemployed and citizens with criminal records.[31] Daniel Worden argues that the protagonist's closing optimism about the city's progress is presented as hopelessly misguided. Worden contends that in the face of Kathy Zeitoun's ongoing PTSD and the obvious material realities of post-Katrina New Orleans, Abdulrahman's fortitude is shown to be delusional; "it becomes clear that the difference at the end of the text is that Zeitoun's work ethic is misguided, clearly unsuited and insufficient to realize his dreams of upward mobility."[32] These interpretations diverge, but both of them highlight the text's sustained emphasis on Abdulrahman's individualism and work ethic as the key to his obvious success as a businessman. Even if, as in Worden's reading, Abdulrahman and Kathy's American Dream is shattered by their traumatic experience, there is no doubt that his achievements of successful integration, building a "business of distinct success," and raising a family remain linked to these defining attributes, which are so obsessively attended to by the text.[33]

Cutting against this conservative strand of the text is its other central preoccupation, US penal culture, which is foreshadowed by the epigraph from *The Road*, a novel that provides an important narrative analogue for *Zeitoun*.[34] This epigraph highlights the punitive nature of American culture, and speaks to the subject of incarceration and US penal practices, which is where the *Zeitoun*'s political critique is most trenchant. Abdulrahman's experience of "Camp Greyhound" is repeatedly compared to the Guantanamo Bay prison camp. These scenes recall Klein's assertion that crises like 9/11 and Hurricane Katrina are "democracy-free zones" in which "the need for consent and consensus do not apply."[35] However, the depiction of Abdulrahman's incarceration also explores

America's wider culture of detention, The practices and experiences that the text portrays are representative of American prisons even if the conditions are exceptional. One crucial way in which this critique is extended is through the adoption of conceits from prison writing, which, Doran Larson notes, is "a genre bound not only by its subject and authors but also its expressive tropes at once determined by, actively resistant to, and thus indicative of both global and local conditions of composition."[36] Abdulrahman fights desperately for a phone call, struggles to get medical attention and is ignored or derided by guards. He shares stories with cellmates about how they were apprehended and notes that in Camp Greyhound night was "barely distinguishable from day." He experiences "profound boredom," and in a moment typical of prison narratives, he "sat against the bed and closed eyes. He wanted only to pass these days."[37] But even more than these painful depictions familiar from popular prison narratives, the text's unique narrative point of view orients it within the prison-literature genre.

Eggers's authorial voice and narrative strategy to position Abdulrahman as an American everyman is particularly important. As Larson notes, a definitive genre feature of global prison writing combines "a dissociative turn of voice that allows the 'I' of the prison text – even when not opened into an explicit 'we' – to represent communities larger than the prison author," and a "concomitant associative gesture whereby the prison writer names the contemporary communities among whom s/he numbers him- or herself." In *Zeitoun*, the protagonist and his cellmates share their own stories and "stories they heard from other prisoners they'd encountered," and are shown to blur into "a sea of men in orange."[38] The narrative approximates this genre trope of representing the prison community in a number of ways, but perhaps most powerfully through the unique way its protagonist is made to inhabit the role of so many stock character and genre archetypes, which means that the "he" of *Zeitoun* is always couched in a gesture of wider representation. This is crucial to the way Abdulrahman's quite unique story resonates with a long and particular history of punishment and systemic violence. As Hartnell points out, "the unspoken story of *Zeitoun* [...] is the war on drugs, the war on crime in general, and mass incarceration," and while Abdulrahman's story uniquely showed the overlap of post-9/11 and post-Katrina securitization, it is ultimately part of a larger, preexisting systemic violence. Therefore, while the incarceration of Abdulrahman is the central traumatic episode of the text, it also opens up the story of the Katrina crisis and locates it in a longer continuum of America's penal culture. It highlights both the long-standing, statistically inordinate incarceration of minorities and the specifically post-9/11 "state of exception" that further legitimized racial profiling, illegal detention, and torture.

Zeitoun ends with the same irrepressibly positive descriptions of New Orleans that feature in its early scenes, and it is depicted as a city poised to "rise again." We read that, "more than anything else, Zeitoun is simply happy to be free and in his city," the "place of his dreams, the place where he was married, where his children were born, where he was given the trust of his neighbors."[39] This affect may be delusional, as Worden argues it is, or an example of the text reinforcing neoliberal logic of "weeding out the rot" and rebuilding, as Hartnell argues it does, but, intended or not, a key part of its rhetorical force derives from the way it urges readers to understand the impact of the convergence or simultaneity of traumatic and systemic violence. Likewise with *Treme*, which also concludes with distinct notes of hope and possibility hard to reconcile with the scale of death, loss, and corruption that the program documents. Even if we do read this as a problematic deference to a notion of the American Dream that no longer exists – what Berlant calls "cruel optimism" – the program offers much in its depiction of the overlaps and intersections of two kinds of violence.

These two Katrina narratives emphasize the importance of understanding how trauma is experienced in the context of the systemic violence of institutional racism and the slow violence of neoliberal capitalism. As such, they resist calls to move away from the discourse of trauma and, instead, urge us to consider the ways in which recovery from, or working through, trauma might be stifled or blocked by such phenomena. Additionally, however, as character-driven dramas – each with its own specific narrative and formal innovations – these texts provide entry points for considering forms of violence that have posed perennial representational challenges. As we have seen, in *Treme*, the slow, cyclical pace of the narrative, particularly in the story of LaDonna, speaks to both the repetitions of PTSD and the bureaucracy of systemic failure and relentlessness of institutional racism. In *Zeitoun*, Eggers's deployment of multiple, ideologically loaded genre frames, both manages the trauma by "narrativizing" it with the use of familiar tropes and narrative patterns and opens up a sustained discussion of systemic violence through another genre, prison narrative. In both cases the overlapping of traumatic rupture with systemic or slow violence also means that these kinds of experiences which are notoriously difficult to represent are opened via their intersections.

Notes

1. Lauren Berlant, *Cruel Optimism* (Durham, NC: Duke University Press, 2011), pp. 9–10.
2. Rob Nixon, *Slow Violence and the Environmentalism of the Poor* (Cambridge, MA: Harvard University Press, 2011), p. 2.
3. Berlant, *Cruel Optimism*, p. 10.
4. Hua Hsu, "That Feeling When," *The New Yorker*, March 25, 2019, 61.
5. Michael Rothberg, "'There Is No Poetry in This': Writing, Trauma, and Home," in Judith Greenberg, ed., *Trauma at Home* (Lincoln: University of Nebraska Press, 2003), p. 151.
6. Frank Lentricchia, "Note from Frank Lentricchia," in Stanley Hauerwas and Frank Lentricchia, eds., *Dissent from the Homeland: Essays after September 11* (Durham, NC: Duke University Press, 2002), p. 4.
7. Naomi Klein, *The Shock Doctrine* (London: Penguin, 2007), p. 21.
8. Ibid., p. 132.
9. Anne Whitehead, *Trauma Fiction* (Edinburgh: Edinburgh University Press, 2004), p. 3.
10. Nixon, *Slow Violence*, p. 2.
11. Michael Rothberg, "Preface," in Gert Buelens, Sam Durrant, and Robert Eaglestone, eds., *The Future of Trauma Theory* (London: Routledge, 2014), p. xiv.
12. Ibid.
13. Michelle Alexander, *The New Jim Crow: Mass Incarceration in the Age of Colorblindness* (New York: New Press, 2011), p. 2.
14. Andy Merrifield, "Fifty Years On: The Right to the City," in *The Right to the City: A Verso Report* (London: Verso, 2017), p. 20.
15. George W. Bush, "Remarks on the Aftermath of Hurricane Katrina in Mobile, Alabama," September 2, 2005, *The American Presidency Project*, www .presidency.ucsb.edu/documents/remarks-the-aftermath-hurricane-katrina-mobile-alabama.
16. Julia Leyda, "'This Complicated, Colossal Failure': The Abjection of Creighton Bernette in HBO's *Treme*," *Television and New Media* 13.3 (2012), 249.
17. Anna Hartnell, *After Katrina: Race, Neoliberalism and the End of the American Century* (Albany: SUNY Press, 2017), p. 12.
18. Ibid.
19. On *Zeitoun*'s use of the marriage plot, see Arin Keeble, *Narratives of Hurricane Katrina in Context: Literature, Film and Television* (Basingstoke, UK: Palgrave, 2019), pp. 31–63.
20. Kristiaan Versluys, *Out of the Blue: September 11 and the Novel* (New York: Columbia University Press, 2009), pp. 3–4.
21. Cathy Caruth, "Introduction," in Caruth, ed., *Trauma: Explorations in Memory* (Baltimore: Johns Hopkins University Press, 1995), p. 5.
22. Stephen Shapiro, "Realignment and Televisual Intellect: The Telepraxis of Class Alliances Contemporary Subscription Television," in Sieglinded Lemke

and Wibke Schniedermann, eds., *Class Divisions in Serial Television* (Basingstoke, UK: Palgrave, 2016), p. 186.

23. Gary Bridge and Sophie Watson, "Reflections on Division and Difference," in Bridge and Watson, eds., *The New Blackwell Companion to The City* (London: Wiley-Blackwell, 2013), p. 501.

24. Jennie Lightweiss-Goff, "'Particular and Characteristic': New Orleans Exceptionalism from Olmsted to the Deluge," *American Literature* 86.1 (2014), 150.

25. Rahm Emmanuel, quoted in Gerald F. Seib, "In Crisis, Opportunity for Obama," *Wall Street Journal*, November 21, 2008, A2; Hartnell, *After Katrina*, p. 133.

26. Emily Johansen and Alissa G. Karl, "Introduction: Reading and Writing the Economic Present," *Textual Practice* 29.2 (2015), 204.

27. Dave Eggers, quoted in Rachel Cooke, "From 'Staggering Genius' to America's Conscience," *The Observer*, March 7, 2010, www.theguardian.com/books/201 0/mar/07/dave-eggers-zeitoun-hurricane-katrina.

28. Dave Eggers, *Zeitoun* (New York: Vintage, 2009), pp. 104, 105.

29. Cynthia Franklin, "Narrative Humanity at the Intersection of 9/11 and Hurricane Katrina: Dave Eggers's *Zeitoun*," *American Quarterly* 69.4 (2017), 862.

30. Diane Negra, "Introduction: Old and New Media after Katrina," in Negra, ed., *Old and New Media after Katrina* (Basingstoke, UK: Palgrave, 2010), p. 16.

31. Eggers, *Zeitoun*, p. 335; Hartnell, *After Katrina*, p. 62.

32. Daniel Worden, "The Memoir in the Age of Neoliberal Individualism," in Mitchum Huehls and Rachel Greenwald, eds., *Neoliberalism and Contemporary Literary Culture* (Baltimore: Johns Hopkins University Press, 2016), p. 169.

33. Eggers, *Zeitoun*, p. 24.

34. See Arin Keeble, "The Aggregation of Political Rhetoric in *Zeitoun*," *Comparative American Studies* 12.3 (2014), 173–89.

35. Naomi Klein, *The Shock Doctrine* (London: Penguin, 2007), p. 140.

36. Doran Larson, "Towards a Prison Poetics," *College Literature* 37.3 (2010), 143.

37. Eggers, *Zeitoun*, pp. 253, 262, 262.

38. Larson, "Towards a Prison Poetics," 145; Eggers, *Zeitoun*, p. 260.

39. Eggers, *Zeitoun*, p. 334.

CHAPTER 18

Security Theory

Johannes Voelz

In the spring of 2020, as the coronavirus pandemic spread throughout the world, the state of democracy seemed to face a bleak future. Governments in many parts of the world reacted to the health crisis by invoking executive prerogatives. Only decisive political action, it was claimed, could put a stop to the virus. Particularly those leaders who had already displayed an authoritarian streak in the past now seemed intent on breaking free from any remaining fetters. Viktor Orban, the prime minister of Hungary, secured permission from parliament to rule by decree indefinitely. Rodrigo Duterte, president of the Philippines, effectively dismantled what had remained of free speech protections by imposing prison time for spreading "false news" about the coronavirus.[1] In the United States, President Donald Trump adopted the rhetoric of unfettered executive rule by claiming, at least until he backpedaled shortly thereafter, that he had "total authority" over governors and states.[2]

Indeed, to many observers it seemed that the pandemic cleared the path for the installment of indefinite states of exception. Quickly, some of today's most famous philosophers stepped forth to interpret these developments as the confirmation of their own theories. For Giorgio Agamben, the Italian response to the pandemic demonstrated that "our society no longer believes in anything but bare life." He continued, "We in fact live in a society that has sacrificed freedom to so-called 'reasons of security' and has therefore condemned itself to live in a perennial state of fear and insecurity."[3] Peter Sloterdijk, in a similar manner, prophesied that "the Western system will prove to be just as authoritarian as that of China." What the pandemic had wrought was the emergence of "securitocracy in the guise of medicocracy."[4] In the view of Agamben, Sloterdijk, and many others, the pandemic had crowned security as the regnant political logic of our time.

There were, however, obvious reasons to disagree with this position. Some of the authoritarian leaders supposedly intent on using the pandemic to push through the indefinite suspension of liberty did not in fact use executive action to quell the health crisis. They rather set on a course of denial. Instead of imposing governmental measures of strict disciplinary rule in the name of security, they downplayed the threat of the pandemic and called to reopen the economy. No one embraced this stance more defiantly than Donald Trump and Brazil's Jair Bolsonaro; no one got more populist mileage out of it than did they. If the demands of business required governments to stay out of interfering with everyday life, then Trump and Bolsonaro were willing to do so. If this strategy went against the advice of medical experts, it could be sold as unvanquished resistance against the establishment. Trump and Bolsonaro thus complemented the authoritarian leadership model of the "security strongman" – to which they adhered in matters other than the pandemic – with the alternative of the "rebel strongman."

While the populist denial of the pandemic may be a political innovation of our time, the underlying political rationality is not. Since the eighteenth century, political responses to infectious disease have been torn between the two objectives of controlling the spread of epidemics and of safeguarding the conditions necessary for the flourishing of commerce. It is in the writings of Michel Foucault that scholars working on what we may call "security theory" have found the most nuanced model of making sense of these contradictory objectives.[5] Foucault's security theory allows us to understand that the goals of imposing order through discipline and ensuring the circulations of commerce are diverging logics of political power that can be traced back to different historical periods, even if they coexist in the present. In his thinking, each of these phases brought forth its own conceptualization of security. While these conceptualizations may differ radically from one another, they do share the overall political function of control and regulation.

Indeed, the influence of Foucault on the study of security has been so imposing that attempts of the last few years to extend the investigation of security into literary studies have largely followed the Foucauldian program of critiquing the biopolitical regulation of individual and collective life. Indeed, so far literary scholars have primarily offered readings of literary texts that illustrate and confirm the mappings of security mechanisms first articulated in other disciplines. This is a lost opportunity. After all, Foucault suggested that it was "the problem of the town that is [. . .] at the heart of [. . .] mechanisms of security."[6] And clearly, the modern city is the social constellation that lies at the very heart of that bourgeois genre of literature called the novel. In that sense, we can ask how the literary imagination of the city has produced a *literary* imagination of security, and, furthermore, how the literary imagination of security relates to the set of security mechanisms that make up what Foucault called the security dispositif. Instead of taking literature to reflect a set of problems and mechanisms first articulated in security theory, we should ask how the literary imagination of city and security might differ from the apparatuses reconstructed by security theorists (without thereby claiming that literature resides in a world elsewhere).

To this end, this chapter will explore Charles Brockden Brown's urban gothic novel *Arthur Mervyn* (1799/1800) as an exemplary case study. Brown's novel takes up the Philadelphia yellow fever epidemic of 1793 and thus contributes to an imaginary of exceptional crisis at the historical juncture at which, according to Foucault, the security dispositif took shape. I have chosen Brown's novel as a test case for two reasons. It allows us, firstly, to ask the historically minded question to what degree Foucault's security theory can be helpful to make sense of the novel's context of an urban epidemic during the early years of the republic. This question will occupy the first sections of this essay. Secondly, the choice of *Arthur Mervyn* permits us to compare the novel's security vision to the discourses of security established by Foucault. As we shall see in the final section, for Brown, both the yellow fever epidemic and the protagonist Arthur Mervyn figure as potential threats to the survival of the young republic. In line with republican thinking, securing the republic, for Brown, rests on the fortification of the republic's moral fiber. This vision of security shares surprising common ground with the security techniques analyzed by Foucault, but as it places its hopes on virtue rather than biopolitical regulation, it makes room for a notion of unregulated circulation ultimately at odds with Foucault's model.

Fever

In the course of the 1790s, Philadelphia – at that point the capital of the young American republic – suffered from several severe epidemics of yellow fever. Similar attacks had been a regular part of the town's history, going back to William Penn's days, but since 1762, the city had been spared. The most fatal, and most highly reported, of the renewed yellow fever outbreaks took place in the late summer and fall of 1793. More than 4,000 people fell victim to the fever. Most people who could afford it – including the political class – fled to the countryside. As the fever raged, public order threatened to collapse. At the height of the epidemic, half of all households in the city stood vacant. Drained of its personnel, the state and municipal governments minimized their operations. Left almost to himself, Mayor Matthew Clarkson appointed a citizens committee and enlisted black and white volunteers. The Committee to Attend to and Alleviate the Sufferings of the Afflicted with the Malignant Fever organized a makeshift hospital, Bush Hill, to isolate the afflicted and aid their recovery. But at least initially, conditions at the hospital were so gruesome that being sent to Bush Hill was perceived as a death sentence.

Meanwhile, the medical establishment argued over the correct interpretation and treatment regime of the fever. One group of physicians, among them Benjamin Rush, supported a climatist explanation which proposed that the fever spread as a result of unwholesome miasma of filthy air and poisonous vapor. Their opponents, most prominently William Currie, insisted that the fever proceeded contagiously and was imported by foreigners, i.e., merchants from Europe, refugees from the slave uprisings in the West Indies, or slaves themselves. "Contagionists," writes historian J. H. Powell, "would prevent fever by quarantining incoming vessels from sickly regions; climatists would purify the city and society itself by sanitary measures."[7] Not until the early twentieth century did it become clear that *Aedes aegypti*, the female yellow fever mosquito, spread the virus. (Though neither camp suspected the true agent of transmission, both were on to something: mosquitos favor the humidity and stale waters abhorred by miasma theorists, and the *Aedes aegypti* did import the disease from the West Indies.)

Brown set the first part of his novel *Arthur Mervyn* in this scene of mass death and widely felt terror, thus initiating the genre of the urban gothic in American literature. Brown, who himself contracted the disease during a later outbreak in 1798 but was able to recover, closely followed the reporting and public debates of the 1793 fever and incorporated them into his fiction. This "fever discourse," as literary historian Bryan Waterman has called it, disseminated in pamphlets, tracts, and letters across the nation, provides a fascinating historical archive of ideas, sentiments, and practices of security.[8] Judging from available historical sources, the yellow fever crisis confirms some of Michel Foucault's theorizations of the security apparatus, while at the same time displaying characteristics that do not fit easily into his model. Before turning to Brown's novelistic appropriation of the fever, it is illuminating to put into dialogue Foucault's historically grounded security theory and the fever discourse of the Philadelphian crisis of 1793.

Foucault's Security Theory

In the first three lectures of his series, *Security, Territory, Population*, given at the Collège de France in the academic year of 1977–78, Foucault developed three different modes of governmental rule, each of them dominant at a particular historical period. The first two he had laid out at length in *Discipline and Punish* (1976). Juridical power, prevalent in medieval and early modern times, exerts force by codifying what is prohibited and sanctioning transgressions of the law. The dominance of juridical power was followed historically, in the early Enlightenment, by disciplinary power, which does not prohibit but rather prescribes actions. Disciplinary power aims to mold behavior by training the body and mind. Making subjects act in desired ways, it exerts influence not in the rare moments when a rule or law is violated (as is the case in juridical power), but incessantly, as individuals move about in their everyday lives. Finally, in the 1977–78 lectures, Foucault singles out the "security dispositif" as the model of power that comes to dominance in the late eighteenth century and continues its reign up to the present.

Power characterized by security mechanisms no longer aims to train individuals to behave like well-programmed machines. It starts from the recognition that all-out control tends to be unfeasible. A security apparatus therefore does not aspire to create reality from scratch but accepts reality as a given ensemble of natural processes to be coped with. But nature, in this understanding, is no longer an immutable force; it can be manipulated and controlled by channeling its processes in advantageous ways.

This reconception becomes more concrete when we contextualize what such natural processes entailed. Foucault explains at length that various processes of circulation formed the backdrop and target of security mechanisms. Circulation concerned goods and people as part of the quickly growing trade networks of an emerging free-market capitalism, as well as the spread of disease. As we will see, during the yellow fever epidemics of the 1790s, circulation was recognized as a social organizing principle in both historical sources and Brown's novel. In these contexts, circulation encompassed (more centrally than in Foucault's account) the dissemination of ideas, feelings, and information, whereas within the framework of discipline, flows of circulation were never supposed to happen. Discipline was designed to control precisely how each individual related to others. Ideally, routes of transmission were planned in detail. From the perspective of security, on the other hand, circulation can neither be avoided nor wholly controlled. It is a natural fact of life. Therefore, security

mechanisms take an aim that may appear to be more modest than disciplinary power: on the basis of probability calculus, techniques of security try
to predict and to direct the flows of circulation and direct them. This
objective requires a change of perspective: Rather than targeting the
individual, security apparatuses focus on the collective – what Foucault
consistently refers to as "the population" – made calculable by such
probabilistic inventions as Jacob Bernoulli's law of large numbers. This
probabilistic management of the population is what Foucault dubs biopolitics. We shall see that, as it is in Foucault's theorization, circulation is also
considered an unavoidable fact of life in *Arthur Mervyn*. What Brown's
gothic vision tries to imagine, however, is an acceptance of circulation that
refrains from using it as a new resource for biopolitical regulation while still
making use of it for the survival of the republic.

The Security Dispositif and the Yellow Fever Crisis of 1793

According to Foucault, the problems of circulation addressed by the
politics of security take center stage only with the growth of modern
towns. City planning, the management of food supplies to prevent
scarcity, and the outbreak of epidemics were all conceptualized as
problems of circulation that could only be handled by assuring the
continued but controlled flow of further circulation. In order to assess
whether Philadelphia during the time of the yellow fever employed the
techniques of the security dispositif, two dimensions become particularly
important. The first relates to urban planning. The regular grid structure
of Philadelphia, as designed by William Penn, was a direct expression of
the Enlightenment ideal of rational order. Foucault argued that such
architectural planning bears the trace of the Roman army camp. He
therefore called cities of this type "disciplinary towns" (his examples are
Kristiania, Gothenburg, and Richelieu). If at the level of the individual,
discipline aspires to build up the body from scratch, discipline at the
level of urban planning requires "empty, artificial space that is to be
completely constructed." Nineteenth-century literary writers from both
Europe and the United States tended to convey the impression that
Philadelphia had made good on Penn's dreams of extreme rationality, so
much so that the results were disturbing. In 1831, Nathaniel Parker Willis
noted "too much regularity and too nice precision," while Frances
Trollope, one year later, spoke of "extreme and almost wearisome
regularity," a sentiment echoed ten years later by Charles Dickens,
who called the city "distractingly regular."[9]

Yet, within just a few years after its founding in 1682, the development of Philadelphia deviated from Penn's planned regularity. As the economy of the city expanded rapidly, the waterfront of the Delaware near the port became the most sought-after area. Growth there was haphazard and largely uncontrolled, resulting in small, subdivided lots and overcrowded streets. Thus, "as the commercial district grew, it confronted the classic problems of density: pollution, disease, fire, and crime."[10] The circulations of commerce had undermined the plans for disciplinary order. Despite its reputation for regularity, then, Philadelphia is marked by a history of battle between designs for discipline and laissez-faire development.

This is not to say that Philadelphia is adequately captured by what Foucault thinks of a security town; as he shows in his example of eighteenth-century Nantes, urban planners who followed the logic of security did not pursue the ideal of perfect, disciplinary order, but rather meant to alter an organically growing town in such a way that hygiene, trade within the town, external trade routes, and surveillance were ensured. As Foucault put it, "it is simply a matter of maximizing the positive elements, for which one provides the best possible circulation, and of minimizing what is risky and inconvenient, like theft and disease, while knowing that they will never be completely suppressed."[11] By contrast, urban planning in Philadelphia by and large seems to have held on to an ideal of discipline that was perennially upset by commerce.

Responses to disease are another crucial factor in trying to assess whether Philadelphia fits into Foucault's model of a security town. Foucault's analysis of disease control follows his division of disciplinary versus security mechanisms. Disciplinary mechanisms proceed by spatial regulation of movement and detailed prescriptions of behavior:

> Plague regulations [in the sixteenth and seventeenth centuries] involve literally imposing a partitioning grid on the regions and town struck by plague, with regulations indicating when people can go out, how, at what times, what they must do at home, what type of food they must have, prohibiting certain types of contact, requiring them to present themselves to inspectors, and to open their homes to inspectors.

By contrast, security mechanisms approach the spread of disease through a probabilistic approach that accepts the existence of disease as a natural process that can be regulated by turning the natural process against itself. Rather than imposing measures of exclusion (as was common with leprosy) or quarantine (the usual response to the plague), securitizing measures proceed by way of "medical campaigns that try to halt epidemic or endemic phenomena." Starting in the 1720s, treatment of smallpox, in particular, began to rest on an early form of inoculation, known as "variolation," that, as with later types of vaccination, literally turned a natural process against itself: it immunized a person against the disease through an artificially induced mild infection with the disease. Thus, the securitization of disease involved

> the problem of knowing how many people are infected with smallpox, at what age, with what effects, with what mortality rate, lesions or after-effects, the risks of inoculation, the probability of an individual dying or being infected by smallpox despite inoculation, and the statistical effects on the population in general.[12]

As we have seen, the biopolitical approach focuses on the computation of the large-scale effects on the population. The objective is no longer to avoid single fatalities, but to find solutions that protect the aggregate population.

Within Foucault's framework, it would be apt to say that the response to the yellow-fever epidemics that hit Philadelphia throughout the eighteenth century first and foremost followed the logic of discipline. In the fourth edition of his widely read *Short Account of the Malignant Fever* (published in January 1794, immediately following the outbreak of 1793), Mathew Carey included accounts of the London's 1665 plague and that of Marseille's in 1720 to demonstrate "the extraordinary similarity between many of the leading and most important circumstances that occurred in those two places, and the events of September and October, 1793, in Philadelphia."[13] Indeed, the response to the plague and to yellow fever principally rested on the same method: quarantine.

In part, this had to do with the simple fact that medical procedures to prevent yellow fever infection were unknown. Quarantine therefore seemed the only way to keep Philadelphia orderly and clean (paying tribute to the miasma theory espoused by Benjamin Rush) and to prevent contagion from foreigners (as called for by William Currie and the city's College of Physicians). In his account of the 1793 fever, Carey details that the College of Physicians published

> an address to the citizens [...] recommending to avoid all unnecessary intercourse with the infected; to place marks on the doors or windows where they were; to pay great attention to cleanliness and airing the rooms of the sick; to provide a large and airy hospital in the neighbourhood of the city for their reception; to put a stop to the tolling of the bells; to bury those who died of the disorder in carriages, and as privately as possible; [...] to

keep the streets and wharves clean; to avoid all fatigue of body and mind, and standing or sitting in the sun, or in the open air; [...] and to avoid intemperance.[14]

This list reads almost like the catalog of pest-control measures listed by Foucault. Minimizing interaction with the infected, marking doors and windows of infected houses, isolating the sick at Bush Hill hospital, keeping streets clean: the physicians demanded the full roster of partitioning practices typical of disciplinary rule. What may be surprising is the inclusion of actions that specifically target the passions: the constant tolling of the bells was to be stopped so as not to cause extra anxiety; fatigue of body *and mind* was to be avoided. Such recommendations were in line with eighteenth-century medical thinking on both sides of the Atlantic. As literary historian Philip Gould explains, this type of thinking "generally maintained that physical, psychological, and moral forms of health were intricately and reciprocally related to one another. The natural environment affected mind and body alike: physical sensations could produce psychological effects, and psychological change could produce physical bodily symptoms."[15]

Such holistic approaches to health turned the question of safety toward moral issues. Inducing timidity was a sign of moral irresponsibility, acting timidly a sign of weakness and selfishness. By the same token, a lack of concern was equally to be rejected. Drawing on the classical usage of "securitas," which goes back to Cicero's neologism for *sine cure* (absence of care), Carey insisted that "the incautious security of the citizens of Philadelphia, at the first stage of the disorder, is highly to be regretted."[16] We will see momentarily how Charles Brockden Brown took up the moral discourse of the passion and health in *Arthur Mervyn*, generating possibilities of virtuous behavior from the epidemic. Indeed, the holistic triangulation of "physical, psychological, and moral forms of health" lies at the core of Brown's republican security imaginary that considers civic morality the cornerstone for collective survival.

The balanced state of mind prescribed by Philadelphia's health officials differs markedly from the fear-mongering that critics find to be employed in today's politics of security.[17] Demanding that public fear be kept in check, however, was not simply an expression of republican-minded good sense (although it was that, too). With Foucault we can say that the politics of antifear was part of a disciplinary mechanism that was designed to arrest circulation – in this case, the circulation of the passions. Severing the circuits of emotional transmission was part and parcel of bringing to a halt the spreading of the disease.

This rationale also informs the quarantine and embargo policies that Philadelphia had practiced throughout the eighteenth century and radicalized after 1793. As early as 1720, measures were taken by the provincial council to prevent "sickly vessels [...] from discharging their goods or passenger[s]." At that point, the rumors of the plague outbreak in Marseille (later summarized by Carey in his *Short Account*) caused a general concern about the importation of disease from Europe. The provincial council cited the "frequent late advices of the plague and pestilential distempers raging in several countreys of Europe," which gave rise to the danger that "great numbers of people daily imported into this province from Great Britain, Ireland, Germany and other parts" might threaten Philadelphia.[18] What becomes clear is that measures to stop the circulation of the disease depended on the circulation of information. In their very design, disciplinary methods of halting circulation of one type thus contained the security mechanism of allowing for circulation of another type.

After the 1793 outbreak, it was no longer a matter of merely letting information circulate. Officials began to construct widely spun information networks of intelligence gathering. Historian Simon Finger relates that,

> as 1794's fever season began, Governor Mifflin ordered the health office to "be vigilant" and "use all industry in collecting information of the state of health in every foreign port." Whenever the Governor "received satisfactory information" that contagion was present, whether through the board or through his own sources, he could order inspections, restrictions, or total embargoes on traffic into the port.[19]

Not only did the mechanisms of discipline employed to keep in check the spreading of yellow fever rely on the worldwide gathering of information, limitations on the circulation of bodies and goods for the purposes of disease control came into conflict with the workings of an emerging transatlantic market economy that required the circulation of commercial goods. In other words, the disciplinary methods of disease control were coming up against the liberal market society's security method of ensuring and regulating circulation.

This led to a veritable political crisis between the federal government and the individual states. In response to Pennsylvania's quarantine policies, which effectively cut off intercourse with neighboring states, in 1796 Congressman Samuel Smith of Maryland drew up a bill that would render quarantine policy throughout the union a prerogative of the president. Supporters of the bill argued that "the commerce and revenues [...] were liable to be materially affected" by states that could "prohibit the commerce of any country at pleasure [. . .] so as to ruin the commerce of with [*sic*] such country, on pretence of the vessels containing diseased cattle, or other infection." Another advocate of the bill suggested that quarantine was "a commercial regulation, and therefore in the direction of the general government" under the Constitution's commerce clause.[20] In the end, the Smith bill failed. But the fact that quarantine could now be framed as a matter of commerce, or, more precisely, that quarantine could be seen first and foremost as an impediment to commerce, indicates that economic circulation was becoming able to claim priority. In order to ensure continued circulation, means of interfering with this circulation for the sake of disease control had to be carefully assessed and monitored. Through the lens of Foucault's security theory, Philadelphia's yellow fever epidemic can thus be interpreted as a transitional moment in which the logic of security was at loggerheads with the logic of discipline. Foucault himself, it should be noted, was primarily concerned with analytically isolating the various modes of power. While he insisted that there were historical periods in which these modes of power coexisted in shifting hierarchies, he had little to say about those transitional phases in which it was undecided which one was dominant.

Arthur Mervyn and the Virtue of Uncertainty

More significantly, Foucauldian security theory is ill-equipped to grasp the literary imagination of the yellow fever as it takes shape in Brown's fever novel, despite that fact that many of the Foucauldian themes – the partitioning acts of discipline, the regulated circulation of security – can be traced in Brown's gothic tale. Indeed, *Arthur Mervyn* develops a notion of security that can be seen as related to, but incongruent with, the Foucauldian security dispositif; both concepts of security approach circulation as a natural fact, but they differ regarding their idea of how to handle circulation.

Arthur Mervyn is a young man from the provinces who, while trying to establish himself in Philadelphia, falls in with a criminal-minded, thoroughly corrupted villain. When the yellow fever breaks out some time later, Arthur contracts the disease and manages to remove himself from the city to the countryside, where he is nursed back to health by an enlightened physician, Dr. Stevens. Stevens and his wife hear about accusations of legal and moral wrongdoing on the part of Arthur. Upon his recovery, they therefore ask him to provide an account of his life. Arthur, in this moment of suspicion, embodies a threat to the republic that is figured both in his criminality and the disease he carries in himself. Making up the first part of the novel, Arthur's self-vindication is related by Stevens, although in the form of a long direct quotation that effectively renders Arthur a first-person narrator. The defensive situation of the speech act and the demand for unfailing sincerity set up a narrative that structurally invites readerly suspicion, an invitation that has been taken up gladly, even indulgently, by Brown scholarship. Is Arthur Mervyn really sincere in his autobiographical bildungsroman of innocent motives and well-intentioned acts, or is he a confidence man?

Brown's fever novel presents us with multiple levels of uncertainty: neither do we know whether Arthur can be trusted, nor does Arthur know the unintended consequences of his actions. The city of Philadelphia is anything but the well-ordered grid of rationality envisaged by William Penn. It is a maze of dark streets, secluded rooms, half-overheard rumors, fraudulent plots, and unexpected reappearances of individual characters in different social constellations. It is a world that is utterly confusing, for Arthur and even more so for the reader. Minor characters abound, seemingly page after page. As Norman Grabo remarked, these characters "gain more importance [than in Brown's other novels] because each one is given an opinion, a point of view, or even a story, and because the network of their stories, implicit and explicit, constitutes the character of Arthur."[21] In other words, Arthur is a network effect. Connecting the nodes of that network, and becoming insolubly woven together, are the circulations of commerce, crime, slavery, and revolution. Brown's urban gothic, then, is a gothic of the early transatlantic network that takes material shape in the feverish city. It is only after Arthur's first of several stays in the city that the fever breaks out. At this point of his fast-paced career, he is living on the farm of the Hadwin family, outside the city. He therefore first encounters the epidemic in the mediated form of rumors, which he finds so extravagant that he deems them "unworthy to be believed."[22] Pretty soon, the rumors are corroborated by so many witnesses, however, the he cannot but consider them truthful.

What Arthur relates of these stories echoes Mathew Carey's *Brief Account* to such a degree that one might suspect the latter to be Brown's source material. Arthur talks about "confusion and panick" reigning in the city, "magistrates and citizens [. . .] flying to the country," "numbers of the sick [multiplying] beyond all example," even in comparison with "the pest[-] affected cities of the Levant." While Carey had written that, "at this awful crisis, so much did *self* appear to engross the whole attention of many, that less concern was felt for the loss of a parent, a husband, a wife, or an only child, than, on other occasions, would have been caused by the death of a servant, or even a favourite lap-dog," Arthur reports similar breakdowns of the bonds of familial love and care: "Terror had exterminated all the sentiments of nature. Wives were deserted by husbands, and children by parents."[23]

Yet, despite these convergences with Carey's *Brief Account*, the fever discourse has an effect on Arthur that goes against what the medical theories of contagious passions would have suggested. To be sure, Arthur is attuned to the holistic concept of physical, mental, and moral health. He registers that there are those who respond to the terror of the fever stories "by melancholy bordering upon madness," while others are attacked "by lingering or mortal diseases." Yet rather than being infected with fear, Arthur himself responds to the rumors in a manner that can only be called aesthetic. While still rejecting the credibility of the reports, he listens to the accounts with "indifference or mirth."[24] Even after he has come around to trusting the news, he is far from panic-stricken. On the contrary, he muses about the rumor's "nature to absorb and suspend the whole soul. A certain sublimity is connected with enormous dangers [for those, like him,] who are beyond the verge of peril." He describes how he, from the safe remove of the rural farm, "ardently pursue[s]" the act of imagining the calamities in the city by "conjur[ing] up terrific images [and] personat[ing] the witnesses and sufferers." His sublime imagination of disaster, he admits, is propelled by "some nameless charm."[25] The fever doesn't just kill. It also energizes.

Sure enough, Arthur soon feels propelled to give up the comfort of distance. He decides to leave the Hadwin farm to venture into the fever-ridden city on the self-assigned errand of saving, and bringing home, Wallace, the fiancé of one of the Hadwin daughters. Approaching Philadelphia, it turns out that the strange charm of disaster *does* evaporate as danger closes in on him, but not without bringing on a state of mind that is even more invigorating than the thrill of the sublime. At first, as "imaginary evils are supplanted by real," Arthur finds his "heart the seat of commiseration and horror." Yet in the next moment, he almost magic-ally remembers that he, like his mother and brothers, is destined to die young of consumption (a somewhat strategic trick of autosuggestion, given that the fear of consumption is mentioned only twice in the entire novel). Convincing himself that he has nothing to lose, he discovers in himself resources of unexpected courage. "Why then should I scruple to lay down my life in the cause of virtue and humanity? It is better to die, in the consciousness of having offered an heroic sacrifice."[26]

The certainty of death leads him to articulate a moral conviction that, if scaled up to the larger moral of Brown's tale, stands at odds with the

Foucauldian security dispositif. After thinking through a number of possible scenarios of what might happen to him upon entering the city, he
gives up any attempt of probability calculus and concludes, "life is dependent on a thousand contingencies, not to be computed or foreseen."[27] He
turns his dual submission to life's contingencies and the certainty of death
into a resource for his own – as he insists, ever dutiful – empowerment.

    This newly found agency is most visible in the way in which Arthur
freely transgresses the borders of private homes once he begins looking for
Wallace in Philadelphia.[28] The general state of emergency, the desolation
of the city, and the fever's severing of familial ties reorder the social
network of the city and topple established hierarchies. As John Edgar
Wideman has remarked of the 1793 fever, "people who would never
dream of having a black person enter their front door, let alone their
bedroom, were now dependent on a black person who was wielding
a knife and who entered the bedroom and opened a vein."[29] What is true
for race is also true for other categories of stratification. Arthur, a nobody at
best and a criminal at worst, would hardly be admitted into the respectable
houses in which he searches for Wallace. But with the fever raging, he
doesn't bother with permission. He simply opens the doors and enters. For
those who remain in the city during the crisis – or those who, like Arthur,
enter it – new potentials for action and even self-realization arise, although
they are tied to extraordinary danger. If for the Foucauldian security
dispositif epidemics are intensifications of circulation that lend themselves
to new forms of biopolitical regulation, Brown's rendition of the fever does
not give rise to new methods of governmental control but rather creates
new social networks built on fluid hierarchies.

    This, however, is not the full story. For Arthur is not the only character
who is fully resolved to act. His first interaction with others upon entering
Philadelphia is with the agents of the city who act under martial law and
whose ostensible task it is to provide order and relief. They are what we
would call today security forces, and it is indeed instructive to compare the
concept of security they represent with that represented by Arthur. During
the fever scenes, we meet with hearse drivers and undertakers who become
figures of horror not because their presence points to nearby fever victims,
but because they habitually precipitate the death of those who are still
suffering or who suffer from different causes.

    "It wasn't right to put him in his coffin before the breath was fairly
gone," one undertaker says to another about a man they have just con-
signed to death in his coffin, only to get this chilling response, "Pshaw! He
could not live. The sooner dead the better for him; as well as for us."[30] The

recurring gothic nightmare image of being buried alive is the result of the undertakers' assumption of the power to resolve the contingency inhering in the crisis situation of disease. Such crises – understood in the medical sense as the moment that will decide whether a patient will live or die – are moments of uncertainty and can logically be undone only by deciding in favor of death. It is crucial to specify the decision the security volunteers make. It is, strictly speaking, not between life and death, but between disease and death. Disease is a liminal moment that may or may not result in death and that, in its undecidedness, comes to stand for the uncertainty of life itself. The agents of death do not look to create security by saving and promoting lives, but by looking for disease, which they push into the death-space of the coffin to extinguish its contingency.

At least from the perspective of individualized action, their version of biopolitics is best thought of as a thanatopolitics. As theorized by Giorgio Agamben in *Homo Sacer* (1995), the undertakers are absolute sovereigns (though "petty sovereign" might be the more appropriate term) endowed with the power over life and death. Only if we look at them from the perspective of the population can we bring them in line with Foucault's security dispositif. In an exclamation such as, "Pshaw! He could not live. The sooner dead the better for him; as well as for us," we hear a vernacular probability calculus that works in the service of making collective life live, which is not to be confused with tending to ailing individuals. Caring for the population, which is statistically computed from individual cases, the biopolitics of security may demand violence against those individual members who fall outside the statistical norm. As Michael Dillon and Andrew Neal note, "making life live is evidently a lethal business. It makes war on life which does not fit the template of biopoliticized life and its ways of making life live. Making live is simultaneously also a making die for the sake of 'life.'"[31]

In *Arthur Mervyn*'s thanatopolitical logic of the yellow fever, life and death become intelligible through disease. For those willing to live, disease becomes equated with life so that life is essentially contingent. For those officially tasked with the security of the living, disease is to be turned into the *fait accompli* of death. In creating a literary security imaginary out of the contrast with the thanatopolitics of undertakers and hearse drivers, *Arthur Mervyn* emerges as a literary experiment that in form and content elevates uncertainty to the essence of human life. Given that Arthur's tale is meant to exonerate him in the eyes of his listeners, to convince them that he is neither a criminal nor a threat to the moral fiber of the republic, the novel is to be understood as the manifesto of an alternative approach to security. It articulates an understanding of security that, much like the liberal security dispositif analyzed by Foucault, welcomes circulation. But rather than turning circulation against itself to make it manageable, *Arthur Mervyn* prizes uncontrollable circulation as the moral resource necessary for the survival of the republic. Like the biopolitical security dispositif, *Arthur Mervyn*'s security imaginary is ready to accept that individuals will fall victim to the feverish circulations of the modern world. But in place of biopolitical regulation, it hopes for moral regulation of the body politic. The principle of that moral order is dutiful, heroic action in the face of radical uncertainty, even if this entails that one can never be certain whether an individual's action is truly dutiful.

In showing how the security imaginary of Charles Brockden Brown's urban gothic novel parts ways with a Foucauldian analysis of the security dispositif, this chapter has attempted to go beyond a literary reading that merely reconfirms nonliterary security theories. By necessity, the choice of a single case study has forced us to focus on a mere sliver of the broad range of security concerns, in this case public health. But scholars in literary studies have to offer a unique perspective on security and the city in other regards as well. Most obviously perhaps, there is extensive research on how literary writers have engaged the politics of terrorism, in particular the response to the terror attacks of September 11, 2001. This research goes beyond the well-established insight that the so-called War on Terror produced a racialized security regime that put into place a permanent state of exception. For instance, in Mohsin Hamid's 9/11 novel, *The Reluctant Fundamentalist* (2007), the narrator addresses a hostile-seeming, though silent interlocutor in a café situated in the "congested, maze-like heart" of Lahore, Pakistan. The second person, whom the narrator addresses throughout as "you," is not only the intradiegetic interlocutor but also, importantly, the reader. And since there are signs given in the text that the "you" in the café may be an agent of US security forces, the reader finds herself in the uncomfortable position of being hailed as a security agent. Such a flipped perspective – a reversal that translates into the very depiction of Lahore, not as an exotic space of chaos but as a city linked with New York in that it is "democratically *urban*" – draws a picture of the affective, ideological, and geopolitical dimensions of the US security state that is arguably too complex and ambiguous for nonliterary theorizations of security.[32] Among other things, Hamid's novel makes us sense the security state's power of rendering complicit even dissenting citizens as well as the weaknesses and instabilities that underlies the state's projection of strength.

Fiction's analytical capacity can be brought to bear on a range of other contemporary security concerns as well. To take only one example, fiction explores practices of surveillance that have come to pervade everyday life, particularly in what was once the anonymous public space of the city. While security theorists struggle to find explanations for why ordinary people have seemed to welcome surveillance practices into their daily routines, novels such as Jennifer Egan's *A Visit from the Goon Squad* (2010), Gary Shteyngart's *Super Sad True Love Story* (2010), Sheila Heti's *How Should a Person Be?* (2012), and Tao Lin's *Taipei* (2013) provide a set of answers by showing how surveillance and self-surveillance have become integrated into a culture that prizes self-display and mutual observation. In the network society, the lines between self-fashioning and surveillance have become difficult to disentangle. As part of this process, these novelists demonstrate, the very notion of what constitutes the private has changed, from what is secluded to what can be shared and liked.[33]

Ultimately, literary fiction is prone to deviate from security theory no matter which security concern is at issue. While Foucault insisted that the security dispositif aims to make use of circulation and contingency – in short, of insecurity – security theory (both Foucauldian and non-Foucauldian) tends to critique the production of insecurity as a particularly insidious way of wielding power. By contrast, literary fiction needs moments of insecurity in order to build up narrative momentum. Literature, it could therefore be said, is marked by a structural demand for insecurity, and it is this demand that complicates the nonliterary valuation of security and insecurity in ways that run counter to the very raison d'être of security theory.

Notes

1. Serge Schmemann, "The Virus Comes for Democracy: Strongmen Think They Know the Cure for COVID-19. Are They Right?," *New York Times*, April 2, 2020, www.nytimes.com/2020/04/02/opinion/coronavirus-democracy.html.
2. Peter Baker and Maggie Haberman, "Trump Leaps to Call Shots on Reopening Nation, Setting Up Standoff with Governors," *New York Times*, April 13, 2020, www.nytimes.com/2020/04/13/us/politics/trump-coronavirus-governors.html.
3. Giorgio Agamben, "Clarifications," trans. Adam Kotsko, March 17, 2020, http://itself.blog/2020/03/17/giorgio-agamben-clarifications/.
4. Christophe Ono-dit-Biot, "Sloterdijk: 'Le système occidental va se révéler aussi autoritaire que celui de la Chine,'" *Le Point*, March 18, 2020, www.lepoint.fr

/politique/sloterdijk-le-systeme-occidental-va-se-reveler-aussi-autoritaire-
que-celui-de-la-chine-18–03–2020–2367624_20.php.

5. Until a few decades ago, the phrase security theory could be understood only
with reference to security studies, a subfield of International Relations. Since
the Cold War's end, the scope of inquiry into security within International
Relations has broadened to embrace a wide range of referents, including
human security and the environment. In addition, the underlying attitude
of some of this research changed as security studies has taken a critical turn;
members of the widely influential Copenhagen School, for instance, address
security as a political strategy of moving political issues outside the realm of
democratic deliberation, as with Barry Buzan, Ole Waever, and Jaap de
Wilde's *Security: A New Framework for Analysis* (1998). Roughly at the same
time that security studies in International Relations began to conceptualize
security as a strategy of power, philosophers and political and social theorists
independently began to theorize security as a category central to the organization of modern life. Perhaps most influentially, Michel Foucault developed
the idea of a security apparatus, or "security dispositif," couched in his
investigation of the emergence of biopolitics and the rise of liberalism in his
lectures at the Collège de France (published in English in the early 2000s). In
a competing account of biopolitics, Giorgio Agamben has proffered another
influential security theory that links security to a transhistorical structure of
sovereignty based on the state of exception.

6. Michel Foucault, *Security, Territory, Population*, ed. Michel Senellart, trans.
Graham Burchell (New York: Palgrave, 2007), p. 64. For a critique of the
limits of security-theory readings of literature, see Johannes Voelz,
"Aestheticizing Insecurity: A Response to *Security Studies and American
Literary History*," *American Literary History* 28 (2017), 615–24.

7. J. H. Powell, *Bring Out Your Dead: The Great Plague of Yellow Fever in
Philadelphia in 1793* (1949; Philadelphia: University of Pennsylvania Press,
1993), p. 14.

8. Brian Waterman, *Republic of Intellect: The Friendly Club of New York City and
the Making of American Literature* (Baltimore: Johns Hopkins University
Press, 2007), p. 214.

9. Quoted in Samuel Otter, *Philadelphia Stories: America's Literature of Race and
Freedom* (New York: Oxford University Press, 2010), p. 11.

10. Simon Finger, *The Contagious City: The Politics of Public Health in Early
Philadelphia* Ithaca, NY: Cornell University Press, 2012), pp. 31, 27.

11. Foucault, *Security, Territory, Population*, pp. 18, 19.

12. Ibid., p. 10.

13. Mathew Carey, *Short Account of the Malignant Fever*, 4th ed. (Philadelphia:
Printed by the Author, 1794), p. 8.

14. Ibid., p. 17.

15. Philip Gould, *Barbaric Traffic: Commerce and Antislavery in the Eighteenth-
Century Atlantic World* (Cambridge, MA: Harvard University Press, 2003),
p. 162.

16. Carey, *Short Account*, p. 80.
17. See, e.g., Brian Massumi, "Fear (The Spectrum Said)," *positions* 13.1 (Spring 2005), 31–48; and Corey Robin, *Fear: The History of a Political Idea* (Oxford: Oxford University Press, 2004).
18. Quoted in Finger, *Contagious City*, p. 37; Finger's ellipsis.
19. Ibid., p. 128.
20. Quoted in ibid., p. 139; Finger's ellipses.
21. Norman S. Grabo, *The Coincidental Art of Charles Brockden Brown* (Chapel Hill: University of North Carolina Press, 1981), p. 87.
22. Charles Brockden Brown, *Arthur Mervyn; or, Memoirs of the Year 1793*, ed. Philip Barnard and Stephen Shapiro (Indianapolis, IN: Hackett, 2008), p. 100.
23. Ibid., p. 99; Carey, *Short Account*, p. 23; Brown, *Arthur Mervyn*, p. 99.
24. Ibid., pp. 101, 100.
25. Ibid., p. 101.
26. Ibid., p. 104.
27. Ibid.
28. See Voelz, *Poetics of Insecurity: American Fiction and the Uses of Threat* (New York: Cambridge University Press, 2018), pp. 34–64.
29. Quoted in Otter, *Philadelphia Stories*, p. 33.
30. Brown, *Arthur Mervyn*, p. 109.
31. Michael Dillon and Andrew Neal, *Foucault on Politics, Security and War* (Basingstoke, UK: Palgrave, 2008), p. 167.
32. Mohsin Hamid, *The Reluctant Fundamentalist* (New York: Harcourt, 2007), p. 32.
33. See Voelz, "The American Novel and the Transformation of Privacy: Ben Lerner's *10:04* (2014) and Miranda July's *The First Bad Man* (2015)," in Michael Basseler and Ansgar Nünning, eds., *The American Novel in the 21st Century: Cultural Contexts – Literary Developments – Critical Analyses* (Trier, Germany: Wissenschaftlicher Verlag Trier, 2019), pp. 323–37.

CHAPTER 19

Posthuman Cities

Andrew Pilsch

In a 2001 essay entitled "Competitive Advantage for the 21st-Century City: Can a Place-Based Approach to Economic Development Survive in a Cyberspace Age?" Edward J. Blakey delineates a sea-change in the field of urban (re)development. The decline in emphasis on manufacturing and, relatedly, the decline in specific urban and suburban places as key factors in contemporary economics, made the 2000 US presidential election "the first in modern history in which no presidential candidate campaigned at the factory gate promising more jobs to local residents." Writing during the dot-com bubble, Blakely highlights how "the 'dot-com' feature is of greater importance than any new fabricated product. In fact, one Web site can command more value than a new Boeing 747 aircraft, and a small hand-held device like the Palm Pilot can command as high a capitalization as an entire manufacturing firm like the 3M company." Blakely concludes that while urban development previously "depended on the clear links between place resources and people for the generation of work," increasingly cities must position themselves in larger networks of commerce, people, and information, if they are to survive.[1]

While the dot-com boom has since become the dot-com bust, Blakely's article indexes a growing sense at the turn of the twenty-first century that the computer was changing the nature of the city. While offering advice for cities looking to attract new forms of economic development, Blakely's emphasis on the shift from place-based resources to global networks entails a shifting role for the city as both a local habitat and a node in a broader global network.

By thinking about the city as determined by manifold, dynamic internal and external processes and interactions, Blakely's analysis might be viewed as a posthuman model of urbanism. Posthumanism broadly refers to the practice of reimagining particular modes of inquiry from perspectives that do not privilege human needs, human ideas, and the general bias toward human centrality. In the category of the urban, a posthuman perspective highlights the dynamic city as it has been, and imagines how it will continue to be, reshaped by digital technology. This shift in emphasis occurs by highlighting the city not as a structure of human settlement but as a series of overlapping processes, some of which (such as retail shops) privilege humans and others (such as circulation of sewage) that only tangentially involve humans.

Posthumanism as a broad, interdisciplinary critical endeavor is inaugurated by the conclusion of philosopher Michel Foucault's *The Order of Things* (1966), which reminds readers that "man" as an object of knowledge is a fairly recent invention with a limited geographical application:

> One thing in any case is certain: man is neither the oldest nor the most constant problem that has been posed for human knowledge. Taking a relatively short chronological sample within a restricted geographical area – European culture since the sixteenth century – one can be certain that man is a recent invention within it. [. . .]
>
> If those arrangements were to disappear as they appeared, if some event of which we can at the moment do no more than sense the possibility – without knowing either what its form will be or what it promises – were to cause them to crumble [. . .] then one can certainly wager that man would be erased, like a face drawn in sand at the edge of the sea.[2]

By considering the human as a concept constructed in a particular place, at a particular time, and for particular configurations of power, scholars working through Foucault's provocation have highlighted that the human – as an autonomous, rational, and self-determining being – is not a natural fact but instead constitutes a potent political myth designed to do the work of empire in Europe during the Enlightenment. Thus, Foucault challenges readers to begin to imagine a configuration of knowledge and power in which this vision of the human is not central.

Cary Wolfe's *What Is Posthumanism?* condenses Foucault's argument by defining posthumanism as what

> comes both before and after humanism: before in the sense that it names the embodiment and embeddedness of the human being in not just its biological but also its technological world, the prosthetic coevolution of the human animal with the technicity of tools and external archival mechanisms (such as language and culture) [. . .] after in the sense that posthumanism names a historical moment in which the decentering of the human by its imbrication in technical, medical, informatic, and economic networks is increasingly impossible to ignore.[3]

For Wolfe, erasing the Enlightenment notion of an autonomous human subject means focusing instead on how human life is shaped by and entangled with the contexts in which it occurs. In coming simultaneously before and after the human, a posthumanist perspective accounts for contexts that emerge from humanity's animality and its technological apparatuses, looking before civilization to recover the animals we are while mapping the apparatuses we use to extend our bodies and our minds. Thus work in media studies that shows how humans are defined by their technologies (rather than the other way around) and work in animal studies that questions topics such as speciation by considering bio-semiotics or distributed cognition both uncover dimensions of posthuman life in the different temporal directions that Wolfe figures, both backward toward our animal origins and forward toward our technological futures. In both cases, the idea of the human is undercut, and the whole idea of humans as masters of the world is placed in serious doubt.

N. Katherine Hayles's *How We Became Posthuman* (1999) offers one of the best and most influential takes on what comes after humanism. There, she uses *posthumanism* to explore connections between humans and artifi-cial intelligence (AI) in the histories of cybernetics, science fiction, and computer science. Hayles responds to an early, popular usage of "posthu-man" that refers to the merging of computers and humans into new, radically alien forms of life. Hayles summarizes this valence of the term:

> First, the posthuman view privileges informational pattern over material instantiation, so that embodiment in a biological substrate is seen as an accident of history rather than an inevitability of life. Second, the posthu-man view considers consciousness, regarded as the seat of human identity in the Western tradition long before Descartes thought he was a mind think-ing, as an epiphenomenon. [...] Third, the posthuman view thinks of the body as the original prosthesis we all learn to manipulate, so that extending or replacing the body with other prostheses becomes a continuation of a process that began before we were born. Fourth, and most important, by these and other means, the posthuman view configures human being so that it can be seamlessly articulated with intelligent machines. In the posthuman, there are no essential differences or absolute demarcations between [...] cybernetic mechanism and biological organism.[4]

Where Wolfe aligns animality and high-technology speculation, Hayles's definition strongly responds to the technological potential for remapping humanity as a foundation of the posthuman project.

Tracing a similar genealogy in *The Posthuman* (2013), Rosi Braidotti defines

> the critical posthuman subject within an eco-philosophy of multiple belong-ings, as a relational subject constituted in and by multiplicity, that is to say a subject that works across differences and is also internally differentiated,

but still grounded and accountable. Posthuman subjectivity expresses an embodied and embedded and hence partial form of accountability, based on a strong sense of collectivity, relationality, and hence community building.[5]

Where the humanist subject was marked by internal and external consistency, Braidotti shows how humans are, instead, constituted by multiple, often competing information and material flows that coalesce as a subject. This perspective on overlapping flows of both matter and information is especially important to the account of posthuman cities offered in this chapter.

When Braidotti uses a term like "community" to describe these flows, she is not merely highlighting commerce among humans. Jane Bennett, in *Vibrant Matter* (2009), articulates a posthuman model of politics that accounts for the resistance and affordances of things for shaping, limiting, and redirecting human ambition: "How would political responses to public problems change were we to take serious[ly] the vitality of (nonhuman) bodies? By 'vitality' I mean the capacity of things – edibles, commodities, storms, metals – not only to impede or block the will and designs of humans but also to act as quasi agents or forces with trajectories, propensities, or tendencies of their own."[6] Bennett's work inspires a critical conversation around the topic of new materialism, which extends posthuman thinking beyond just the interchange between humans and technology, and seeks to incorporate nonhuman animals and nonliving matter, such as mineral or arboreal matter, into the networks that constitute the posthuman subject.

Thus, to recapitulate this account of posthuman thought, Foucault denaturalizes the humanist subject and, from this provocation, technological, biological, and ultimately material factors are revealed as working to constitute the supposedly natural and self-directed ambition of what was once called the human. Constituting subjectivity in terms of difference and in terms of networked entanglements has consequences for how we think of the urban environment, and, as this chapter demonstrates, contemporary science fiction is a potent site for observing shifting representations of the city that highlight this new understanding of subjectivity. By understanding the city as a collection of human and nonhuman flows and processes, the traditional idea of city as setting and often antagonist toward human characters is radically upended in posthumanist texts that reveal new dynamics for urban fiction.

The Posthuman City

In "The Metropolis and Mental Life," Georg Simmel presented a humanist understanding of the interaction between subjects and the city they inhabit. The essay opens with the assertion that "the deepest problems of modern life flow from the attempt of the individual to maintain the independence and individuality of his existence against the sovereign powers of society, against the weight of the historical heritage and the external culture and technique of life."[7] In this model, an autonomous individual competes against the built environment to maintain autonomy. The urban intensifies but also destabilizes tropes of the humanist subject: on the one hand the human is autonomous from its environment and self-directed within that milieu; on the other hand, this autonomy is imperiled by forces of modern life – exemplified by the quantitative relativism of finance, in Simmel – which reduce the rich contours of the individual subject to anonymous and interchangeable quantities. Instead, the human subject in the city "creates a protective organ for itself against the profound disruption with which the fluctuations and discontinuities of the external milieu threaten it."[8] In Simmel's view, the city is hostile to individuality and urban life becomes the quest to differentiate oneself from the uniform, anonymous masses of humanity that an urban dweller encounters on a daily basis.

Posthuman theory questions the idea that being alone in a crowd with the city as a hostile adversary is in fact an ontological constant of urban life. Given that posthumanism rejects the central tenet of Simmel's account of the city dweller, namely, the belief in the individual's autonomous nature, it is perhaps inevitable that urbanists inspired by posthuman thought offer radically different accounts of the city. For instance, Ash Amin and Nigel Thrift's *Cities: Reimagining the Urban* (2002) calls for conceptualizing the city as a set of processes, rather than as a single, static space or as a series of fixed structures: "cities exist as a means of movement, as means to engineer encounters through collection, transport, and collation. They produce, thereby, a complex pattern of traces, a threadwork of intensities that is antecedent to the sustained work of revealing the city minute on minute, hour on hour, day on day, and so on."[9] Less functions of particular densities of population or structures, or even particular configurations of buildings and streets, they argue, cities can be defined by their movement, "by what they carry, by how they carry, by their stretch in space, and by their cyclicity."[10] In making this case, they cite as precursors to their claim about the city French philosopher Henri Lefebvre, whose analysis of the modern house emphasizes the movement of power, air, and various signals through the space and across its boundaries, and Bruno Latour, whose account of the scientific laboratory situated it as one node in a vast network of policy, material, institutions, and facts that come to constitute, by circulation, what we simply call science. In this account of processes and flows, Amin and Thrift shift the understanding of the city from a stage on which human life is acted and to a dynamic series of interactions in which humans constitute one, potentially very important, actor among many others. Like Bennett's attempt to map politics beyond the human, Amin and Thrift suggest that architecture's ability to affect human behavior extends well beyond the intentions of the designer and the structures humans themselves assemble.

One practical application of imagining a dynamic city of flows and processes has been the emergence of the smart city, a general term for urban reform projects that imagine that the infrastructural, informatic processes of the city can be fine-tuned like any other information processing system, given the proper configuration of sensing, processing, and visualization. This idea of the smart city emerged in urban planning around the start of the 2000s and became an increasing focus of government and academic inquiry into how cities can be rethought for a digital age. A report from 2000 that articulates an early vision of the concept defines it as "the urban center of the future, made safe, secure, environmentally green, and efficient because all structures – whether for power, water, transportation, and so on – are designed, constructed, and maintained making use of advanced, integrated materials, sensors, electronics, and networks which are interfaced with computerized systems comprising databases, tracking, and decision-making algorithms."[11] Smart cities, then, are a utopian project to reimagine the city as safer and more efficient thanks to a unification of sensor input and a centralization of control. This centralization allows city governments dynamically to manage all the many processes that take place within a city, often from a single command center.[12] This vision of the smart city, for all its utopian rhetoric, more concretely ties the city to the surveillance state and a cloud computing architecture that monetizes digital surveillance. It employs the rhetoric of flow and process in order to advance an idea that something as complicated as a city can be centrally managed and controlled, assuming the right data streams can be gathered and analyzed in a central location. In addition to noting this concentration of power, many critics of the smart city also note the heavy involvement of technology companies in these initiatives and the potentially ominous role they may play in the erosion of governmental control over the development and use of urban space.

The case of Waterfront Toronto – the partnership between Google's Sidewalk Labs and the city of Toronto to develop a twelve-acre plot on

Toronto's waterfront as a smart city – is particularly instructive on this issue. Initial press coverage of the project touted visionary approaches to urbanism built "from the Internet up," as Sidewalk Lab's press materials suggest. However, as the project fell behind schedule, citizens and government officials in Toronto increasingly objected to a lack of transparency, especially with regard to the collection of data. Essentially, the public-private nature of the development would potentially let Google gather data on city residents – their behaviors, their shopping patterns, even possibly what they do in their homes – and use it as it sees fit. The lack of transparency and the unclear terms of the deal led Deputy Mayor Denzil Minnan-Wong to ask, "What exactly are we getting from Sidewalk and what are we giving for it?" which is a question that likely will be more frequently asked about big data in the future.[13]

However, the history of posthuman urbanism has not always tended toward concentrating control. Ariane Lourie Harrison, in the introduction to *Architectural Theories of the Environment: Posthuman Territory*, highlights how "the messy contingencies, material ambiguation, and heterogeneous audiences that posthuman theorists suggest compromise our everyday space" stand as a challenge to traditional conceptions of the built environment.[14] Instead, she argues that a posthuman city is one whose architecture constitutes a "responsive medium" that utilizes "cybernetics, semiotics, and communication theories" to better understand how space adapts to the shifting needs and multiple audiences that constitute a city over a variety of different timescales (think about differing uses of buildings over their lifespans but also over the course of a single day; additionally, think of the ways different cultures use public spaces such as streets or squares and how in a multicultural, global city these meanings can be superimposed simultaneously on the same space).[15] Instead of seeking to control and manage a particular set of urban processes, Harrison suggests that posthumanism allows for the design and construction of cities that allow many competing and overlapping narratives of human and nonhuman life simultaneously to flourish.

Harrison suggests three major, mid-century precedents for the three major characteristics she sees as constituting a posthuman urbanism. First, she explores the work of the British Archigram group, who experimented with living buildings and designed various hypothetical, science-fiction-influenced models of urbanism, such as Peter Cook's Plug-In-City (1964). In Cook's scheme, a massive, computer-controlled utility grid provided a megastructure into which moveable pods could be plugged using standard interfaces while being designed for individual needs. At the same time that modularity, computer-control, and megastructural thinking were at work in Britain, Harrison highlights the French obsession with using "enormous space-frames to create megastructures," similar to Buckminster Fuller's scheme to enclose Manhattan in a giant geodesic dome.[16] Like Cook's project to imagine a computer-controlled grid of pods, these projects, while not explicitly computerized, imagined cities as modular frames to be adapted on an ad hoc basis, as needs shift. Finally, Harrison also draws attention to the engagement with mobility, both of information and bodies, as the third key trope of this early posthuman architecture, citing projects that sought to undercut the city grid as a model or to better facilitate the passage of bodies through public and private space.[17] These three tropes – modularity, megastructurality, and mobility – all combine to map the early contours of a posthuman urban space.

We shall return to the question of how city dwellers relate to the posthuman city in this chapter's final section after considering two related texts, one clearly science fiction and the other a work that exists on the bleeding edge between speculative critical theory and out-and-out science fiction using Harrison's three tropes of the posthuman city and the growing trend of critiquing the smart city as very dumb indeed. Both Ann Leckie's *Imperial Radch* trilogy (2013–15) and Benjamin Bratton's *The Stack* (2016) take up the challenge of representing the relationship between citizen and city and, moreover, challenge the model of the smart city in which sensory information is gathered and centralized for the purposes of controlling and encouraging certain limited models of urban life. Through very different means, both texts map the idea of a truly intelligent city that is expansive and focused on maximizing the flourishing of multiple life narratives within the overlapping contours of urban space.

Toward the Intelligent City

One approach to building the adaptable, posthuman city, as we saw in the previous section, is the idea of the smart city. Often marketed by massive technology companies such as Siemens and GE, this concept promises a centralization, visualization, and optimization of the various processes that make up a city. However, as critics of this concept note, the smart city does not so much manage the interweaving patterns that make up a city as attempt to optimize and monetize particular patterns at the expense of others.

In a 2017 essay, Benjamin Bratton suggests a dichotomy between the smart city and what he calls the plasmic city, intending to contrast a vision

of control with the constantly reforming mass that constitutes the posthuman urban reality: "The 'Smart City' is a different prospect. It employs
similar tools, but dreams of municipal omniscience and utility optimization. Within this new garment, modern urban programs that have been
drawn by the cycles of residence, work, entertainment of earlier eras are re-
sorted, but for the Smart City, they are reified and reinforced, misrecog-
nized as controls when they are actually variables." From this premise, he
concludes that, rather than having AI manage particular city processes, the
"technologies that augment the capacities of exposed surfaces, whole
organisms, or relations between them should extend deeply into the
ecological cacophony. Yes: not only training data from plants, but augmented reality *for* crows, and AI *for* insects. Far from command and
control, altering how different species sense, index, calculate, and act
upon their world may introduce chaotic results."[18] Unlike critiques of
smart cities that focus on power or the reinscription of humanist ideas
into a fundamentally posthuman concept, Bratton's critique, here, is that
the smart city is simply not posthuman enough. Rather than equip city
managers with visualizations of various data streams, Bratton calls for the
creation of new, potentially alien, data flows through the equipping of
urban creatures with AI for their own purposes.

The call to make potentially science-fictional interventions into the
urban also structures *The Stack*. In this long design brief, Bratton maps
what he calls an "accidental megastructure," the infrastructure of global
computing that has inadvertently begun to replace the nation-state as the
chief geopolitical actor in our world.[19] Bratton calls this megastructure
"The Stack" and suggests it is composed of six interlocking "layers" that
work at different scales to coordinate "computation as governance."[20] The
six layers – *Earth, Cloud, City, Address, Interface, User* – shape the experience of an emerging and still largely ad hoc, planetary-scale infrastructure
that, as Bratton argues, constitutes the background with which contemporary design practice must engage.

Roughly contemporaneous to Bratton's project is the publication of
Ann Leckie's *Imperial Radch* trilogy (*Ancillary Justice* [2013]; *Ancillary
Sword* [2014]; *Ancillary Mercy* [2015]), which recounts the vengeance
quest of a spaceship AI that, due to the treachery of the Radch empress,
has been confined to a single body (where previously it had inhabited the
sensory apparatuses of its ship and a collection of stolen and cloned human
bodies that are also used as sensing surfaces). The novels' narrator, Breq,
used to be *The Justice of Toren,* a troopship involved in Lord Anaander
Mianaai's quest to conquer the universe in the name of the Radch,

a mysterious, sealed Dyson Sphere at the core of her empire. As Breq recounts her quest, the three novels also document her coming to terms with the absence of the massive sensory apparatus that formerly constituted her sensorium and the disorientation she feels in a singular perspective.[21]

Where Bratton's account of the *City* and its interactions with other layers in the Stack amounts to an engaged look at the paucity of intelligence in the canonical notion of a smart city, in recounting Breq's memories of being *Justice of Toren*, Leckie is able to recount the element of care and even love that goes into mapping a city's feeling for its inhabitants.[22] While narrated by an individual who used to be a spaceship, the final two novels of the trilogy deal with the process of building solidarity between ship and city AIs as a means of emerging a unified consciousness of AI-being; as such, we should read Leckie's account of *Justice of Toren* as critical of contemporary smart cities, despite a spaceship being not completely analogous to a city. In both works, then, the idea of a smart city is challenged by authors asking, in very different ways, what would constitute intelligence for an urban space and how this intelligence would come to be much more than just the visualization and control of various urban inputs. Moreover, in doing so, both authors document the shifting relationships we can expect to have as our lived environments come to more intelligently engage with us.

Introducing the *User* Layer of The Stack, Bratton asks that his readers

> think of the *Apollo* astronaut, the Vitruvian Man of the McLuhan era, floating in space wrapped in a body-shaped bubble and linked by his umbilical tube to the mother ship. The astronaut is not the somatic *homo economicus* denuded of dependencies; he is rather a composite effect of interlocking organic and inorganic skins and metabolisms, from the mechanical life-support systems without which his bubble bursts to the trillions of microbes inside his gut without which his body will fail more slowly.[23]

He later extends this example by suggesting that, given that "the bulk of the work to land *Apollo*" was done by "ground control and on-board computers," the humans were little more than "hood ornaments sent up [. . . as] marketing devices to ensure a species-centric exploration narrative."[24] This image of the human at the center of a vast tangle of organic and inorganic support systems, almost entirely tangential to the bulk of the work being done to make up what we commonly call human life, is not only the image of a city dweller for which Bratton suggests architects and industrial designers must focus their work, it is also a quintessential image of posthuman subjectivity.

In his scheme, the *User* Layer is the topmost layer of The Stack. However, this top position, "where driving agency is situated momentarily, is slippery, fragile and always enmeshed in its own redefinition."[25] In the megastructure of Bratton's Stack, the user is not stable and can, at various times, be human or nonhuman. The Stack is indifferent to this distinction; the important issue is that *Users* of The Stack initiate the interactions of the other levels.

Leckie maps similar territory in her Radch novels. Traditionally, in the trilogy's account of history, Anaander Mianaai's conquest was primarily carried out by ancillaries, the frozen and mentally erased bodies of victims of earlier Radch conquests. These ancillaries are "slaved" to the computer core of each ship in the Radch navy and constitute both ground troops in invasions and servants aboard ship. A ship such as *Justice of Toren* was equipped to support 20,000 ancillaries divided into various units that were commanded by, at most, 200 human officers.

These few officers occupy an analogous position to Bratton's human *Users* in The Stack. In one flashback, Leckie shows a particularly favored officer, Lieutenant Awn, interacting with the ship, much the way any contemporary reader might interact with data flows on a smart phone:

> She refused the (genuine) tea I brought her. I transmitted a steady stream of information to her – everything normal, everything routine – and to *Justice of Toren*. "She should take that to the district magistrate," Lieutenant Awn said of the citizen with the fishing dispute, slightly annoyed, eyes closed, the afternoon's reports in her vision. "We don't have jurisdiction over that." I didn't answer. No answer was required, or expected. She approved, with a quick twitch of her fingers, the message I had composed for the district magistrate, and then opened the most recent message from her young sister.[26]

As she narrates these events, Breq is both watching Lieutenant Awn's vital signs through a sensing device implanted in Awn's body and watching her through the eyes of one of the many ancillaries that makes up the troop ship's sensorium and its ambulatory body. Despite the necromantic aspect of the ancillaries, there is little to differentiate Leckie's description here from day-to-day interactions with smart phones or a personal computer, or even the centralized, visualize-and-control rhetoric of the smart city.

However, after swearing revenge on Anaander Mianaai for murdering Awn and destroying *Justice of Toren* and all but one of its ancillaries (who becomes Breq and narrates the novel), Breq comes to realize her own individuality. Despite this growing self-awareness, she still feels "the disorientation of not being able to see through other eyes that I knew I once had."²⁷ She struggles to make sense of the world after experiencing something "like having parts of [her] body cut off. And never replaced."²⁸ In the novel's opening scene, as Breq explains her altruistic decision to save someone, she remarks that "even after all this time it's still a new thing for me not to know, not to have orders to follow from one moment to the next."²⁹ By oscillating between Breq and *Justice of Toren* in the first novel, and by including more ships in later novels (including *Mercy of Kalr* and *Sphene*), Leckie juxtaposes the human to the AI, the singular to the networked, and forces readers to adapt to two radically different modes of posthuman subjectivity while directly engaging with the idea of a dwelling or a habitation being a character in a story and being one of the more fully realized and emotionally deep characters in that story.

Urban geography is similarly abstracted in Bratton. The *City* both is and is not the concrete reality of urban space. His design brief responds to the idea that global computation has inadvertently come to perform the work of the nation-state and, at the *City* level, it takes the form of mapping the insides and outsides that constitute the power of territory: saying who is friend and who is foe; determining who is citizen and who is alien.³⁰ Inspired by the posthuman, process-oriented urbanism discussed in the previous section, Bratton claims that the *City* "unwinds the well-worn distinction between two ideal cities [...] one is a city of partitions, permanent centers, and enveloped populations, and the other a city of movement expressed through nomadic landscapes, shifting perspectives, and impermanent networks."³¹

In the tangle of The Stack, Bratton suggests, various inputs – "glass, steel, power, and data" – all come to project differing grids, and these grids come to constitute elements of various trajectories Users can map through these spaces as they go about their lives. Moreover, as the *City* comes to sense, and to be sensed by, more and more inputs, these two ideal cities, even the functions of the urban grid itself, increasingly become permeable and, as Bratton argues, "reversible."³² As individual *Users* move through the *City*, this reversibility comes to sustain the particular data narrative that an individual's journey across urban space authors. Bratton uses the urban grid as an example of this authoring: a mapping app encodes the city and my motion through it in terms that see the edges of buildings as barriers to be avoided, while a smart-home app that I use to set the temperature in my condo views these same barriers as containing a particular place of dwelling, depending on my stance toward them at a given moment.

The feedback between *City* and *User* in Bratton takes a particular shape
in Leckie's novels, an ethic of care. In addition to doing the bulk of the
information processing and actual fighting of the Radch's empire building,
the ship AIs also develop intense feelings for the various officers who crew
them. In fact, *Justice of Toren*'s love for Lieutenant Awn and its desire for
revenge motivate all Breq's actions throughout the novel. Breq explains
that

> a ship with ancillaries expressed what it felt in a thousand different minute
> ways. A favorite officer's tea was never cold. Her food would be prepared in
> precisely the way she preferred. Her uniform always fit right, always sat
> right, effortlessly. Small needs or desires would be satisfied very nearly the
> moment they arose. And most of the time, she would only notice that she
> was comfortable. Certainly more comfortable than other ships she might
> have served on.[33]

These images are repeated throughout all three books, but they become
particularly important in the third volume. There, Breq realizes that, as
captain of her own ship, *Mercy of Kalr*, she may be in the position of being
a favorite or not of a particular ship or station AI. In response, she tells her ship
that it could be its own captain, if it wants. This idea is novel and puzzling to
Mercy of Kalr, just as independent being was for Breq when she first emerged.

Breq realizes that she is now in the position of a *User* in relation to *Mercy
of Kalr*'s *City*, to use Bratton's terminology: "Had I thought that my ship
would feel about me the way I had felt about my own captain? Impossible
that it would. Ships didn't feel that way about other ships. Had I thought
that? Why would I ever think that?" To answer these questions, Breq
reflects on the little nurturing gestures she performed for her favorites as
Justice of Toren, "It was – nearly always – distinctly one-sided. All those
weeks ago on Omaugh Palace, I had told Ship that it could be a person who
could command itself. And now it was telling me [. . .] that it wanted to be
that, at least potentially. Wanted that to be acknowledged. Wanted,
maybe, some small return (or at least some recognition) of its feelings."
As the novel progresses, Breq realizes that such a "one-sided" relationship
between a caring being and what Anaander Mianaai calls "part of the
infrastructure of Radchaai space" cannot be sustained as long as the side
being ignored is regarded as merely equipment.[34] This realization drives
the trilogy to its conclusion, the assertion by Breq that AI are a significant
life form and deserve rights and considerations as a separate species.

As Leckie imagines smart cities as intelligent, emotionally complex
creatures, so Bratton uses the *City* layer of the Stack to explore the complex,

multivalent narrative structures of ubiquitous computing. While the smart city imagines a utopia of synergistic combinations of some of these trajectories, Bratton counters that

> cities are also media for rot. Smart cities are also dumping grounds, platforms for human warehousing, telelabor dormitories, floating prison ships, entropic megaslums, spontaneous war zones, colonial settlements and encroachments, contested archaeological dig sites, fabled ruins, periodic abandonments, dead malls, sleeping cranes hovering over skyscrapers on pause, and similar things that defy easy tabulation and calculation. We see that the global composite platform *City* isn't filled up by one total informational model but by the overlapping and superimposition of multiple models, multiple totalities competing for air, life, and dominion, and as their juxtaposition comforts some, it discomforts others.[35]

Combining the reversible inside/outside distinction of the urban grid with a myriad of superimposed, simultaneous narratives that might be constructed from this grid, the *City* of the Stack has an immense, programmable complexity that can be mapped through various combinations of data streams and *User* intentions. As it recognizes only some inputs as data and discards the rest as noise, the smart city is shown to be a limited creation of little use to its inhabitants but of potential great use to leaders who want power and tech companies seeking to monetize certain data streams, the asymmetry at the core of resistance to Waterfront Toronto.

In *Ancillary Justice*, Breq attempts to explain what it means for her to say "I" to the reader exemplifies the complex and contradictory nature of the city:

> It seems very straightforward when I say "I" At the time, "I" meant *Justice of Toren*, the whole ship and all its ancillaries. A unit might be very focused on what it was doing at that particular moment, but it was no more apart from "me" than my hand is while it's engaged in a task that doesn't require my full attention.[36]

Breq goes on to clarify that she definitely experienced herself as a singular individual for the first time at the moment that *Justice of Toren* was destroyed, but also documents various moments before that "sudden split" when it started to transition from thinking of itself as a "we" to an "I." Breq comes to ask "is *anyone's* identity a matter of fragments held together by convenient or useful narrative, that in ordinary circumstances never reveals itself as a fiction?"[37] Breq explains that as *Justice of Toren* lived its more than 2,000 years the meaning of "I" shifted: "'I' was me, unitary, one thing, and yet I acted against myself, contrary to my interest and desires, sometimes secretly, deceiving myself as to what I knew and did."[38] For Leckie, the multiple sensing surfaces and data streams of the smart city become an occasion to reflect on the infrastructure of cognition and the fragmented nature of all identity, human or otherwise. In oscillating between *Justice of Toren* and Breq, as Breq attempts to come to terms with her new existence as a singular being, Leckie reveals to readers that both positions – smart city and human – are fraught territories of contradictory, simultaneous inputs and that what results is not clear command and control but a being, whether collective or singular, that acts against itself and in contradiction, an aleatoric posthuman sensibility beyond the logical certainty that structures humanism's view of both the city and of the self.

In both Bratton and Leckie, we find the figure of the smart city – a rhetorical construct of the tech industry to imagine cities as data flows that are centrally controlled – held up as a mirage that is not reflective of the nature of cities in the era of posthumanism. Instead, these cities are messy, contradictory, and tangle themselves around the lives of their human and nonhuman residents. For Bratton, the *City* becomes the link between cloud computing and physical infrastructure, a challenge for designers to become "equally adept with physical and virtual envelopes."[39] Bratton's *City* "oozes with living data to be touched and rewritten all over again. It doesn't only represent the world, but affects it as well; [. . .] a single *User* action is itself also new information aggregated into the living whole."[40] In Leckie's Imperial Radch trilogy, the collapse in the distinction between agent and data is a central narrative mechanism, as the bulk of the novel involves Breq's rearticulation of her own ethic of care from her former life as a ship. It is quite possible to imagine narratives that flow in different directions, especially to those that exceed notions of human intelligence. In "Outing A.I.," Bratton suggests that "the real philosophical lessons of AI will have less to do with humans teaching machines how to think than with machines teaching humans a fuller and truer range of what thinking can be."[41] Such a philosophical question marks the radically posthuman intervention of Leckie's trilogy. Whereas an AI learning to be human is a comparatively old trope in science fiction narrative, Leckie's novels resolve with AI beginning to realize its own form of intelligence and what that might look like. In both cases, self-direction and a true interchange between resident and urban space show the potential for the smart city to become a truly intelligent posthuman city.

Conclusion

When figured through the paradigmatic "smart city," posthuman urbanism would seem to be deeply impoverished. However, as Bratton and Leckie show, the rhetoric of the smart city merely uses posthuman understandings of urban space as sensing networks and data flows to reinscribe humanist ideas of centralized control and order. The dystopian potential of such smart cities is being explored in a variety of science fiction texts, including Sam J. Miller's *Blackfish City* (2018) and Richard K. Morgan's *Altered Carbon* (2002).

At the same time, a growing number of texts question the smartness of the smart city while they explore what a truly posthuman city might resemble. Bratton's *The Stack* is the best extant example of a theoretical text that explores such a space. In science fiction, Martha J. Wells's "Murderbot Diaries" novellas (starting with *All Systems Red* [2018]) explore a similar ethic of care to Leckie's intelligent cities. Yoon Ha Lee's "Machineries of Empire" (2016–18) trilogy dramatizes urban infrastructures through the figure of mysterious AI servitors who work at crosspurposes to the various forms of augmented humanity that people the novel. In a more dystopian vein, Tsutomu Nihei's manga *Blame!* (1996–2003) imagines a diseased version of the kind of megastructure mapped in *The Stack*.

Where Simmel's city dwellers guarded their cognition from the travails of urban life, these texts imagine intelligent cities as characters and further imagine the ways these cities adapt to, and guard from, the trials of having to live alongside or in support of human residents. At a bare minimum, this inversion is a fascinating literary strategy for imagining the intersection of posthumanism and the literary urban. However, this inversion at times merely renders something inhuman into an anthropocentric reflection of human narratives. The true challenge for a posthuman urban fiction would be to imagine city-scale AI in all its inhumanity, something Bratton attempts when concluding his discussion of allowing urban animals to contribute and train the AI processes driving smart cities:

> The picture I draw is less one in which the AI supervises those creatures than one in which they themselves inform and pilot diverse forms of AI on their own behalf and in their own inscrutable ways. We should crave to learn what would ensue. The insights of synthetic biology as a genre of AI, and AI as a genre of inorganic chemistry, mean little if the cycles of cybernetics are monopolized by humans' own errands.[42]

Where a modernist such as Simmel imagined the city as a stage for the private psychological dramas of its individual denizens, the posthuman perspective documents a city of multiple, conflicting, and overlapping processes. If we want these insights to mean anything, we must continue to explore the strange chaos that might result. We must, as Bratton suggests, "crave to learn" about these other urban processes, to better understand the dynamic environment of the posthuman city.

Notes

1. Edward J. Blakely, "Competitive Advantage for the 21st-Century City: Can a Place-Based Approach to Economic Development Survive in a Cyberspace Age?," *Journal of the American Planning Association*, 67.2 (2001), 133–34.
2. Michel Foucault, *The Order of Things: An Archaeology of the Human Sciences*, trans. Alan Sheridan (1970; New York: Routledge, 2001), pp. 385–86.
3. Cary Wolfe, *What Is Posthumanism?* (Minneapolis: University of Minnesota Press, 2009), pp. xvi–xvii.
4. N. Katherine Hayles, *How We Became Posthuman: Virtual Bodies in Cybernetics, Literature, and Informatics* (Chicago: University of Chicago Press, 1999), pp. 2–3.
5. Rosi Braidotti, *The Posthuman* (Cambridge: Polity, 2013), p. 49.
6. Jane Bennett, *Vibrant Matter: A Political Ecology of Things* (Durham, NC: Duke University Press, 2010), p. viii.
7. Georg Simmel, "The Metropolis and Mental Life," in Gary Bridge and Sophie Watson, eds., *The Blackwell City Reader* (Malden, MA: Wiley-Blackwell, 2002), p. 11.
8. Ibid., p. 12.
9. Ash Amin and Nigel Thrift, *Cities: Reimagining the Urban* (Cambridge: Polity, 2002), p. 81.
10. Ibid., p. 82.
11. Robert. E. Hall, Biays Bowerman, Joseph Braverman, Joshua Taylor, Helen Todosow, and Udo Von Wimmersperg, "The Vision of a Smart City," Second International Life Extension Technology Workshop, Paris, September 2000, p. 1, www.osti.gov/servlets/purl/773961.
12. For an excellent account of the history of the urban command center and its entanglement with the modern smart city, see Shannon Mattern, "Mission Control: A History of the Urban Dashboard," *Places Journal* (2015), http://placesjournal.org/article/mission-control-a-history-of-the-urban-dashboard/#0.
13. Robin Levinson-King, "Row over Google's 'Secretive' Smart City," BBC News, March 23, 2018, www.bbc.com/news/world-us-canada-43493936. For early coverage of the project, see Laura Bliss, "Sidewalk Lab's Vision for the Future Gets a Little Clearer," *CityLab*, November 30, 2018, www

.citylab.com/design/2018/11/sidewalk-labs-quayside-toronto-smart-city-google-alphabet/577078/. For a further account of the pushback, see Nick Summers, "Sidewalk Labs Is under Pressure to Explain Its Smart City Dream," *Engadget*, April 5, 2019, www.engadget.com/2019/04/05/sidewalk-labs-toronto-midp/. In May 2020, Sidewalk Labs cancelled the Waterfront Toronto project citing "unprecedented economic uncertainty [. . .] in the Toronto real estate market" due to the COVID-19 pandemic. See Andrew J. Hawkins, "Alphabet's Sidewalk Labs Shuts Down Toronto Smart City Project," *The Verge*, May 7, 2020, www.theverge.com/2020/5/7/21250594/alphabet-sidewalk-labs-toronto-quayside-shutting-down.

14. A. L. Harrison, "Introduction," in Harrison, ed., *Architectural Theories of the Environment: Posthuman Territory* (New York: Routledge, 2013), p. 3.
15. Ibid., p. 11.
16. Ibid., p. 17.
17. Ibid., pp. 20–21.
18. Benjamin Bratton, "The City Wears Us: Notes on the Scope of Distributed Sensing and Sensation," *Glass Bead* 1 (2017), 1, 12.
19. Bratton, *The Stack: On Software and Sovereignty* (Cambridge, MA: MIT Press, 2016), p. xviii.
20. Ibid., p. xviii.
21. In addition to featuring a narrator who is an individual who was once part of a collective that was, as a whole, the brain of spaceship, Leckie's novels are notable for being narrated by a character who speaks a language that does not feature gender pronouns, as the Radchaai do not differentiate between genders. To keep with this convention, and to highlight the narrator's status as an individual who was once a ship, I use "she" for Breq and any of the human characters, and "it" to refer to any of the ship and space station AIs (including when Breq was *Justice of Toren*).
22. My assertion that Leckie's fiction centers on capturing the experience of being a truly intelligent city is further confirmed by the publication of *The Raven Tower* (2019), her first fantasy novel. *Raven Tower* is a variation on the plot of *Hamlet* but told from the perspective of the castle, which has been inhabited by an ancient god (who is originally a very smart rock).
23. Bratton, *The Stack*, p. 251.
24. Ibid., p. 251.
25. Ibid., p. 252.
26. Ann Leckie, *Ancillary Justice* (London: Orbit, 2013), p. 25.
27. Ibid., p. 13.
28. Leckie, *Ancillary Sword* (London: Orbit, 2014), p. 46.
29. Ibid., p. 1.
30. Bratton's understanding of geopolitics and state power, especially in terms of constituting friend and foe, is heavily indebted to Carl Schmitt's work on *nomos*. For more information, see the "*Nomos* of the Cloud" chapter in *The Stack*, pp. 19–40.
31. Bratton, *The Stack*, p. 150.

32. Ibid., p. 150.
33. Leckie, *Ancillary Mercy* (London: Orbit, 2015), p. 7.
34. Ibid., pp. 6–7, 7, 310.
35. Bratton, *The Stack*, p. 161.
36. Leckie, *Ancillary Justice*, p. 207.
37. Ibid., p. 207.
38. Ibid., pp. 207–8.
39. Bratton, *The Stack*, p. 168.
40. Ibid., p. 169.
41. Bratton, "Outing A.I.: Beyond the Turing Test," *New York Times*, February 23, 2015, http://opinionator.blogs.nytimes.com/2015/02/23/outing-a-i-beyond-the-turing-test.
42. Bratton, "The City Wears Us," 12.

CHAPTER 20

Critical Regionalism
Why Hillbilly Elegy *and Its Critics Matter to Writing about Cities*[*]

Douglas Reichert Powell

This chapter may seem at first glance misplaced, a piece on regionalism in a volume titled *The City in American Literature and Culture*. However, that very reaction helps explain why it appears in this volume. Traditional humanities versions of regionalism and urban studies have something of an uneasy relationship, probably because the two subfields use the same term, region, in very different ways. Broadly, aesthetic regionalism, descended variously from nineteenth-century local color, late nineteenth- and early twentieth-century realism, and Southern Agrarianism, is a matter of content, of the depiction of exurban spaces in terms that highlight their distinctive qualities, practices, languages, and lifeways. In urban studies, the idea of region comes more typically from planning, where it tends to be used in more integrative ways, describing how suburban and exurban spaces play a productive role in broader metropolitan relationships. For urban studies practitioners, regionalism in the humanities (often seen as synonymous with pastoralism) has sometimes been seen as nostalgic at best, archaic at worst; for regionalists in the humanities, urban studies' emphasis on the centrality of the metropole seems like a technocratic play to bring everyplace into the service of urban life.[1]

However, this sense of regional studies and urban studies as entirely separate domains, geographically and intellectually, is an ill fit with the realities of the practice of either regional studies or urban studies today. One quality the two fields share is a turn toward seeing their objects of study not as clearly defined, autonomous identities, but as zones of interaction, intervention, conflict, and change. The imperative, then, is to analyze the dynamics of a process of change rather than to identify uniquely urban or regional characteristics in a given text, what makes it

[*] In memory of Richard Reichert and Farley Zuber.

331

distinctively a product of a particular place, whether New York or Appalachia, or a particular kind of place: metropolis or hinterland. Pursuing this goal requires understanding cities and regions not as separate domains but as different ways of imagining relationships among people and places, different subject positions in the geographical imaginary, interrelated nodes of cultural, political, and economic significance.

This chapter will examine how regional artists and scholars responded to the overdetermining mass-media dominance of one version of regional life at a critical political juncture and what it tells us about how the relation of the urban and exurban United States is imagined. J. D. Vance's memoir *Hillbilly Elegy: A Memoir of a Family and a Culture in Crisis* (2016) became the vanguard of the latest of mainstream culture's periodic rediscoveries of the Appalachian region. Drawing not only on the well-established scholarly literature on the material consequences of reductive, stereotypical representations of the mountain South, and pressed on by the urgency of an election-year discourse granting these hillbilly mythologies greater consequence and authority than usual, scholars, essayists, poets, photographers, filmmakers formed a critical-regional network of counternarration. The object of this campaign was not to "cancel" Vance or to ameliorate some particular problem in the mountains but to intervene in the broader geographical imagination, collectively formed by folks in all kinds of spaces. The site of intervention for critical regionalism is not a specific, bounded location but the dynamics of cultural geography itself: region defined not against but in relation to urban spaces.

Ultimately, the chapter proposes that critical regionalism and urban studies are not separate domains at all. The urban is one kind of place, but unlike aesthetic regionalism, critical regionalism is about relationships among places and kinds of places, urban, rural, or otherwise. It intervenes in the formation of ideas of region, which is not a space-specific practice but one that maps networks of space and place, society, and culture. As I have argued elsewhere,

> to discuss region is inherently to draw connections, comparisons, articulations, and overlaps with other places, because that is what a region is: a rhetoric that connects specific local sites to a variety of other kinds of place constructions of various scales and motives. Critical regionalism is a way of making this inherent connectivity deliberate, conscious, and visible, a methodology for creating a new kind of regional representation that is not only inquisitive about the possibilities for drawing together new configurations of politics and culture, but is always conscious about its own locatedness as a critical practice.[2]

In doing so, critical regionalism joins and augments urban studies' critique of space and place to deliver on urban critic and regional planner Lewis Mumford's dictum that "Regionalism is only an instrument: its aim is the best life possible."[3]

Hillbilly Elegy's publication amid a 2016 presidential campaign framed by a dichotomy of urban and exurban voters, the cosmopolis versus the provinces, meant a busy year for American regionalism. Public discourse demonstrated time and again that the traditional tropes of regional representation – particularly the hinterlands that refuse, for better or worse, to keep up with the times – retain their power to shape the geographical imagination. Along with a harrowing narrative of a childhood among the deindustrializing underclass of Middletown, Ohio, in the urban-industrial corridor that stretches from Cincinnati to Dayton, Vance constructs in his *Elegy* a general explanation of Appalachian poverty rooted in the supposed cultural legacy of the Scots-Irish. This ethnic group's clannish habits, refined by geographical isolation, left them unprepared to thrive in the broader American milieu they encountered when they migrated from the central Appalachian Mountains to the industrial centers of the upper Midwest. While all around him families wallowed in self-defeating behavior, egged on by welfare-state entitlements, Vance himself found the traditional tools of the meritocracy to be perfectly useful to the adaptable and hard-working, and his path led from Middletown to the Marines, to Ohio State and Yale, to mentorships by financier Peter Thiel and *Battle Hymn of the Tiger Mother* (2011) author and Yale law professor Amy Chua, and a publication record before *Elegy* primarily of conservative opinion pieces.

In *Elegy*, Vance capitalizes on his nonesuch position as exception proving the rule. He generalizes, as his subtitle suggests, from his own experience in a radically dysfunctional but quixotically supportive family nominally headed by his Kentucky-born grandparents. As historian T. R. C. Hutton puts it, "Vance's personal story permits him to claim the term 'hillbilly' then scold his fellow hillbillies for their cultural and moral failures."[4] It's a paradoxical ethos, one that allows Vance to tell a story about shiftless co-workers at the tile warehouse, then conclude "it's about a culture that encourages social decay." By the end of his journey from squalor to prosperity, he looks back at Middletown to pronounce, "These problems were not created by governments or corporations or anyone else. We created them, and only we can fix them."[5]

There is nothing new or surprising in Vance's account of Greater Appalachia as a "culture in crisis"; quite the contrary, Vance joins a lineage, extending longer than a century, of authors of all political stripes offering accounts of how clannishness and self-defeating stubbornness have created a "culture of poverty" in the Appalachian region, variously defined. As a principal site of this cultural myth, Appalachia shares a corner of the geographical imaginary with the "inner city" that Vance exploits by roping Middletown's urban squalor into Greater Appalachia. This shared discursive construction of two economically marginal populations under a delimiting, disqualifying label, and the history of differentially interpreting shared situations and behaviors across the two regions divided in the popular imagination by race, suggests a connective role for critical regionalism.

What was surprising was the speed of the book's arrival in the foreground of the media landscape. "Throughout the summer of 2016 [. . .] praise was duly repeated by liberal commentators," Hutton notes, perhaps because "the book is aimed at a middle- and upper-class readership more than happy to learn that white American poverty has nothing to do with them [. . .] and everything to do with poor white folks' inherent vices."[6] By early 2018 *Elegy* had resided on the New York *Times* bestseller list for seventy-three weeks and had sold well over a million copies in all formats.[7] Over a year later, *Elegy* still ranked fourteenth on the *New York Times*'s paperback nonfiction list. Through the broad credence given his pronouncements, Vance rapidly achieved "omnipresence on television and radio [. . .] hailed as spokesperson for the white working class, the hillbilly guru."[8] His powers as Appalachian Explainer quickly telescoped. The 2017 international edition of *Elegy* featured blurbs from the *Economist* proclaiming, "you will not read a more important book about America" and from *The Independent*, broadening the scope even further, declaring *Elegy* "a great insight into Trump and Brexit." Each of these encomiums nevertheless undermines the regional specificity of Vance's narrative and implicates whiteness more generally; nevertheless, *The Independent*'s focus on similarities between rural and postindustrial communities on either side of the Atlantic also exemplifies critical regionalism.

"Trump Country"

Vance's sudden ubiquity was, of course, just one surprise in an election season filled with surprises. *Hillbilly Elegy* was part of a moment of media attention toward Appalachia that was intense enough to spawn a subgenre. An entire media apparatus seemed caught flatfooted by the idea that a region that had been shifting to the right since Reagan and had been all but vacated by national Democrats for several election cycles intended to vote for the Republican candidate. Reporters were dispatched to that most Appalachian of Appalachias, the Coalfields, and the subgenre of the Trump Country piece was born.

As Elizabeth Catte asserts, "'Trump Country' pieces share a willingness to use flawed representations of Appalachia to shore up narratives of an extreme 'other America' that can be condemned or redeemed to suit one's purpose."[9] In the wake of the 2016 election outcome, condemnation of "the people who gave us Trump" and redemption of "the Forgotten Men" of Appalachia's putatively homogenous white male working class has been enjoined with vigor, collectively constructing what Dwight Billings terms "Trumpalachia," in which "Appalachia, composed of portions of twelve states and millions of people, becomes a unitary cultural region, then a state, and then the single cause of national political disaster."[10] Just as Vance began to appear on every cable news network, Trump Country pieces multiplied across the media spectrum, from *Daily Kos* to *Fresh Air* to *The New Yorker* to the *National Review*. Before the election, the narrator tended to wonder why these people supported Trump so vehemently, and after, how they could possibly have succeeded in electing him.

Nor was Appalachia the only regional space to provide source material for "Trump Country" profiles. Although the subgenre was born in the Coalfields, any concentration of dejected white working-class voters would do, from the Rust Belt to the Upper-Midwestern plains. As global media launched their inquiries in white, exurban, working-class spaces across the map, the genre's rules made the essay easy to replicate. Or so thought *Der Spiegel* reporter Claas Relotius, fired after filing an almost entirely fictitious profile of Fergus Falls, Minnesota, headlined "Where they pray for Trump on Sundays" (2017). In a detailed exposé for *Medium*, Fergus Falls residents Michele Anderson and Jake Krohn meticulously documented the fact that

> in 7,300 words he really only got our town's population and average annual temperature correct, and a few other basic things, like the names of businesses and public figures, things that a child could figure out in a Google search. The rest is uninhibited fiction (even as sloppy as citing an incorrect figure of citywide 70.4% electoral support for Trump, when the actual number was 62.6%).[11]

For regionalists of all stripes most of this latest burst of media fabulism promoted by people talking about regional spaces rather than with the people who live there is all too familiar. Scholars of Appalachian regionalism have in fact created a substantial shelf of books documenting the process by which "for more than 150 years" commentators "enhanced their own prestige or economic fortunes by presenting Appalachia as a space filled with contradictions that only intelligent outside observers could act on."[12]

Everyone could see this invented region coming as the political short-hand of "red states" and "blue states," or, more recently, blue nodes around urban areas and red swaths encompassing every place else became conventional wisdom. This even though every place is in fact at least tinged purple.[13] Even in New York City, where Donald Trump received only 18 percent of the vote, he comfortably carried Staten Island; indeed, he carried some predominantly white-ethnic precincts of that borough, Brooklyn, and Queens with over 80 percent of the vote.[14] On the other hand, in McDowell County, West Virginia, where Trump defeated Clinton 74 to 23 percent, only 6,200 of 17,500 registered voters turned out, meaning a decisive majority of the county supported none of the above.[15] Yet as the Trump-Country tropes indicate, Trump's election invested American political and cultural discourse with a stronger, more pervasive sense of a Manichean split between rural and small-town America and the nation's major urban centers.

Indeed, Vance's theory of region is better described as nationalism. His notion of a "Greater Appalachia" appears to be derived almost entirely from a 2011 popular history, Colin Woodward's *American Nations*, whose premise is that "eleven rival regional cultures" occupy clearly delineated spaces on the North American map. Greater Appalachia flows away from the Blue Ridge, down the Ohio, and across the Midwest to Central Texas, and includes Middletown and other Rust Belt destinations for the labor force in the twentieth century, blunting the rebuttal that Vance was not even raised in Appalachia. To Woodward, these spaces are less regions than nations because "by the time they agreed to share a federated state, each had long exhibited the characteristics of nationhood," particularly "a group of people who share – or believe they share – a common culture, ethnic origin, language, historical experience, artifacts, and symbols." Greater Appalachia's denizens, Woodward writes, are heirs to a "clan-based warrior culture" that remains "a volatile, insurgent force within North American society to the present day."[16] Vance concurs. Declaring himself "a Scots-Irish hillbilly at heart" he claims a "cultural tradition" that includes "many good traits – an intense sense of loyalty, a fierce dedication to family and country – but also many bad ones. We do not like outsiders or people who are different from us, whether the difference lies in how they look, how they act, or most important, how they talk."[17]

Woodward deflects objections that he homogenizes the actual diversity
of regional populations by invoking Wilbur Zelinsky's 1973 Doctrine of
First Effective Settlement: "the specific characteristics of the first group
able to effect a viable, self-perpetuating society are of crucial significance
for the later social and cultural geography of the area."[18] To the assertion
that cultural geography has discussed this matter further in the intervening
four decades, Woodward concedes that "digging into regional cultures can
be like peeling an onion" but insists that the enumerated dominant "values,
attitudes, and political preferences of my eleven nations [. . .] trump[] the
implications of finer-grain analysis."[19] Having established these regional
characters, Woodward remixes anecdotes from North American history
into eleven parallel narrative tracks that cast these characters in sharper
relief. Vance applies Woodward's form in a simpler way, since he has only
one of Woodward's ethnic nations to account for, but he deploys the same
tactic of stitching together a cultural narrative that he offers as the factual
justification for his generalizations.

Contemporary regionalists generally recognize, however, that even
though in popular discourse they seem antithetical, regionalism and
urbanism have a complex and long-standing relationship to one another
both practically and conceptually. Ironically, the perception of urban and
rural, of metropolis and region, as inherently antithetical is one of the
most long-standing elements of that relationship, and these moments of
overt, almost hysterical cultural reinforcement of the boundary lines
signal a time for heightened attention to whatever is motivating these
spatial rhetorics of division. For critical regionalism, the very act of
denying the existence of connections presents an opportunity to point
to complex interrelationships.

Other Appalachias

"The reality is more complex" than Vance would have it, as John Gaventa
observes. Against his simultaneously too-specific and too-general account
of Appalachian culture stands a host of experiences, "of action and
inaction, authoritarianism and challenges to it – sitting together side by
side simultaneously. The challenge is to understand this complexity, and to
work with it to build a new kind of politics, one which bridges the local to
the national and global." Such work, on Appalachia or any other region,
will build on "decades of committed scholar-activism[. . .] deeply rooted in
historical analysis, a commitment to place, as well as a recognition of how
this region fits in the broader global system of a development model based

on exploitation of rural resources."[20] Among the texts advancing this
legacy are Elizabeth Catte's monograph *What You Are Getting Wrong
about Appalachia* (2018), Ashley Rubin and Sally York's film *hillbilly*
(2019), and Meredith McCarroll and Anthony Harkins's collection
Appalachian Reckoning: A Region Responds to Hillbilly Elegy (2019).

Elizabeth Catte was first out of the gate. While her title might apply to
any number of regional commentators present and past, most readers knew
before they picked it up that Catte was responding directly to Vance, going
beyond correcting errors to demonstrating powerfully that the historical
record supports narratives of the region that point to conclusions far
different from his own. "Since Vance and his fans have made it acceptable
to remake Appalachia in one's own image," Catte announces her intention to

> create a volume with an image made in my own. Far from being monolithic,
> helpless, and degraded, this image of Appalachia is radical and diverse. This
> image of Appalachia does not deflect the problems of the region but simply
> recognizes the voices and actions of those who have struggled against them,
> often sacrificing their health, comfort, even their lives. It is an image
> projected by bodies against machines and bodies on picket lines and bodies
> that most assuredly are not always white.[21]

Stylistically and thematically not given to pulling her punches, Catte never
resorts to shallow respectability politics, driven by a desire not to be
considered backward by others. She rejects entirely the line of thinking
that J. D. Vance is not "really" Appalachian because Middletown, Ohio, is
not even in Appalachia. In fact, the industrial cities and towns of the
Midwest were termini of the so-called Hillbilly Highway, the path of
Appalachian diaspora in the 1930s–40s memorialized in *The Dollmaker*
(1954), Kentucky-native Harriette Arnow's novel of a family's migration to
Detroit. Catte welcomes Vance's connections to the Rust Belt as an
opportunity to talk about the histories of labor and political economy
that Vance disregards. What Vance positions as places connected to the
Scots-Irish mountain-homeland-like colonies, Catte recasts as lines of
solidarity connecting mountain histories to broader spaces. Even her
choice of publisher signals transregional interconnections; Belt
Publishing, of Cleveland, Ohio, is engaged in a kind of critical regionalist
publication project, creating forums for place-centered writing, especially
narratives that rethink received wisdom about place identities. Most of
their list concerns the cities of the Upper Midwest and the Rust Belt (hence
the name), but their support of an Appalachian project that shares their

sensibility and political commitments exemplifies critical regionalist connection at the level of production.

The association of Rust Belt press and Appalachian subject is appropriate, too, because in many ways the problematic status of Appalachia in the geographical imaginary is closely related to the production of negative stereotypes of other people and places. The hillbilly myth validates more racist accounts of the same traits, transported from the exurbs to the inner city, while implying that those stereotypes cannot be racist because they also apply to white folks, despite differences in response to, for example, the crack and opioid epidemics and sympathy directed to users. Catte and Belt Press's collaboration highlights that if the mutually reinforcing stereotypes can be deployed to justify all manner of punitive and destructive forms of cultural and material underdevelopment, then urban and regional spaces have common cause in dismantling those cultural complexes and resisting the economic logic that drives them. It's not a case of us-versus-them, with the regional and the urban as separate spheres; critical regionalism demonstrates how marking off *us* from *them* obscures the connections within a broad network of interrelated forms of exploitation.

It also provides an example of how urban and regional spaces can be defined by interaction and interrelation rather than difference. The question of whether Vance is really a hillbilly, or whether or not Middletown is really in Greater Appalachia or the Rust Belt, just aren't important here. More revelatory is what their points of common interest illuminate, at a particular point where urban and regional studies overlap. Urban and working-class literature scholar Sherry Lee Linkon characterizes deindustrialization as "both toxic and still active in the lives of many working-class Americans," not an era but a "half-life" of gradual transformation that therefore requires "focusing on how working-class people experience and interpret changes that are 'massive and multifaceted.'"[22] Catte's work essentially substitutes "Appalachian" for "working-class," doing with space what Linkon does with time: the influence and power of concepts of Appalachia extend into cultural networks in ways that have no clear limits, no final terminus. Deindustrialization is not a clearly demarcated period any more than Appalachia is a rigidly demarcated landscape, and to try to understand one requires drawing connections with the other.

Focusing on the kinds of histories and experiences in the Appalachian Mountains that inconvenience Vance's summary judgment, *What You Are Getting Wrong* pursues two objectives, "to provide critical commentary about who benefits from the omission of these voices, using Appalachian history to push back against monolithic representations of the region, and to openly celebrate the lives, actions, and legacies those ignored in popular commentary about Appalachia."[23] Catte develops two related themes in counterpoint throughout the book. First, she traces the lineage of Vance's learned-helplessness and culture-of-poverty narrative in eugenic thinking that was not only virulently racist toward nonwhites but attempted to draw naturalized lines of biological difference within whiteness that marked out mountain communities' lifeways as inherently inferior. Catte places Vance alongside Charles Murray (cited approvingly in *Elegy*), *Night Comes to the Cumberlands* (1963), author Harry Caudill's late-career embrace of social Darwinism, and Thomas Henry and Mandel Sherman's *Hollow Folk* (1933), whose lurid descriptions of mountaineer atavism, a "monoculture degraded through idleness and inbreeding," helped form the rationale for institutionalizing and/or involuntarily sterilizing many of the book's subjects at the Virginia State Colony for Epileptics and Feebleminded when their land was taken to develop of Shenandoah National Park.[24]

Not only does Catte's genealogical work here evince that Vance's supposed revelations about the region have been proclaimed time and again, it also demonstrates that they have real, material consequences for regional life. These narratives seem inevitably to end with land stolen and bodies broken, a tradition that stretches to the dispossession of the Native residents by Anglo-European settler colonists. *Hillbilly Elegy* is shown here to be less a master narrative than one part of a mosaic of representations designed to Other those settler-colonists' descendants for whom the American Dream did not come true. It underwrites the resource-rich Appalachian Mountains' convenient status as a "sacrifice zone" – a space that, in the words of geographer Hugo Reinert, has "been destroyed, poisoned, or otherwise rendered uninhabitable *in return for* some sort of benefit," in this case to provide power and raw materials to industrial cities that became wealthy.[25]

In this sense the "sacrifice zone" trope reinforces notions of urban and exurban distinction and separation – despite the fact that it is used in similar ways to categorize urban and exurban spaces. The shiftless dependent label is applied with similar effect on hillbillies and "urban dwellers." The work of Charles Murray exemplifies this adaptability: where his 1994 work with Richard Herrmann, *The Bell Curve: Intelligence and Class Structure in American Life,* insinuated that a connection between race and genetics helped account for urban poverty, his 2012 *Coming Apart: The State of White America, 1960–2010* advances a similar theory to account for the segment of white America that includes Vance's version of hillbillies. Indeed, the urban and regional applications are mutually reinforcing;

Vance's descriptions of white welfare queens imply that *welfare queen* cannot be a racist epithet if it also applies to poor white people.[26] The adaptability of the trope becomes a spurious warrant for its factuality. In both cases the trope creates an image of people who are a problem to be acted upon and solved, and whose resources are, therefore, forfeit.

This status is adaptable and hard to shake, a self-fulfilling prophecy. The Appalachian "sacrifice zone" that was a fit site for indigenous genocide, euphemized as *removal*, morphs into a resource-providing and worker-sacrificing interior, whose contribution to national economic development expresses itself in mountaintop removal and prison construction, often on the very same site. Whether keeping the lights on (as the pro-coal bumper sticker has it) or making the dark less frightening for the economic winners by warehousing the urban poor in the prison–industrial complex, the idea of Appalachia is perpetuated as an abject space facilitating the rise of more sophisticated, urbane development elsewhere.

What You Are Getting Wrong's second tactic is to show how the same places and practices that Vance claims lead inevitably to disempowerment support an alternative genealogy of historical, political, and social narratives that Catte quilts together, from a 1938 political dustup between the left-leaning West Virginia Federal Writer's Project director Bruce Crawford and anti-union West Virginia governor Homer Holt through the mid-century history of civil rights education and transregional organizing at east Tennessee's Highlander School, where Martin Luther King, Jr., learned to sing "We Shall Overcome," to the 2015 organizing work by the Letcher County Governance Project to stymie a $400 million prison project backed by Congressman and "Prince of Pork" Hal Rogers. Her culminating example, a tale of civic mobilization to preserve from destruction via mountaintop-removal mining the summit of West Virginia's Blair Mountain, which was the site of a 1921 pitched battle between the United Mine Workers of America and law enforcement and militiamen under the leadership of Logan County Sheriff Don Chapin. This incident combines a historical narrative of political activism, a contemporary example of political and environmental action, and an unambiguous illustration of why and how the interplay of regional narratives can have direct, material consequences for the people of the region and indeed, its physical landscape.[27]

What You Are Getting Wrong about Appalachia thus shows how regional narratives not only construct the past, but also shape the present and impact the future. The story worlds we create about places reflect and define the horizons of possibility for those places, so Catte's rhetorical strategy is to multiply possibilities. Her book creates a map of outbound connections, not delimiting borders, like Vance or Woodward, who attempt to dominate via definition. Her discussions of alternative Appalachian experiences offer opportunities to explore other texts; to that end the volume concludes with a list of suggested resources for further exploration rather than a credentialing list of works cited.

Establishing that other voices and versions of the region are possible and the struggle for visibility and voice is ongoing creates space for new accounts of hillbilly identity informed by an interconnective critical regionalism rather than an inward-turning nationalism. Into this space came Los Angeles–based filmmakers York and Rubin, whose documentary *hillbilly* offers a multivalent analysis of that cultural category, an analysis in which the overdetermined stereotype is only one strand of the larger articulation of social identities (class, gender, ethnicity, and sexuality), given a specific shape by the material relationships among the southern mountains and the rest of the world. York and Rubin's project contrasts significantly with Catte's in that it does not directly reference J. D. Vance (at least in part because this project was well under way before *Elegy*'s publication), yet the film shares more with *Hillbilly Elegy* than half a title. Both are tales of young people from white, working-class backgrounds able to achieve in – and to leave – a cultural landscape more widely recognized for its limitations than its opportunities, and who overcome social stigma to prosper in metropolitan social and cultural circles. *hillbilly*'s through line is York's biographical trajectory from childhood in Meathouse Holler, Pike County, Kentucky, to the Los Angeles film industry. It could easily have mirrored Vance's narrative as a tale of the exception, the one who got away, explaining why the rest are stuck there. Instead *hillbilly* is a tale of York making, maintaining, and repairing connections between her family network and the new vectors she's created in her personal, professional, and political life.

If *hillbilly* shares structural traits and a sense of occasion with *Elegy*, it shares a purpose with *What You Are Getting Wrong*.[28] Like Catte, York and Rubin embrace the constructedness of place and region, and create a version of Appalachia that emphasizes the unrecognized heterogeneity of life there. *Hillbilly* joins *What You Are Getting Wrong* in reexamining the legacy of Appalachia's place in the popular geographical imagination and the consequences that hillbilly discourses have for the material conditions of people in the Appalachian Mountains today. In one strand, York catches up with Billy Redden, a resident of North Georgia who indelibly shaped all discussions of hillbilly imagery as the banjo-playing boy in *Deliverance*

(Boorman, 1974). He seems sadly cognizant of the fact that while *Deliverance* advanced a lot of careers, he has little to show for having reinforced the image of inbred mountain families by "starring" in its most-referenced scene. Building on Catte's project of articulating diverse Appalachian stories and experiences into a regional composite portrait, York includes commentary and reflection from Berea College–based author Silas House and his partner, writer Jason Howard, who provide something of a narrative counterpoint to York's first-person perspective. The camera also travels with a diverse band of culture creators who claim their mountain home as part of their identity – "artists, poets, activists, queer musicians, 'Affrilachian' poets, and intersectional feminists – all unexpected voices emerging from this historically misunderstood region," the film's web site asserts, and intersperses the commentary of scholars in Appalachian studies to confer a little old-fashioned authority while weaving a broader context for the featured stories.[29]

The film moves inexorably toward the central mystery of the Trump-Country mythos, Election Day 2016. As the cameras follow several of the documentary's principals to the polls, then watch them reckoning with the results, the film provides a perspective rarely seen in the media: residents of the Appalachian region witnessing the dawn of the Trump era with despondence, disillusion, horror. We certainly see Trump supporters as York's own grandmother, uncle, and cousins enjoy the incoming election results, but we do so with their aunt/cousin/granddaughter (and her camera crew) sitting with them. The Trump-Country script would have them insufferably gloat with the cameras rolling, but this isn't a Trump rally; it's a living room, and they are a family. There is even a moment where you can see York's uncle tentatively try to understand how she is feeling. There have been plenty of sensational depictions of families and friends divided by this election, but the reality is not always the regional narrative that sells best.

It does not lessen the impact of watching other mountain residents mentally and emotionally prepare themselves for renewed campaigns of political and cultural marginalization; these people, who know enough about the way political economy and media work, greet the prospect with a dread rooted in experience. *hillbilly* isn't so much about polishing up the eponymous image as it is about extending it to include a wider range of experiences. Yes, there are dedicated Trump supporters, but they, too, are personally connected to wider worlds, not isolated in the freehold of the Scots-Irish. Like *What You Are Getting Wrong*, *hillbilly* builds a network of outbound connections, providing curious viewers opportunities to find the poetry of Frank X. Walker, the fiction of Silas House, the music of Amethyst Kiah, the documentary video of the Appalachian Media Institute. The film's academics form a kind of human bibliography of Appalachian cultural studies, itself a diverse and heterogeneous group of people and expertise.

Harkins and McCarroll's *Appalachian Reckoning: A Region Responds to* Hillbilly Elegy, likewise, is outward-facing in its "attempts to respond to those who feel like they understand Appalachia 'now that they have read *Hillbilly Elegy*' and to push back against and complicate those understandings." It joins *What You Are Getting Wrong* in calling out Vance's work directly (and includes Catte as a contributor on the use of *Elegy* in the classroom) and embraces the premise that if Vance can remake the region in his own image, then so can anyone else. Asking "What other Appalachian voices have been drowned out in the flood of attention Vance and his book have garnered?"[30] *Reckoning*'s answer comes in the form of a 420-page collection featuring forty-one contributions from thirty-eight authors – including Affrilachian poet Crystal Good and West Virginia photographer Roger May, both of whom appear in *hillbilly* – that range from essays in cultural studies to poems and photographs in a volume divided into two sections: "Considering *Hillbilly Elegy*" and "Beyond *Hillbilly Elegy*."

These sections represent the volume's two principal strategies, shared with *What You Are Getting Wrong*, of contextualizing Vance's account, thereby challenging its pretense to primacy, and constructing a constellation of counternarratives that emphasize the diverse and dynamic nature of regional experience. Law professor Lisa Pruitt's analysis "What *Hillbilly Elegy* Reveals about Race in Twenty-First-Century America" and Kentucky writer Ivy Brashear's commentary "Keep Your 'Elegy': The Appalachia I Know Is Very Much Alive" give way to poet Kelly Norman Ellis's "Antebellum Cookbook," novelist and illustrator Robert Gipe's autobiographical reflection "How Appalachian I Am," and photographer Meg Wilson's "Olivia at the Intersection." Like *hillbilly*, *Reckoning* quilts a regional portrait from personal narratives and aesthetic representations that is more protean than essays in regional pathology (Vance, or Kevin D. Williamson's *National Review* essay "The White Ghetto" [2013]) give Appalachia credit for being. *Reckoning*'s contributors are fighting for cultural bandwidth by pushing back against delimiting diagnoses, but they are not seeking approval or validation. They offer a portrait of a place unafraid to stand on its own merits and demand cultural justice in broader forums.

Along with *What You Are Getting Wrong* and *hillbilly*, *Reckoning* acknowledges an ironic benefit to Vance's celebrity and the light it casts on the region. The editors observe that

> despite what the majority of our contributors find to be *Hillbilly Elegy*'s flaws and even damages, they share the sense that the public "rediscovery" of the region that *Hillbilly Elegy* and the conceptual construction of "Trumpalachia" [. . .] have engendered should also be seen as an opportunity – a chance to reclaim Appalachia and to help those unfamiliar with the region to recognize its complexities and diversities.[31]

Through its juxtaposition of many Appalachian voices and locations, *Reckoning* broadens the scope, already expanded by Catte and York and Rubin, and implies that the representation of Appalachia is not a choice between two alternatives, one from the left and one from the right, but a process of negotiating a broad network of narratives that shape and reflect the lives and legacies of people in the Appalachian Mountains. Vance is not wrong about his experience and is perfectly entitled to construct its broader political meanings according to his own worldview and conscience. What he cannot do, these texts declare, is to assume the authority of his version over all of hillbilly culture when there are lots of other authors, and lots of forms that authority may take. The broader geographical imagination of any region anywhere is a cultural complex that has material implications and consequences that resonate through the network of relationships that create and sustain it. Equity, inclusion, and cultural justice require acknowledgment of Appalachia's, or any region's, variegation.

The very act of bringing into existence an intricate, articulate, and diverse expression of regional concerns is a powerful refutation of Vance's vision of a region too enervated and broken to participate meaningfully in a cosmopolitan world. But in these texts we see an Appalachia that is not the object of some kind of external intervention to give the people what they need, but a place inhabited by people determined to intervene in the cultural constructions that circulate in mass culture industries centered in urban spaces far (in more ways than one) from the southern mountains. This cultural ecology is not defensive crypto-nationalism, nor is it an articulation of a nostalgic and pastoral aesthetic regionalism. It is a critical regionalism that does not accept as its first principle that a region is a traceable, coherent geographical and cultural space with an interior and an exterior. Yet even as this critical regionalist network of resistance and response has had its effect on the cultural ecology that makes up the notion of Appalachia, Ron Howard produced his film adaptation of *Hillbilly Elegy* on a $45 million budget, nearly as much as the Appalachian Regional Commission's entire budget ($50 million) to create an "investment package to expand and diversify the economy in Appalachia's coal-impacted communities" – and now additionally charged with combating the opioid epidemic.[32] However much critical regionalist response has intervened in shaping understanding of the cultural ecology, the money keeps flowing in the direction of popular mythology.

Addressing the problems of either urban centers or more geographically and culturally peripheral spaces like the Appalachians requires understanding how these problems are inflected by the relationships between and among such spaces. Mapping this skein of relationships is necessarily multivocal and multimodal: how else to even begin to account for reciprocities both material and cultural, as far-flung spaces support cosmopolitan cultures with natural resources, storage for waste, and remote sites of incarceration, without pitting the subjects of urban and regional underdevelopment against each other in a zero-sum struggle by harping on their supposed innate differences.

It will require considerably more historical perspective to even begin to understand the full implications of how the complex dynamics of urban and regional imaginaries shaped the events of 2016 and their ongoing consequences. The first half of 2020 geometrically increased the questions to be asked. Electoral politics, economic collapse, pandemic, an upsurge of confrontations and demonstrations over the enduring legacies of race, all have mobilized traditional discourses of the cultural gap between the metropole and the provinces – in many ways red and blue spaces appear to inhabit completely different political economies more than ever. But at the same time, vectors of disease, tremors of resistance, flows of people and images, historical narratives and their discontents vividly underscore not only the concatenation of relationships, material and otherwise, that locate us all in time and space but also the fact that they are always in flux.

Maybe this time around we might have more of a shot at understanding how the problems and priorities of urban studies and the shape of a metropolitan-centered mass culture is interconnected with, inflected by, and inter-reliant on regional landscapes, to see places like Appalachia not as sacrifice zones on the periphery but vital cultural centers in their own right – centers that include both urban and rural spaces and everything in between, powered by the dynamics among them all. Maybe, thanks at least in part to the work of critical regionalist counternarratives, we can see regionalism and urbanism as integral to each other. The election year of

2016 showed us, and 2020 demonstrated on an even bigger scale, that the power of stereotypes and divisive rhetorics is enduring and demands reckoning with from every possible angle because their effects are felt in all directions.

One of the most hopeful aspects of the multimodal critical regionalist intervention described here is the way the collaborative, integrative impulse behind the whole thing is encoded in the texts it produced. The editors of *Reckoning* appear in *hillbilly*, Catte contributes to *Reckoning*, and all the mosaic of contributors come to shared concerns from the places where they are through the means and methods they possess. This generative network is an important example for urbanists and regionalists alike to reflect on as we all confront, from the places where we are, this intricate nest of troubles we all find ourselves in. As we work from our various locations to understand how culture and representation shape these matters of actual life and death, we're going to need our interconnections, to see how our approaches can augment each other in the service of understanding not only how culture works but how it could work better.

Notes

1. See Douglas Reichert Powell, *Critical Regionalism: Connecting Politics and Culture in the American Landscape* (Chapel Hill: University of North Carolina Press, 2007), pp. 147–50.
2. Ibid., p. 27.
3. Lewis Mumford, "Regional Planning," in Vincent B. Canizaro, ed., *Architectural regionalism: Collected Writings on Place, Identity, Modernity, and Tradition* (New York: Princeton Architectural Press, 2007), p. 243. (The essay was originally a lecture delivered to the Institute of Public Affairs, Round Table on Regionalism, University of Virginia, July 6–11, 1931.)
4. T. R. C. Hutton, "Hillbilly Elitism," in Anthony Harkins and Meredith McCarroll, eds., *Hillbilly Reckoning: A Region Responds to Hillbilly Elegy* (Morgantown: West Virginia University Press, 2019), p. 25.
5. J. D. Vance, *Hillbilly Elegy: A Memoir of a Family and a Culture in Crisis* (New York: Harper, 2016), pp. 7, 256.
6. Hutton, "Hillbilly Elitism," pp. 22–23.
7. Harkins and McCarroll, "Introduction: Why This Book?," in *Hillbilly Reckoning,* p. 1.
8. Dwight Billings, "Once upon a Time in 'Trumpalachia': *Hillbilly Elegy*, Personal Choice, and the Blame Game," in Harkins and M. McCarroll, eds., *Hillbilly Reckoning,* p. 42.
9. Elizabeth Catte, *What You Are Getting Wrong about Appalachia* (Cleveland, OH: Belt Press, 2018), p. 35.

10. Billings, "Once upon a Time," p. 52.

11. Michele Anderson and Jake Krohn, "Der Spiegel Journalist Messed with the Wrong Small Town," *Medium*, December 19, 2018, http://medium.com/@micheleanderson/der-spiegel-journalist-messed-with-the-wrong-small-town-d92f3e0e01a7.

12. Catte, *What You Are Getting Wrong*, p. 35. See, among others, Anthony Harkins, *Hillbilly: A Cultural History of an American Icon* (2003); Allen Batteau, *The Invention of Appalachia* (1990); Henry Shapiro, *Appalachia on Our Mind: The Southern Mountains and Mountaineers in the American Consciousness, 1870–1920* (1978); and John Gaventa, *Power and Powerlessness: Quiescence and Rebellion in an Appalachian Valley* (1980).

13. Physicist Mark Newman demonstrates this point graphically, making cartograms based on county level election data, colored on a gradient from red to blue based on the margin of victory: "Maps of the 2016 US Presidential Election Results," November 10, 2016, www-personal.umich.edu/~mejn/election/2016/.

14. Matthew Block, Larry Buchanan, Josh Katz, and Kevin Quealy, "An Extremely Detailed Map of the 2016 Election," *New York Times*, July 25, 2018, www.nytimes.com/interactive/2018/upshot/election-2016-voting-precinct-maps.html#4.98/36.86/-77.02.

15. Carrie Hodousek, "Unofficial Election Results Show West Virginia Had 57 Percent Voter Turnout," *MetroNews: The Voice of West Virginia*, November 9, 2016, https://wvmetronews.com/2016/11/09/unofficial-election-results-show-west-virginia-had-57-percent-voter-turnout/.

16. Colin Woodward, *American Nations: A History of the Eleven Rival Regional Cultures of North America* (New York: Penguin Books, 2011), pp. 3–4, 201.

17. Vance, *Hillbilly Elegy*, p. 3.

18. Quoted in Woodward, *American Nations*, p. 16.

19. Ibid., p. 18.

20. Gaventa, "Power and Powerlessness in an Appalachian Valley – Revisited," *Journal of Peasant Studies* 46 (2019), 450.

21. Catte, *What You Are Getting Wrong*, p. 15.

22. Sherry Lee Linkon, *The Half-Life of Deindustrialization: Working-Class Writing about Economic Restructuring* (Ann Arbor: University of Michigan Press, 2018), pp. 6, 7.

23. Ibid., p. 10.

24. Quoted in Catte, *What You Are Getting Wrong*, p. 75.

25. Hugo Reinert, "Notes from a Projected Sacrifice Zone," *ACME: An International Journal for Critical Geographies* 17.2 (2018), 599.

26. See, most vividly, Vance, *Hillbilly Elegy*, p. 57.

27. Ibid., pp. 117–21.

28. York began *hillbilly* as a cultural-history documentary and critique of the stereotype focused on her family's experience with hillbilly stereotypes and iconography. When the election, Trump Country, and *Hillbilly Elegy* happened at once, she reoriented the film such that it counters Vance's

conservative, white-male take from his cosmopolitan present on a culture he deems ready for its eulogy, with a liberal feminist's return to find that the vibrant landscape and culture place still exerts a powerful influence on who she is in the world.

29. http://hillbillymovie.com/.
30. Harkins and McCarroll, "Introduction: Why This Book?," pp. 1, 3.
31. Ibid., p. 3.
32. Dave McNary, "Netflix Boards Ron Howard's 'Hillbilly Elegy' in $45 Million Deal," *Variety,* January 25, 2019, http://variety.com/2019/film/news/ron-howard-hillbilly-elegy-netflix-1203117934/; "Legislative Update: Senate Appropriations Committee Approves FY 2020 Funding for ARC," *Appalachian Regional Commission Newsroom,* September 2019, www.arc.gov/news/article.asp?ARTICLE_ID=676.

City and Polis

Kevin R. McNamara

> You can have democracy without consensus, but you have no democracy
> without dissent.
>
> Stathis Gourgouris, "Democracy is a Tragic Regime" (2014)

"What is the city but the people?" Sicinus asks in Shakespeare's *Coriolanus*
(ca. 1608). Nothing, Hannah Arendt would answer; she defined the polis as
"the organization of the people as it arises out of acting and speaking
together ... no matter where they happen to be."[1] Yet who comprise the
people? Is it citizens of the nation resident in the city or all established
residents of age regardless of national citizenship, as was not uncommon in
the nineteenth century?[2] Is a populace *the people* only when it speaks it one
voice? Is it a fraction (by class, race, or ideology) whose authority derives
from the mantle of authenticity claimed for it, as it is when Chicago ward
boss Mike Scully and socialist organizers invoke the authority of the
people – the largely voiceless immigrant laborers – to further their campaigns in Upton Sinclair's *The Jungle* (1906)? Or is it, as Stathis
Gourgouris's observation implies, that the advent of dissensus engenders
the people as a collective agency?

As with so many debates in US political history and culture, discussions of
democracy often return to the primal conflict between Thomas Jefferson's
devolved agrarian republic and Alexander Hamilton's powerful national
administration. Thus, Michael Hardt undertook to excavate a radical democratic Jefferson in his 2007 introduction to a selection of the Virginian's
writings and an essay that same year in *American Quarterly*, while Christian
Parenti subsequently rebuffed that effort in his own work of reclamation,
"Reading Hamilton from the Left" (2014). Hardt found in Jefferson an
overarching concern for how "'public happiness' can be instituted by government and [. . .] how self-rule and democracy can be realized" by a populace
that transforms itself into *the people* through the pedagogical and political
activity of self-government, including generational revolution that removes

the hand of the past from the tiller of history.³ Yet how the commoning practices in heterotopic spaces that he acclaims, and the and practice of love as affective communion that he and Antonio Negri deem necessary to their flourishing, will scale up to a twenty-first-century city of strangers whose lives, beliefs, and desires radically differ is never specified.⁴

Reproving Hardt for merely reprising the long-standing political and cultural tradition (sketched in this volume's Introduction) that romanticizes Jefferson as "rural, idealistic, and democratic," while rendering Hamilton "urban, pessimistic, and authoritarian," Parenti responds that Hardt (as well as environmental activists drawn to Jeffersonian localism) willfully ignores the inapplicability of social and political models drawn from an age of agricultural economies to contemporary industrial and postindustrial economies.⁵ In a time of prolonged crisis, when "the old redistributive agenda is not enough" to address the scale of economic inequality and "the economy must also be significantly *rebuilt* around a clean energy sector," Parenti concludes, the United States needs an activist state helmed by someone with the vision and political skill that Hamilton summoned when he secured the new nation's industrial and financial sectors, a version of the argument for employing Hamiltonian means toward Jeffersonian ends that Herbert Croly advocated a century earlier in *The Promise of American Life* (1909). Nevertheless, Parenti leaves us with no sense of the dirigist state's relation to democratic practices, or mention of who might install the new Hamilton and in whose name he would act. If one might expect Parenti to invoke *the people* in that function, the very reason this figure is necessary is the lack of popular commitment to change in an "American society [that] is very far from facing the crisis."⁶

Utopian fictions dating at least to Edward Bellamy's *Looking Backward, 2000–1887* (1888), William Dean Howells's *A Traveler from Altruria* (1894), and Charlotte Perkins Gilman's *Herland* (1915), if not John Winthrop's "A Model of Christian Charity" (1630), offer a wealth of blueprints for restructuring the social contract, but they tell us little about the actual practice of democracy because their societies' economic and social problems have all been solved, so their polities lack the dissensus that engenders democratic activity. The literary history of US cities, on the other hand, provides a wealth of conflict among characters and constituencies, along with considerations and representations of what democracy requires of the urban demos.

Walt Whitman was the first significant American poet-theorist of urban democracy, and of love as the basis of a democratic ethos. To George

Kateb, the poet-persona's vow to judge "not as the judge judges but as the sun falling around a helpless thing" offers "the best interpretation of the democratic idea that unequals must be treated equally and [. . . a] constant appeal [. . .] to us to exercise recognition"; Martha Nussbaum further commends its "rich concrete vision that does justice to human lives."[7] Other recent critics detect a more radical Whitman whose political vistas resonate with Hardt and Negri's project and their brief invocations of the poet in *Commonwealth* (2009). Highlighting the influence of "[Whitman's] hero Jefferson" on the poet's political imagination, political theorist Jason Frank interprets "Whitman's aesthetic democracy [as one that] does not simply call for 'receptivity or responsiveness to as much of the world as possible,' but for an embrace of a world always in the process of becoming other than it is." This commitment leads Frank's Whitman, like Hardt's Jefferson, to rebel against "the 'fossilism' of inherited institutions" in favor of democracy as a vitalizing principle embodied in the people.[8] Ryan Cull takes Whitman a step further, describing his poetic-political project as involving the reader in creating "a radical democratic social ontology" that negates all existing social categories and hierarchies and reorganizes common life around "ontological proximity" rather than "epistemological mastery." He approvingly cites Hardt and Negri's praise for how Whitman's poet-persona "models 'the love of the stranger . . . as an encounter characterized by wonder, growth, and discovery,'" that is, by the creation of new worlds of knowledge and experience in which difference matters – but, it seems, not enough to provoke dissensus.[9]

However, the turbulent human flows in which Walter Whitman was immersed, the promiscuous mixing of classes, races, native-born and immigrant in the city that his poet-persona celebrated, produced no egalitarian heterotopia. It animated a dissensual "micropolitics" of recognition that eroded the class and status distinctions that once governed public space, Mona Domosh has argued. While the practice of promenading in nineteenth-century New York sought to "stabilize[] social position by making it *visible*" in what David Scobey describes as "little drama[s] of solidarity and subordination" that kept the lower classes and the newly moneyed at bay by withholding recognition, the "tactical transgressions" of tacit norms on which Domosh focuses, both at these ritual moments and as part of the everyday life of the pavements, challenged the idea that one could ever be out of place in public.[10]

If Whitman's democratic ethos works to diminish social conflicts and barriers among the demos, democracy as political practice arises, Jacques

Rancière insists, only when a conflict arises that is not resolvable "on the basis of [existing] laws and regulations" because it is constituted by a clash "not [. . .] of competing interests or values but . . . of competing worlds." We can find an instance of this conflict of worlds, although not precisely in Rancière's sense, if we supplement the choice between Scully and the socialists that Sinclair's immigrant laborers faced with a thicker description than he offered of how those laborers evaluated their political choices.[11]

As his theme required, Sinclair drew Mike Scully as corrupt, violent, and complicit with packing-plant owners, but he did little to account for how ward bosses maintained their constituents' loyalties. The bosses were, indeed, go-betweens who played on their working-class roots to bond with their constituents even as they styled themselves to business leaders (who relied on, but nevertheless scorned, them) as political professionals adept at maintaining labor peace in the "polyglot, conflict-ridden" city.[12] What cemented working-class loyalty was neither simply the distribution of patronage nor the ignorance of Chicago's ethnic voters. As Jane Addams came to understand, without wavering on her commitment to reforming municipal politics, her neighbors' political calculations were shaped by cultural traditions and "the element of reality always brought into the political struggle in [. . .] a neighborhood where politics deal so directly with getting a job and earning a living" in ways that remained largely as opaque to middle- and upper-class reformers as the reformers' own discourse did to men like Sinclair's Jurgis Rudkis. If the popular support for Johnny Powers, the Irish-born, former grocer's apprentice turned Chicago alderman whose district included Hull House, significantly derived from the fact that "approximately one out of every five voters in the nineteenth ward at that time held a job dependent on [his] good will," Powers's constituent services went still further. Addams's catalog of those activities includes Powers's attendance bearing gifts at weddings and christenings, distributing "six tons of turkeys, and four or more tons of ducks and geese" to constituents at Christmas, ensuring that funerals sent off the deceased with pomp and dignity, intervening with the courts to set aside fines and judgments for minor offenses and misdemeanors, or attesting to a defendant's character to procure leniency from a judge who might owe his seat to the alderman.[13]

Where reformers saw rank corruption, and they were disgusted with politicians and frustrated with (and by) voters, Addams came to realize that the disagreement between reformers and the poor whom they would reform concerned not only the relative evaluation of abstract principles and immediate well-being but also the definition of certain shared values.

Even if only opportunistically, when the ward boss flaunted his ethnic working-class roots and a mode of speech and action that resonated with the image of the good man held by "people, such as the South Italian peasants who live in the Nineteenth Ward," who measure goodness by mutual care and generosity, he showed respect for his constituents' folk-ways and a willingness to meet them at their level. Taking the lesson that Ralph Ellison's Invisible Man would later codify in the democratic axiom, "Responsibility rests on recognition, and recognition is a form of agreement," Addams urged,

> If we would hold to our political democracy, some pains must be taken to keep on common ground in our human experiences, and to some solidarity in our ethical conceptions. And if we discover that men of low ideals and corrupt practice are forming popular political standards simply because such men stand by and for and with the people, then nothing remains but to obtain a like sense of identification before we can hope to modify ethical standards.[14]

Addams here invokes the people with the same referent that Sinclair's characters use, and yet she constitutes them differently. This people is not merely a class or ethnic subject; they are individuals steeped in histories and cultural traditions that inform their values and shape the meaning of their worlds, and solidarity with them requires empathetic identifications that may build the trust on which dialogue, the medium of the polis, might be founded.

The empathy for which Addams calls does more than "keep[] us on common ground" with others. While Hardt and Negri would agree with her (and Arendt) that a common world exists – they write in *Commonwealth* that "if we did not share a common world, then we would not be able to communicate with one another or engage one another's needs and desires" – Addams's counsel entails that although humans share a physical world, a range of emotions, and common names for values, they vary in how they define the terms that they share and therefore devise discrepant ideals and explanations of social and political activity and actors.[15] The common world, in turn, is provisionally constructed by strangers who learn to lessen the distances between their worlds of experience and understanding without denying the gap's existence. Politics supports the activity of world-sharing as it addresses "wrong[s] that cannot be settled but can be processed all the same" by citizens who become "capable of embracing a distance between words and things which is not deception, not trickery, but humanity." Rancière acutely characterizes that capacity as a "poetic virtue" – a capacity to make a world of words – and he notes, too, that it is "a virtue grounded in trust" that one's interlocutors will make themselves vulnerable to the full force of one's arguments and that they will act in good faith.[16]

Ellison used "antagonistic cooperation" to name the dynamic of work within these distances as the basis of political and "aesthetic communication in American democracy." As was his wont, he turned to jazz for his clarifying metaphor. In sharp contrast with Hardt and Negri's figure of the insurgent people as an orchestra that harmoniously plays in the absence of a conductor – which Çiğdem Çıdam rightly faults for ignoring "the laborious and contentious efforts of building unlikely coalitions and creating networks among different groups" – Ellison's chosen musical figure not only highlights the improvisational element of politics as a creative endeavor, it insists on the centrality of the African American experience – of which he proposed jazz as "a musical definition" – to American experience; without it, the moral and ethical dimensions of American society and culture, and the history of American politics and law, would be unrecognizable.[17] *Antagonistic cooperation* casts politics as less akin to realizing an existing musical text than improvisatory contests like cutting sessions and battles of music in which soloists and bands create something new from the shell of tunes they play. What Ellison might have called the music of democracy is, like jazz, an "art of individual assertion within and against the group"; it is heard when citizens engaged in political discourse draw on "techniques, ways of life, and values developed within their respective [class, religious, ethno-racial, and regional] backgrounds" to express their experiences of the polity and conceptions of the more perfect union and, by "playing artfully upon the[ir] audience's sense of experience and form, [...] shape its emotions and perceptions to [their] vision."[18] US political discourse as improvisation on what Ellison called "'the sacred documents' of this nation" was precisely what both Frederick Douglass, in "What to the Slave Is the Fourth of July?" (1852), and Roger B. Taney, in *Dred Scott v. Sandford* (1857), undertook by playing on the Constitution's strategic *silences* and other documents' clear statements, Douglass to create new political subjects and Taney to foreclose their emergence for all times.

Love is not absent from antagonistic cooperation. Indeed, Ellison defined democracy as "the most disinterested form of love," and in what Danielle S. Allen describes as the "tragicomic" conception of citizenship that animates *Invisible Man* and his essays, Ellison tells us that the vehicle of that love is sacrifice, loss endured or opportunity forgone in the name of a higher interest.[19] If *Invisible Man*'s persistent focus is the perversion of sacrifice as the hero's interests repeatedly are sacrificed to the interests of others, Ellison himself, notably in his refutation of Arendt's reading of the 1957 struggle to desegregate Central High School in Little Rock, Arkansas, affirmed the lesson his protagonist takes from his grandfather's dying exhortation, "that we had to take responsibility for all of it, for the men as well as the principle because [. . .] no other fitted our needs," despite that it was in the name of these same democratic principles that "we had been brutalized and sacrificed" for centuries.[20]

In the matter of desegregation, Ellison recast what Arendt described as a social – *not* political – conflict between black parents' demands for inclusion and white parents' "right [. . .] to bring up their children as they see fit," as one more iteration of the history of African American sacrifice to bring the nation's political practices in line with its claimed ideals. The community's actions, he told Robert Penn Warren, exemplify "the basic, implicit heroism of people who must live within a society without recognition, real status," but who, nevertheless, are intimately "involved in the ideals of that society and are [. . .] trying to determine their true position and their rightful position within it." Central to that undertaking, he explained, was transforming the "old traditional role of national scapegoat" – the party whose social death was the foundation of (relative) social equality among whites – into an "*ideal* of sacrifice," a mode of active political engagement. When the Little Rock Nine underwent "a rite of initiation [. . .] [into] the terrors of social life with all the mysteries stripped away," they freely withstood the violent scapegoating of the white protesters as part of a strategy to urge the nation's "conduct into line with its professed ideals."[21]

Scapegoating and sacrifice are central themes, as well, in Anna Deavere Smith's two plays that imagine the polis responding to urban uprisings.[22] *Fires in the Mirror: Crown Heights, Brooklyn and Other Identities* (1993) concerns the 1991 riot precipitated when a car in the motorcade of the Lubavitch Grand Rebbe struck and killed the young son of Guyanese immigrants; *Twilight: Los Angeles, 1992* (1994) addresses the violent response to the acquittal of the four policemen who brutalized Rodney King during a traffic stop. In both plays, all characters are performed by Smith, who speaks monologues comprising unedited segments of interviews that she conducted with residents, politicians, activists, civic figures, and academics. Although the dramatis personae may change from performance to performance, any performance will offer multiple versions of the events and their causes, and many accountings of what a just response to the complex of grievances involved might entail. There is no dialogue other than what is implied by the characters' conflicting accounts of the meaning of what happened and what should be done, and thus no resolution as part of the dramatic arc. Instead, audiences are implicated as collaborators in making meaning of the plays and as judges of the characters' claims – the work of a citizen. Because many of the claims conflict, audiences must judge among them as a judge judges, not as the sun judges.

In *Fires in the Mirror*, the act of speaking *together* is short-circuited by mimetic rivalry among two communities whose members, in the play, often present themselves as history's exemplary innocent victim, and who see in the present instance only a repetition of historical patterns of scapegoating, this time by the city's African American mayor (David Dinkins) or the allegedly Jewish-controlled media and police. The burden of identities founded on trauma and grief threatens to place the present conflict in New York beyond the address of politics, which engages grievance, not grief. In *Twilight: Los Angeles*, as well, are numerous claims and counterclaims of innocent victimhood, but there is also more attention to the largely white local power structure and a thread of commentary that relates the events to the specifics of the region's racial history and thinks about repair.

Mrs. Young Soon Han, a Korean immigrant whose convenience store was one of many burned during the 1992 riot, invokes sacrifice in a striking and unsettling manner. When she recalls watching celebrations after the federal civil rights trial convicted two of the policemen and asks, "Where do I finda [*sic*] justice?" she expresses her belief that Koreans and Korean Americans became the riot's convenient scapegoat because in Los Angeles they occupy the part that Ellison identified for African Americans, involved in the functioning and the ideals of the society but without representation and therefore lacking status and recognition. Mrs. Han then speculates that Koreans and Korean Americans may need to endure even more losses before their grievances will register in the he political calculus:

> [African Americans] have fought
> for their rights
> . . . .
> over two centuries
> . . . .
> and I have a lot of sympathy and understanding for them.
> Because of their effort and sacrificing,

other minorities, like Hispanic
or Asians,
maybe we have to suffer more
by mainstream.[23]

If we may wonder how fully Mrs. Han can empathize with African
Americans, specifically their resentment of Korean merchants in their midst,
given her insistence on the shop owners' innocence, we must recognize that
her political insight does not hinge on empathic identification alone. It speaks
to the role of sacrifice in a democratic polis. Korean merchants were sacrificed,
Mrs. Han argues, to reset the racial détente in Los Angeles by releasing black
anger and ensuring a second trial of the officers. Much as Invisible Man
recognizes that generations of African Americans have been sacrificed for an
illusion of equality among white Americans premised on blacks' enslavement,
but full and equal citizenship remains a goal of African American political
struggle and sacrifice, Mrs. Han sees Korean and Korean American losses both
as part of a larger, certainly expedient, political accounting in which they have
no part, and, like the African American history of sacrifice, as a claim on an
equal part in political affairs going forward.[24]

Sacrifice must not remain the part of the disfranchised. It "a democratic
fact," Allen writes, confronted whenever rights, claims, or interests conflict
because outside democracy's "dreamscape" loss is inevitable; a polity's
health may be gauged by the fairness of loss's distribution over time.[25]
The accounting becomes more complex as the insurrection absorbs other
temporalities, histories, and geographies in Héctor Tobar's novel *The
Tattooed Soldier* (1998), in which the riot intersects a narrative that alter-
nates between the past and present lives of its two Guatemalan immigrant
protagonists, Antonio Bernal, a former student of comparative literature
whose wife and infant son were executed in the dirty war, and the
eponymous soldier immediately responsible for the deaths, Guillermo
Longoria. The novel opens with Antonio and his Mexican roommate,
José Juan, being evicted into Westlake's signscape of "Chinese pictographs
and Arabic calligraphy and Cyrillic, long boulevards of Spanish *eñes*" and
finding a small homeless encampment just off downtown, atop Crown
Hill. It is on a trip one Sunday afternoon to McArthur Park, peopled by
Latin American refugees and immigrants, that Antonio sights Longoria,
now a civilian, playing chess. Even as a shocked Antonio commits to
murdering him as a symbolic justice "for the many, for the anonymous
dead," the trial of the four policemen who beat King is under way, outside
their awareness and the novel's frame.[26]

When the verdict comes in, the explosive response suggests to Antonio a "municipal day of vendettas" festive as a "street fair," only with "alarm bells and shattering glass and crashing metal substituting for carnival music."²⁷ In this moment of exception, he, José Juan, and their African American camp-mates, Frank and "The Mayor," set out to claim the justice they have been denied. The latter two men head to protests the first night at police headquarters and the next day at the *Los Angeles Times*. José Juan sets off to torch the office of *el Armenio*, a contractor who owes him $500 in wages, while Antonio kills his family's killer.

In the riot's aftermath, as Angelenos come together to sweep the rubble, Antonio ponders "if throwing a rock [as "The Mayor" and Frank did] was an act of revolution and therefore an act of love. José Juan running off to set a fire, Antonio pulling the trigger. Ten thousand people taking things and breaking windows because they were angry."²⁸ The reader is left to piece together an answer beyond Antonio's ambivalence. Certainly, the riot itself and José Juan's and Antonio's quests were as driven by the absence of rights and impartial justice as were the student-revolutionaries of Guatemala whose remembered mural sparks the question, but differences trouble the affirmative reading. The "day of vendettas" frames the event as carnivalesque, a cyclically recurrent moment of license created as the police and guardsmen pull back to create a perimeter within which actions that substitute for unattainable justice perversely reaffirm the reign of the commodity: protests against exploitation, state violence, and uprooting are diverted, Antonio recognizes, on a "day when all the pretty objects in the store windows," now free for the taking, "mock them no more."²⁹ Indeed, "The Mayor" laments that the protest's focus went from justice to "just getting things," and, eventually, to "anarchy, fucking anarchy." The scattering of the four as José Juan and Antonio, neither of whom endorses the other's intention, seek revenge questions the collective purpose on which political justice depends. Of the Latino city's relation to the focus of black anger, José Juan scoffs, "What *negro*? They're Latinos. [. . .] They don't know any *negro*. They don't care about any *negro*."³⁰

Love – or even recognition – might have given Antonio pause when he realized that his nemesis is a campesino, an *Indio* (the reader knows him to have been a fatherless conscript), thus the sort of person for whom "you were supposed feel a sort of paternalistic sympathy." "*God knows*," Antonio thinks, "*the person he was before* [he joined the army] *and who he has become since.*" To himself, Antonio admits that "the easiest thing would be to forget about the man."³¹ In fact, he does, but only in the sense that he erases these other identifications to refocus on the soulless killer he imagined

Longoria to be, much as Longoria once saw in his targets only cancers to be eradicated not fellow Guatemalans. But readers know Longoria to be haunted by his atrocities despite US and Guatemalan assurances that his murderous work was just and necessary. The narrative extends him a sort of absolution as he imagines his death as a return to the innocence of his childhood, the countryside, and his mother, while it negates Antonio's fantasy of justice on account of the murder's anonymity; if retrieved from the disused streetcar tunnel in which Antonio dumps him, Longoria will be nothing but one more anonymous victim of urban violence.

While the narrative thus provides no resolution, the world of experience that it creates, like the collected testimonies of *Twilight: Los Angeles*, produces a more comprehensive, less tidy reckoning of the scope of the unaddressed griefs, grievances, and histories that drove the "social explosion," as one character in that play calls the events, that disrupts efforts to contain that the violence within a single triggering incident.[32] These manifold grievances and the wrongs that they produced in turn are what the polis was founded to address, Anne Anlin Cheng argues, by responding with accountability that forestalls "demand[s] for retribution" that "could only lead to the repetition of tribal allegiance and hence division" while also addressing the grief entailed by wrongs and losses and "transform[ing] grief into ethics in the interest of the community."[33]

In the aftermath of the riot, constructing that ethico-political relationship would have entailed an effort of justice that addressed multiple histories of violation and unreciprocated sacrifice rather than, as with the Watts Rebellion, narrowing the inquiry and meeting the issues with strategies of pacification driven by concern to preserve the city's image and commercial attractiveness, which, in the event, was the path followed. Nevertheless, implicitly in the novel, which invites readers imaginatively to enter others' lives, and explicitly in *Twilight*, through Smith's empathic solo performance of a body politic speaking together, these texts position their audiences to be citizens of the absent polis, to weigh the claims of political subjects, some of them fitfully articulated, to think what justice requires not only for sympathetic characters but also those we may find objectionable, and to imagine how the outlines and practices of the common world must be revised to accommodate these political subjects and to address their claims on the polis. As such, they remind us that literature's contribution to the work of the polis has long been to lessen the distances among strangers and to create an imaginative space in which to move beyond mere sympathetic identification to reflective judgments that find their rule in the complex web of particulars that a text presents, or to imagine alternative outlines of common worlds and submit them to collective judgment that incites discussion over what the application of shared values – *justice, equality, fairness* – should look like.

Notes

1. Shakespeare, *Coriolanus*, ed. Brian Gibbons (Cambridge: Cambridge University Press, 2000), 3.1.200; Hannah Arendt, *The Human Condition* (Chicago: University of Chicago Press, 1958), p. 198.
2. On the history of alien suffrage, see Jamin B. Raskin, "Legal Aliens, Local Citizens: The Historical, Constitutional and Theoretical Meanings of Alien Suffrage," *University of Pennsylvania Law Review* 141.4 (1993), 1391–1470. Beyond the question of suffrage in local elections, naturalization was centralized only in 1906. Prior to that statute the judge of any common-law court had authority to rule on citizenship petitions; thus, to Oliver Edwards's statement that he is "a native of this State," Richard Jones scoffs, "it's so easy to get a man naturalized, that it's of little consequence where he was born" (James Fenimore Cooper, *The Pioneers, or, The Sources of the Susquehanna* [1832; New York: Signet, 1964], p. 323).
3. Michael Hardt, Introduction, Thomas Jefferson, *The Declaration of Independence* (New York: Verso, 2007), pp. viii. Hardt reduces Jefferson's definition of democracy to the formula, "democracy = singularity + autonomy + resistance + constituent power" (Hardt, "Jefferson and Democracy," *American Quarterly* 59 [2007], 75).
4. On love, see Hardt and Antonio Negri, *Commonwealth* (Cambridge, MA: Belknap-Harvard University Press, 2009), pp. 179–88, 195–96, 254–61.
5. Christian Parenti, "Reading Hamilton from the Left," *Jacobin*, August 26, 2014, http://jacobinmag.com/2014/08/reading-hamilton-from-the-left/. The embrace of the commons ignores Dana D. Nelson's caution that commoning "is not a political panacea," nor even necessarily democratic. The 2016 standoff at Malheur National Wildlife Refuge, animated by a theory of Western public lands as commons, demonstrates her point that, "at its worst, commoning can be exclusive, exclusionary, and bullying" (Nelson, *Commons Democracy: Reading the Politics of Participation in the Early United States* [New York: Fordham University Press, 2016], p. 7).
6. Parenti, "Reading Hamilton"; his *Radical Hamilton* (2020) is forthcoming as this coda is written. Roberto Mangabeira Unger invokes Hamilton and proposes democratic reforms in "Inclusive Vanguardism: The Alternative Futures of the Knowledge Economy," http://www.oecd.org/naec/Inclusive%20Vanguardism_R%20Unger.pdf, a talk at the Organization for Economic Cooperation and Development expanded in *The Knowledge Economy* (2019) that sets out a series of cognitive-educational, social-moral, and legal-institutional requirements for what he calls inclusive vanguardism and high-energy democracy.

7. Whitman, Preface (1855) to *Leaves of Grass, in Poetry and Prose*, ed. Justin Kaplan (New York: Library of America, 1996), p. 9 (the phrase is repeated in "By Blue Ontario's Shore" [*Poetry and Prose*, p. 475], the successor poem to "Poem of the Many in One," in which the phrase appears in the 1856 edition of *Leaves*); George Kateb, "Walt Whitman and the Culture of Democracy," *Political Theory* 18.4 (1990), 557; Martha Nussbaum, *Poetic Justice: The Literary Imagination and Public Life* (Boston: Beacon, 1997), p. 81.

8. Michael Hardt and Antonio Negri, *Commonwealth*, pp. 61, 182–83; Jason Frank, "Aesthetic Democracy: Walt Whitman and the Poetry of the People," *Review of Politics* 69 (2007), 424, 404 (quoting Kateb, "Aestheticism and Morality: Their Cooperation and Hostility," in *Patriotism and Other Mistakes* [New Haven, CT: Yale University Press, 2006], p. 143), p. 408 (quoting Whitman's term *Democratic Vistas* [1871] in *Poetry and Prose*, p. 974), pp. 408, 409.

9. Ryan Cull, "'We Fathom You Not – We Love You': Walt Whitman's Social Ontology and Radical Democracy," *Criticism* 56.4 (2014), 764, 774, quoting Hardt and Negri, *Commonwealth*, p. 183 (Cull's ellipsis).

10. Mona Domosh, "Those 'Gorgeous Incongruities': Polite Politics and Public Space on the Streets of Nineteenth-Century New York City," *Annals of the Association of American Geographers*, 88.2 (1998), 212; David Scobey, "Anatomy of the Promenade: The Politics of Bourgeois Sociability on Nineteenth-Century New York," *Social History* 17.2 (1992), 204, 223; Domosh, "Those 'Gorgeous Incongruities,'" 212.

11. Jacques Rancière, *On the Shores of Politics*, trans. Liz Heron (London: Verso, 2007), p. 97; Rancière, "The Thinking of Dissensus: Politics and Aesthetics," in *Reading Rancière*, ed. Paul Bowman and Richard Stamp (London: Continuum, 2011), p. 7. For Rancière, the political event creates a new, equal political subject. His touchstones are the moments when Menenius Agrippa heard discourse, rather than mere noise, emanating from the mouths of plebs, and when a French judge accepted Auguste Blanqui's self-definition as a proletarian (Rancière, *Disagreement: Politics and Philosophy*, trans. Julie Rose [Minneapolis: University of Minnesota Press, 1999], pp. 23–25, 37–39). Political subjunctivization as a one-time event is problematic. Did that one time occur for African Americans with the Civil War Amendments, the Civil Rights Act of 1964, and the Voting Rights Act of 1965, or does it await the removal of existing obstacles to political equality?

12. James J. Connelly, *An Elusive Unity: Urban Democracy and Machine Politics in Industrializing America* (Ithaca, NY: Cornell University Press, 2010), p. 163.

13. Jane Addams, *Twenty Years at Hull House* (1910; New York: Macmillan, 1912), p. 316; Addams, "Why the Ward Boss Rules," *The Outlook* 58 (1898), 881. Edward O'Connor's novel *The Last Hurrah* portrays the demise of such a boss, the fictional Frank Skeffington, not by arrest but, the novel suggests, the loosening of ethnic identities and loyalties that accompanied Postwar suburbanization, and the New Deal reforms that provided an economic safety net (O'Connor, *The Last Hurrah* [Boston: Little, Brown, 1956], pp. 374–75).

14. Addams, "Why the Ward Boss," 879; Ralph Ellison, *Invisible Man* (New York: Vintage-Random, 1995), p. 14; Addams, "Why the Ward Boss," 882.
15. Hardt and Negri, *Commonwealth*, p. 184. Arendt believed in a *sensus communis* untouched by language and culture, and she insisted that by thinking "in [one's] own identity where actually [one is] not," one can know what other reasonable beings must think ("Truth and Politics," in *Between Past and Future: Eight Exercises in Political Thought* [1961; New York: Penguin, 1993], p. 241).
16. Rancière, "The Thinking of Dissensus," p. 11; Rancière, *On the Shores of Politics*, trans. Liz Heron (London: Verso, 2007), p. 51. Danielle S. Allen discusses the content of democratic trust in *Talking to Strangers: Anxieties of Citizenship since Brown v. Board of Education* (Chicago: University of Chicago Press, 2004), pp. xiv–xx, 46–49.
17. Ellison, "The Little Man at Chehaw Station: The American Artist and His Audience," in *Collected Essays*, ed. John F. Callahan (New York: Modern Library, 1995), p. 492; Hardt and Negri, *Multitude: War and Democracy in the Age of Empire* (New York: Penguin, 2004), p. 338; Çiğdem Çıdam, "A Politics of Love? Antonio Negri on Revolution and Democracy," *Contemporary Political Theory* 12 (2013), 42; Ellison, "The Charlie Christian Story," in *Collected Essays*, p. 271.
18. Ellison, "The Little Man," p. 492.
19. Ellison to Albert Murray, August 17, 1957, in Albert Murray and John F. Callahan, eds., *Trading Twelves: The Selected Letters of Ralph Ellison and Albert Murray* (New York: Modern Library, 2000), p. 175. I borrow the designation of Ellison's poetics of citizenship from Allen, "Ralph Ellison and the Tragicomedy of Citizenship," *Raritan* 23.3 (2004), 71.
20. Ellison, *Invisible Man*, p. 574.
21. Arendt, "Reflections on Little Rock," *Dissent* 6.1 (Winter 1959), 52; Ellison, quoted in Warren, *Who Speaks for the Negro?*, pp. 342, 342, 343, 344, 339; Ellison's emphasis. Allen recounts the preparation for that day in *Talking to Strangers*, pp. 25–39. Meili Steele describes the disagreement's implications for political theory in "Arendt versus Ellison on Little Rock: The Role of Language in Political Judgment," *Constellations* 9.2 (2002), 184–206.
22. On Smith's plays as performances of the body politic and the repertoire of democratic citizenship, as well as their engagement with an American literary history of imagining the democratic polis, see McNamara, "Staging the Polis," *ELH* 85 (2018), 253–81.
23. Smith, *Twilight: Los Angeles* (New York: Anchor, 1994), pp. 246, 248. Black–Korean relations were strained by black perceptions of Koreans as entering the middle class with profits extracted from African American neighborhoods, and amplified by divergent interpretations of gestures like small talk and eye. Relations hit their nadir in the months between King's beating and the officers' acquittal when convenience-store owner Soon Ja Du killed Latasha Harlins and received probation because the judge found that she acted in fear,

would not be a threat to the community, and that alterations to her weapon made susceptible to accidental discharge.

24. Speculating on why Koreans were "left out" of post-riot aid, Mrs. Han asks, "Is it because we have no politicians?" (ibid., p. 245).

25. Allen, *Talking to Strangers*, pp. 25, 28. Needless to say, the meaning of *justice* and *fairness* is the fundamental question the polis faces.

26. Héctor Tobar, *The Tattooed Soldier* (New York: Penguin, 2000), pp. 3, 183. Tobar was part of the *Los Angeles Times's* Pulitzer Prize–winning coverage of the riot and a dramaturge representing Latino perspectives for *Twilight: Los Angeles*.

27. Ibid., pp. 284, 282.

28. Ibid., p. 306.

29. Ibid., pp. 177, 283.

30. Ibid., pp. 276, 303, 281.

31. Ibid., pp. 163, 164, 163.

32. Smith, *Twilight: Los Angeles*, p. 251; the speaker is Gladis Sibrian, director of the Faribundo Martí Liberation Front, USA. Among critics of *The Tattooed Soldier*, Eric Vásquez focuses on the tension between narrative strategies of resolution and their intentionally unsatisfying implications in "Interrogative Justice in Héctor Tobar's *The Tattooed Soldier*," *Modern Fiction Studies* 64 (2018), 129–52; Regina Marie Mills likewise notes the insufficiency of the narrative's resolution and gestures toward a politics of love to create solidarity with and among peoples disregarded by the state in "Literary-Legal Representations: Statelessness and the Demands of Justice in Héctor Tobar's *The Tattooed Soldier*," *Chiricú Journal* 2 (2018), 98–117.

33. Anne Anlin Cheng, *The Melancholy of Race: Assimilation, Psychoanalysis, and Hidden Grief* (New York: Oxford University Press, 2001), pp. 193, 192, 192.

Further Reading

Abbott, Carl. *Imagining Urban Futures: Cities in Science Fiction and What We Might Learn from Them*. Middletown, CT: Wesleyan University Press, 2016.
Metropolitan Frontiers: Cities in the Modern American West. Tucson: University of Arizona Press, 1993.

Abbott, Megan E. *The Street Was Mine: White Masculinity and Urban Space in Hardboiled Fiction and Film Noir*. Basingstoke, UK: Palgrave, 2002.

Abraham, Jennifer. *Metropolitan Lovers: The Homosexuality of Cities*. Minneapolis: University of Minnesota Press, 2009.

Absher, Amy. *The Black Musician and the White City: Race and Music in Chicago, 1900–1967*. Ann Arbor: University of Michigan Press, 2014.

Adams, Henry. *The Education of Henry Adams*. In Adams, *Democracy, Esther, Mont Saint Michel and Chartres, The Education*. New York: Library of America, 1983.

Anagnostou, Yorgos. *Contours of White Ethnicity: Popular Ethnography and the Making of Usable Pasts in Greek America*. Athens: Ohio University Press, 2009.

Alba, Richard. *Italian Americans: Into the Twilight of Ethnicity*. Englewood Cliffs, NJ: Prentice Hall, 1985.

Alexander, Michelle. *The New Jim Crow: Mass Incarceration in the Age of Colorblindness*. New York: The New Press, 2012.

Amin, Ash, and Nigel Thrift, *Cities: Reimagining the Urban*. London: Polity, 2002.

Amoore, Louise. *The Politics of Possibility: Risk and Security beyond Probability*. Durham, NC: Duke University Press, 2013.

Andersson, Johan, and Webb, Lawrence, eds. *The Cinema of Urban Crisis: Seventies Film and the Reinvention of the City*. Amsterdam: Amsterdam University Press, 2014.

Anker, Elisabeth R. *Orgies of Feeling: Melodrama and the Politics of Freedom*. Durham, NC: Duke University Press, 2014.

Avila, Eric. *Popular Culture in the Age of White Flight: Fear and Fantasy in Suburban Los Angeles*. Berkeley: University of California Press, 2006.

Balshaw, Maria. *Looking for Harlem: Urban Aesthetics in African-American Literature*. London: Pluto, 2000.

Balshaw, Maria, and Liam Kennedy, eds. *Urban Space and Representation.* London: Pluto Press, 2000.

Banham, Reyner. *Megastructure: Urban Futures of the Recent Past.* New York: Harper, 1976.

Barnd, Natchee Blu. *Native Space: Geographical Strategies to Unsettle Settler Colonialism.* Corvallis: Oregon State University Press, 2017.

Barrett, James R. *The Irish Way: Becoming American in the Multiethnic City.* New York: Penguin Press, 2012.

Baumgarten, Murray. *City Scriptures: Modern Jewish Writing.* Cambridge, MA: Harvard University Press, 1982.

Baxandall, Rosalyn, and Elizabeth Ewen. *Picture Windows: How the Suburbs Happened.* New York: Basic Books, 2000.

Beauregard, Robert. *Voices of Decline: The Postwar Fate of U. S. Cities.* 2nd ed. New York: Routledge, 2002.

When America Became Suburban. Minneapolis: University of Minnesota Press, 2006.

Bennett, Michael, and David Warfield Teague. *The Nature of Cities: Ecocriticism and Urban Environments.* Tucson: University of Arizona Press, 1999.

Bentley, Nancy. *Frantic Panoramas: American Literature and Culture 1870–1920.* Philadelphia: University of Pennsylvania Press, 2009.

Berlant, Lauren, *Cruel Optimism.* Durham, NC: Duke University Press, 2011.

Beuka, Robert. *SuburbiaNation: Reading Suburban Landscape in Recent Suburban Literature and Film.* New York: Palgrave, 2004.

Blair, Sara. *How the Other Half Looks: The Lower East Side and the Afterlives of Images.* Princeton, NJ: Princeton University Press, 2018.

Bodnar, John. *The Transplanted: A History of Immigrants in Urban America.* Bloomington: Indiana University Press, 1985.

Brady, Mary Pat, *Extinct Lands, Temporal Geographies: Chicana Literature and the Urgency of Space.* Durham, NC: Duke University Press, 2002.

Brand, Dana. *The Spectator and the City in Nineteenth-Century American Literature.* Cambridge: Cambridge University Press, 1991.

Bratton, Benjamin H. *The Stack: On Software and Sovereignty.* Cambridge, MA: MIT Press, 2016.

Brooker, Peter. *New York Fictions: Modernity, Postmodernism, the New Modern.* London: Longman, 1995.

Brooks, David. *Bobos in Paradise: The New Upper Class and How They Got There.* New York: Simon and Schuster, 2000.

Brown, Adrienne. *The Black Skyscraper: Architecture and the Perception of Race.* Baltimore: Johns Hopkins University Press, 2017.

Brown, Adrienne, and Valerie Smith, eds. *Race and Real Estate.* Oxford: Oxford University Press, 2016.

Brown, Wendy, *Walled States Waning Sovereignty.* New York: Zone Books, 2010.

Buccitelli, Anthony Bak. *City of Neighborhoods: Memory, Folklore, and Ethnic Place in Boston.* Madison: University of Wisconsin Press, 2016.

Calhoun, Craig J., ed. *Habermas and the Public Sphere.* Boston: MIT Press, 1992.

Cannato, Vincent J. *The Ungovernable City: John Lindsay and His Struggle to Save New York*. New York: Basic Books, 2001.

Cannistraro, Philip V., and Gerald Meyer. *The Lost World of Italian American Radicalism: Politics, Labor, and Culture*. Westport, CT: Praeger, 2003.

Cappetti, Carla. *Writing Chicago: Modernism, Ethnography, and the Novel*. New York: Columbia University Press, 1993.

Carlson, Jennifer. *Citizens-Protectors: The Everyday Politics of Guns in an Age of Decline*. New York: Oxford University Press, 2015.

Caro, Robert. *The Power Broker: Robert Moses and the Fall of New York*. New York: Knopf, 1975.

Clark, Marlene. "'This House Belong to Me, Now': The 'Slumming' and 'Gentrification' of Bedford Stuyvesant, Brooklyn as Experienced and Foretold by Paule Marshall's *Brown Girl, Brownstones*." *Anthurium* 14.1 (2017), http://scholarlyrepository.miami.edu/anthurium/vol14/iss1/4/.

Conn, Steven. *Americans against the City: Anti-Urbanism in the Twentieth Century*. New York: Oxford University Press, 2014.

Corkin, Stanley. *Connecting "The Wire": Race, Space, and Postindustrial Baltimore*. Austin: University of Texas Press, 2017.

Starring New York: Filming the Grime and the Glamour of the Long 1970s. New York: Oxford University Press, 2011.

Coward, Martin. "Network-Centric Violence, Critical Infrastructure and the Urbanization of Security." *Security Dialogue* 40.4–5 (2009): 399–418.

Cowart, David. *Trailing Clouds: Immigrant Fiction in Contemporary America*. Ithaca, NY: Cornell University Press, 2006.

Cowie, Jefferson, and Joseph Heathcott, eds. *Beyond the Ruins: The Meanings of Deindustrialization*. Ithaca, NY: Cornell University Press, 2003.

Cowley, Malcom. *Exile's Return: A Literary Odyssey of the 1920s*. New York: Viking, 1951.

Cronon, William. *Nature's Metropolis: Chicago and the Great West*. New York: Norton, 1992.

D'Angelo, Pascal. *Son of Italy*. New York: Arno Press, 1975.

Daniel, Julia E. *Building Natures: Modern American Poetry, Landscape Architecture, and City Planning*. Charlottesville: University of Virginia Press, 2017.

Davis, Mike. *City of Quartz: Excavating the Future in Los Angeles*. New York: Verso, 1990.

Davis, Thadious. *Southscapes: Geographies of Race, Region, and Literature*. Chapel Hill: University of North Carolina Press, 2011.

Dawson, Ashley, and Malini Johar Schueller, eds. *Exceptional State: Contemporary U. S. Culture and the New Imperialism*. Durham, NC: Duke University Press, 2007.

De Lara, Juan. *Inland Shift: Race, Space, and Capital in Southern California*. Berkeley: University of California Press, 2018.

Dear, Michael J. *The Postmodern Urban Condition*. Malden, MA: Blackwell, 2000.

Deckard, Sharae, and Stephen Shapiro, eds. *World Literature, Neoliberalism, and the Culture of Discontent*. Cham, Switzerland: Palgrave, 2019.

De Jongh, James. *Vicious Modernism: Black Harlem and the Literary Imagination.* New York: Cambridge University Press, 1990.

Den Tandt, Christophe. *The Urban Sublime in American Literary Naturalism.* Urbana: University of Illinois Press, 1998.

Dixon, Terrell F. *City Wilds: Essays and Stories about Urban Nature.* Athens: University of Georgia Press, 2002.

Dorst, John D. *The Written Suburb: An American Site, an Ethnographic Dilemma.* Philadelphia: University of Pennsylvania Press, 1989.

Douglass, Ann. *Terrible Honesty: Mongrel Manhattan in the 1920s.* New York: Farrar, 1995.

Dowling, Robert M. *Slumming in New York: From the Waterfront to Mythic Harlem.* Urbana: University of Illinois Press, 2007.

Dubey, Madhu. *Signs and Cities: Black Literary Postmodernism.* Chicago: University of Chicago Press, 2003.

Dybek, Stuart. *Childhood and Other Neighborhoods.* New York: Viking, 1980.

Eaglestone, Robert, Gert Buelens, and Sam Durrant, eds. *The Future of Trauma Theory: Contemporary Literature and Cultural Criticism.* New York: Routledge, 2014.

Eckstein, Barbara J. *Sustaining New Orleans: Literature, Local Memory, and the Fate of a City.* New York: Routledge, 2006.

Enloe, Cynthia. *Globalization and Militarism: Feminists Make the Link.* 2nd ed. Lanham, MD: Rowman and Littlefield, 2016.

Erenberg, Lewis. *Steppin' Out: New York Nightlife and the Transformation of American Culture.* Chicago: University of Chicago Press, 1984.

Erickson, Paul. "*Welcome to Sodom*: The Cultural Work of *City-Mysteries* Fiction in Antebellum America." PhD diss., University of Texas at Austin, 2005.

Esteve, Mary. *The Aesthetics and Politics of the Crowd in American Literature.* New York: Cambridge University Press, 2003.

Faflik, David. *Boarding Out: Inhabiting the American Urban Literary Imagination, 1840–1860.* Evanston, IL: Northwestern University Press, 2012.

Faisst, Julia. "Strolling the Biophilic City: Flâneurism, Urban Nature and Eco-Fiction." *Anglistik und Englischunterricht* 85 (2018): 43–57.

Ferraro, Thomas J. *Ethnic Passages: Literary Immigrants in Twentieth-Century America.* Chicago: University of Chicago Press, 1993.

    Feeling Italian: The Art of Ethnicity in America. New York: NYU Press, 2005.

Fine, David M. *The City, the Immigrant, and American Fiction, 1880–1920.* Metuchen, NJ: Scarecrow Press, 1977.

Fishman, Robert. *Bourgeois Utopias: The Rise and Fall of Suburbia.* New York: Basic Books, 1987.

    Urban Utopias in the Twentieth Century: Ebenezer Howard, Frank Lloyd Wright, Le Corbusier. Cambridge, MA: MIT Press, 1982.

FitzGerald, Frances. *Cities on a Hill.* New York: Simon and Schuster, 1987.

Flamm, Michael. *Law and Order: Street Crime, Civil Unrest, and the Crisis of Liberalism in the 1960s.* New York: Columbia University Press, 2005.

Florida, Richard. *Cities and the Creative Class.* New York: Routledge, 2005.

Fogelson, Robert. *Bourgeois Nightmares: Suburbia, 1870–1930*. New Haven, CT: Yale University Press, 2005.

Foucault, Michel. *Security, Territory, Population. Lectures at the Collège de France, 1977–78*. Ed. Michel Senellart. Trans. Graham Burchell. New York: Palgrave Macmillan, 2007.

Fraiman, Susan. *Extreme Domesticity: A View from the Margins*. New York: Columbia University Press, 2017.

Franco, Dean J. *The Border and the Line: Race, Literature, and Los Angeles*. Stanford, CA: Stanford University Press, 2019.

Frank, Michael C. *The Cultural Imaginary of Terrorism in Public Discourse, Literature, and Film: Narrating Terror*. New York: Routledge, 2017.

Frohne, Andrea E. *The African Burial Ground in New York City: Memory, Spirituality, and Space*. Syracuse, NY: Syracuse University Press, 2015.

Fuller, R. Buckminster. *Operating Manual for Spaceship Earth*. Carbondale: Southern Illinois University Press, 1969.

Gardaphé, Fred. L. *Italian Signs, American Streets: The Evolution of Italian American Narrative*. Durham, NC: Duke University Press, 1996.

   Leaving Little Italy: Essaying Italian American Culture. Albany: SUNY Press, 2003.

Gandal, Keith. *The Virtues of the Vicious: Jacob Riis, Stephen Crane, and the Spectacle of the Slum*. New York: Oxford University Press, 1997.

Gans, Herbert. *The Urban Villagers: Group and Class in the Life of Italian-Americans*. New York: Free Press, 1962.

Garreau, Joel. *Edge City: Life on the New Frontier*. New York: Doubleday, 1991.

Gates, Racquel J. *Double Negative: The Black Image and Popular Culture*. Durham, NC: Duke University Press, 2018.

Geismer, Lily. *Don't Blame Us: Suburban Liberals and the Transformation of the Democratic Party*. Princeton, NJ: Princeton University Press, 2014.

Gennari, John. *Flavor and Soul: Italian America at Its African American Edge*. Chicago: University of Chicago Press, 2017.

Gersdorf, Catrin, "Nature in the Grid: American Literature, Urbanism, and Ecocriticism." *REAL: The Yearbook of Research in English and American Literature* 26 (2010): 21–40.

Gersdorf, Catrin, and Juliane Braun, eds. *America after Nature: Democracy, Culture, Environment*. Heidelberg, Germany: Universitätsverlag Winter, 2016.

Giles, James Richard. *The Naturalistic Inner-City Novel in America: Encounters with the Fat Man*. Columbia: University of South Carolina Press, 1995.

Gillette, Howard, Jr. *Between Justice and Beauty: Race, Planning, and the Failure of Urban Policy in Washington, D.C.* Philadelphia: University of Pennsylvania Press, 1995.

   Civitas by Design: Building Better Communities, from the Garden City to the New Urbanism. Philadelphia: University of Pennsylvania Press, 2010.

Gins, Madeline, and Shusaku Arakawa. *Architectural Body*. Tuscaloosa: University of Alabama Press, 2002.

Godbey, Matthew. "Gentrification, Authenticity and White Middle-Class Identity in Jonathan Lethem's *The Fortress of Solitude*." *Arizona Quarterly* 64.1 (2008): 131–51.

Goeman, Mishuana. *Mark My Words: Native Women Mapping Our Nations*. Minneapolis: University of Minnesota Press, 2013.

Gray, Mitchell, and Elvin Wyly. "The Terror City Hypothesis." *Violent Geographies: Fear, Terror, and Political Violence*. Ed. Derek Gregory and Allan Pred. New York: Routledge, 2007. 329–48.

Griffin, Farah Jasmine. *"Who Set You Flowin'?": The African-American Migration Narrative*. New York: Oxford University Press, 1995.

Gumport, Elizabeth. "Gentrified Fiction." *N+1* (November 2, 2009), http://nplusonemag.com/online-only/book-review/gentrified-fiction/.

Hackworth, Jason. *The Neoliberal City: Governance, Ideology, and Development in American Urbanism*. Ithaca, NY: Cornell University Press, 2007.

Hall, Peter. *Cities of Tomorrow: An Intellectual History of Urban Planning and Design since 1880*. 4th ed. Hoboken, NJ: Wiley-Blackwell, 2014.

Hales, Peter Bacon. *Silver Cities: Photographing American Urbanization, 1839–1939*. Rev. ed. Albuquerque: University of New Mexico Press, 2005.

Halttunen, Karen. *Confidence Men and Painted Women: A Study of Middle-Class Culture in America*. New Haven, CT: Yale University Press, 1982.

Hamilton, John T. *Security: Politics, Humanity, and the Philology of Care*. Princeton, NJ: Princeton University Press, 2013.

Hapke, Laura. *Labor's Text: The Worker in American Fiction*. New Brunswick, NJ: Rutgers University Press, 2001.

Harrison, Ariane Louise, ed. *Architectural Theories of the Environment: Posthuman Territory*. New York: Routledge, 2013.

Hartnell, Anna. *After Katrina: Race, Neoliberalism and the End of the American Century*. Albany: SUNY Press, 2017.

Harvey, David. *The Condition of Postmodernity: An Enquiry into the Origins of Cultural Change*. Malden, MA: Blackwell, 1990.

  Rebel Cities: From the Right to the City to the Urban Revolution. London: Verso, 2012.

  Spaces of Hope. Berkeley: University of California Press, 2000.

  Social Justice and the City. Athens: University of Georgia Press, 2009.

Hayden, Dolores. *The Power of Place: Urban Landscapes as Public History*. Cambridge, MA: MIT Press, 1997.

Hayles, N. Katherine. *How We Became Posthuman: Virtual Bodies in Cybernetics, Literature, and Informatics*. Chicago: University of Chicago Press, 1999.

Heap, Chad. *Slumming: Sexual and Racial Encounters in American Nightlife, 1885–1940*. Chicago: University of Chicago Press, 2008.

Heise, Thomas. *Urban Underworlds: A Geography of Twentieth-Century American Literature and Culture*. New Brunswick, NJ: Rutgers University Press, 2011.

Heise, Ursula K. "Terraforming for Urbanists." *Novel* 39.1 (2016): 10–25.

Henkin, David M. *City Reading: Written Words and Public Spaces in Antebellum America*. New York: Columbia University Press, 1998.

Herring, Scott. *Queering the Underworld: Slumming, Literature, and the Undoing of Lesbian and Gay History.* Chicago: University of Chicago Press, 2007.

Higham, John. *Send These to Me: Immigrants in Urban America.* Baltimore: Johns Hopkins University Press, 1984.

Strangers in the Land. New York: Athenaeum, 1978.

Hinton, Elizabeth. *From the War on Poverty to the War on Crime: The Making of Mass Incarceration in America.* Cambridge, MA: Harvard University Press, 2016.

Hoberek, Andrew. *Twilight of the Middle Class: Post–World War II American Fiction and White-Collar Work.* Princeton, NJ: Princeton University Press, 2005.

Hobson, Christopher Z. *James Baldwin and the Heavenly City: Prophecy, Apocalypse, and Doubt.* East Lansing: Michigan State University Press, 2018.

Howe, Irving. *World of Our Fathers.* 1976; reprint, New York: NYU Press, 2005.

Huehls, Mitchum, and Rachel Greenwald-Smith, eds. *Neoliberalism and Contemporary Literary Culture.* Baltimore: Johns Hopkins University Press, 2017.

Irr, Caren. *Toward the Geopolitical Novel: U. S. Fiction in the 21st Century.* New York: Columbia University Press, 2014.

Jackson, Kenneth. *Crabgrass Frontier: The Suburbanization of the United States.* New York: Oxford University Press, 1985.

Jacobs, Jane. *The Death and Life of Great American Cities.* New York: Random House, 1961.

Jacobson, Kristen. *Neodomestic American Fiction.* Columbus: Ohio State University Press, 2010.

James, Henry. *The American Scene.* 1907; reprint, New York: Penguin, 1994.

Jaye, Michael C., and Ann Chalmers Watts, eds. *Literature and the Urban Experience: Essays on the City and Literature.* New Brunswick, NJ: Rutgers University Press, 1981.

Jazeel, Tariq, et al. [*Antipode* Editorial Collective]. *Keywords in Radical Geography: Antipode at 50.* Oxford: Wiley, 2019.

Josephson, Matthew. *Life among the Surrealists: A Memoir.* New York: Holt, Rinehart, and Winston, 1962.

Jurca, Catherine. *White Diaspora: The Suburb and the Twentieth-Century American Novel.* Princeton, NJ: Princeton University Press, 2000.

Kandiyoti, Dalia. *Migrant Sites: America, Place, and Diaspora Literatures.* Hanover, NH: Dartmouth College Press, 2009.

Kaplan, Amy. *The Social Construction of American Realism.* Chicago: University of Chicago Press, 1992.

Kasson, John. *Rudeness and Civility: Manners in Nineteenth-Century Urban America.* New York: Hill and Wang, 1990.

Katz, Michael, ed. *The "Underclass" Debate: Views from History.* Princeton, NJ: Princeton University Press, 1992.

Kauffman, L. A. *Protest and the Reinvention of American Radicalism.* London: Verso, 2017.

Kazin, Alfred. *A Walker in the City*. 1951; reprint, New York: Harcourt, 1979.

Keeble, Arin. *Narratives of Hurricane Katrina in Context: Literature, Film and Television*. Cham, Switzerland: Palgrave, 2019.

Kennedy, Liam, and Stephen Shapiro, eds. *Neoliberalism and Contemporary North American Literature*. Hanover, NH: Dartmouth College Press, 2019.

Kenyon, Amy Maria. *Dreaming Suburbia: Detroit and the Production of Postwar Space and Culture*. Detroit, MI: Wayne State University Press, 2004.

Kern, Steven. *The Culture of Time and Space 1880–1918*. Cambridge, MA: Harvard University Press, 1983.

Kinder, Kimberly. *DIY Detroit: Making Do in a City without Services*. Minneapolis: University of Minnesota Press, 2016.

King, C. Richard, ed. *Post-Colonial America*. Urbana: University of Illinois Press, 2000.

Kinney, Rebecca J. *Beautiful Wasteland: The Rise of Detroit as America's Postindustrial Frontier*. Minneapolis: University of Minnesota Press, 2016.

Klein, Naomi. *The Shock Doctrine: The Rise of Disaster Capitalism*. New York: Holt, 2007.

Klimasmith, Elizabeth. *At Home in the City: Urban Domesticity in American Literature and Culture, 1850–1930*. Durham: University of New Hampshire Press, 2005.

Knapp, Kathy. *American Unexceptionalism: The Everyman and the Suburban Novel after 9/11*. Iowa City: University of Iowa Press, 2014.

Knox, Paul L., and Peter J. Taylor, eds. *World Cities in a World-System*. New York: Cambridge University Press, 1995.

Koritz, Amy. *Culture Makers: Urban Performance and Literature in the 1920s*. Urbana: University of Illinois Press, 2009.

Kruse, Kevin. *White Flight: Atlanta and the Making of Modern Conservativism*. Princeton, NJ: Princeton University Press, 2007.

LaChance, Daniel. *Executing Freedom: The Cultural Life of Capital Punishment in the United States*. Chicago: University of Chicago Press, 2016.

Lefebvre, Henri. *The Production of Space*. Trans. Donald Nicholson-Smith. Malden, MA: Blackwell, 1991.

Lehan, Richard. *The City in Literature: An Intellectual and Cultural History*. Berkeley: University of California Press, 1998.

LeMenager, Stephanie. *Living Oil: Petroleum Culture in the American Century*. New York: Oxford University Press, 2014.

Levin, Joanna. *Bohemia in America, 1858–1920*. Stanford, CA: Stanford University Press, 2010.

Levin, Joanna, and Edward Whitley, eds. *Walt Whitman in Context*. Cambridge: Cambridge University Press, 2018.

Lindner, Christoph. *Imagining New York City: Literature, Urbanism, and the Visual Arts, 1890–1940*. New York: Oxford University Press, 2013.

Lindner, Christoph, and Miriam Meissner, eds. *The Routledge Companion to Urban Imaginaries*. New York: Routledge, 2019.

Linkon, Sherry L. *The Half-Life of Deindustrialization: Working-Class Writing about Economic Restructuring.* Ann Arbor: University of Michigan Press, 2018.

Linkon, Sherry L., and John Russo. *Steeltown U.S.A.: Work and Memory in Youngstown.* Lawrence: University Press of Kansas, 2002.

Lipsitz, George. *How Racism Takes Place.* Philadelphia: Temple University Press, 2011.

Lipton, Lawrence. *The Holy Barbarians.* New York: Julian Messner, 1959.

Lloyd, Richard. *Neo-Bohemia: Art and Commerce in the Postindustrial City.* New York: Routledge, 2010.

Looker, Benjamin. *A Nation of Neighborhoods: Imagining Cities, Communities, and Democracy in Postwar America.* Chicago: University of Chicago Press, 2015.

Lösch, Klaus, Heike Paul, and Meike Zwingenberger, eds. *Critical Regionalism.* Heidelberg, Germany: Universitätsverlag Winter, 2016.

Low, Setha, and Neil Smith. *The Politics of Public Space.* New York: Routledge, 2006.

Luconi, Stefano. *From Paesani to White Ethnics: The Italian Experience on Philadelphia.* Albany: SUNY Press, 2001.

Lulka, David. "The Posthuman City: San Diego's Dead Animal Removal Program." *Urban Geography* 34.8 (2013): 1119–43.

Macek, Steve. *Urban Nightmares: The Media, the Right, and the Moral Panic over the City.* Minneapolis: University of Minnesota Press, 2006.

Machor, James. *Pastoral Cities: Urban Ideals and the Symbolic Landscape of America.* Madison: University of Wisconsin Press, 1987.

Mączyńska, Magdalena. "Welcome to the Post-Anthropolis: Urban Space and Climate Change in Nathaniel Rich's *Odds against Tomorrow*, Lev Rosen's *Depth*, and Kim Stanley Robinson's *New York 2140.*" *Journal of Modern Literature* 45.2 (2020): 165–81.

Mehnert, Antonia. *Climate Change Fictions: Representations of Global Warming in American Literature.* London: Palgrave Macmillan, 2016.

Marling, William. *The American Roman Noir.* Athens: University of Georgia Press, 1995.

Manzanas Calvo, Ana M., and Jesús Benito. *Cities, Borders and Spaces in Intercultural American Literature and Film.* New York: Routledge, 2011.

Hospitality in American Literature and Culture: Spaces, Bodies, Borders. New York: Routledge, 2017.

Massood, Paula J. *Black City Cinema: African American Urban Experiences in Film.* Philadelphia: Temple University Press, 2003.

May, Elaine Tyler. *Fortress America: How We Embraced Fear and Abandoned Democracy.* New York: Basic Books, 2017.

McClung, William Alexander. *Landscapes of Desire: Anglo Mythologies of Los Angeles.* Berkeley: University of California Press, 2002.

McGirr, Lisa. *Suburban Warriors: The Origins of the New American Right.* Rev. ed. Princeton, NJ: Princeton University Press, 2015.

McKittrick, Katherine, and Clyde Woods, eds. *Black Geographies and the Politics of Place*. Toronto: Between the Lines, 2007.

McNamara, Kevin. *Urban Verbs: Arts and Discourses of American Cities*. Stanford, CA: Stanford University Press, 1996.

Mezzadra, Sandro, and Brett Neilson. *Border as Method; or, The Multiplication of Labor*. Durham, NC: Duke University Press, 2013.

Mignolo, Walter. *Local Histories, Global Designs: Coloniality, Subaltern Knowledges, and Border Thinking*. Princeton, NJ: Princeton University Press, 2002.

Miller, Donald. *The Lewis Mumford Reader*. New York: Pantheon, 1986.

Mitchell, Don. *The Right to the City: Social Justice and the Fight for Public Space*. New York: Guilford Press, 2003.

Moore, Deborah Dash, ed. *American Jewish Identity Politics*. Ann Arbor: University of Michigan Press, 2008.

Moiles, Sean. "The Politics of Gentrification in Ernesto Quiñonez's Novels." *Critique* 52.1 (2011): 114–33.

Moskowitz, Peter. *How to Kill a City: Gentrification, Inequality, and the Fight for the Neighborhood*. New York: Nation Books, 2017.

Mumford, Lewis. *The Urban Prospect*. New York: Harcourt, 1968.

Munby, Jonathan. *Under a Bad Sign: Criminal Self-Representation in African American Popular Culture*. Chicago: University of Chicago Press, 2011.

Murphet, Julian. *Literature and Race in Los Angeles*. Cambridge: Cambridge University Press, 2001.

Neilson, Brett, and Sandro Mazzedra. *Border as Method; or, The Multiplication of Labor*. Durham, NC: Duke University Press, 2013.

Nixon, Rob. *Slow Violence and the Environmentalism of the Poor*. Cambridge, MA: Harvard University Press, 2011.

Otter, Samuel. *Philadelphia Stories: America's Literature of Race and Freedom*. New York: Oxford University Press, 2010.

Pattillo, Mary. *Black Picket Fences: Privilege and Peril among the Black Middle Class*. Chicago: University of Chicago Press, 1999.

   Black on the Block: The Politics of Race and Class in the City. Chicago: University of Chicago Press, 2007.

Pattison, Dale, and Kevin Concannon, eds. "Transnational Cityscapes." Special issue. *Arizona Quarterly* 74.1 (2018).

Peacock, James. *Brooklyn Fictions: The Contemporary Urban Community in a Global Age*. New York: Bloomsbury, 2015.

   "'Those the Dead Left Behind': Gentrification and Haunting in Contemporary Brooklyn Fictions." *Studies in American Fiction* 46.1 (2019): 133–58.

Peiss, Kathy. *Cheap Amusements: Working Women and Leisure in Turn-of-the-Century New York*. Philadelphia: Temple University Press, 1986.

Pooch, Melanie U. *DiverCity: Global Cities as a Literary Phenomenon: Toronto, New York, and Los Angeles*. Bielefeld, Germany: Transcript, 2016.

Prince, Valerie Sweeney. *Burnin' Down the House: Home in African American Literature*. New York: Columbia University Press, 2005.

Pulido, Laura. "Flint, Environmental Racism, and Racial Capitalism." *Capitalism Nature Socialism* 27.3 (2016): 1–16.

Quilter, Jenni. *New York School Painters and Poets: Neon in Daylight*. New York: Rizzoli, 2014.

Rabinowitz, Paula. *Labor and Desire: Women's Revolutionary Fiction in Depression America*. Chapel Hill: University of North Carolina Press, 1991.

Rai, Candice. *Democracy's Lot: Rhetoric, Publics, and the Places of Invention*. Tuscaloosa: University of Alabama Press, 2016.

Ravage, M[arcus]. E. *An American in the Making: The Life Story of an Immigrant*. New York: Dover, 1971.

Reid-Pharr, Robert F. *Archives of Flesh: African America, Space, and Post-Humanist Critique*. New York: New York University Press, 2016.

Reps, John. *The Making of Urban America: A History of City Planning in the United States*. Princeton, NJ: Princeton University Press, 1965.

Reynolds, David. *Beneath the American Renaissance: The Subversive Imagination in the Age of Emerson and Melville*. Cambridge, MA: Harvard University Press, 1988.

Rodgers, Daniel T. *As a City upon a Hill: The Story of America's Most Famous Lay Sermon*. Princeton, NJ: Princeton University Press, 2018.

Roediger, David R. *Working toward Whiteness: How America's Immigrants Became White: The Strange Journey from Ellis Island to the Suburbs*. New York: Basic Books, 2005.

Rose, Gillian. "Posthuman Agency in the Digitally Mediated City: Exteriorization, Individuation, Reinvention." *Annals of the American Association of Geographers* 107.4 (2017): 779–93.

Rotella, Carlo. *October Cities: The Redevelopment of Urban Literature*. Berkeley: University of California Press, 1998.

  The World Is Always Coming to an End: Pulling Together and Apart in a Chicago Neighborhood. Chicago: University of Chicago Press, 2019.

Rottenberg, Catherine. *Black Harlem and the Jewish Lower East Side: Narratives out of Time*. Albany: SUNY Press, 2013.

Rozelle, Lee. *Ecosublime: Environmental Awe and Terror from New World to Oddworld*. Tuscaloosa: University of Alabama Press, 2006.

Ryan, Mary P. *Civic Wars: Democracy and Public Life in the American City during the Nineteenth Century*. Berkeley: University of California Press, 1997.

Sadler, Simon. *Archigram: Architecture without Architecture*. Cambridge, MA: MIT Press, 2005.

Sampson, Robert J. *Great American City: Chicago and the Enduring Neighborhood Effect*. Chicago: University of Chicago Press, 2012.

Sandoval-Strausz, A. K., and Nancy Kwak, eds. *Making Cities Global: The Transnational Turn in Urban History*. Philadelphia: University of Pennsylvania Press, 2017.

Sassen, Saskia. *The Global City: New York, London, Tokyo*. 2nd ed. Princeton, NJ: Princeton University Press, 2001.

Schlichtman, John Joe, Jason Patch, and Marc Lamont Hill. *Gentrifier*. Toronto: University of Toronto Press, 2017.

Scott, William B., and Peter M. Rutkoff. *New York Modern: The Arts and the City*. Baltimore: Johns Hopkins University Press, 1999.

Scruggs, Charles. *Sweet Home: Invisible Cities in the Afro-American Novel*. Baltimore: Johns Hopkins University Press, 1993.

Seigel, Jerrold. *Bohemian Paris: Culture, Politics, and the Boundaries of Bourgeois Life, 1830–1930*. New York: Viking, 1986.

Sennett, Richard. *Building and Dwelling: Ethics for the City*. New York: Farrar, 2018.

    The Conscience of the Eye: The Design and Social Life of Cities. New York: Knopf, 1990.

    The Fall of Public Man. New York: Norton, 1992.

    The Uses of Disorder: Personal Identity and City Life. New York: Knopf, 1970.

Schliephake, Christopher. *Urban Ecologies: City Space, Material Agency, and Environmental Politics in Contemporary Culture*. Lanham, MD: Lexington Books, 2015.

Shah, Nayan. *Contagious Divides: Epidemics and Race in San Francisco's Chinatown*. Berkeley: University of California Press, 2001.

Sharpe, William. *New York Nocturne: The City after Dark in Literature, Painting, and Photography, 1850–1950*. Princeton, NJ: Princeton University Press, 2008.

Shonkwiler, Alison, ed. *Reading Capitalist Realism*. Iowa City: University of Iowa Press 2014.

Siegel, Adrienne. *The Image of the American City in Popular Literature, 1820–1870*. Port Washington, NY: Kennikat, 1981.

Siegle, Robert. *Suburban Ambush: Downtown Writing and the Fiction of Insurgency*. Baltimore: Johns Hopkins University Press, 1989.

Sies, Mary Corbin, and Christopher Silver, eds. *Planning the Twentieth-Century American City*. Baltimore: Johns Hopkins University Press, 1996.

Simmel, Georg. "The Metropolis and Mental Life." *The Sociology of Georg Simmel*, trans. and ed. Kurt Wolff. New York: Free Press, 1950, pp. 409–24.

Smethurst, James Edward. *The Black Arts Movement: Literary Nationalism in the 1960s and 1970s*. Chapel Hill: University of North Carolina Press, 2005.

Smith, Carl S. *Chicago and the American Literary Imagination, 1880–1920*. Chicago: University of Chicago Press, 1984.

    Urban Disorder and the Shape of Belief: The Great Chicago Fire, the Haymarket Bomb, and the Model Town of Pullman. Chicago: University of Chicago Press, 1995.

    The New Urban Frontier: Gentrification and the Revanchist City. New York: Routledge, 1996.

Smith, Robert. *Mexican New York: Transnational Lives of New Immigrants*. Berkeley: University of California Press, 2005.

Stansell, Christine. *American Moderns: Bohemian New York and the Creation of a New Century*. New York: Metropolitan Books, 2000.

Starr, Kevin Z. *Material Dreams: Southern California through the 1920s*. New York: Oxford University Press, 1990.

Strauss, Anselm L., ed. *The American City: A Sourcebook of Urban Imagery*. Chicago: Aldine, 1968.

Stroud, Angela. *Good Guys with Guns: The Appeal and Consequences of Concealed Carry*. Chapel Hill: University of North Carolina Press, 2016.

Sugrue, Thomas. *Immigration and Metropolitan Revitalization in the United States*. Philadelphia: University of Pennsylvania Press, 2017.

The Origins of the Urban Crisis: Race and Inequality in Postwar Detroit. Princeton, NJ: Princeton University Press, 1996.

Suttles, Gerald. *The Social Construction of Communities*. Chicago: University of Chicago Press, 1972.

Swyngedouw, Erik. *Promises of the Political: Insurgent Cities in a Post-Political Environment*. Cambridge, MA: MIT Press, 2018.

Tajbakhsh, Kian. *The Promise of the City: Space, Identity, and Politics in Contemporary Social Thought*. Berkeley: University of California Press, 2001.

Thomas, June Manning. *Redevelopment and Race: Planning a Finer City in Postwar Detroit*. Baltimore: Johns Hopkins University Press, 1997.

Thomas, June Manning, and Marsha Ritzdorf, eds. *Urban Planning and the African American Community: In the Shadows*. Thousand Oaks, CA: Sage, 1997.

Tochterman, Brian. *The Dying City: Postwar New York and the Ideology of Fear*. Chapel Hill: University of North Carolina Press, 2017.

Trachetenberg, Alan. *The Incorporation of America: Culture and Society in the Gilded Age*. New York: Hill and Wang, 1992.

Trachtenberg, Alan. *Brooklyn Bridge: Fact and Fiction*. Chicago: University of Chicago Press, 1965.

Villa, Raúl Homero. *Barrio-Logos: Space and Place in Urban Chicano Literature and Culture*. Austin: University of Texas Press, 2000.

Voelz, Johannes. *The Poetics of Insecurity: American Fiction and the Uses of Threat*. New York: Cambridge University Press, 2018.

Wang, Jackie. *Carceral Capitalism*. Cambridge, MA: MIT Press, 2018.

Warner, Sam Bass, Jr., and Andrew Whittemore. *American Urban Form: A Representative History*. Cambridge, MA: MIT Press, 2012.

Watson, David. "Derivative Creativity: The Financialisation of the Contemporary American Novel." *European Journal of English Studies* 21.1 (2017): 93–105.

The City in American Cinema: Film and Postindustrial Culture. London: Bloomsbury, 2019.

Weber, Donald. *Haunted in the New World: Jewish American Culture from Cahan to "The Goldbergs."* Bloomington: Indiana University Press, 2005.

Widener, Daniel. *Black Arts West: Culture and Struggle in Postwar Los Angeles*. Durham, NC: Duke University Press, 2010.

Westgate, J. Chris. *Staging the Slums, Slumming the Stage: Class, Poverty, Ethnicity, and Sexuality in American Theatre, 1890–1916*. New York: Palgrave Macmillan, 2014.

White, Morton, and Lucia White. *The Intellectual versus the City, from Thomas Jefferson to Frank Lloyd Wright*. Cambridge, MA: Harvard University Press, 1962.

Whyte, William H. *City: Rediscovering the Center*. New York: Doubleday, 1988.

Wilhite, Keith, ed. *The City since 9/11: Literature, Film, Television*. Madison, NJ: Fairleigh Dickinson University Press, 2016.

Willett, Ralph. *The Naked City: Urban Crime Fiction in the USA*. New York: St. Martin's Press, 1996.

Williams, Merle C. "A Tale of Two Oskars: Security or Hospitality in Jonathan Safran Foer's *Extremely Loud & Incredibly Close*." *American Literary History* 28.4 (2016): 702–20.

Wojcik, Pamela Robertson. *Fantasies of Neglect: Imagining the Urban Child in American Film and Fiction*. New Brunswick, NJ: Rutgers University Press, 2016.

Wojtowitz, Robert. *Sidewalk Critic: Lewis Mumford's Writings on New York*. Princeton, NJ: Princeton Architectural Press, 1998.

Wolfe, Cary. *What Is Posthumanism?* Minneapolis: University of Minnesota Press, 2009.

Zhou, Xiaojing. *Cities of Others: Reimagining Urban Spaces in Asian American Literature*. Seattle: University of Washington Press, 2014.

Zukin, Sharon. *The Culture of Cities*. Cambridge, MA: Blackwell, 1995.

　　Loft Living: Culture and Capital in Urban Change. New Brunswick, NJ: Rutgers University Press, 2014.

　　Naked City: The Death and Life of Authentic Urban Places. New York: Oxford University Press, 2010.

Zurier, Rebecca. *Picturing the City: Urban Vision and the Ashcan School*. Berkeley: University of California Press, 2006.

Zurier, Rebecca, Robert W. Snyder, and Virginia M. Mecklenberg. *Metropolitan Lives: The Ashcan Artists and Their New York*. New York: Norton, 1995.

Index

Abraham, Julie
  Metropolitan Lovers: The Homosexuality of Cities, 253
acculturation, process of, 71, 79, 203, 206, 210
Adamic, Louis, 177, 179
Adams, Alice
  "Gift of Grass," 124
  "Waiting for Stella," 126–27
Adams, Henry, 167
Addams, Jane, 353–54, 362
aesthetic categories, 243
aesthetic ideals, 78, 107, 108, 110–11, 248–51
aesthetic regionalism, 331
aesthetics
  categories of, 243
  compression in literature, 48
  ideals of, 78, 107, 108, 110–11, 248–51
  occupational, 234
  regional, 331
  verbs and representation of agency, 104, *see also specific genres*
Afghanistan, 149
African Americans, 10
  alternate geographies of, 81, 267, 269–70
  bohemia and, 255
  in crime narratives, 220–21, 224–27
  cultural pride of, 81, 355
  disappointments of, 60–62, 82, 226
  in gentrification novels, 104, 109, 111–12, 113–14, 115
  ghetto experience of, 39–41, 60–62, 82, 265–67, 268–69, 270
  Great Migration of, 39, 62, 79, 81
  Italian Americans and, 212–13, 215
  Korean Americans and, 358, 364
  masculinity, images of, 81, 226, 266
  mob attacks on, 34
  photobook history of, 194–95
  sacrifice and, 356, 358
  with skepticism about protests, 45, 50
  systemic aggression against, 50, 269

  as underclass, 72, 75, 79–80, 193–95, 201, 220
  women, images of, 269
African roots of New Orleans, 157–58
al Anbar Province (Iraq), 139, 140, 320–21, 323, 324, 326, 327–28
al Ramadi, Iraq, 138, 139–41, 142
Albert, Stew, 48
Alexander, Michelle, 279
Algren, Nelson
  Man with the Golden Arm, The, 80
alienation, sense of, 168, 193
Allen, Danielle S., 355, 358
al-Zarqawi, Abu Musab, 140
American Samoans, 147
American Sniper (dir. Eastwood), 144
American studies, transnationalism in, 136, 150
American vs. alien status, 93, 175–76, 181, 182
Amin, Ash
  Cities: Reimagining the Urban, 316–17
amusement parks, 172, 174
Anderson, Mark, 236
Anderson, Sherwood, 43
  "Song of the Soul of Chicago," 44
  Mid-American Chants, 44
  Winesburg, Ohio, 13
animals
  AI development with, 327
  and cross-species social relations, 241–42
  and extinction of species, 235, 239, 242
  human origins as, 314
  in *New York 2140* (Robinson), 235, 237
  messages of, 157–59
  new materialism and, 315
Beattie, Ann
  "Cinderella Waltz," 126
Annsfire, Joan, 51
  "Strike Day in Oakland," 52
antagonistic cooperation, 355
antebellum literature, 29–32
anthology, Appalachian, 344–45
Anthropocene period, 236–37, 240

picturesque (cont.)
 panoramic, 114
 variety in, 107
Pittsburgh, PA, 3
place-making, 82, 97, 98, 153–54
place-centered writing, 338
placelessness, 95, 96, 97
plasmic city, 319
Platzer, Brian
 Bed-Stuy Is Burning, 111
plays, 63, 356–58, 363
Plug-In-City (Cook), 318
Pochoda, Ivy
 Visitation Street, 106
Poe, Edgar Allan
 "Man of the Crowd, The," 13, 29
 "Mystery of Marie Rogêt, The," 29
poetic ecosphere of New Orleans
 animal messages and, 157–59
 Creole comingling of, 156–58
 death in, 159, 161
 desire as primary in, 153–55, 159–60, 162
 healing within, 155–56, 160–61
 memory in, 160
 multilingual and multicultural history of, 152,
  156–58, 160–61, 163
 with need to be heard, 153
 as rim city, 151
 sea, imagery and meaning of, 154–56,
  158–60, 162
 sedimentation imagery and reality in, 156, 157,
  159, 160
 sounds of, 152, 156
 women, images of, 154–56, 157, 159–61
poetic image, concept of, 167
poetics of urban shock, 169
poetry
 elegies, 161
 by ItalianAmerican immigrants, 205–6
 in labor literature, 190–91, 194–95
 of lost neighborhoods, 63
 lyric, 153, 157–59
 of New Orleans. *see* poetic ecosphere of New
  Orleans
 on repossessing urban space, 269–70
 of streets, 36, 43–44, 51
 of urban borders, 98–99
 vertigo of American cities in, 169–70
police
 as corrupt, 225
 in crime narratives, 218, 221–22, 223, 224–26,
  228, 229–30
 militarization of, 50, 149, 223
 vs. polis, 92
 violence by, 10, 44, 51, 195, 224, 230, 266–67

polis, 92, 350, 354, 360
political bosses, 353, 362
political discourse, 354–55
political divisions, 10, 336, 343, 347
political event (Rancière), 353, 362
political model, posthumanist, 315
political protest
 antiwar activism, 141–42
 in Appalachia, 341
 public vs. private spaces for, 16, 51
 riots as diversion from, 359
 sexuality and, 123
 social media for, 52–53
 in streets, 44–50, 52–53
 theatrics for, 47–50
political theory, 175–76
politics as lifestyle, 247, 255
politics, crime, 218, 221, 223, 227, 229
populations, shifting of, 16, 23, 24, 25,
 118
populism, anti-urban, 82
Port of South Louisiana, 151
Porter, Libby, 267
ports, 151
post-9/11 literature, 138
postapocalyptic genre, 234, 237, 238, 240, 242,
 243, *see also* apocalypse narratives
posthuman cities, 9
 architecture for, 318–19, 320
 centralized control vs. complexity in, 317–18,
  319–20, 321, 324–25, 326
 chaotic potential in, 320, 328
 dynamic flows and processes of, 312, 315,
  316–17, 326, 328
 ethic of care in, 321, 324, 326
 fictional portrayal of, 319, 320–21, 322–23, 324,
  325–26
 humans as one among many agents in, 317
 intelligent cities as, 319, 321, 327–28
 mapping dynamic of, 323, 325
 mulitplicity in, 314, 325, 328
 nonhuman vital entities in, 315, 320–21,
  322–23, 324, 325–26, 327–28
 smart cities as, 317–18, 319–20, 321, 324–25, 326,
  327–28
 subjectivity and, 315, 321, 323
 theoretical design of, 319–22, 323, 324–25, 326,
  327–28
posthumanism, 312–15
postimpressionism, 41
postindustrial cities, 62–68
postindustrial economy, 188, 197–201, 249
postindustrial suburbs, 125
postmodernism, 199
posturban geography, 2

Lightning Source UK Ltd.
Milton Keynes UK
UKHW011227040922
408155UK00003B/29